CLASH
OF
FLEETS

CLASH
OF
FLEETS

NAVAL BATTLES OF THE GREAT WAR, 1914–18

VINCENT P. O'HARA
AND LEONARD R. HEINZ

Naval Institute Press • Annapolis, Maryland

Naval Institute Press
291 Wood Road
Annapolis, MD 21402

Library of Congress Cataloging-in-Publication Data

Names: O'Hara, Vincent P., 1951- author. | Heinz, Leonard R., co-author.
Title: Clash of fleets : naval battles of the Great War, 1914-18 / Vincent P. O'Hara and Leonard R. Heinz.
Description: Annapolis, Maryland : Naval Institute Press, 2017. | Includes bibliographical references and index.
Identifiers: LCCN 2016054316| ISBN 9781682470084 (hardback : alkaline paper) | ISBN 9781682470190 (ePub) | ISBN 9781682470190 (MOBI)
Subjects: LCSH: World War, 1914-1918—Naval operations. | BISAC: HISTORY Military / Naval. | HISTORY / Military / World War I.
Classification: LCC D580 .O35 2017 | DDC 940.4/5—dc23 LC record available at https://lccn.loc.gov/2016054316

♾ Print editions meet the requirements of ANSI/NISO z39.48-1992 (Permanence of Paper).

Printed in the United States of America.

25 24 23 22 21 20 19 18 17   9 8 7 6 5 4 3 2 1

First printing

Contents

Illustrations

Photos

Maps

Figure

Tables

Acknowledgments

The authors wish to thank Stephen McLaughlin, who generously provided comments, translations, and much valuable information regarding the Imperial Russian Navy. Enrico Cernuschi and Michael Yaklich gave unstintingly of their time in reading and reviewing the manuscript. John Roberts and James Goldrick graciously shared source information; John Brooks reviewed points relating to fire control; Sergei Vinogradov provided information from his research on the Russian navy; Cernuschi, Roberts, Vinogradov, and Peter Schenk also allowed the reproduction of photographs from their collections. Rick Russell and Tom Cutler of the Naval Institute Press supported this project and brought it to print. The authors would also like to acknowledge the many organizations and individuals involved in the digitization and online publication of source material. They have created a treasure trove of relevant documents. Irrespective of the many people whose input helped improve this book, the authors are solely responsible for the content and any errors that may occur.

Finally, and most importantly, the authors would like to acknowledge the support of their families, which is the true foundation of any project of this sort: for O'Hara, his son Vincent and daughter Yunuen and most especially his wife Maria; for Heinz, his wife Meg, son David, daughter Julia, and granddaughter Maggie, who thought there should be pirates.

Introduction

Deprived of [seaborne trade] Great Britain could neither
maintain her industries, nor equip her armies, nor feed her people.
—CHARLES E. FAYLE

A Google image search of World War I brings up picture after picture of trenches, machine guns, gas masks, primitive tanks, and the occasional biplane. Warships are conspicuously absent. These pictures reflect the collective memory of the Great War a century later. They are accurate in showing that the vast majority of deaths occurred on land but disguise the fact that events at sea played a crucial role in determining the victor.

World War I was so deadly and so long a stalemate because, in part, it was the first total war of the industrial age. The ingredients of the victory won by the Entente powers in 1918 proved to be technology, resources, and stamina—not, as expected in 1914, the best-trained divisions or the most efficient mobilization plan. Because no nation had all the resources necessary to fight a modern total war it was largely on the seas that the required coal, iron ore, phosphates, and foodstuffs arrived. The Entente powers, especially the United Kingdom, clearly relied upon maritime communications to maintain their economies but even the Ottoman Empire, for example, required sea transportation to meet its energy needs, and Germany needed it to get the iron ore for its war industries. Had the Entente powers lost control of the seas, their supply of resources would have been imperiled and their ability to fight on would have quickly faded. The Central Powers survived longer without sea control (although Germany controlled the Baltic Sea to the very end), but the Entente's oceanic naval blockade ultimately wreaked great privation in Germany and caused starvation in the Austro-Hungarian and Ottoman Empires. Germany's best chance of victory was to defeat the United Kingdom, but this could only be done at sea—most effectively by imposing a counter-blockade. The German navy's attempt to do this via unrestricted submarine warfare inflicted hardship and panic but ultimately backfired when it provoked the United States to declare war. This, and the Entente's defeat of the submarine offensive, tipped the balance and ultimately doomed the Central Powers.

Clash of Fleets is a naval history of the Great War. It focuses on naval surface combat as the frame of its narrative and the instrument of its analysis. Naval surface combat commonly evokes an image of battleships proceeding majestically in column with massive guns roaring in great gouts of smoke and fire—and it could be like this, but not very often. *Clash of Fleets* details 144 naval engagements fought between major surface warships engaged mostly in the mundane but vital tasks that sustain sea power like patrol, escort, mine warfare, or raiding. Such an account reveals, in its cumulative detail of success, failure, and near run affairs, in its record of fleeting encounters and battleship clashes, how the combatants conducted the war at sea, what they considered important, on what they were willing to hazard their assets, and how the management of risk evolved throughout the war. This history illustrates how weapons performed, how doctrine met operational requirements, and how the naval and land wars intertwined. This work also illuminates one of the great watershed periods of naval development. For decades weapons, processes, and tactical thought had evolved at breakneck speeds in relative peace. In the subsequent trial by fire some systems did not work as expected, some were not used as anticipated, and others established an unexpected importance. The analogies between 1914 and 2017 are striking in that powerful new platforms and weapons have again evolved untested by a full-blooded naval war. Doctrine and training have raced to anticipate the realities of what combat will be like should another war occur. There is much for today's naval professional to consider in the conflict that occurred one hundred years ago.

The general themes of this work are:

- That sea power played a vital role in World War I
- That surface combat and the ability to impose surface combat power was a key capability of navies throughout the war
- That surface combat was fundamental to the application of sea power in all its aspects
- That new technology was difficult to apply and sometimes diminished rather than enhanced naval combat power

The book contains seven chapters: The first introduces the weapons and the fleets of the Great War while the following five cover individual years. The final chapter compares surface combat of the Great War to the wars that preceded and followed it, assesses the performance of the combatant navies, and draws certain conclusions. The chronological chapters are divided into sections corresponding to major geographic areas in which fighting occurred: the North Sea, the Baltic Sea, the Black Sea, the Mediterranean and Adriatic Seas, and non-European waters. The components of these geographic subchapters are the battles themselves. This organization allows the massive sweep of action to be presented in a structured format. Space limitations restrict the detail in some cases but at the minimum every description contains a header of basic facts, an order of battle, and a broad outline of what transpired. Certain key or interesting actions are presented in greater detail and their consequences assessed. The objective is a holistic overview of the war at sea through which the themes of this work resonate.

For the purposes of this book, a naval engagement is defined as an encounter between opposing warships of at least 100 tons standard displacement (the smallest-sized oceangoing torpedo boats) in which guns or torpedoes were used. Each of the belligerents had its own terminology for ship types, ranks, and measurements; reconciling these for the modern, nonspecialist reader has led the authors to adopt certain conventions. For example, a 1,000-ton warship armed with torpedoes and

4-inch guns would be called a torpedo boat destroyer or destroyer in the British navy, a contre-torpilleur (or roughly a torpedo boat killer) in the French navy, a cacciatorpediniere (torpedo boat hunter) in the Italian navy, a squadron torpedo carrier in the Russian navy, and a hochseetorpedoboot (high-seas torpedo boat) in the German navy. Such diverse terminology fosters ambiguity and therefore, regardless of what a ship might have been called in its own navy, ship nomenclature is standardized in this book as follows:

Ship Nomenclature, Standard Abbreviations, and General Characteristics:

- Battleship or Dreadnought (BB): An armored vessel constructed after 1905 with a uniform main battery of at least eight guns of 11-inch bore or larger
- Battlecruiser (BC): An armored vessel constructed after 1905 with similar displacement and main battery, but lighter armor and higher speed than a dreadnought
- Old battleship or predreadnought (OBB): An armored vessel generally constructed before 1906 with a mixed main battery and four or fewer 10- to 12-inch guns
- Armored cruiser (CA): Generally a pre-1906 vessel with an armored belt and deck and armed with a main battery of 6- to 10-inch guns and a secondary battery of 4- to 6-inch guns
- Protected cruiser (CP): Generally a pre-1906 vessel with a protected deck and armed with 4- to 6-inch guns
- Light cruiser (CL): Generally a high speed, post-1906 vessel with light deck or belt armor and a main battery of 4- to 6-inch guns
- Scout cruiser (CLS): A small, post-1906 cruiser with no armor and a main battery of 4- or 4.7-inch guns
- Destroyer leader (DL): A large destroyer generally displacing more than 1,300 tons
- Destroyer (DD): A ship generally displacing from 350 to 1,300 tons and armed with guns of 3-inch bore or greater and two or more torpedoes
- Torpedo boat (TB): A ship displacing less than 350 tons, armed with guns 3.4-inch or smaller and at least one torpedo

Each action described in this book is preceded by a header. Its purpose is to facilitate reference and comparison. Each header includes (to the extent known):

- Action name and date (in many cases the authors have assigned a name based on location)
- Conditions (weather, visibility, sea state)
- Mission (describing the reason a ship was at sea just prior to the start of the surface combat, as further defined below)
- Entente order of battle (ship names, formations and force commanders)
- Central Powers order of battle, in the same format.

The mission types are broadly descriptive and their main intent is to allow comparison and analysis. Missions are defined as follows:

Offensive Missions:

- Raid or bombardment: at sea to attack a known target or objective
- Sweep: at sea to seek nonspecific targets in enemy or contested waters (includes reconnaissance)
- Interception: at sea to find and attack a specific or anticipated enemy formation (includes convoy attack)
- Offensive minelaying (generally in enemy waters).

Defensive Missions:

- Transit: at sea en route from one point to another with no other mission (includes in port or transportation mission)
- Patrol: at sea to exert sea control (includes positional defense and blockade)
- Escort: at sea to protect friendly or neutral ships
- Minesweeping: at sea to sweep mines
- Defensive minelaying (generally in friendly waters)

In the header order of battle, "★" after a ship's name indicates it was sunk in the action, "#" indicates that the ship sustained enough damage to affect its combat effectiveness, and "+" indicates that the ship was slightly damaged. A "†" after a commander's name signifies that he was killed in action.

The primary references for each action are given in one note at the end of the section describing that action except that direct quotations may be noted as they appear. Miles always refer to nautical miles unless otherwise specified; the Imperial system of yards is preferred over the metric system. Gun sizes, however, are presented in the native format: inches, centimeters, or millimeters. Displacements are normal: that is, full outfit with two-thirds of all supplies and fuel, unless otherwise specified. Ranks are translated into English. Names omit noble titles. The book refers to Great Britain, France, Russia, and Italy as the Entente Powers, although technically Italy was an "Allied Power." For actions involving British and German forces British times are used; German and Russian actions use German times. Otherwise, times are local. Abbreviations for ship types and formations are defined in Appendix 2. They appear in every description and readers may wish to review them. The authors have translated any quotations from non-English language works. Many place names used in the text do not appear in a modern atlas. For example, the important Albanian seaport of Durazzo will be found as Durrës on a modern map, while Ösel, the scene of much naval action in the Baltic is now Saaremaa. The authors have retained the English-language usage prevalent at the time, relying on the Hammond Home and Office *Atlas of the World* (1913 edition) and other contemporary sources such as the U.S. Naval Institute *Proceedings*. With only a few common exceptions, the reader will find every place name mentioned in the text on one of the maps included in this work. Ship names are presented in their native format (*Köln* not *Cologne*). Russian ship and personal names are transliterated according to the Library of Congress system. Ottoman names follow those presented in *Conway's All the World's Fighting Ships* series. Specifications of ships that participated in surface combat are given in Appendix 1. This includes a silhouette of each class of ship drawn to scale and the basic characteristics such as year of launching, normal displacement, armament, armor, engine type, fuel type, and speed. This appendix does not show every ship of every nation, only those that participated in surface combat.

In all cases, these conventions strive for consistency and ease of understanding.

I

The Fleets

Anyone brought up in the oil fuel age can have no idea of the physical
effort required of the stokers of a coal-fired ship steaming at high speed.
With the fans supplying air to the boilers whirring at full speed the
furnaces devoured coal just about as fast as a man could feed them.
—BRIAN SCHOFIELD, HMS *INDOMITABLE*

This chapter introduces the ships, weapons, and technology of 1914 as well as the tactics, doctrine, and expectations of the men tasked with the job of fighting and winning a war at sea.

Technology

The technology of the early twentieth century was one of steam and steel, forging and casting, milling and machining, of the open hearth and the factory floor, and of new types of engineering: chemical, electrical, hydraulic, and optical. This confluence of young technologies transformed the material aspects of sea warfare and confronted navies on the eve of Europe's first general war in a century with a host of new challenges.

Navies of the era had three means of sinking enemy ships: guns, mines, and torpedoes. Guns had been in use for centuries but recent developments had vastly expanded their capabilities. Mines first appeared in the eighteenth century but came of age in the decade before the First World War. Torpedoes were the newest weapons and their capabilities seemed tremendous, but were in fact uncertain.

Guns

A series of developments transformed gunnery in the decades before the war. Advances in chemistry provided propellants that burned consistently and predictably. Progress in metallurgy allowed the fabrication of longer, stronger guns. Precision manufacturing techniques meant that the new guns and their projectiles were more accurate. Constantly improving hydraulic and electrical systems meant that big guns could be controlled more precisely and could sustain higher rates of fire. Advanced optics revolutionized sighting and range finding. Theoretical battle ranges grew from 3,000 yards at the beginning of the century to 8,700 yards in 1907 and 15,000 yards or more on the eve of World War I.[1]

While the big guns in the new battleships could shoot to a mark eight miles away, hitting an opposing warship at such a distance was another matter. The guns themselves were subject to the pitch, yaw, and roll of the ship they were mounted upon as well as that ship's progress through the water. Meanwhile, the target was also in motion, and could have traveled three hundred yards or more between the time the guns were fired and the shells arrived. To hit at long range thus required firing the shells to the point where the target ship would be when the shells arrived, not where it had been when the guns were fired. To do this successfully a host of variables needed to be considered. The most important were range to the target and the target's course, bearing, and speed as well as one's own course and speed. To determine and account for these variables navies developed an array of sophisticated devices. Optical rangefinders measured range although their accuracy varied, sometimes by hundreds of yards as ranges lengthened, as in the case of the 9-foot rangefinder that equipped most British dreadnoughts in 1914. Mechanical devices—early analog computers—abounded. Some tracked a target's apparent motion and the rate at which the range changed based on estimations of the target's course, speed, and bearing relative to the firing ship's known course, bearing, and speed; others continuously indicated the current best estimate of the range to the target based on the rate at which the range was changing; while still others plotted range and bearing over time.

Other factors that affected hitting included shell drift, imparted by the stabilizing spin that resulted from the gun barrel's rifling; wind speed and angle to the shell's path; barrel wear; humidity; the characteristics of the charge used; spread of the salvo; and, most importantly, the skill of the fire control parties and gun crews.

Devices improved the accuracy of long-range gunnery but no system could automatically hit at long range, so gunners relied upon a process called spotting. Spotting was the correction of an instrument-derived fire control solution by observing where the shells hit water. Ideally, fire was adjusted until the shells could be seen to straddle the target with some falling over, some short and—hopefully—some on the target itself. The better the initial fire control solution and the quicker the shells could be spotted onto the target, the better the chance of hitting. Effective use of fire control instruments and control of guns required the centralization of functions that had once been handled by individual gun crews. The Royal Navy in particular adopted systems that allowed one fire control team to direct and shoot a ship's entire main gun battery, but all navies centralized gun control as the war progressed.[2] A British publication summarized the process as follows: "Briefly, the rangefinder equipment was used to feed the Dreyer fire control table (which plotted target range and compass-bearings against time) and the latter was relied upon to furnish the requisite information for successful attack on a moving target. In conjunction with this the bracket system of spotting was universally used to correct the best mean range into the actual gun range after opening fire. The correction of the remaining factors, such as rate and deflection, was primarily dependent upon observation of fire."[3]

Range-taking, determining an enemy's course and speed, and spotting all depended on optical instruments. Visibility conditions greatly affected these instruments. A pall of funnel and gun smoke, wind-whipped spray and shell splashes, twilight and night, fog and mist, the glare of sunlight at dawn or dusk, all could profoundly degrade the accuracy of a ship's gunnery.

This description of naval fire control refers to the heavy weapons of capital ships. The fire control problem of course applied to lighter ships as well. However, while they might be expected to fight at shorter ranges, light cruisers and flotilla craft entered the war with rudimentary systems that did not meet the requirements of combat. Of cruisers the British Admiralty noted that although they commenced "the war with

Figure 1.1 Fire Control and Formations

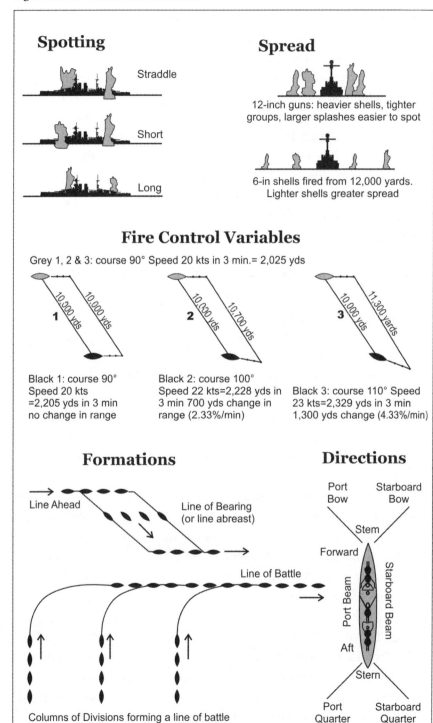

Spotting

Straddle

Short

Long

Spread

12-inch guns: heavier shells, tighter groups, larger splashes easier to spot

6-in shells fired from 12,000 yards. Lighter shells greater spread

Fire Control Variables

Grey 1, 2 & 3: course 90° Speed 20 kts in 3 min.= 2,025 yds

1 10,300 yds / 10,000 yds

2 10,000 yds / 10,700 yds

3 10,000 yds / 11,300 yards

Black 1: course 90° Speed 20 kts =2,205 yds in 3 min no change in range

Black 2: course 100° Speed 22 kts=2,228 yds in 3 min 700 yds change in range (2.33%/min)

Black 3: course 110° Speed 23 kts=2,329 yds in 3 min 1,300 yds change (4.33%/min)

Formations

Line Ahead

Line of Bearing (or line abreast)

Line of Battle

Columns of Divisions forming a line of battle

Directions

Port Bow   Starboard Bow

Stem

Forward

Port Beam   Starboard Beam

Aft

Stern

Port Quarter   Starboard Quarter

a system of control efficient for the accepted standards of the day, the pre-Jutland period was spent in developing that system to meet the harder standards imposed by actual battle experience." Destroyers were seen as not likely to fight at ranges beyond six thousand yards. Thus the primary fire control instrument on destroyers at the outbreak of the war was the seaman's eye "although a few ships were fitted with telaupad (headphones) or voice pipe control, or visual rangeboards."[4]

Armor technology made significant advances in the late 1800s and early 1900s, but the hitting power of large guns advanced even faster. Even when heavy shells did not penetrate, they could still wreck delicate fire control systems, jam turrets, smash command facilities, burst steam lines, and slaughter crews. Ironically, technology extending battle ranges actually increased the value of armor, as shells penetrated less at longer ranges. But still, the balance favored the big gun, and navies concluded that they could punish any target the big guns could hit. This all assumed that shells functioned as intended, which was not always the case.

Mines

In a 1797 demonstration William Pitt, the British prime minister, watched a mine sink a warship and then enthused about the new weapon. The First Sea Lord, who was also there, remarked, "Pitt is the greatest fool that ever existed, to encourage a mode of war which they who commanded the seas did not want, and which, if successful, would deprive them of [their command]."[5]

Mines first saw widespread use in the Crimean War and sank several ships in the American Civil War. Modern mine warfare dated from the Russo-Japanese War of 1904–1905, when mines sank one Russian and two Japanese battleships. The mines used in World War I were even more potent. Older battleships and cruisers proved highly vulnerable to them, and they posed a serious threat even to the higher standards of underwater protection found on modern dreadnoughts. Such ships might survive one, two, or even three mine hits, but would be a long time in dockyard hands before they were fit to fight again. Most World War I mines had contact-activated fuzes. They were held below the surface by a steel cable connected to an anchor. At the start of the war, the standard German mine could be laid in water no deeper than 380 feet. By the end of the war, prototypes could be moored in depths up to a thousand feet. The combatants used mines defensively, to protect a port or shipping lanes, or offensively by laying them across the expected track of enemy ships. Major navies deployed purpose-built minelayers; all used warships from light cruisers down to torpedo boats fitted with mine racks. Merchant vessels also served as auxiliary minelayers.

At the start of the war minesweeping was a primitive business. Navies pressed fishing trawlers and old torpedo boats into such service, using rudimentary wire sweeps to cut mine mooring cables and rifle fire to detonate the mines that bobbed to the surface. As the war progressed navies recognized the need for purpose-built minesweepers and more effective sweeping gear. Even with the best equipment, however, clearing minefields was dangerous work and mines claimed many minesweepers.[6]

Torpedoes

The last major weapon of World War 1 navies was the torpedo. A British warship fired the first locomotive torpedo used in combat in 1877 (it missed). The weapon evolved in the following thirty-seven years to have larger warheads, longer ranges, and faster speeds. On the eve of the war theoretical ranges had reached ten thousand yards and warheads rivaled mines in explosive power, meaning that a single torpedo could cripple or sink a capital ship. In World War I torpedoes were carried on surface warships ranging in size from 12-ton motorboats to the largest dreadnoughts. Some strategists predicted massed torpedo attacks would damage or sink up to 30 percent of the battle line at the start of an action. The fear of such an attack was a strong impetus for extending gun ranges beyond the maximum torpedo range.[7]

Propulsion

The navies of World War I relied on steam power to move their ships, with a few exceptions such as gasoline engines in motorboats and diesels in submarines. There were important differences, however, in the details of the various steam systems. In the early 1900s the steam turbine began to replace the reciprocating steam engine. The reciprocating engine was large, needed extensive maintenance, and was unable to sustain high speeds for long periods. The steam turbine was more compact for the same power output and better able to accelerate ships to high speeds and then maintain those speeds. As one Royal Navy admiral put it: "No greater step towards efficiency in war was ever made than the introduction of the turbine. Previous to the turbine's adoption every day's steaming at high speed meant several days' maintenance in harbor. All this changed as if by magic."[8] The turbine, however, had downsides. It was complex to manufacture and its fuel consumption was high.

The supply and consumption of fuel was an overriding consideration in all naval operations. In 1914 most ships used coal to fire their boilers and generate steam. Coal was bulky, it was dirty, and it was difficult to work with. Ships needed large crews because the coal had to be continuously moved by hand from distant bunkers to near bunkers and then to boilers and finally shoveled into boilers at rates of up to twenty tons an hour. It polluted the air, the machinery, the entire ship. Coaling a ship was a long and laborious task. One British captain noted that "the first maxim in coaling should be to get every single officer and man that can be spared, into the collier to dig out the coal." There they shoveled coal into bags that could hold 220 pounds. These were slung on board the warship and emptied into the vessel's bunkers. Coal was moved this way at rates of up to 300 tons (nearly three thousand bags) per hour. Long as it took to coal, it generally took longer to clean men and ship afterwards.[9]

Battleship *Dreadnought* carried nine hundred tons of coal under normal conditions but could accommodate two thousand tons in a pinch. At full speed, she consumed 17.5 tons an hour; at 11 knots that dropped to 5.5 tons an hour. Carrying two thousand tons and steaming at an average speed of 15 knots (submarines made lower speeds dangerous) *Dreadnought* had a practical range of 2,700 nautical miles and an endurance of seven days. This was not much and limited autonomy was the one great disadvantage modern navies suffered in comparison to their Napoleonic forbears. The hardness and carbon/energy content of coal also mattered. In 1914 Great Britain had the world's greatest supply of premium bunker coal—so-called Welsh steam coal. Lesser coals produced more smoke and ash and less energy, preventing ships from reaching their designed speeds, and fouling boilers and tubes more quickly. All the major navies began the war with hoarded stockpiles of Welsh steam coal.

At the turn of the century a slow transition to oil fuel began. Oil provided more energy than coal for the same weight. It could be pumped rather than shoveled, which eased refueling and eliminated the need for large gangs of stokers to feed the boilers. Oil increased the temperature in a boiler's firebox more rapidly, allowing a ship—particularly a turbine-equipped ship—to accelerate more quickly. It burned more cleanly, which meant less fouling of boilers, smaller smoke clouds from a ship's funnels during the day, and less flame showing at night. The major issue with oil was supply. Continental Europe produced little oil, with most coming from Romania. The major world producers were Burma, Persia, Russia, and the United States—sources unavailable to the Central Powers in wartime. A lesser issue was protection. Coal bunkers helped protect a ship from gunfire whereas oil tanks did not. While all major navies of World War I used oil fuel the Royal Navy used the most.[10]

Signaling

The last area of technology directly relevant to surface combat is signaling. World War I navies used flags, lights, and radio to communicate between ships. Higher speeds, larger fleets, greater distances between ships and formations, and billowing clouds of coal and gun smoke made flag communication increasingly problematic. The development of electricity allowed ships to carry powerful signaling lights but visibility conditions likewise limited their effectiveness. Radio at first glance might seem a solution, but it came with its own set of problems. Radios of the era relied on delicate networks of antennas and were restricted in frequencies. Limited frequencies increased the possibility of successful jamming and allowed the enemy to receive traffic almost as readily as the intended recipient. The risk of interception meant that important traffic had to be ciphered. Encoding, transmitting, and decoding messages took time and, in the heat of battle, time was always a scarce commodity.

Despite its limitations, radio revolutionized naval operations. Before the advent of radio, warships had to call at ports or rely on dispatch vessels to get orders and intelligence. Radio rapidly changed all that, with the range of shipboard sets growing from only ten miles in the mid-1890s to more than a thousand miles by the turn of the century.[11] Twin revolutions in command and intelligence resulted. The revolution in command was obvious. For good or ill radio communications allowed central staffs to exert more control over ships at sea. The revolution in intelligence was more subtle but no less profound.

Radio quickly became both a source of intelligence and a means of rapidly disseminating it. Properly used, radio gave commanders at sea unprecedented access to information about an enemy's plans and dispositions. Used carelessly, it could provide that information to the enemy. As early as the Russo-Japanese War, both the Russians and the Japanese monitored each other's radio communications to get a rough sense of the enemy's location and proximity, and the Russians at least took the next step of gathering and acting on intelligence from intercepted Japanese signals.[12] The Austrians also made an early start in the business of intercepting and decoding enemy radio transmissions, while the British, Germans, and Russians built efficient interception services soon after the start of the war, with British and Russian decryption efforts particularly helped by captured German code books. Before the war was over, all the major naval powers except (apparently) the Ottomans had developed some ability to crack enemy codes. Moreover, as the war continued, radio direction-finding techniques became increasingly sophisticated, allowing transmission sources to be pinpointed. The combatants practiced increasingly strict radio discipline to counteract signals intelligence, but improvement in radio security generally lagged behind improvements in intelligence gathering. The net result was an intelligence revolution.

Submarines and Aircraft

Two technologies relatively untested by war and indirectly related to surface combat also merit mention: submarines and aircraft. Submarines by 1914 had graduated from oddities to potentially useful weapons. Many naval officers regarded them as mobile minefields, useful to defend ports and possibly, for the longer-ranged types, to lay in ambush off a hostile coast. Their as yet theoretical capabilities affected war plans, being one of the factors that convinced the British to mount a distant blockade of German ports. Expectations that submarines would operate as an adjunct to the surface fleet in combat proved false; nonetheless, the submarine's role evolved rapidly during the war, profoundly influencing fleet operations and seaborne commerce.

Aircraft development during the war was likewise astounding, but at its start the most useful aircraft were vast engine-propelled gasbags: Germany's Zeppelins and the dirigibles of other navies. These could carry a worthwhile payload, including some of the first airborne radios. So equipped, they were useful scouts. Heavier-than-air aircraft began as puny, unreliable things but improved radically, creating another class of radio-equipped aerial scouts and a new threat capable of at least harassing surface ships.

Ships

The first single-battery capital ship, HMS *Dreadnought*, was constructed, launched, and commissioned in 1906; she was a revolutionary vessel. With few exceptions, navies stopped building mixed-battery capital ships, armored cruisers, and protected cruisers after 1905, with the result that every major fleet had two elements: its predreadnought and its post-dreadnought vessels. New types such as battlecruisers, light cruisers, scouts, and destroyer leaders first appeared after 1906. Torpedo boats and destroyers doubled in size in the years before 1914. This section sorts through the various types of ships and compares them across nationalities and over time to highlight subtle but sometimes very important differences.

Dreadnoughts

Amidst all the uncertainty of 1914 the definition of naval power seemed clear. Every fleet measured its strength, indeed its relevance, in terms of its dreadnoughts. HMS *Dreadnought* represented a distinct break from prior battleship classes; she was larger and faster but most importantly, her main battery was composed entirely of guns of one caliber. That meant similar flight times for shells and similar corrections for all firing guns. This was key because accurate gunnery required effective spotting, which in turn required guns of the same type firing salvos under centralized control. By 1914, the world's major navies and a number of smaller ones had dreadnought battleships in service, were building them, or were trying to buy them.

The last of the British predreadnought battleships, *Lord Nelson*, was laid down on 18 May 1905. She displaced 16,090 tons. Her main battery of four 12-inch guns and ten 9.2-inch guns fired a 5,300-pound broadside. She could steam at 18 knots. *Dreadnought* was laid down on 2 October 1905. She displaced 18,110 tons (13 percent more than *Lord Nelson*). Her main battery of ten 12-inch guns fired a broadside of 6,800 pounds (28 percent more) and her turbines gave her a speed of 21 knots (a 17 percent increase). *Iron Duke*, launched eight years later (five months before the war's start) steamed at 21 knots like *Dreadnought*, but her broadside was 14,000 pounds on a displacement of 25,000 tons. When the first "super-dreadnought," *Queen Elizabeth*, was commissioned in 1915 her broadside was 15,360 pounds: nearly three *Lord Nelsons*. Moreover she was faster, better armored, harder to sink, and could fight at ranges significantly beyond those attainable by *Lord Nelson* (or *Dreadnought*). Given these differences it was little wonder that admirals, governments, and nations embraced the dreadnought standard, cost be damned. In fact, *Dreadnought* cost £1.8 million—only 20 percent more than *Lord Nelson's* £1.5 million, so if a ship's worth was measured by how much metal she could hurl at the enemy, then *Dreadnought* was cheaper.[13] And, as ships grew in size, so did the savings, at least according to this measurement.

British battlecruiser *Princess Royal*. She fought in the battles of Heligoland Bight, Dogger Bank, and Jutland. (Library of Congress)

Queen Elizabeth cost £2.5 million. She could fire 290 percent of *Lord Nelson*'s metal at just a 67 percent increase in cost.

Battlecruisers

Battlecruisers were dreadnought derivatives; they carried nearly as much firepower but sacrificed armor to gain 5 or 6 knots more speed. At the war's start only the Germans and British had battlecruisers in service (the Japanese had what might be termed semi-battlecruisers). They saw extensive action, and their greater speed proved its value time and time again. Postwar battleship designs (with the exception of the *Nelson* class) were all capable of 27 knots or better.

Predreadnoughts

These were the ships that the dreadnoughts replaced. They were smaller and slower, but still carried powerful guns and thick armor. Great Britain relegated its predreadnoughts to secondary duties, but the rest of the powers included their more serviceable predreadnoughts in the line of battle, with the Russians making especially active frontline use of their older ships. Despite an alarming and frequently demonstrated tendency to sink from a single mine or torpedo hit, predreadnoughts served until other manning requirements, advanced age, and hard usage caused many to be paid off.

Armored Cruisers

Armored cruisers were an obsolescent type by the start of the war, essentially being to battlecruisers as predreadnoughts were to dreadnoughts. They were typically armed with four 8-inch to 10-inch guns and around a dozen 6-inch weapons. They had deck and belt armor and were generally around 5 knots faster than contemporaneous predreadnoughts. They had served in the line of battle as recently as 1905, but dreadnoughts completely outmatched them. None were launched after 1908. Navies used these ships to support light forces and serve in trade protection and on blockade lines. They shared with the old battleships a susceptibility to underwater damage. A large armored cruiser such as *Warrior* cost £1.18 million. When one considers that an armored cruiser cost £470/broadside pound, battlecruiser *Indefatigable* £223/broadside pound, and

Russian armored cruiser *Admiral Makarov*. The Russians got good use out of their older cruisers. (Wiki Public Domain)

the super-battlecruiser *Lion* "only" £209/broadside pound it is clear why the type was superseded.

Small Cruisers

Small cruisers were maids of all work, performing screening and reconnaissance functions for the fleets, leading and supporting destroyer flotillas, and acting as commerce raiders and minelayers. Most light cruiser classes had a minimal armor belt with a maximum thickness of from one to three inches and a thin armored deck, but some carried deck armor only. Their armament consisted of torpedoes and up to a dozen guns ranging from 3.9- to 6-inch. They could reach speeds ranging from 25 to 29 knots.

Scout cruisers were an early type of light cruiser that generally lacked belt armor. They also tended to be smaller and more lightly armed. Protected cruisers were the predecessors to the light cruiser type. These had deck armor (which was what made them "protected") and could be quite large. The Imperial Russian Navy in particular got good service from its *Bogatyr*–class protected cruisers. Italy and Austria-Hungary each had only three light/scout cruisers on hand or finishing when the war began. Britain and Germany had many light cruisers, built more, and used them hard. France, Russia, and the Ottoman Empire did not have any, although the French and Russians had such cruisers building or in design while the Ottomans acquired a German light cruiser at the war's beginning.

The Italian scout cruiser (*esploratore*) *Nino Bixio*. Small cruisers were the capital ships in the Adriatic's hit-and-run naval war. (Courtesy of Ufficio Storico Marina Militare)

Flotilla Craft (torpedo boats, destroyers, and flotilla leaders)

The first torpedo boat dated from the mid-1870s, displaced 33 tons, was marginally seaworthy, and was armed with torpedoes only. By the First World War, this simple boat had spawned many descendants. Most common was a type displacing from 400 to 1,200 tons, with a mixed armament of torpedo tubes and guns ranging up to 4.1-inch. The Royal Navy fielded ships with fewer tubes and heavier guns; it called them "torpedo boat destroyers" and regarded their primary function as the neutralization of enemy torpedo boats. The Kaiserliche Marine favored vessels with more tubes and lighter guns; it dubbed them ocean-going torpedo boats (*hochseetorpedoboote*) and considered their primary role as launching torpedo attacks against larger warships. Theoretical maximum speeds varied considerably with the slowest Royal Navy destroyers of the immediate prewar period rated for 27 knots and the fastest for 35.

While the trend was for larger ships, there were exceptions. The Kaiserliche Marine, K.u.K. Kriegsmarine, and Regia Marina made much use of small (100–350 ton) torpedo boats. These typically mounted a few torpedo tubes and some light guns. The Germans dubbed theirs

British Tribal-class destroyer *Viking* steaming at full speed. She received with a single 6-inch piece in 1916 but this proved unwieldy and was replaced. (Courtesy of John Roberts Collection)

"A-boats," and designed some so they could be transported in sections by rail for assembly at bases such as Zeebrugge.

At the other end of the spectrum were flotilla leaders. These were essentially enlarged destroyers used as scouts and (with their larger staff accommodations) as leaders for destroyer flotillas. The Royal Navy built a number of these ships in a variety of classes, with the originals being scarcely larger (and actually less well armed) than the destroyers being built by the end of the war. The Regia Marina also used this type, dubbing theirs *esploratori* and emphasizing their independent scouting role.

Other Types

During the First World War the major navies greatly expanded their mine warfare capabilities. Smaller warships or converted merchant vessels often served as minelayers, while some navies built vessels specifically for that purpose. While much effort was spent in laying mines, even more was expended in clearing them. At the start of the war some navies planned to use older torpedo boats as minesweepers. As the minefields proliferated so too did the numbers of minesweepers. The British and the Germans in particular built specialized ships for sweeping mines. Many were lost while conducting their dangerous work.

Monitors arose from the need to bombard shore targets without risking valuable battleships and cruisers along a hostile coast. The basic concept was to put the largest possible gun on the smallest possible hull. The result was a slow, ungainly vessel unsuited for a sea fight, although the type participated in several surface actions. The larger monitors were armored and protected against mines and torpedoes. The Royal Navy commissioned a number of purpose-built monitors, while the Regia Marina extemporized gun platforms from whatever weapons, hulls, and engines it found at hand.

Gunboats, another special class of ship, were armed with guns ranging from 4-inch to 6-inch; however, they were slow and lacked torpedoes. The larger ships were armored. The Russians, in particular, got good service from gunboats in the Baltic Sea's coastal waters.

These ship types were the major playing pieces on the naval chessboard, but the navies wielding them could only speculate about the rules of the game. Technology untried in battle meant that tactics for using the technology were also untested.

Intellectual Foundations

Sea power may be broadly defined as the ability to freely transport men and materiel on the seas and the capacity to deny an enemy the same ability. Sea power as a principle and as a national goal was very much on the mind of the world's governments, militaries, and even publics in 1914. In part this was due to a perception, first articulated in the decades prior to World War I, that the capacity to exert sea power was a prerequisite or a path to national greatness—even survival. An American naval captain, A. T. Mahan, propounded this belief in his 1890 work *The Influence of Sea Power upon History 1660–1783*. His work was translated into six major languages and went through fifty editions. He became the prophet of navalism, a philosophy that was espoused not just by naval professionals, but by the public of many nations. The British Navy League, established in 1894, was the first public association established to advance navalism, followed by the German navy league, Deutscher Flottenverein, in 1898. They both had hundreds of thousands of members. The U.S. Navy League was founded in 1902. By 1909 there were also French, Italian, Russian, Austrian, and Ottoman navy leagues. With large and influential segments of the public in all the major powers actually demanding that their governments build more battleships, naval budgets grew to unprecedented levels.

Mahan wrote that there were two major ways navies exerted sea power: the decisive battle and blockade. Mahan wrote: "The proper main objective of the navy is the enemy's navy," and that the objective of all naval activity is the destruction of the enemy's naval forces.[14] This evolved into the principle of the decisive naval battle and was accepted by the naval leadership of all the great navies of 1914. The British Royal Navy's staff appreciation of the Battle of Jutland, written shortly after the war, precisely summarized this naval philosophy. "Naval warfare has only four principal aspects, vis: Invasion, and counter invasion; attack of trade and defence of trade. These ends, which loom behind every naval operation, can only be completely achieved by the destruction of the enemy's forces."[15] The principles of concentration and economy of effort dictated that power should be concentrated in the largest groups of the heaviest ships possible. Of course, there was one problem with the underpinnings of Mahan's conclusions that he himself brought forth in the very beginning of his book: he had to study "the history and experience of naval warfare in the days of sailing-ships" because "steam navies have as yet made no history which can be quoted as decisive in its teachings."[16]

If steam navies had no history in 1890 this was no longer true by 1914. Based on the results of several recent major wars including the Sino-Japanese War of 1894–1895, the Spanish-American War of 1898, and the Russo-Japanese War of 1904–1905, the proponents of the decisive battle were able to conclude that Mahan's principles still applied inasmuch as all three of these wars had included a major "decisive" naval battle in which one side established sea power and ultimately claimed victory.

Tactics

While admiralties generally believed that naval battles could be war-winning events, in 1914 battle tactics were, for the most part, theoretical. Only the Japanese and the Russians had experienced full-scale twentieth century naval warfare. Dreadnoughts had never fought.

No one was completely sure what long-range gunnery really was, how submarines would perform, how flotilla craft could best work with the fleet, how to deploy divisions of battleships, how much punishment the new armored ships could really take. For these subjects recent history provided little guidance.

The naval battles of the Sino-Japanese War and the Spanish-American War had been fought within two decades of the outbreak of the Great War, but technology had changed so drastically in that brief period that few lessons could be drawn. Italy and the Balkan states had fought the Ottoman Empire in 1911 and 1912, but the modest naval actions of those wars again held few lessons for navies focused on the clash of dreadnought battle fleets. The Russo-Japanese War, however, was much studied given that it featured many of the ingredients of modern naval war: battles ranging from skirmishes between light forces to battle fleet actions, commerce raiding, blockades and the costs of maintaining blockades, fleets operating at great distances from their bases, mines used defensively and offensively, torpedoes, radio, and relatively long-range gunnery. In particular, the Battle of Tsushima, in which a Japanese fleet annihilated a Russian fleet that was far from home and trying reach the safety of Vladivostok, was held up as the finest example of a decisive victory since the British crushed a Franco-Spanish fleet a century before at Trafalgar. But even the decade since the Russo-Japanese War saw developments such as the dreadnought, longer gunnery ranges, and more effective torpedoes that changed the likely complexion of naval combat.

In 1914 a British naval officer speculating about a future war complained, "To those who have been, and who are trying to prepare for the day of battle, the difficulty has for long been that they could not get any authoritative statement on the principles of tactics, and the uses of the various types of ships in the fleet." In 1913 another officer wrote, "In reviewing the field of existing tactical thought . . . [it] would seem that ideas upon the employment of warlike forces have not kept pace with the tremendous development of material." Naval intellectuals even wondered whether big guns were the preeminent naval weapon. The same author stated that: "No question in modern naval war is more difficult than the relative importance and battle winning value of the gun and the torpedo."[17] His contemporaries debated the tactical impact of variables such as rapidity of fire, dispersion, and range. They debated whether all-big-gun armaments were best, the likelihood of hitting at long ranges, what long ranges actually were, and the relative merits of different gun arrangements. One officer, for example, believed that the eight 15-inch guns armament of the new *Queen Elizabeth* was a mistake and that the fourteen 12-inch guns of *Rio de Janeiro* better addressed the need to hit promptly. "It seems certain that the ship with the larger number of guns will at any probable range obtain a greater number of hits" and "annihilation will not be effected at extreme range."[18]

The impact of torpedoes on a future naval battle generated even more debate than did gunnery. Some authorities advocated daylight torpedo attacks while others dismissed them as suicidal. Regarding the matter of torpedo range, one author cautioned that some future fleet actions may "*commence* with torpedo fire. This change in conditions does not appear to be fully recognized yet, and even among those who realise it, there is considerable divergence of view as how best to deal with the new state of affairs."[19] In 1912 the Royal Navy's Admiral Louis Battenberg opined that German battleships opposing a British line would probably hit the British ships with 30 percent of the torpedoes they fired. This was at a time when maximum range of torpedoes was approaching the gunnery engagement ranges considered realistic for the North Sea. Admiral John Jellicoe, commander of the Royal Navy's Grand Fleet for much of the war, wrote that the starting point for evaluating the danger of German torpedoes was the assumption that a single torpedo boat might get hits on a line of battleships with three or four torpedoes for every six launched.[20]

Formations, maneuver, and communications were other sources of uncertainty and debate. Most admiralties believed that the anticipated decisive battle would be a matter of keeping the heavy ships concentrated in a single line and blasting away at a similar line of the enemy's capital ships. "Within the last few years a general opinion has gradually crystallized in the service that the conventional 'column' is the best fighting formation." However, a minority dissented: "The single line is entirely defensive, and a weak defensive at that." This minority endorsed divisional tactics whereby formations of capital ships operated independently against the enemy line as the tactical situation required. Even if battleships fought in a long column, the roles of battlecruisers, light cruisers, armored cruisers, and especially destroyers within the grand framework of the line of battle were matters of intense debate.[21]

Although admiralties were mostly preoccupied with fleet actions, they also wrestled with the tactical implications of submarines, aircraft, and mines. The belief that submarines would play an integral role in surface combat turned out to be wrong. Prewar ideas about mine warfare were also largely wrong. Of this weapon, the most prolific of prewar British tactical writers echoed the 1797 sea lord by stating, "Tactically there is very little doubt that the mine is a two-edged weapon for use under exceptional circumstances only."[22]

Doctrine, Expectations, and Goals
Each nation approached the problems of sea power differently depending upon its force structure, geography, and national requirements.[23]

Austria-Hungary: Kaiserliche und Königliche (K.u.K.) Kriegsmarine
The Austro-Hungarian (hereinafter Austrian) navy was the world's seventh largest with a fleet of 3 dreadnoughts, 9 predreadnoughts, 5 old and 2 new cruisers, 64 flotilla craft, and 5 submarines. A fourth dreadnought was nearing completion. Prewar, it planned to cooperate with Italy against France outside the Adriatic. When Italy stayed neutral, the navy's main jobs became supporting the army's operations against Montenegro and keeping the French out of the Adriatic. The navy's leadership sensibly ignored German urgings to fight in the Mediterranean and as far afield as the Black Sea and instead planned for war against Italy. In this case, the fleet would ideally gain dominance of the Adriatic by means of a decisive battle shortly after the war's outbreak, should the Italians offer battle on terms favorable to Austria or attempt to land forces in Istria.

The Austrian naval command considered superiority in speed, concentration of fire on the weakest point, and superior morale as the building blocks of their naval combat doctrine. The battle fleet would seek combat sailing in columns of divisions and deploy into a single battle line just before combat. Austrian planners considered nine thousand yards long range and sixty-five hundred as ideal battle range. Flotilla craft would stay

Map 1.1 Europe at War

Affiliation as of war's end

- **Central Powers**
- **Entente Powers or controlled**
- **Neutral**

Abbreviations

A - P of Albania
B - K of Belgium
D - K of Denmark
Fr - France
G - K of Greece
It - Italy

K - Kingdom
M - K of Montenegro
N - K of Netherlands
P - Principality
Rep - Republic
S - Rep of Switzerland
UK - United Kingdom

O'Hara 2016

out of the way until required to sink damaged enemy ships or support friendly cripples.

Germany: Kaiserliche Marine

The German Kaiserliche Marine was a relatively new institution, having expanded from the amalgamated coastal defense forces of the German states to the world's second largest navy in a mere forty-five years. In August 1914 it could deploy 14 dreadnoughts, 4 battlecruisers, 22 predreadnoughts, 32 old and 16 new cruisers, 132 flotilla craft, and 27 submarines.

The German army and navy did little joint planning and, in effect, fought separate wars. The army hoped for a short campaign. Kaiser Wilhelm, who kept a tight rein on the navy, did not wish to see his expensive fleet decimated in a brief conflict. Nonetheless, the purported purpose of the German navy was to break an anticipated British blockade and establish naval superiority by winning a decisive battle in the North Sea. There was little planning for offensive actions into the Baltic and no intention to invade England as much of the British public (and some in government) feared.

The Germans planned to fight a potentially superior foe in line ahead formation with destroyers making torpedo attacks to reduce enemy strength. The Germans believed they could obtain an advantage by fighting at six thousand yards and that superior armor would allow their damaged ships to return to nearby ports.

Ottoman Empire: Osmanli Donanmasi

On 1 August 1914, the navy of the Ottoman Empire could deploy 2 old battleships, 2 old coast-defense ships, 3 cruisers, 18 flotilla craft, and 19 gunboats. The navy had been bested by Italy in the war of 1911–12, then by Greece in the First Balkan War, and most experts did not consider it efficient or effective. The outbreak of war deprived it of two modern dreadnoughts that were ready to sail and one more that was building, all three still in Great Britain. In August, however, Germany's Mittelmeer Division—a battlecruiser and a light cruiser—joined the Ottoman navy, at least in title. In September 1914 a German became fleet commander and nearly every warship of any size received German officers. As the war evolved, the fleet's major missions were to dispute the Russians for control of the Black Sea, supply troops on the Anatolian coast, protect the critical traffic in coal from Zonguldak to Constantinople, and protect the Bosporus and Dardanelles.

Great Britain: Royal Navy

The British navy was the world's largest in 1914 and considered itself the gold standard to which other navies aspired. In August 1914 the British Royal and Dominion navies included 21 dreadnoughts, 9 battlecruisers, 41 predreadnoughts, 86 old cruisers, 24 modern light cruisers and scouts, 323 flotilla craft, and 76 submarines.

The mission of the Royal Navy was foremost to contain the German High Seas Fleet, and, if challenged, to defeat the Germans in a decisive battle. Success in this mission would protect the British Empire's seaborne trade, secure the passage of troops and supplies to France, and stifle enemy traffic.

The British, having the most battleships, had the biggest problem in ensuring that their superior numbers could be brought to bear in any action. The fleet would sail to contact in columns of divisions screened by scouts, and then deploy into line ahead at the proper moment. The fleet would then engage at long range to employ its presumed superiority in big guns and fire control. After the enemy had been damaged, the line would close to decisive ranges. Flotilla craft and their light cruiser leaders would prevent torpedo attacks by enemy flotillas.[24]

France: Marine Nationale

In 1914 France had the world's fourth largest navy but it was an unbalanced fleet with no modern cruisers and few large destroyers. There were 2 dreadnoughts with 10 building (5 of which entered service), 17 predreadnoughts, 36 old cruisers, 214 flotilla craft, and 50 submarines. The French navy's mission changed once it became clear that Great Britain would be a wartime ally. In August 1914 the fleet had responsibility for the Mediterranean and planned to fight the combined Austrian and Italian fleets. Its first priority, however, was to ensure the safe transit of France's North African troops from Algeria to France. Italy's neutrality and the flight of Germany's Mediterranean squadron to Constantinople reduced France's naval obligations to a blockade of the Austro-Hungarian fleet inside the Adriatic and support of Serbia and Montenegro. France also maintained some light flotillas in the North Sea and English Channel.

The Marine Nationale paid lip service to the doctrine of the decisive battle. The main fleet operated in divisions of battleships. These divisions would unite before combat and engage the enemy in line ahead. The fleet expected to fight at six thousand meters. Gun elevation limitations meant that 12,000 meters was extreme range. Prewar exercises convinced the French they could hit quickly and obtain up to 40 percent hits at their battle range.[25]

Italy: Regia Marina

Italy's Regia Marina was a relatively new service founded after the unification of the peninsula in 1866. In 1914 it was the world's sixth largest navy having 3 dreadnoughts, 13 predreadnoughts, 19 old cruisers, 3 scout cruisers, 96 flotilla craft, and 21 submarines.

Italian prewar naval planning was based on two opposite situations: that the Habsburgs would be allies or they would be foes. In the first case, a united Austro-Italian fleet would concentrate in Sicily under Austrian command to confront the French and interfere with traffic from Africa. In the second case, Italy envisioned dominating the Adriatic via submarines and flotilla craft and protecting its maritime traffic. There was no plan to seek a decisive battle.

Italian battle doctrine called for its dreadnoughts, best predreadnoughts, and the four best armored cruisers sailing to contact in divisions, deploying into line ahead formation just before contact and then fighting at ranges not to exceed ten thousand meters.

Russia: Rossiiski Imperatorskii flot

The Russian navy had two main fleets: one in the Baltic and the other in the Black Sea. In 1914 the Baltic Fleet deployed 4 predreadnoughts, 9 old cruisers, 64 flotilla craft, and 8 submarines. There were four dreadnoughts building. The Black Sea Fleet had 5 predreadnoughts, an ancient coastal defense ship, 2 old cruisers, 36 flotilla craft, and 11 submarines, with 3 dreadnoughts and a number of big destroyers under construction.

Because Russia had to operate in separate, non-supporting theaters, the fleets had different objectives. In the Baltic the navy had to protect the capital, Petrograd (the name changed from St. Petersburg in 1914), from the much stronger German navy. The mainstay of Petrograd's protection would be a mine-artillery barrier blocking entry into the Gulf of Finland. The navy was also to support the army's flank with expendable ships such as gunboats spared from the fleet's main defensive task.

In the Black Sea the navy's mission was not clear. The ultimate Russian goal was to control the Bosporus and prevent the transit of enemy forces into the Black Sea. The 1914 war plan envisioned a stronger Ottoman fleet, anticipating that Constantinople would take delivery of the British-built dreadnoughts. The Russians planned to "take up a favorable position for battle near Sevastopol and fight a decisive engagement from this position."[26] When the three British-built ships failed to appear, Russian plans for the Black Sea went into a bit of a freefall.

Russian doctrine differed from the European norm, based in part on the Russians' relatively recent battle experience. They intended to fight in independent divisions rather than in a massive line ahead formation. In the case of the Black Sea Fleet the Russians planned to engage at as much as 20,000 yards. The modern destroyers carried heavy torpedo batteries and would attack the enemy during a fleet engagement.

1914: Trial by Fire

If I lose one of these valuable ships the country will not forgive me.
—ADMIRAL DAVID BEATTY, 28 AUGUST 1914

Overview

The war that began on 28 July 1914 did not end before Christmas as many assumed it would. Instead, the Franco-British armies stopped a rapid German advance short of Paris after which both sides became stalemated with neither able to force a decision. There were massive back-and-forth battles in the east that saw the Germans repulse the Russians from East Prussia and advance to threaten Warsaw while the Russians occupied Austrian Galicia up to the Carpathian passes. In the Balkans, Serbia successfully stood off superior Austro-Hungarian forces.

Two factors determined the initial course and the ultimate outcome of this conflict that became the First World War. The first factor was that the war erupted spontaneously, in reaction to events rather than in a deliberate manner by a great power trying to shape events. Second was the prevailing expectation that the war would be of short duration. These factors particularly affected Imperial Germany and Imperial and Royal Austria-Hungary, the continental powers with the most restricted access to the sea. These powers had sophisticated and effective plans to mobilize their armies but they did not have plans to mobilize their economies. Germany expected the British to impose a naval blockade,

32

but did not have proper stockpiles of strategic materials (other than coal) required to fight under the constraints of an embargo. In 1939 Germany went to war with 6.5 million tons of food stockpiled. In 1914, there was nothing.[1]

The Admiralstab, Germany's naval staff, expected Britain to impose a close blockade of Germany's short North Sea coast. They anticipated this would expose the blockading ships to opportunistic attacks and allow Germany to whittle down Britain's margin of superiority under favorable conditions. Once the odds had been thus improved staff planned to seek a decisive fleet action. The British, however, frustrated German expectations by implementing a distant blockade, intercepting enemy traffic far from German shores. The Royal Navy already had sea control and did not need to risk the fleet to keep it.

Once the Admiralstab realized there was no blockade line around Wilhelmshaven it was forced to reconsider the navy's fundamental strategy. Interestingly the greatest threat perceived by the British during this period—a German attack against the transports carrying the British Expeditionary Force (BEF) to the continent—was something the Germans, for a number of good reasons, never considered.[2] Of the six

Table 2.1 Forces Deployed in the North Sea and Atlantic Coast of France and the UK

Type	France	Britain	Germany
Dreadnought	0	22	14
Battlecruiser	0	4	4
Predreadnought	0	35	22
Armored Cruiser	6	32	5
Light Cruiser	0	18	20
Protected Cruiser	1	18	4
Destroyer	33	179	91
Torpedo Boat	20	48	61
Submarine	21	56	25

Sources: British as of 5 August 1914 per Pink List. French and German, http://www.gwpda.org/naval/n0000000.htm#swt.

regular army divisions available in August 1914 the British sent only four to France and retained two in England to guard against a German invasion—another activity the Admiralstab never seriously contemplated.

Germany's fleet faced not only the North Sea but the Baltic and, thanks to the Kiel Canal, could quickly deploy from one sea to the other. The Baltic was Russia's major maritime theater because it fronted Petrograd, the capital. Given Germany's naval superiority, Russian planners developed a barrier called the Central Position to defend Petrograd. This consisted of a dense minefield in the Gulf of Finland west of Revel supported by artillery batteries on islands to the north and south. Cruiser patrols would detect a German fleet trying to force the Central Position; flotilla craft would deliver mass torpedo attacks on its flanks while battleships formed the final defense to the east.

While Russia began the land war with an offensive into East Prussia and Galicia, the navy's posture was entirely defensive. When war seemed imminent the Russian Baltic Fleet began laying hundreds of mines. But despite the Kaiserliche Marine's ability to outnumber the Imperial Russian Navy at will, it never considered a serious attack against Petrograd.

Table 2.2 Forces Deployed in the Baltic, 1 August 1914

Type	Germany	Russia
Predreadnought	0	4
Armored Cruiser	1	5
Protected Cruiser	1	4
Light Cruiser	7	0
Destroyer	9	14
Torpedo Boat	7	50
Minecraft	0	6
Submarine	4	8

Sources: Sources vary. The table is based on War at Sea (http://www.gwpda.org/naval/ n0000000.htm#swt), Stephen McLaughlin, correspondence. See also Firle, *Ostsee*, 1:4; Halpern, *World War I*, 15 (which includes vessels not in service).

Table 2.3 Forces in the Mediterranean and Black Sea, 1 August 1914

Type	France	Britain	Italy	Germany	Austria-Hungary	Ottoman Empire	Russia
Dreadnought	2	0	3	0	3	0	0
Battlecruiser	0	3	0	1	0	0	0
Predreadnought	15	0	8+5★	0	9+3★	2	4+2★
Armored Cruiser	7	4	10	0	2	0	0
Light Cruiser	0	4	3	1	2★★	0	0
Protected Cruiser	10	0	9	0	3	2	1
Destroyer	37	16	28	0	19+6^	9	26
Torpedo Boat	6	16	68	0	39	9	10
Submarine	15	6	21	0	5	0	11

Sources: Halpern, *Mediterranean*; Weyer, *Taschenbuch der Kriegsflotten.*

★indicates old armored coast defense ships.

★★one more completed in August 1914.

^old.

The most important naval event in the Baltic was the Russian capture of German code books from a stranded cruiser. This and other captures helped the Russians and British (with whom they shared their windfall) break German wireless codes, which in turn yielded intelligence about many naval operations. The Germans never realized their codes had been deeply compromised.

The Mediterranean was vital to many nations. It united France's North African possessions with its European Métropole; Italy's central position and dependence on seaborne imports made Mediterranean events critical to that nation's security; Ottoman territory dominated the sea's eastern littoral; and Russia's best access to the world's oceans passed through Ottoman-controlled straits. The Mediterranean gave access to the Austro-Hungarian sea frontier on the Adriatic. Finally, it provided the most direct route from India and Australia to Great Britain.

The biggest uncertainty in the Middle Sea was Italy's attitude. With Italy a member of the Triple Alliance, plans originally called for the Italian and Austrian fleets to unite under Austrian command and then seek to control the Mediterranean. But, as old rivals, Rome and Vienna both doubted whether the plan would ever materialize. In the opening days of the war, the Entente's greatest concern in the Mediterranean was to ensure the safe passage of French colonial troops from Algeria to France.

Uncertainty ruled the Black Sea as well. From a naval perspective, the Russians had less at stake in the Black Sea than in the Baltic and, with its armies already fully committed against Germany and Austria-Hungary, Russia did not want war with the Ottoman Empire. Although it had long-standing territorial ambitions on the Black Sea littoral, Petrograd was willing to suspend these and to placate the Ottomans pending events elsewhere.

The Ottoman government's attitudes toward war were complicated: one party wanted to join the Central Powers, one the Entente, one supported impartial neutrality, and yet another backed armed, anti-Russian neutrality. Russia was an old enemy, however, and Great Britain had outraged public opinion by seizing without compensation battleships that British yards were completing for the Ottoman navy. Relations with the Entente powers deteriorated after Germany gifted its Mediterranean squadron to the Ottomans. The Porte closed the Black Sea to foreign shipping on 26 September and Great Britain declared a blockade on 2 October.

The addition of a German battlecruiser and light cruiser greatly enhanced Ottoman naval power but German involvement went beyond material reinforcement. German Rear Admiral Wilhelm Souchon became an Ottoman vice admiral and Germans assumed key command and technical positions. On October 29 Souchon used the war minister's carte blanche to launch a surprise attack against Russian Black Sea ports. War with Russia followed on November 2.

At the start of the war Britain and Germany had the world's two largest merchant fleets: Britain's with more than 9,200 vessels displacing over 19 million GRT and Germany's with 2,400 ships and 5.5 million GRT.[3] In terms of naval power, the Germans had only light cruisers on the Mexican Pacific coast, in the West Indies, and in East Africa. At their major base in Tsingtau, China, they had a light cruiser, gunboats, a torpedo boat, and an old Austrian protected cruiser, and elsewhere in China they had two more gunboats. The East Asiatic Squadron with two armored cruisers was at sea and a light cruiser was under way to Mexico. In comparison the British deployed the Australia Squadron with a battlecruiser and three light cruisers, a New Zealand Division with three protected cruisers, an East Indies Squadron with a predreadnought, two cruisers, and some sloops, and a China Squadron with a predreadnought, two armored and two protected cruisers, eight destroyers, and two sloops. In French Indochina the Marine Nationale mustered two armored cruisers, a torpedo gunboat, and three torpedo boats. Japan's late August entry into the war added two dreadnoughts, eleven predreadnoughts, six battlecruisers, twenty-seven cruisers, and eighty flotilla craft.

The threat of German raiders caused the Entente much inconvenience and forced them to deploy squadrons in every ocean and near every choke point, but the British, at least, had the navy for the job. The campaign against German raiders provoked many of the year's naval actions and while the Germans temporarily disrupted trade in limited areas, they could not stop it. By year's end the campaign was largely over with just a few fugitive raiders still afloat. The end of 1914 also saw the great majority of the German merchant marine seized, interned in neutral ports, or idled by the British blockade.

North Sea 1914
Action in the Broad Fourteens: 18 August, 0540–0700
   Conditions: Fine and clear, light northern wind
   Missions: British, patrol; Germans, raid
   British Force (Captain Wilfred Blunt): 1st Destroyer Flotilla (DF): CL *Fearless*; DD *Acheron, Attack, Ariel, Badger, Beaver, Defender, Druid, Ferret, Forester, Goshawk, Hind, Hornet, Hydra, Jackal, Lapwing, Lizard, Phoenix, Sandfly, Tigress.*
   German Force (Captain Viktor Harder): CL *Stralsund.*

Several weeks of reconnaissance by submarines and explorations by small cruisers and destroyers out to a distance of 120 miles from Heligoland established that the British were not closely investing Heligoland Bight as expected. The Admiralstab therefore determined to undertake a foray toward the Dutch coast in the area of the Broad Fourteens. It sent the light cruisers *Strassburg* and *Stralsund* to slip past British destroyers it assumed were patrolling in the area. They would then backtrack separately and surprise the enemy at dawn. *Kolberg* would wait near Terschelling while *U19* and *U24* lurked to the northeast to attack ships lured their way. Battlecruisers raised steam, but remained in Schillig Roads.

The German cruisers reached the far point in their sweep between 0330 and 0400 and came about as planned. *Strassburg*, the northernmost ship, encountered the British submarines *E5* and *E7*, which quickly dived when she answered their recognition signals with gunfire. To the south *Stralsund* collided with the Royal Navy's 1st DF. This force was sweeping southwest in a line of five columns, each three miles apart. *Stralsund* and the westernmost column—*Lizard, Lapwing, Goshawk,* and *Phoenix*—spotted each other at 0540 and exchanged long-range broadsides for a half hour. The British destroyers reported the enemy fire as heavy while *Stralsund* observed only three or four enemy rounds falling close aboard; the rest dropped fifty to two thousand yards short. The German ship also noted four torpedo tracks. *Fearless* steamed toward the

Map 2.1 North Sea

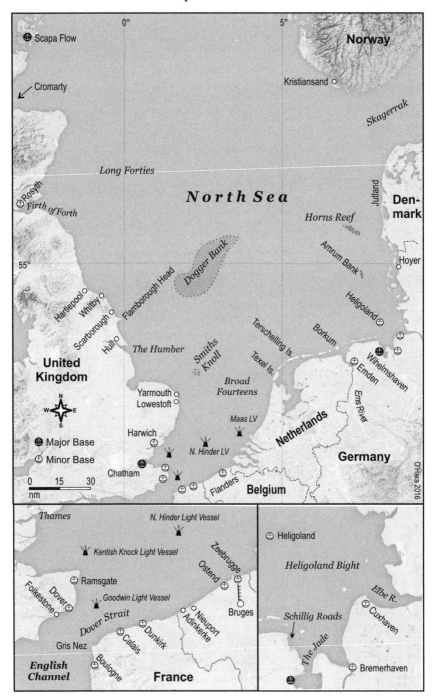

Scapa Flow

Cromarty

0°

5°

Norway

Kristiansand

Skagerrak

Long Forties

Rosyth
Firth of Forth

North Sea

Jutland

Den-mark

Horns Reef

Hoyer

55°

Dogger Bank

Amrum Bank

Hartlepool
Whitby
Scarborough
Hull
Flamborough Head

Heligoland

Borkum

The Humber

Smiths Knoll

Terschelling Is.

Texel Is.

Wilhelmshaven
Emden

United Kingdom

Yarmouth
Lowestoft

Broad Fourteens

Maas LV

Netherlands

Ems River

N
W E
S

Harwich

N. Hinder LV

Germany

⊕ Major Base
⊕ Minor Base

Chatham

Flanders

Belgium

0   15   30
nm

O'Hara 2016

Thames

N. Hinder Light Vessel

⊕ Heligoland

Kentish Knock Light Vessel

Zeebrugge
Ostend

Heligoland Bight

Folkestone
Dover
⊕ Ramsgate

Goodwin Light Vessel

Bruges

Elbe R.

Cuxhaven

Schillig Roads

Dover Strait

Nieuport
Adinkerke

Gris Nez
Calais
Dunkirk

The Jade

English Channel

Boulogne

France

Bremerhaven

action and misidentified *Stralsund* as an armored cruiser. At 0610 Blunt turned away to the southwest to collect his force before engaging such a superior foe. "This produced a tirade of signals from the closest (and bitterly disappointed) destroyers, asserting that the enemy was not an armored cruiser."[4]

As *Fearless* concentrated her flotilla, *Stralsund*'s Harder turned north at 0637. He assessed his opponents as two cruisers and ten destroyers. He believed he had hit two enemy ships and concluded his ship alone "could not hold out longer against an enemy considerably superior in numbers." The 1st DF pursued and another flotilla tried to cut *Stralsund* off, but it was too late and the German cruisers reached base unmolested.[5]

The Admiralstab had been tentative in its first offensive effort and as the official history noted, the small force deployed "rendered inadmissible from the start a complete success." In fact, the Germans had been lucky, delivered from a far superior foe because Blunt exaggerated his opponent. The tendency to overestimate enemy forces would be a leitmotif of the surface war. It prevented action from being joined or attacks being pressed, and reflected a widespread belief that a superior force would inevitably annihilate an inferior force. This indeed proved true in some actions, but more often the superior force struggled against factors that prevented a decisive victory, including command and control difficulties, the fog of war, poor visibility, and bad weather.[6]

First Battle of Heligoland Bight: 28 August, 0653–1300

Conditions: Light northwest wind, many patches of fog

Missions: British, raid; Germans, patrol

British Forces: Grand Fleet forces (Vice Admiral David Beatty): BC *Lion, Princess Royal, Queen Mary*. 1st Light Cruiser Squadron (LCS) (Commodore William Goodenough): CL *Southampton, Birmingham, Nottingham, Lowestoft, Falmouth, Liverpool*.

Force K (Rear Admiral A. C. Moore): BC *Invincible, New Zealand*; DD *Badger, Beaver, Jackal, Sandfly*.

Harwich Force (Commodore Reginald Tyrwhitt): 3rd DF: CL *Arethusa*[#]; DD *Lookout, Leonidas, Legion, Lennox, Lark, Lance, Linnet, Landrail, Laforey, Lawford, Louis, Lydiard, Laurel*[#], *Liberty*[#],

Lysander[+], Laertes[#]. 1st DF: CL *Fearless*[+]; DD *Acheron, Attack, Hind, Archer, Ariel, Lucifer, Llewellyn, Ferret, Forester, Druid, Defender, Goshawk*[+], *Lizard, Lapwing, Phoenix*.

Harwich Submarines (Commodore Roger Keyes): DD *Lurcher, Firedrake*; SS *D2, D8, E4, E5, E6, E7, E8, E9.*

German Forces (Rear Admiral Franz Hipper, Rear Admiral Leberecht Maass†): Outer Patrol: I Torpedo Boat Flotilla (TBF) (Frigate Captain Wallis): DD *G193, G196, G194, V187*[*], *V188, V190, V191, G197, V189*. Inner Patrol: Minesweeper Flotilla (MSF) III (Corvette Captain Eberhard Wolfram): TB *D8*[#]; MS *T36, T29, T40, T31, T34, T33*[#], *T37, T35, T25, T71*. V TBF: DD *G9, V1*[+], *S13, G12, V6, V3, G11, V2, G10, G7*. Light Forces: CL *Köln*[*], *Stettin*[#], *Frauenlob*[#], *Ariadne*[*], *Stralsund, Strassburg, Mainz*[*].

The German navy conducted another raid ten days later when two light cruisers and a destroyer flotilla probed to the edge of the Dogger Bank and sank eight fishing trawlers. The Admiralty regarded such pinprick actions as proof that the High Seas Fleet had no intention of challenging the Grand Fleet any time soon. The question of provoking action on favorable terms in the face of such a strategy led Commodore Roger Keyes, commander of the Harwich submarines, and Commodore Reginald Tyrwhitt, commanding the Harwich light forces, to propose an attack on the enemy's defenses of the Heligoland Bight. These consisted of one ring of destroyers patrolling twenty-five miles from the fortress island of Heligoland and another of torpedo boats and minesweepers twelve miles out. The German dispositions were designed to detect enemy submarines penetrating their base area and force them to submerge and use up their batteries. The two commodores devised a scheme in which three submarines would provoke the patrolling destroyers into chasing them while five more crept in to ambush ships emerging in support. Meanwhile, two light cruisers and thirty-one destroyers would sweep in from the north and hit the enemy's rear. Force K, consisting of two battlecruisers, and Force C, five armored cruisers and one small cruiser, would support the raiders in case they encountered serious opposition.

The Admiralty approved the plan and set the date for 28 August but rejected Admiral John Jellicoe's request to support the operation with most of the Grand Fleet. In response to Jellicoe's continued entreaties, however, the Admiralty finally allowed all of the available battlecruisers to participate. Jellicoe immediately ordered Vice Admiral David Beatty, with three battlecruisers and the six light cruisers of Commodore William Goodenough's 1st LCS, to rendezvous with Force K in the northern bight. Keyes and Tyrwhitt would have welcomed this reinforcement had they known of it, but a communications breakdown left them unaware of Beatty's participation. Tyrwhitt found out only when his force saw Beatty's ships at 0330 on 28 August; he came close to attacking before establishing their identity. Even then, he had no idea Goodenough's cruisers would follow him into the battle area. Keyes would learn of Beatty's presence only during the battle itself.

Keyes, on board *Lurcher*, and Tyrwhitt, flying his broad pennant in *Arethusa*, inserted their forces into the bight as planned. The German outer patrol consisted of nine destroyers while the inner patrol included nine old torpedo boats serving as minesweepers and a torpedo boat leader. Light cruisers available to support the smaller ships included *Stettin*, anchored near Heligoland, and *Frauenlob* and *Ariadne* farther south. Heligoland Island itself contained batteries of 21-cm, 10.5-cm, and 88-mm guns.

At 0500 a British submarine attacked *G194*. The destroyer reported the incident ("false alarm inadmissible") to Rear Admiral Leberecht Maass, commanding the German flotilla craft from light cruiser *Köln*. At 0610 Maass summoned V TBF's ten destroyers to reinforce the patrol line and steer for *G194*'s position, sixteen miles northwest of Heligoland Island.[7]

The Harwich flotillas had already turned south at 0400 to penetrate the bight, steaming through a still sea and patchy fog. The 3rd DF sighted *G194* at 0653 and Tyrwhitt dispatched *Laurel*, *Liberty*, *Lysander*, and *Laertes* to attack. They soon disappeared into the mist. The British also encountered *G196* and then from 0725 collided with units of the V TBF that were racing out to hunt the reported submarine. When they came under fire from a clearly superior force the surprised German ships turned and ran for Heligoland.

The first confirmation of British surface forces was *G196*'s 0706 message that enemy cruisers were chasing *G194* in grid square 142ε, fifteen miles northwest of Heligoland Island. Then between 0723 and 0730

Map 2.2 Battle of Heligoland Bight: 28 August 2014

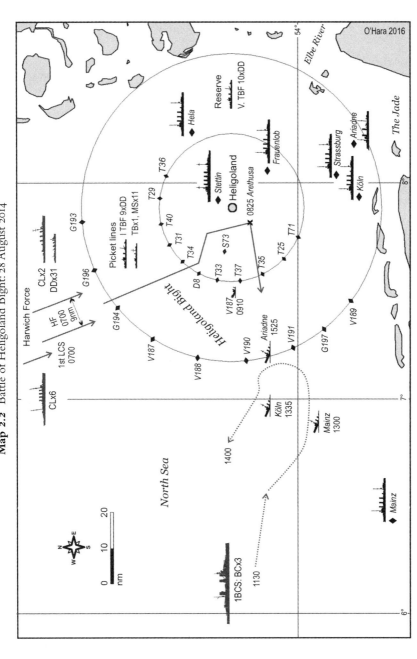

Maass received a series of signals from the picket destroyers. They had to be decoded and took as long as a quarter hour to reach the bridge after receipt and in some cases arrived out of chronological sequence. They indicated a submarine steering northeast by east, no location given; a solitary enemy vessel (type unspecified, square, 142ε) steering northeast by east; enemy cruisers steering south in square, 142ε; two destroyers, location thirty-five miles northwest of Heligoland; and enemy forces, type and location unspecified, steering south-southeast. Moreover, the weather at the German bases was clear and no one there appreciated the chaos that the fog was producing in the battle zone. After further reports mentioned large cruisers and twenty destroyers Maass ordered his flotilla craft to retire under Heligoland's guns.

As Maass struggled to grasp the situation the British destroyers were quickly shooting through their allloment of 360 4-inch rounds per ship in the target rich environment. The German destroyers on the other hand, with their 88-mm weapons generally being outranged, expended far fewer rounds, except for *V1* and *S13*, which lagged behind due to not having full steam up. They fired forty and fifty-one rounds respectively. The inner picket minesweepers heard the gunfire, but maintained position thinking the commotion was due to the submarine hunt. The minesweeper commander only learned differently when at 0730 friendly destroyers suddenly emerged out of the mist from the north, racing hell bent for Heligoland. When enemy warships appeared in chase *D8* and the sweepers in her vicinity turned for Heligoland at top speed. However, top speed was only fifteen knots and the British quickly closed. *D8* estimated she was the target of up to six hundred shells. "Most of the shells on striking the water did not detonate, but rebound[ed] after striking, keeping on and skipping up to 20 m high in the air without doing any damage." Nonetheless, five shells did hit the old torpedo boat, killing thirteen, wounding twenty, and leaving her dead in the water. *D8* fired eighty-five 50-mm rounds in her own defense and was eventually towed back to Heligoland. *T33*, *T34*, *T37*, *T35*, and *S73* also found themselves under fire. Of these, however, only *T33* suffered. She was first hit at 0800. Her captain reported: "The engine stopped and the water rose very rapidly in the engine room. I now drifted helplessly and the enemy rushed on at high speed."[8]

Rear Admiral Franz Hipper, commander of the scouting forces, ordered *Stettin* and *Frauenlob* to investigate the reports of enemy forces. *Stettin* did not have far to go. She got under way at 0740 with three of eleven boilers cold and minutes later, just four miles northwest of Heligoland, came upon *V1*. The destroyer was in distress having been hit twice, with a boiler out and steering gear damaged. At 0758 *Stettin* engaged a group of destroyers from nine thousand yards. Five minutes later she switched to *Arethusa* as the cruiser came up and then targeted *Fearless* on a reciprocal course at ranges that dropped to seven thousand yards. One report noted the splashes from the enemy's shells in *Stettin*'s immediate vicinity "gave the impression that the *Stettin* was in boiling water." At 0812 *Fearless* turned away whereupon *Stettin* circled east to build pressure in all her boilers so she could fight at full speed.[9]

At 0808 *Frauenlob* arrived south of Heligoland Island and, heading southwest, encountered *Arethusa*. She opened fire at nine thousand yards on a converging course, likely saving *D8* and *T33* in the process. *Arethusa*, a new ship and not fully worked up, was soon in trouble. Materiel defects silenced some of her guns while *Frauenlob*'s good shooting disabled others. Splinters cut down the flagship's signal officer at Commodore Tyrwhitt's side. By 0815 only one of *Arethusa*'s guns remained in action. She was losing speed due to a damaged main freshwater feed tank and an engine room was flooding. *Arethusa* had hit *Frauenlob* ten times in return but many British shells were duds and *Frauenlob* suffered little harm. At 0825 with the range just 3,400 yards *Arethusa* vanished into the fog and *Frauenlob* turned away.

V187 was the only German ship sunk in the initial assault. She sailed into clear air where *Goshawk*, *Lizard*, *Lapwing*, and *Phoenix* spotted her. They chased the German south until *V187* suddenly veered north right into the path of the oncoming *Ferret*, *Forester*, *Druid*, and *Defender*. In fact the German had found herself running right toward *Nottingham* and *Lowestoft* and had to pick the lesser of two evils. The British swarmed the unfortunate vessel, leaving her dead in the water. *Goshawk* then approached to rescue survivors but a German gun tagged the British ship with a single round. This provoked a renewed pounding and *V187* sank at 0910. Rescue operations were under way when *Stettin* emerged from a fog bank and scattered the British destroyers, causing them to abandon some of their boats.

Commodore Reginald Tyrwhitt, who led the Harwich Force throughout the war and participated in more surface actions than any other commanding officer. (Library of Congress)

With the action an hour old, nothing larger than a small cruiser reported, and no knowledge of the battle area's conditions, Hipper concluded that he was facing just a raid by light forces. He first ordered *Stralsund*, *Danzig*, and *München* to reinforce the cruisers already engaged. Orders to *Mainz* followed twenty minutes later. Finally, between 0900 and 1000 Hipper sent *Köln*, *Strassburg*, *Kolberg*, and *Ariadne* to join the battle. In their rush to intervene, the light cruisers did not attempt to concentrate or coordinate their movements. Battlecruisers *Moltke* and *Von der Tann* were raising steam by 0908, but had to wait for high water due at noon before they could clear the Jade River bar to reach the open sea.

A lull following the first flurry of actions allowed *Arethusa* to repair most of her gun and some of her machinery problems. At 1000 Tyrwhitt even took time to scold Goodenough for joining the action. "I was not informed you were coming into this area; you run great risk from our submarines. . . . Your unexpected appearance has upset all our plans."[10] Fume he might; Keyes, cruising off Heligoland in *Lurcher*, had three times reported Goodenough's cruisers as enemy, while they had almost run down one friendly submarine and had come perilously close to being attacked by another. Tyrwhitt even urged Goodenough's light cruisers to chase the light cruisers that Keyes reported were chasing him, not realizing they were all the same ships.

At 1048 *Strassburg* encountered *Arethusa* and briefly engaged her from six thousand yards in a sharp but inconclusive action. After *Strassburg* withdrew northwards Tyrwhitt elected to keep his forces concentrated rather than chase. Shortly after, *Köln* appeared and lobbed a few salvoes at the British. Tyrwhitt mistook her for an armored cruiser and at 1128 urgently radioed Beatty for support. Next *Strassburg* returned and again targeted *Arethusa*. Tyrwhitt reported: "We were receiving a very severe and almost accurate fire from this cruiser; salvo after salvo was falling between ten and thirty yards short, but not a single shell struck."[11] The British commodore ordered a full-blooded torpedo attack from eight 3rd DF destroyers. They closed to 4,500 yards and launched starting at 1135. All torpedoes missed as *Strassburg* sheered north and disappeared from view. The British remained concentrated and awaited the next development.

At 1130 1st DF, steaming four to five miles west of *Arethusa* and *Fearless*, spotted *Mainz* farther west. *Mainz* chased the destroyers north, peppering them with 10.5-cm rounds but not hitting. During this action, *Stralsund* contributed a few salvoes from the north and then lost sight of the enemy. At 1145 *Mainz* turned south after sighting Goodenough's cruisers to the west, only to find herself sandwiched between four ships of that squadron and the two Harwich cruisers to the east. The British opened fire at ten thousand yards and quickly registered hits. At 1200 *Laurel*, *Liberty*, *Lysander*, and *Laertes* raced in to attack. As *Laurel* put four torpedoes into the water an enthusiastic officer related: "[*Mainz*'s] shells were dropping, some of them just 20 yards short, and others 20 yards over us, I got drenched by the spray from one of them. Heaps of times we heard the buzzing of a shell just above our heads. It was most marvelous!"[12] However, it was not so marvelous when a shell punched into *Laurel*'s engine room and another struck near her foremost gun. Shells in the gun's ready rack exploded, damaging a funnel, wreathing the ship in smoke, and killing eleven men. *Liberty* next astern plunged through the unexpected smoke and also launched four torpedoes but then a shell slammed into her bridge, toppled the mainmast, and killed her captain along with seven other crewmen. The third destroyer, *Lysander*, fired her torpedoes and withdrew undamaged but *Mainz* hammered *Laertes*, the last ship, with four shells, holing her boilers and bringing her to a complete stop. However, one of the twelve torpedoes fired smacked the German cruiser and this proved her death-blow. Commodore Keyes, who was nearby, described the scene: "She had settled considerably by the bows, the after part was crowded with men, many terribly wounded, the battery was a ghastly shambles, amidships she was a smoldering furnace, two of her funnels had collapsed and the wreckage appeared to be red hot, the heat scorched one's face as far off as the bridge of the *Lurcher,* everything was dyed saffron with the fumes of our lyddite shells."[13] *Lurcher* eventually rescued 220 of *Mainz*'s crew.

At 1230 *Köln,* followed by *Strassburg,* sighted the enemy to the south. *Köln* attacked *Arethusa,* then to her southwest, and was engaged in turn by *Fearless* to her southeast. *Strassburg* reported targeting British destroyers but lost contact after a brief exchange. Then Beatty's battle-cruisers, responding to Tyrwhitt's earlier calls for support, appeared out of the mists. At 1238 they turned their main batteries against *Köln* from six thousand yards. As *Köln* temporarily escaped into the fog, *Ariadne* was sailing toward the sound of gunfire and entered the fight from the north at 1256. A 13.5-inch shell exploded in the small cruiser's boiler room and cut her speed to 15 knots. Then, as her captain reported, "The *Ariadne* received many hits from large guns, among them a series of hits in the stern, which burst into flames. . . . How many hits there were in all can not be estimated."[14] After a half hour *Ariadne* escaped, cloaked in smoke from her own fires. At roughly the same time, however, *Köln* emerged from a fog bank only four thousand yards from *Lion.* The battlecruiser's first salvo wrecked the German cruiser; *Köln* sank at 1335 with only one survivor. *Ariadne* eventually capsized at 1525. After savaging *Köln,* the British forces withdrew. They had raised havoc off the German anchorages for more than seven hours and it was time to be off. *Moltke* and *Von der Tann* finally reached open water at 1400, too late to intervene.

The Battle of Heligoland Bight was a British victory. There were certainly grounds for criticism, especially the Admiralty's failure to inform Keyes and Tyrwhitt of Beatty's participation. The faults on the side of the Kaiserliche Marine were more glaring: ineffective communications, disjointed attacks by individual light cruisers and inadequate plans to intervene with heavy units if needed. The battle did cause the Admiralstab to reconsider how it would protect its bases. Maintaining a constant picket line had been taking a toll on the torpedo boat flotillas. Hipper had been reluctant to lay extensive minefields for fear that this would inhibit German forces almost as much as the British. After this battle, he was more amenable to defensive mining and to using low-value trawlers on the picket line rather than destroyers. Amongst the officers of the fleet the reaction was more personal. *München*'s executive officer wrote: "The effect of this day was an immense loss of confidence in the leadership of the fleet, but a gain of confidence in our training and weapons."[15]

Part of the Admiralstab plan for a naval offensive against Great Britain was a series of mining operations. The auxiliary minelayer *Könige Luise* opened the war by laying a field off the mouth of the Thames on 5 August but was caught and sunk shortly thereafter by scout cruiser *Amphion* and destroyers *Lance*, *Landrail*, and *Laurel*. Ironically, while returning to base, *Amphion* struck two mines in the newly laid field and sank with the loss of 151 of her crew and eighteen of the twenty *Könige Luise* survivors she had rescued.

The purpose-built minelayers *Nautilus* and *Albatross* laid a pair of fields off the Humber on 26 August. On 16 October *Nautilus*, *Kolberg*, and the auxiliary minelayer *Berlin* set out to mine the Firth of Forth and the Clyde, on Scotland's west coast. The first two aborted their mission, while *Berlin* was forced to lay her field off Northern Ireland's Lough Swilly instead. This ultimately resulted in the loss of dreadnought *Audacious*.

The British scout cruiser *Amphion*. She sank *Könige Luise*, the first German auxiliary minelayer to venture to the English coast, and was in turn sunk by one of her victim's freshly laid mines. (Courtesy of John Roberts Collection)

Battle off Texel: 17 October, 1350–1630
Conditions: Clear
Missions: British, patrol; Germans, offensive minelaying
British Force (Captain Cecil Fox): CL *Undaunted*; DD *Lance*⁺, *Lennox*,
  Legion, *Loyal*.
German Force (Corvette Captain Georg Thiele†): 7 TBHF: TB *S115*★,
  S117★, *S118*★, *S119*★.

The German capture of the Belgian ports of Zeebrugge and Ostend allowed short-ranged flotilla craft to participate in offensive minelaying efforts. In the first such operation the minelayers would start in the Heligoland Bight and end in Flanders with their target being the Downs, an important roadstead northeast of Dover. The Admiralstab assigned the dangerous mission to a half flotilla of old torpedo boats, the smallest vessels practical. They landed nonessential personnel, loaded a dozen mines each, and left the Ems at 0330 on 17 October.

British forces actively patrolled the waters through which the minelayers needed to transit. This vigilance was rewarded at 1340 when light cruiser *Undaunted*, leading four destroyers, sighted smoke to the northeast and turned to investigate. Ten minutes later the forces spotted each other; the Germans came hard about and the chase was on. The torpedo boats were outmatched, particularly as a condenser defect in *S118* limited the formation's speed to 18 knots. *Undaunted* engaged at 1405 from eight thousand yards whereupon the Germans began zigzagging violently. *Undaunted* ceased fire to conserve ammunition and Captain Fox signaled general chase. On the right *Lennox* and *Lance* headed to block *S115* from Heligoland Bight while on the left *Loyal* kept *S119* from breaking to the open waters to the north. *Legion* pursued *S117* and *S118* in the center. By 1500 the range had dropped to 2,500 yards and the action became general. Gunfire quickly left *S115* dead in the water; *S117* soon suffered the same fate. The other two torpedo boats turned back and *S119* launched torpedoes. One struck *Lance*, leaving a 3-inch bulge in her plating six feet below the water line but failing to explode. *Undaunted*, *Loyal*, and *Legion* reported being near-missed by torpedoes in numbers greater than the Germans actually carried.[16] By 1630 every German ship was sunk. The British expended seventy-six 6-inch and 1,043 4-inch rounds, and had five men wounded. Two hundred and twenty-two Germans died and only thirty-six were rescued.[17]

The Battle off Texel had an unexpected postscript when a British trawler fishing over the German wrecks dragged up a lead-lined chest. The chest contained secret documents, including a copy of the Verkehrbuch—the Kaiserliche Marine flag officer code and the last of the three major German naval codes to be acquired by British intelligence.[18]

The Yarmouth Raid: 3 November, 0710–0731

Conditions: Misty

Missions: British, patrol; Germans, bombardment

British Force (Commander G. N. Ballard): TGB *Halcyon*[+]; DD *Leopard*, *Lively*.

German Force (Rear Admiral Franz Hipper): BC *Seydlitz*, *Von der Tann*, *Moltke*; CA *Blücher*; CL *Stralsund*, *Kolberg*, *Graudenz*, *Strassburg*.

The loss of four torpedo boats and an auxiliary minelayer in the war's first two months led the Germans to ponder other ways to mine British coastal waters. For the next major effort Admiral Friedrich Ingenohl, commander of the High Seas Fleet, tried a combined operation. Battlecruisers would bombard Yarmouth, a small English port of minor military value, while the light cruiser *Stralsund* would use the distraction to lay a minefield that would hopefully pass unnoticed. Ingenohl also believed the operation would embarrass the British, and "afford gun crews some much needed practice."[19] Because the Germans were not sure of the Grand Fleet's location, most of the High Seas Fleet would trail 120 miles behind the bombardment force just in case. In fact, most British dreadnoughts were at far-off Lough Swilly while their intended base at Scapa Flow was being secured against submarine attack. Only the battlecruiser force at Cromarty was within striking distance.

After waiting for suitable weather, the bombardment/minelaying force left the Jade at 1630 on 2 November followed by the rest of the fleet at 1800. The heavy ships and three light cruisers of the advance force were bound for Yarmouth, while *Stralsund* headed for the shipping channel off Smith's Knoll. All ships reached their assigned locations

without incident, although *Stralsund*'s navigation was off and she began
to lay her mines prematurely.

At 0710 as the German battlecruisers approached Yarmouth in misty
conditions *Halcyon*, an elderly torpedo gunboat serving as a minesweeper,
appeared and challenged the raiders. Almost immediately she came under
a deluge of fire from ranges of 9,000 to 13,000 yards. An officer on *Von
der Tann* observed: "Due to a misunderstood signal, in addition to *Seydlitz*,
Moltke, *Blücher*, *Graudenz*, and *Strassburg* also opened fire on *Halcyon* and
only to this circumstance does the small vessel owe its life, as the fire of five
ships on only one target from five different directions could not expect success."[20] Patrolling nearby the antique destroyers *Leopard* and *Lively* heard the
gunfire and rushed to investigate.

As the Germans made a broad loop, sailing from southwest to south-
southeast they engaged the little ships and also the intended target, Yarmouth, ten miles to the west. On board *Lively* a crewman recalled, "One
watched for the flash, waited with eyes turned to the skies to catch a
sight of the shells as they came hurtling towards us—for they could be
plainly seen in the clear morning air . . . those big, brown, red-banded
shells, some bursting with an awful crash overhead; one especially I recall,
almost knocking us down with its blast and concussion as it burst not 20
yards from our stern." At 0735, Admiral Hipper turned east northeast and
continued with *Stralsund* scattering the last of her mines in the formation's
wake. A large shell fragment struck *Halcyon*'s bridge and her aerial was shot
away; otherwise, the British were shaken but unharmed. Fire against the
town had been blind and damage was entirely random.[21]

Other British forces were at sea that morning. The light cruiser *Undaunted*
(Captain Francis Gerald St. John having replaced Captain Fox in October)
leading four destroyers encountered the raiders at 0950. However, St. John,
believing the Germans might overwhelm his little force, immediately broke
contact, something he did so well that he could not find the Germans again
when ordered to shadow the enemy and report.[22]

Heavy fog in Heligoland Bight compelled the German fleet to
anchor outside its bases on the evening of 3 November. That night
armored cruiser *Yorck* developed engineering problems. She attempted
to transit a "friendly" minefield, lost her way, hit two mines, and sank
with heavy loss of life. In addition, the British quickly discovered *Stralsund*'s

minefield and, after losing a trawler in an attempt to sweep it, opened an alternate route.

The Yarmouth raid accomplished little but it did suggest a possible way for the High Seas Fleet to attack isolated elements of the British fleet. With this as the principal objective, Admiral Ingenohl planned another foray. The battlecruiser force would bombard Scarborough, Hartlepool, and Whitby while light cruiser *Kolberg* laid a minefield to the south. The High Seas Fleet would follow, alert for an opportunity to pounce on any British force—short of the entire Grand Fleet—responding to the bombardment.

Admiral Ingenohl was still operating with poor intelligence regarding British dispositions and movements but by the time he issued the raid's final orders, the Royal Navy's radio interception and decoding group, based in Room 40 of the Old Admiralty Building in London, was rapidly honing its ability to read German radio communications. In this case Room 40 gave warning of Ingenohl's sortie, but no precise information about the forces involved or their target. Admiral Jellicoe guessed the objective would be in the vicinity of Scarborough and selected an almost perfect interception point. He wanted to bring the entire Grand Fleet but the Admiralty incorrectly assumed the High Seas Fleet would not sail because no wireless intercepts indicated that it would. Thus, the Admiralty allowed only one of the Grand Fleet's battleship divisions to sail—an example of how intelligence could deceive as well as reveal.

The Scarborough Raid—Destroyer Battle: 16 December, 0515–0800

Conditions: Moonless and overcast, wind WNW Force 2, sea state
    moderate

Missions: British, interception; Germans, raid

British Force: 4th DF (Commander R. S. P. Parry): DD *Ambuscade*[#],
    Unity, *Hardy*[#], *Lynx*[#], *Shark*, *Acasta*, *Spitfire*.

German Forces: High Seas Fleet Screen. Engaged units: DD *V155*.
    Then CL *Hamburg*[+]; DD *V158*, *V160*. Then CA *Roon*; DD *V161*,
    V150, *V153*, *V154*, *V151*. Finally CL *Stuttgart*, *München*.

Rear Admiral Hipper, commanding four battlecruisers, one armored and four light cruisers, and two destroyer flotillas, left the Jade at 0220 on 15 December. Ingenohl followed that evening with fourteen dreadnoughts, eight predreadnoughts, two armored and six light cruisers, and five destroyer flotillas bound for a point just short of Dogger Bank. The British, meanwhile, sent six battleships under Vice Admiral George Warrender, four battlecruisers under Vice Admiral David Beatty, four light cruisers, four armored cruisers, and seven destroyers to intercept the German raiders as they returned. Unwittingly, this force was bound to a position thirty miles south of Ingenohl's rendezvous point.

An hour before dawn Warrender's force crossed just twenty miles ahead of the High Seas Fleet as the two forces steamed toward their respective destinations around Dogger Bank. The 4th DF was ten miles northeast of the 2nd Battle Squadron (BS). The High Seas Fleet battleships were proceeding west in a long column flanked by light cruisers and a few destroyers to the north and with the rest of the screen ahead, south, and astern. At 0515 *Roon*, which was leading the German screen, dispatched *V155* to investigate a Dutch steamer. *V155* soon found herself alongside the 4th DF. Challenges flashed back and forth and the first shots, at ranges under two thousand yards, followed at 0525. *V155* veered north with the British in chase off her port quarter. This prevented them from deploying their superior firepower while *V155*, shooting well in the pre–dawn murk, hit *Lynx*, the British leader, twice, flooding her forward magazine and holing an oil tank. At 0537 *Lynx's* helm jammed, spinning her in a half circle to port away from *V155*. As the rest of the line followed *V155* hit *Ambuscade*, holing her forward. The 4th DF was completely disrupted. *Ambuscade* staggered off to the west, *Lynx* and *Unity* headed southwest and *Hardy*, *Shark*, *Acasta*, and *Spitfire* made off to the south-southwest while the unharmed German destroyer disappeared to the northeast.

When *V155* reported her encounter Ingenohl was naturally concerned that it signified the Grand Fleet's arrival. Instead of pushing his flotillas forward to find out, he turned southeast at 0542. This put the German fleet on a course parallel to Warrender's ships, which were just out of sight ten miles southwest of Ingenohl's screen. Then, at 0620, without advising Hipper, Ingenohl turned further east and shaped course for the Jade. Warrender, meanwhile, got sighting reports but no position reports. He thus knew there were German ships about but not where. He decided (without advising Beatty or the Admiralty) to continue to his destination before turning north to cut the enemy off. Had he swung

Map 2.3 Scarborough Raid: 16 December 1914

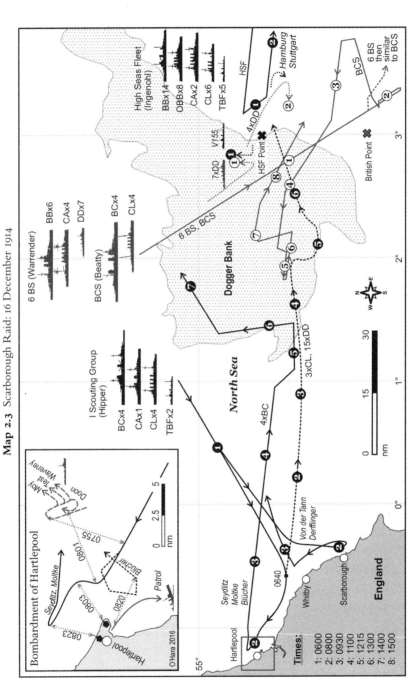

Bombardment of Hartlepool

I Scouting Group (Hipper)

BCx4
CAx1
CLx4
TBFx2

6 BS (Warrender)

BBx6
CAx4
DDx7

BCS (Beatty)

BCx4
CLx4

High Seas Fleet (Ingenohl)

BBx14
OBBx8
CAx2
CLx6
TBFx5

North Sea

Dogger Bank

England

Hartlepool
Whitby
Scarborough

Times:
1: 0600
2: 0800
3: 0930
4: 1100
5: 1215
6: 1300
7: 1400
8: 1500

O'Hara 2016

north immediately he would have encountered the High Seas Fleet. However, given that Ingenohl withdrew after hearing enemy destroyers were nearby it is legitimate to question whether he would have responded more aggressively to the sight of battleships.

During Ingenohl's withdrawal the light forces continued to wrangle. *V155* had called for help and *Hamburg* with *V158* and *V160* in train veered northwest in response. *Hamburg* encountered *Hardy* and *Shark* at 0553 and pounded *Hardy* at ranges down to four hundred yards, wrecking her steering gear and her forward gun. In return, the destroyers hit *Hamburg* twice. *Hardy* uncorked a torpedo that *Hamburg* veered to avoid, losing contact in the process. At 0616, *Roon* sighted *Lynx* and *Unity*. Initially the large cruiser was uncertain of their identity and turned away to keep out of torpedo range. By the time she had reached a safe distance the British destroyers had vanished.

Ambuscade, *Lynx*, and *Unity* were out of the fight but *Hardy* made temporary repairs. *Shark* then led *Hardy*, *Acasta*, and *Spitfire* east toward *Roon*'s smoke. By 0708, they had closed the cruiser's escort, which was now trailing the fleet, and engaged at four thousand yards. When *Roon* emerged from the mist the British withdrew to eight thousand yards and shadowed as *Roon* followed the fleet eastward. This ended at 0750 when *Hamburg* and *Stuttgart* came up and *Stuttgart* chased the British destroyers off to the west. The 4th DF's reports delayed the British admirals from appreciating the situation and when, at 0805, Beatty at last understood that the destroyers were tangling with German cruisers he immediately turned to the east-northeast to intervene.

The Scarborough Raid—Bombardment of Hartlepool: 16 December, 0755–0832

Conditions: Strong winds and chop

Missions: British, patrol; Germans, raid/bombardment

British Forces: Patrol force (Commander H. M. Fraser): DD *Doon*[+], *Test*, *Waveney*, *Moy*. In harbor (Captain A. C. Bruce): CL *Patrol*[*], *Forward*. Shore batteries.

German Forces (Rear Admiral Hipper): BC *Seydlitz*[+], *Moltke*[+]; CA *Blücher*[#].

Conditions along the coast were dreadful on the morning of 16 December, even by North Sea standards. A strong wind pushing against an ebb tide created a short, violent chop that played havoc with the German light forces. Neither the light cruisers nor the destroyers could work their guns and the destroyers were forced to unload their torpedo tubes. At 0642 Hipper ordered them to abandon the mission and join Ingenohl at the Dogger Bank rendezvous. He sent *Kolberg* south to lay mines and *Von der Tann* and *Derfflinger* to bombard Scarborough and Whitby while *Seydlitz*, *Moltke*, and *Blücher* headed north to shell Hartlepool, the only one of the three targets that was defended and had some military facilities. Hipper was approaching Hartlepool when a patrol of four old destroyers spotted his ships passing seven thousand yards to the south.

Seydlitz engaged the destroyers at 0755. *Doon* turned to starboard and led the column southeast as the Germans headed northwest. *Doon's* captain wanted to deliver a torpedo attack but could approach no closer than five thousand yards before heavy gunfire forced him to flee. *Moltke* shot thirty-eight 28-cm and 154 15-cm shells in just five minutes while *Seydlitz* expended approximately one hundred 15-cm rounds; *Blücher* also fired. This barrage wounded eleven in *Doon* with splinters but scored no direct hits. The Germans reported they avoided three torpedoes but the British fired none.[23]

The bombardment itself began at 0803. While *Seydlitz* and *Moltke* continued northwest along the coast, *Blücher* veered southwest toward Hartlepool harbor. This put her in position to engage *Patrol*, which was just then sailing to support the British destroyers while *Forward* raised steam. *Blücher* smacked her target at 0818 with a pair of 21-cm shells that badly holed the small cruiser, killing four, and forced her to run aground south of the harbor at the mouth of the Tees. At 0832 Hipper's force withdrew. The three 6-inch guns of the shore batteries had returned fire landing three nonpenetrating hits on *Seydlitz* that caused mostly splinter damage. On *Moltke* one shell inflicted considerable blast damage to the crew accommodations forward and caused some flooding. *Blücher* took four shells and had two secondary guns knocked out and a 21-cm turret damaged. The bombardment killed 93 and wounded 441, mostly civilians. The other two targets, Scarborough and Whitby, were undefended towns and there were no clashes with British forces.[24]

News of these bombardments reached Warrender and Beatty shortly before 0900. It was the first hard evidence of the battlecruiser force they were at sea to trap and caused each of the admirals to abandon their pursuit of German cruisers reported to their east. They both came about, first to the northwest and then west. It seemed the trap had snared the prey and that a great victory must surely follow.

The Scarborough Raid—Light Cruisers Fight: 16 December, 1125–1155

Conditions: Strong winds and chop

Missions: British, interception; Germans, transit

British Force: 1st LCS (Commodore William Goodenough): CL *Southampton, Birmingham, Falmouth, Nottingham.*

German Forces (Captain Harder): CL *Stralsund*; DD *V191, G196, G195, G192, G 194.* CL *Graudenz*; DD *V186, V190, V188, G197, V189.* CL *Strassburg*; DD *V28, S31, V27, V25, V26.*

Proceeding east in a line of bearing *Graudenz, Stralsund,* and *Strassburg,* each followed by a clutch of destroyers, had been steaming through a wicked following sea for nearly five hours heading toward their expected rendezvous with the High Seas Fleet. At 1125 *Southampton,* the southern-most ship of the screen preceding Beatty's battlecruisers and, at the time, just ten thousand yards ahead of *Lion,* spotted *Stralsund* to the northwest. To one observer it seemed the Germans destroyers were "bobbing about like corks."[25] Goodenough reported the contact and turned to starboard as *Stralsund* veered south. Both ships opened fire. The range dropped to five thousand yards and then began to open again as they passed on opposite courses. Then *Southampton* turned south and *Birmingham* fell in behind her with the British cruisers following *Stralsund* off her port quarter while *Strassburg* and *Graudenz* paralleled *Stralsund*'s course to the west. *Stralsund*'s destroyers attempted to lay smoke.

For ten minutes the cruisers traded broadsides at ten thousand yards. On *Southampton* an officer recalled: "We opened fire with all guns bearing, but the gunlayers became confused at the number of targets and each gun was firing more or less independently. This, added to the fact that owing to the sea and spray the telescopes were useless and they had to use open sights, made accurate shooting impossible."[26] At 1145, *Strassburg* and *Graudenz* emerged into view as the Germans bent to the southeast trying to get around the enemy. The ineffectual gunnery exchange ended when Beatty saw *Nottingham* heading south to join Goodenough. He ordered her back to her station in the screen but the searchlight signal was addressed to the light cruisers generally and repeated to Goodenough. Accordingly, Goodenough turned *Southampton* and *Birmingham* back to the west at 1155 while the Germans continued southeast. At 1210 when *Southampton* came into view of *Lion* Beatty signaled "What have you done with the enemy light cruisers?" Goodenough replied, "They disappeared south when I received your signal to resume station."[27] Beatty was furious at Goodenough for not maintaining contact regardless of his orders. In any case, Beatty was more intent on getting at Hipper's heavy ships, which he assumed were behind the cruisers.

As the battlecruisers continued west the German light cruisers suddenly emerged into full view of Warrender's six dreadnoughts. Having noted the two-character recognition signal previously flashed at her by *Southampton*, *Stralsund* immediately made the same signal, gaining time until a squall allowed the Germans to break contact. Warrender, realizing he had been duped, signaled their presence at 1235 whereupon Beatty immediately came about to the east and gave chase. *Birmingham* was only twelve miles away from Hipper, who was steering straight for Beatty, but she could not see the German battlecruisers in the poor conditions. *Stralsund*'s sighting report had alerted Hipper to the possibility that he might be heading toward a British force and at 1245 the German admiral turned 90 degrees from east to north, once he confirmed his light cruisers were clear of the British. Although Beatty and Warrender dashed about east, west, north, and south for another three hours, Hipper had given them the slip. The British trap had sprung on empty seas.[28]

Several ironies marked this operation. The Royal Navy's superior intelligence could have led to the very result that the Germans were trying to achieve: contact between a detached British force and the whole German fleet. Jellicoe's interception point was near perfect, except that it exposed ten British capital ships to attack by twenty-six German capital ships. But a few destroyers were enough to spook Ingenohl. This raises the question of how the admiral was ever to know his force was superior. Given problems of visibility and ambiguous and erratic reporting, no amount of scouting could give the absolute assurance Ingenohl apparently needed before he would accept combat. This action also reflected poorly on Beatty's leadership, marked as it was by reactive decisions and ambiguous communications. Bad weather forced Hipper to detach his screening forces, but that allowed them to give him sufficient warning that a Royal Navy force blocked his return route to the Jade. Had Hipper been following his screen closely, he might well have been drawn into an action with a superior British force and Ingenohl would have been unable to intervene. The operation could have been a great victory for either side, but fate and the uncertainties of naval operations decreed otherwise.[29]

Baltic 1914

The Russians lost an opportunity to engage the Germans on favorable terms early on when two armored cruisers surprised minelayer *Deutschland*, light cruisers *Augsburg* and *Magdeburg*, and three destroyers on 17 August as they were steaming to lay a minefield near the entrance of the Gulf of Finland. The Russian commander failed to engage believing he faced armored rather than light cruisers and was sacked for his lack of aggression.

Probing the Gulf: 18 August, 1903–

Conditions: Clear

Missions: Russians, patrol; Germans, bombardment

Russian Force: CA *Admiral Makarov, Gromoboi.*

German Force: DD *V25, V26, V186.*

The Germans were back the next day when three destroyers ventured into the gulf to bombard a lighthouse and cover *Magdeburg* and *Augsburg* as they inspected merchant traffic. *Admiral Makarov* and *Gromoboi* spotted the flotilla and opened fire at 1903 from 11,000 yards. Their shells fell short as the destroyers quickly fled and rejoined the light cruisers outside the gulf.[30]

The Loss of **Magdeburg:** *26 August, 0910–0930*

Conditions: Thick fog but clearing, calm

Missions: Russians, interception; Germans, raid

Russian Force: CA *Pallada*; CP *Bogatyr*; DD *Leitenant Burakov, Rianyi.*

German Force: CL *Magdeburg*★ (Corvette Captain Richard Habenicht); DD *V26*#.

Map 2.4 Baltic Sea

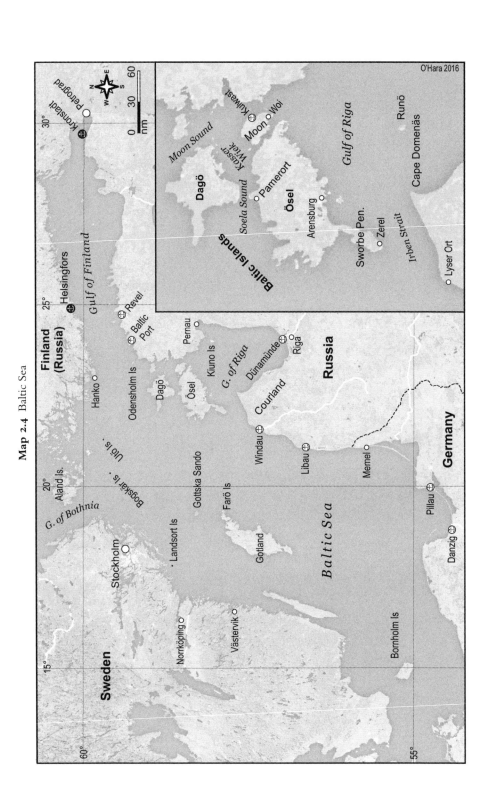

The Germans returned to the Gulf of Finland in late August. The plan was for *Augsburg* and *Magdeburg* accompanied by *V26* and *V186* to inspect shipping and shell Baltic Port. The Russians had mined the gulf's entrance so the German force ran southeast along the edge of the barrage from the Finnish coast toward Estonia, intending to turn into the gulf north of Odensholm Island. *Magdeburg* was following *Ausburg* through dense fog and was a mile farther south than plotted. Due to this error and a delay in reading a signal, *Magdeburg* did not turn when she was supposed to and ran hard aground two hundred yards off Odensholm at 0037 on 26 August. For the rest of the night Captain Habenicht labored to free his command, ordering ammunition, coal, extra fittings, and water over the side. The crew rocked the ship and gathered aft to lift the bow as the engines went full astern, but nothing worked. At 0800, to salvage something from the fiasco, *Magdeburg* fired 120 rounds at the island, nicking the lighthouse and setting the signal station on fire. *V26* finally arrived at 0830 after spending several valuable hours searching through the dark and fog for the stranded vessel. However, after securing a line, she could not free the cruiser either. Meanwhile, the destroyers *Leitenant Burakov* and *Rianyi* had departed Revel at 0500 followed at 0625 by *Bogatyr* and *Pallada*. More destroyers and *Riurik* followed as they raised steam.

German light cruiser *Magdeburg* hard aground off Odensholm Island. In the chaos of being abandoned while under fire the crew failed to properly dispose of secret code books, leading to an intelligence windfall for the Russians and British. (Courtesy of Sergei Vinogradov Collection)

By 0900 the air was buzzing with Russian transmissions and Habenicht reluctantly decided to scuttle his command after a second attempt by *V26* failed to budge *Magdeburg*. The destroyer came alongside and personnel began transferring. At 0959, however, *Bogatyr* and *Pallada* spotted the Odensholm lighthouse and the Germans through the fog. Minutes later they fired a few rounds. This caused pandemonium on board *Magdeburg*. Many crewmen jumped into the water including one man carrying the cruiser's secret code book. As *V26* backed away Habenicht ordered the scuttling charges lit. Russian reports time the subsequent explosion at 1015. In fact, only the forward charges exploded, but this was enough to break the ship's back and shower men with metal debris. The aft charges were apparently never lit as crewmen were still gathered aft. *V26* waited at a distance while most of *Magdeburg*'s men struggled to board. Then *Bogatyr* and *Pallada* reappeared out of the fog just 2,500 yards away.

V26 got under way as the cruisers opened fire. Crowded with survivors, the destroyer could not deploy her torpedoes. In a twenty-minute exchange at ranges out to four thousand yards the cruisers near-missed *V26* once, sweeping eight men overboard, and hit her at least twice. The first blow smashed into an officer's wardroom, which was being used as a sick bay, while another damaged her steam lines and forced the turbine room's evacuation. Still making 23 knots, *V26* escaped west and rendezvoused with *Augsburg*. *Augsburg* would eventually have to tow the destroyer home. The Russians failed to pursue.

At 1040, destroyers *Leitenant Burakov* and *Rianyi* arrived. Neither Russian force expected to see friendly vessels and before identities were established *Pallada* drenched *Burakov* with an 8-inch near miss while *Bogatyr* dodged one of *Burakov*'s torpedoes. The Russians captured fifty-seven members of *Magdeburg*'s crew, including Habenicht. Far worse, from the German point of view, was that the Russians recovered two copies of the German *Signalbuch der Kaiserlichen Marine* code book and current code key from the wreck or the waters nearby. From this, Russian (and British) intelligence developed the ability to routinely intercept and decode many German naval radio messages. The Germans went through the whole war without discovering this security breach, and ascribed to espionage or treachery the many instances where the enemy seemed aware of their plans.[31]

Chase of Augsburg: 1 September, 2210–2304

Conditions: Clear

Missions: Russians, interception; Germans, patrol

Russian Force (Admiral N. O. Essen): CA *Riurik*, *Rossiia*; CP *Bogatyr*, *Oleg*; DD *Novik*.

German Force (Rear Admiral Ehler Behring): CL *Augsburg*.

After messages decoded with the help of the captured signal book gave indications that the German Baltic Fleet was weaker than previously believed, Admiral Essen, the Russian commander, received approval to attack the German picket line extending east to west across the Baltic at the level of Gotland. Essen sailed with four cruisers and five destroyers, but a storm off the Gulf of Finland forced all the destroyers except the big, new *Novik* to turn back. Once the storm abated, the cruisers and *Novik* steamed south under a moon two nights short of full.

Three German light cruisers were on patrol: *Amazone* west of Gotland, *Gazelle* east, and *Augsburg* farther east toward the Courland coast. *T124* was west of *Gazelle* and *V25* east of *Augsburg*. The ships were spaced sixteen miles apart. *Augsburg* was heading north when at 2210 she saw the Russians' smoke ahead. She turned south ten minutes later, running but trying to maintain contact.

Essen saw *Augsburg* as well and detached *Novik* to attack her. *Novik* chased the light cruiser at her top speed of 32 knots and finally fired four torpedoes at 2304 at maximum range. An officer on *Novik* described the scene: "[A] signal bell sounded from the poop. Four bright flashes of light appeared, and the buzzing torpedoes fell heavily into the water. At the same moment the cruiser abruptly turned upon us and by that maneuver avoided the torpedoes."[32] *Augsburg* in fact saw the flashes as *Novik* launched and tried to illuminate the Russian destroyer with her searchlight, but found the range too great.

There were no further attacks that night, despite another brief meeting of *Augsburg* and *Novik*, but Essen was not done. At 0630 as the sky lightened *Augsburg* again saw smoke clouds to the north. *Bogatyr* and *Oleg* appeared over the horizon and chased the German vessel until 0930 without being able to draw within range. The Russians then gave up and returned to Revel. Although the foray caused no damage it did make the Germans move their picket line south.[33]

Trap off the Gulf of Finland: 6 September, 1256–1622

Conditions: Clear and calm

Missions: Russians, patrol; Germans, interception

Russian Force: CA *Baian*, *Pallada*.

German Force (Grand Admiral Heinrich Hohenzollern): CA *Blücher*,
    CL *Strassburg*, *Augsburg*; DD *V25*, II TBF.

The appearance of Russian cruisers in the central and southern Baltic prompted Grand Admiral Heinrich, Kaiser Wilhelm's brother and commander of Baltic naval forces, to set a trap. Heinrich sent *Augsburg* and *V25* into the Gulf of Finland on the morning of 6 September to lure any patrolling Russian cruisers into range of his fleet, which had been reinforced for the occasion by *Blücher* and a group of predreadnoughts.

The bait flotilla saw smoke at 1230 and by 1256 *Augsburg* was fleeing south before the patrol cruisers *Baian* and *Pallada* as planned. The sighting report found Heinrich flying his flag on board *Blücher* twenty miles south of Bogskär. He got his forces in motion with *Blücher*, *Strassburg*, and II TBF leading the way. Quickly outpacing the old battleships, *Blücher* built up to 24 knots and followed *Strassburg* into the gulf.

The Russians spotted *Blücher*'s enormous smoke cloud at 1340 from thirty-five miles away and veered north. *Strassburg* saw the Russians ten minutes later and, followed by *Blücher*, gave chase. By 1530 *Blücher* had the enemy in sight. *Baian* and *Pallada* increased speed, but at 1617 *Blücher* engaged from 17,000 yards. She fired for five minutes before breaking off when she reached a predetermined stop line. The operation reminded the Russians that the Germans could confront them with superior force at any time but one of the faster battlecruisers would have had been better for the job.[34]

The Germans transferred more predreadnoughts to the Baltic in late September to cover a possible diversionary landing on the Latvian coast. Responding to intelligence about this activity, Russian destroyers scouted south and on the night of 25 September encountered two German destroyers six miles south of Windau, although there was no exchange of fire. Shortly thereafter the Germans canceled the landing because reports of British activity caused the Admiralstab to recall the battleships. The Germans did enjoy one major success on 11 October when *U26* torpedoed *Pallada*. The armored cruiser blew up and went down with all hands, a demonstration of the type's extreme vulnerability to underwater damage.

Ships in the Night: 6 November, 0135–
Conditions: Poor visibility
Missions: Russians, transit; Germans, patrol
Russian Force (Commander P. Paletskii): DD *Novik.*
German Force (Frigate Captain Paul Nippe): CL *Thetis.*

In November, with the nights growing longer, Russian minelayers began venturing into the southern Baltic. On the night of 5/6 November four destroyers laid a 150 mines forty miles off Memel while *Novik* sowed 50 off Pillau. That evening *Thetis* was steaming south thirty miles off Memel hunting a submarine. At 0135 she encountered *Novik* heading north. *Thetis* challenged with recognition lights; *Novik* responded by accelerating to 32 knots. *Thetis* snapped on her searchlight, slewed to port to open gun arcs, and discharged fifteen rounds at ranges of one to two thousand yards before *Novik* disappeared in funnel smoke and darkness. The Russian mining operation was a success, sinking the armored cruiser *Friedrich Karl* off Memel on 17 November.[35]

Activity in the Baltic diminished as winter set in but the Russians continued mining into February 1915 when ice finally ended activity until spring. These weapons had further successes, most prominently on the night of 24/25 January 1915 when the light cruisers *Augsburg* and *Gazelle* struck mines in separate fields. The armored cruiser *Prinz Adalbert* also ran aground, making it a costly night for the Germans. The Germans sowed mines as well, although their offensive efforts were directed against the trade routes between Sweden and Russia. Sweden was a valuable trading partner of both Germany and Russian, sending high-quality iron ore from Stockholm south and trans-shipping goods to Russia across the Gulf of Bothnia. The belligerents harassed each other's Swedish trade, but had to avoid flagrant violations of Swedish neutrality.

Black Sea 1914
On 25 October, after months of uneasy peace, Ismail Enver, the Ottoman minister of war, instructed his navy's German commander in chief,

Map 2.5 Black Sea

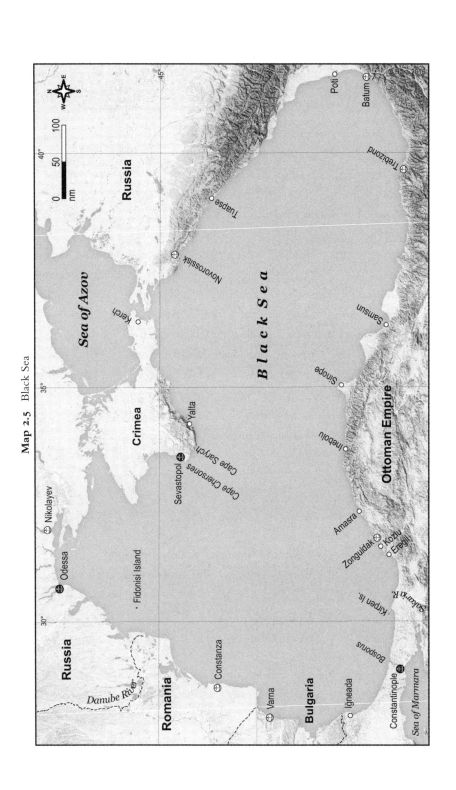

Vice Admiral Souchon, to create an incident that would incite war with Russia. Souchon did a thorough job, conducting a four-pronged attack on Russian bases using every operational Ottoman warship of any size.

Raid on Odessa: 29 October, 0330–0410

Conditions: Poor visibility

Missions: Russians, none; Ottomans, raid

Russian Force: GB *Donets*★, *Kubanets*#; ML *Beshtau*+.

Ottoman Force (Corvette Captain Rudolf Maldung): DD *Gairet, Muavenet*.

In the first of the multiple Ottoman strikes *Gairet* and *Muavenet* boldly sailed into Odessa harbor with navigation lights burning. *Gairet* spotted the gunboat *Donets* moored at the end of the breakwater and launched a torpedo from just a hundred yards. This detonated and sank the small warship. The intruders then doused their lights and headed deeper into the harbor where *Muavenet* shot up *Kubanets* docked at the navy pier. *Kubanets* responded but her return fire was wild. *Muavenet* doubled back and sent a dozen rounds toward *Beshtau*. Given her cargo of mines *Beshtau* did not answer. In their wild forty minute raid the destroyers also shelled shore installations and some commercial vessels before retiring. While they played havoc, the old minelayer *Samsun* laid twenty-eight mines outside the port.

Raid on Sevastopol: 29 October, 0633–0730

Conditions: Foggy

Missions: Russians, transit; Ottomans, bombardment

Russian Forces: In port: CB *Georgii Pobedonosets*. At sea: DD *Kapitan Saken*#; TB *Zharkii, Zhivuchii*; ML *Prut*★.

Ottoman Force (Vice Admiral Wilhelm Souchon): BC *Yavuz Sultan Selim*+; TB *Tazos, Samsun*.

Yavuz targeted the main Russian base at Sevastopol. As the battlecruiser approached the harbor two torpedo boats preceded her, sweeping for mines. At 0633 *Yavuz* opened fire from eight thousand yards and continued in action for seventeen minutes, expending forty-seven 28-cm and twelve 15-cm rounds. Forty-four coast defense guns ranging in size from 11-inch to 9.56-inch replied, firing 360 rounds, while the venerable battleship *Georgii Pobedonosets* added another three. This defensive fusillade hit the battlecruiser three times: a 10.7-in howitzer and two 11-inch rounds left several holes and caused some blast and splinter damage, but did not reduce the ship's fighting ability. *Yavuz*'s group was returning to base when, at 0707, it encountered a destroyer and two torpedo boats that tried to attack the battlecruiser under the cover of the morning fog. *Yavuz*'s secondary batteries quickly zeroed in on *Kapitan Saken*, scoring several hits that started fires and disabled her steering control. That ended the Russian attack. *Yavuz* then spotted minelayer *Prut* at 0715. She quickly set the small ship aflame and *Prut* sank at 0840.

In addition to these actions, protected cruiser *Hamidieh* lobbed 150 shells into the port of Feodosia, auxiliary minelayer *Nilüfer* laid a minefield off Sevastopol and light cruiser *Midilli* mined the Kerch Strait and then joined torpedo-gunboat *Berk-i-Satvet* in shelling Novorossisk. The minefields sank two Russian merchantmen. These raids accomplished Enver's goal of provoking a Russian declaration of war. They did not, however, reduce Russian sea power in the Black Sea.[36] In fact, the Imperial Russian Navy immediately began an energetic program of minelaying, bombardments, and anti-shipping sweeps, including one that sank three unprotected Ottoman troop transports.

The Russian Black Sea Fleet's commander, Admiral A. A. Ebergard, recognized that *Yavuz* and *Midilli* could run from a superior force and run down an inferior force. The fleet's gunnery officers, who had been planning to fight the Ottoman dreadnoughts building in British yards, had already devised a potential solution to the problem of fighting a modern dreadnought with the predreadnoughts, which were the heaviest ships the Russians could deploy until their dreadnoughts entered service the next year: a system to allow three predreadnoughts to fire as one. The central ship in a three-ship line controlled the fire of all by a special radio circuit, with the goal of functioning as if they were a single twelve-gun ship. As long as the ships could coordinate their maneuvers and their fire, they could confront *Yavuz* with roughly equal firepower but triple the defensive capacity. The opportunity to test this system arrived quickly.[37]

Battle of Cape Sarych: 18 November, 1219–1239

Conditions: Calm, patchy fog

Missions: Russians, transit; Ottomans, interception

Russian Force (Admiral A. A. Ebergard): OBB *Evstafii*[#], *Ioann Zlatoust*, *Panteleimon, Tri Sviatitelia, Rostislav*; CP *Kagul, Pamiat Merkuriia*; DS *Almaz*; DD *Gnevnyi, Bespokoinyi, Pronzitelnyi, Leitenant Shesta-kov, Kapitan-leitenant Baranov, Leitenant Zatsarennyi, Kapitan Saken*; TB *Zhutkii, Zhivoi, Zharkii, Zhivuchii, Zvonkii, Zorkii*.

Ottoman Force (Vice Admiral Wilhelm Souchon): BC *Yavuz*[#]; CL *Midilli*.

The Russian fleet sortied at noon on 15 November and at 0700 on 17 November bombarded Trebizond, the main Ottoman port for the Caucasus front. According to a British eyewitness, "the harbour works, cranes + military pontoons &c., for landing troops and war material were destroyed."[38] Responding to the Russian foray, Vice Admiral Souchon had left Constantinople with *Yavuz* and *Midilli* at 1300 that afternoon and shaped a course to intercept. Ebergard knew of Souchon's departure and was thus alert for an encounter.

On the morning of 18 November the Russian fleet was returning to Sevastopol on a northwesterly course. The visibility was improving after dense morning fog but was still variable. The Russian ships were steaming with *Almaz* and the cruisers leading, the battleships seven thousand yards behind, and the flotilla craft trailing them. *Zorkii* lagged behind with a fouled propeller shaft with *Zhivoi* in attendance. At 1140, when *Almaz* reported smoke to the west, Ebergard closed his formation and ordered the screen to fall back. By 1205 *Midilli* had *Almaz* in sight. *Almaz* reported seeing *Midilli* at 1210 five degrees off her port bow and immediately turned to starboard. Souchon worked *Yavuz* up to full speed and passed the light cruiser. The Russian cruisers eventually took station on the disengaged side of the battleline.

Ebergard wanted to engage with his three leading battleships using the centralized fire control system, but his formation's present course would allow *Yavuz* to cross his T and engage *Evstafii* without the rest of his column being able to respond. To prevent this Ebergard had to turn his formation. His problem was that he did not know the enemy's exact course or distance, which left the question of when to change course, how far, and in which direction a matter of guesswork. Nonetheless,

Ebergard decided quickly. He rang up 14 knots—close to the maximum of the old battleships—and turned 90 degrees to a southwesterly course. His ships began turning in succession at 1219.

Map 2.6 Battle of Cape Sarych: 18 November 1914

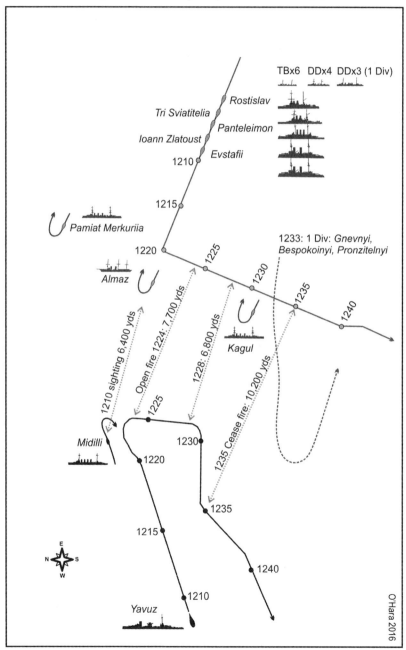

This proved an astute move as Souchon turned *Yavuz* south minutes later, about nine thousand yards west of Ebergard's line. This put the Ottoman battlecruiser on a gradually converging course slightly behind the Russians. If Souchon wanted to use his ship's superior speed to run past the enemy, he would have to travel the length of the Russian line exposed to their combined fire. Rangefinders and fire control officers on both sides struggled to find and fix targets as the already variable visibility was made worse by funnel smoke being belched out by ships steaming at maximum power.

At this point the Russian multi-ship fire control system broke down. The battleships using the system were, in order, *Evstafii, Ioann Zlatoust* (control ship), and *Panteleimon. Tri Sviatitelia*, the fourth ship in line, was in reserve while *Rostislav* at the rear had 10-inch guns that were incompatible with the system. The problem came from *Zlatoust* being in an area of poorer visibility than *Evstafii*. In *Evstafii*, Ebergard could see *Yavuz* turning to parallel his course, but *Zlatoust* was struggling to get the range. She kept signaling 12,000 yards when the Russian admiral had it as less than eight. At 1224 Ebergard decided to wait no longer and ordered *Evstafii* to engage independently. She fired a two-gun salvo at 7,700 yards and immediately hit *Yavuz*. The 12-inch shell penetrated the armor of a 15-cm gun casement. One eyewitness recalled, "In a moment an appalling [sheet] of flame swept through the ammunition hoist below and endangered the magazine in the bottom of the ship."[39] The blow ignited a serious powder fire and temporarily disabled *Yavuz*'s secondary battery on the engaged side, reducing her firepower at the ranges over which the action was being fought.

At 1226 *Yavuz* replied. Her first salvo fell up to two hundred yards over but one shell holed *Evstafii*'s central funnel and disabled her fire control radio. *Zlatoust* joined in but continued to broadcast incorrect ranges. Not surprisingly, all of her shells fell well over. Having found the range, *Evstafii*'s 8- and 6-inch guns roared into action and raised shell splashes all around *Yavuz*. *Yavuz* continued to target *Evstafii*: two 28-cm rounds from the Ottoman ship's third salvo struck 6-inch gun casements forward and amidships. The second caused a serious fire. The Russians, mistaking *Yavuz*'s gun flashes for impact explosions, believed they were punishing the enemy battlecruiser. This impression was heightened when, at 1229, *Yavuz* turned west. Farther back, *Tri Sviatitelia* and *Rostislav* engaged *Midilli,* but she quickly ducked into a fog bank. At 1233 Ebergard ordered *Gnevnyi, Bespokoinyi,* and *Pronzitelnyi,* his fastest destroyers, to mount a torpedo attack. Meanwhile, before ceasing fire at 1235, *Yavuz* scored on *Evstafii* one last time—a near miss riddled the battleship's hull with fragments. By 1239 *Yavuz* had vanished and the three destroyers returned shortly thereafter unable to locate *Yavuz* in the poor visibility. The battle lasted less than fifteen minutes.

Yavuz fired nineteen 28-cm shells: twelve during the four minutes she held a steady course parallel to the enemy and seven more after she turned away, for a total of three hits and a damaging near miss. *Evstafii* fired twelve 12-inch, fourteen 8-inch, and nineteen 6-inch rounds for one hit on *Yavuz.* *Zlatoust* and *Sviatitelia* expended six and twelve 12-inch rounds respectively but these all missed. Bad visibility prevented *Panteleimon* from engaging. *Rostislav* fired two 10-inch and six 6-inch rounds at *Midilli,* while *Sviatitelia* directed some 6-inch rounds at the light cruiser. *Evstafii* lost thirty-four men killed and twenty-four wounded. Her damage took a month to repair. *Yavuz* lost thirteen men and was back at sea within three weeks.

Damage suffered by the Russian predreadnought *Evstafii*'s forward casemate from a 28-cm round fired by *Yavuz* at the November 1914 Battle of Cape Sarych. (Courtesy of Sergei Vinogradov Collection)

Souchon never explained his decision to break contact when he had the superior ship and was inflicting more damage. He knew in advance that he would be facing five Russian battleships and probably expected to leverage *Yavuz*'s 10-knot superiority into a tactical advantage over the course of the engagement. The accuracy of Russian gunnery may have been an unpleasant surprise as his ship took potentially fatal damage right at the start of the action. Despite Souchon's eagerness to end the battle, and the fact that the Russians claimed a dozen hits on the Ottoman vessel, Ebergard received most of the after-action criticism. Higher command viewed Cape Sarych's indecisive result as the product of excessive caution and considered Ebergard's refusal to resume operations until *Evstafii* was repaired as proof. How he could have forced a decision given *Yavuz*'s great speed advantage is not clear. In fact, Ebergard made a difficult maneuver at exactly the right time and drove off a dangerous foe, despite the failure of the fire control system designed to fight that foe.[40]

Raid on Zonguldak: 24 December, 0300–25 December, 1030

Conditions: Storms early

Missions: Russians, raid; Ottomans, transit

Russian Forces: Blocking Force (Captain K. A. Porembskii): OBB *Rostislav*; DS *Almaz*; TB *Stremitelnyi, Strogii, Svirepyi, Smetlivyi*; blockships *Atos★, Erna★, Istok★, Oleg★*. Minelaying Force: OBB *Evstafii, Ioann Zlatoust, Panteleimon, Tri Sviatitelia*; CP *Kagul, Pamiat Merkuriia*; DD *Kapitan Saken, Kaptain-leitenant Baranov, DDx12*; ML *Kseniia, Konstantin, Aleksei, Grigorii*.

Ottoman Force: (Frigate Captain Paul Kettner): CL *Midilli*.

The Black Sea Fleet sortied on 20 December with the dual mission of mining the entrance to the Bosporus and blocking the harbor at the coal port of Zonguldak. Anatolia's poor transportation system meant that coal for Constantinople had to be shipped by sea. If Zonguldak could be blocked or shipments otherwise disrupted, the Ottomans would face serious difficulties; thus traffic between this harbor and the capital was a prime target of the Russian navy.

Ebergard planned to close the port using four old merchant vessels: *Atos, Erna, Istok,* and *Oleg.* They would be accompanied by *Rostislav,*

Almaz, and four torpedo boats. While *Almaz* and *Rostislav* shelled the town, the blockships would scuttle in the harbor mouth and the torpedo boats would then dash in to rescue their crews. The rest of the fleet would mine the entrance to the Bosporus and then cover the Zonguldak force.

The blocking force met the fleet's main body north of the target on 23 December as planned. But things quickly began to go awry. Rising seas separated the formations. *Erna* suffered a machinery breakdown and *Rostislav* had to take her in tow. Then, at 0300 on 24 December *Midilli*, which had sailed to join *Yavuz* in the eastern Black Sea, encountered the blockship formation. *Midilli* lit up *Oleg* with her searchlight and riddled the ship with a flurry of gunfire. *Oleg* did not sink, but *Midilli's* attack further scattered the group. When *Rostislav* approached the cruiser retreated out of range but not out of the area. At dawn *Midilli* found *Atos*, which had become separated from the main body, and forced her to scuttle.

The three remaining blockships and their escort approached the coast at 0930, only to come under what they reported as an intense barrage from newly sited shore batteries that made it too risky for them to continue in daylight. With the operation thus stalled, the Russians saw smoke in the west. They assumed *Yavuz* was about to appear over the horizon and so scuttled the blockships. The smoke actually belonged to *Midilli*. She followed the enemy squadron as it withdrew north and rendezvoused with the rest of the Russian fleet. At 1300 she engaged the destroyers in an ineffectual firefight at 13,000 yards when they tried to close her. Kettner broke contact at nightfall, but picked up the fleet the next morning as it approached Sevastopol. There followed another profitless long-range exchange of fire between *Midilli* and the Russian destroyers whereupon, at 0852 on 25 December, the battleships flung some salvoes at the Ottoman cruiser. *Midilli* veered off but then turned yet again to regain touch. The hyperactive cruiser finally watched the Russians steam out of sight at 1030 after dogging them for more than twenty-four hours.

The blocking mission failed (as did most blocking operations), but *Yavuz* struck two mines in the newly laid field on her return to Constantinople. She was severely damaged and not fully repaired until

May 1915. Fortunately for the Ottomans, a series of careful deception efforts convinced the Russians that *Yavuz* remained operational.[41]

Mediterranean 1914

In the Mediterranean Sea the British navy responded to the building crisis by concentrating at their main base at Malta while the French prepared to cover the movement of XIX Corps from Algeria to Marseilles. As early as 30 July the British Mediterranean commander in chief, Admiral Berkeley Milne, received intelligence that Italy would stay neutral. This guaranteed Entente superiority in the theater. That same day the Admiralty cabled Milne that his first priority was to assist the French transports; only after their arrival could he engage the German Mediterranean squadron and then only so long as he had the superior force. On 2 August, with only Austria-Hungary and Serbia officially at war, Italy declared its neutrality. German battlecruiser *Goeben* and light cruiser *Breslau* had just arrived at Messina from the Adriatic. The commander of the German squadron, Rear Admiral Wilhelm Souchon, anticipated Germany's declaration of war against France and took his ships to sea. On 3 August he learned that war had indeed been declared and that Berlin and Constantinople had concluded an alliance. The Admiralstab ordered him to proceed to Constantinople and not into the Atlantic as he had planned. Being only several hours north of the Algerian coast Souchon decided to first bombard the nearby French ports of Philippeville and Bône. This he did at dawn on 4 August. The German ships then feinted west but turned for Messina, needing coal to reach Constantinople.

Milne had already received instructions to find and shadow *Goeben*. On the afternoon of 3 August he sent the 1st Cruiser Squadron's (CS) Rear Admiral Ernest Troubridge to reinforce the ships guarding the mouth of the Adriatic. Milne repeated the Admiralty's instructions to avoid combat with superior forces. Lacking news of the Germans, the Admiralty had ordered the battlecruisers *Indomitable* and *Indefatigable* to make for Gibraltar to prevent the Germans from breaking out into the Atlantic trade routes. They were north of Bône and heading west at 22 knots when, at 1032 on 4 August, the German squadron appeared on a reciprocal course. War between Germany and Great

Britain was still pending, and so the battlecruisers passed each other at high speed, guns manned but silent. Then the British ships came about to follow.

The German ships were faster and over the course of nine hours slowly drew out of sight. Milne, unaware that the French fleet had deployed en masse between Sardinia and Tunisia to keep the Germans away from the transport routes, still believed *Goeben* intended to eventually break west and that he bore the burden of stopping her. The Germans, meanwhile, arrived in Messina where they stayed for thirty-six hours and coaled from a German vessel.

Pursuit of Goeben: *6 August, 1800–7 August, 1640*

Conditions: Calm and clear

Missions: British, interception; Germans, transit

British Forces: Shadowing: CL *Gloucester* (Captain Howard Kelly). Attack Force (Captain John Kelly): CL *Dublin*; DD *Beagle, Bulldog*.

German Force: (Rear Admiral Wilhelm Souchon): BC *Goeben*; CL *Breslau*[+].

Orders to commence hostilities against Germany arrived in the Mediterranean at 0115 on 5 August. Milne deployed his battlecruisers to block the route between Messina and the western Mediterranean and relied on Troubridge to cover the Adriatic. Only the light cruiser *Gloucester* guarded the southern exit of the Straits of Messina. As Winston Churchill expressed it, "We hoped to sink [*Goeben*] the next day. Where could she go? Pola seemed her only refuge throughout the Mediterranean. According to international law nothing but internment awaited her elsewhere."[42] As the British waited the battlecruiser took on 2,100 tons of coal and at 1700 on 6 August Souchon headed south. At 1800 *Gloucester* spotted the Germans, broadcast the alarm, and turned to follow. This sparked a reaction from the other British forces but Milne still assumed the enemy intended to make for the Adriatic or double back to the west.

After dark *Gloucester* maintained contact and *Dublin*, in company with two destroyers, attempted to intercept and deliver a torpedo attack. *Dublin* encountered *Breslau* but held fire anticipating the larger prey. However, *Goeben* passed the little flotilla unseen. Troubridge, meanwhile, had positioned armored cruisers *Defence, Warrior, Duke of Edinburgh,* and *Black Prince* and eight destroyers to stop *Goeben* from entering the Adriatic. He finally turned in pursuit at 0008 on 7 August when it became clear that *Goeben* was in fact heading southeast but at 0347 gave up the chase. The German ships were only making 17 knots and Troubridge could have cut them off, but he considered *Goeben* the superior force in good visibility because with her larger guns (ten 28-cm weapons to the twenty-two 9.2-inch (23.4-cm) guns of the British cruisers) and greater maximum speed he believed *Goeben* could stand off and sink the armored cruisers one by one. Troubridge also felt it "inexpedient to quit his position [covering the Adriatic] in the absence of specific instructions."[43] The Austro-Hungarian fleet sailed south on the morning of 7 August to support the Germans. They turned back 220 miles north of the Entente blocking force when fleet commander Admiral Anton Haus learned *Goeben* was making east and not north.

Gloucester continued to shadow. Souchon was having trouble with *Goeben*'s boilers and wished to elude the enemy cruiser so he ordered *Breslau* to drop back. *Gloucester* opened fire on *Breslau* at 1335 with her foremost 6-inch gun at 11,500 yards. *Breslau* replied. Her salvos fell close while *Gloucester*'s gunnery inflicted several casualties. This caused *Goeben* to reverse course to assist. *Gloucester* backed off and the action ended at 1350 as ranges opened. At 1640 *Gloucester* terminated her chase. She was running low on coal and Milne had ordered her to stay west of Cape Matapan. She joined Troubridge, who had anchored his force in Zante Bay.

Milne continued to expect that *Goeben* would eventually head west. *Goeben*, in fact, loaded 2,445 tons of coal in the Aegean near Naxos from a German collier, and then made for the Dardanelles, entering the straits on 10 August. On 12 August she and *Breslau* officially joined the Ottoman navy under the names of *Yavuz Sultan Selim* and *Midilli*. Both vessels retained their German crews, leavened with a few Ottomans. On 24 September Souchon assumed command of the Ottoman navy. The episode caused Souchon's star to shine, but blighted the careers of Milne and Troubridge, neither of whom ever again served at sea. As Churchill expressed it: "The explanation is satisfactory; the result unsatisfactory."[44]

Following *Goeben*'s escape France and Great Britain executed an agreement that gave France command of Mediterranean naval operations. War against the Austro-Hungarian Empire followed on 12 August. The French admiralty instructed Vice Admiral Augustin Boué de Lapeyrère, commander of the French Mediterranean Fleet, to act against the Austrians while avoiding offense to the Italians. Accordingly Lapeyrère sailed his fleet into the Adriatic with the intention of breaking the Habsburg blockade of Montenegro, which was being enforced by a rust flotilla based at Cattaro, Austria's base located on the southern extremity of Dalmatia, while the main Austrian fleet kept to the heavily fortified harbor of Pola in the north.

Battle of Antivari: 16 August, 0700–0837

Conditions: Calm and clear

Missions: French, interception; Austrians, blockade

French Force (Vice Admiral A. Boué de Lapeyrère) BB *Courbet, Jean Bart*; OBB *Diderot, Danton, Vergniaud, Voltaire, Condorcet*#, *Vérité, République, Patrie, Justice*#, *Démocratie*; CA *Jules Michelet, Ernest Renan, Edgar Quintet, Léon Gambetta, Victor Hugo, Jules Ferry*; BR CA *Defence, Warrior*; CP *Jurien de la Gravière*; DDx40, BR DD *Scorpion, Beagle* class DDx3.

Austrian Force (Frigate Captain Paul Pachner): CP *Zenta*★; DD *Ulan*+.

The French battle fleet steamed into the Adriatic along the Italian coast. As one British participant recorded, "the whole horizon was covered with French tricolours. . . . It was certainly a most impressive sight."[45] They then dashed across the narrow waters toward Cattaro and swept south to trap the enemy against a cruiser force advancing north. At 0700 the Austrian predreadnought *Monarch*, the old torpedo cruiser *Panther*, and two destroyers spotted the enemy armada and fled to Cattaro. However, the pincers snared the protected cruiser *Zenta* and the destroyer *Ulan* off the Montenegrin port of Antivari. The Habsburg ships were fleeing the southern force when the French battleships appeared barring their path. Opening fire at 0803 from 13,000 yards, they deluged *Zenta* with more than five hundred 12-inch shells. She exploded at 0825 and sank fifteen minutes later with heavy loss of life. *Courbet* and *Jean Bart* peppered *Ulan* with their secondary batteries, but the destroyer escaped with only splinter damage. The French did not come off unscathed. Shells exploded prematurely in both barrels of *Condorçet*'s No. 5 240-mm turret and in a 194-mm casemate gun in *Justice.* There were no casualties but all three barrels required replacement. *Justice* collided with *Démocratie* the day after; they both had to return to Malta for docking. The French fleet withdrew having ended the Austrian blockade of Montenegro but disappointed their show of force had not returned better results.[46]

L'Armée Navale proceeded to blockade the Strait of Otranto, using Greece's Ionian islands as coaling stations and Malta as their main base. In September the French briefly occupied the island of Lissa and bombarded Cattaro's outer forts. They laboriously dragged a battery of old 6.1-inch guns to the summit of Lovčen Mountain overlooking Cattaro to shell Austrian ships in harbor. They also periodically swept the southern Adriatic, generally to cover small convoys into Antivari. For example, on 1 November 1914 a freighter escorted by three cruisers and five destroyers entered the tiny harbor. The battle fleet stood off the port in case the semi-dreadnought *Radetzky*, which was present at Cattaro to shell the Lovčen battery, tried to intervene. Another section of French armored cruisers and destroyers headed north to threaten Lesina, Lagosta, and Lissa. The scout cruiser *Helgoland* and the destroyers of I TBF sortied from Sebenico and approached to within 11,000 yards of the French squadron before withdrawing. The French operation continued through the 3rd. On that day Austrian submarines unsuccessfully attacked the armored cruisers *Waldeck-Rousseau* and *Jules-Ferry* and the fleet withdrew that night.[47]

The great frustration for French arms was that the Austrians had no intention of being provoked into a fleet action. They conducted pinprick raids with their flotilla craft but generally relied on mines and submarines to disrupt Entente traffic. The fact that each day the French fleet consumed five thousand tons of coal and a thousand tons of fuel oil meant that logistics quickly became a burden. Moreover, Lapeyrère received a first-hand lesson on the hazards of operating large warships in narrow waters during the next convoy operation when on 21 December the Austrian submarine *U12* torpedoed his flagship, *Jean Bart.* The battleship returned to Malta down by the bow. That ended French battleship operations in the Adriatic.

Non-European Waters 1914
First Action off Tsingtau: 22 August, sunset
Conditions: Unknown
Missions: British, patrol; Germans, patrol
British Force (Lieutenant Commander F. A. Russel): DD *Kennet*[#].
German Force (Captain Lieutenant Paul Brunner): TB *S90*.

Upon the outbreak of war an Entente squadron that included the pre-dreadnought *Triumph*, the cruiser *Yarmouth*, the French armored cruiser *Dupleix*, and three British destroyers sailed from Hong Kong to blockade Germany's main Asian base at Tsingtau on China's Shandong Peninsula. The German governor, meanwhile, summoned to Tsingtau the gunboats *Luchs* and *Jaguar* from other parts of China while he sent *Emden* along with eight colliers to reinforce Vice Admiral Maximilian Spee's East Asiatic Squadron in the Marianas. The raider *Cormoran* likewise departed Tsingtau before the Entente blockade clamped down.

On 15 August, Japan issued an ultimatum demanding Tsingtau's surrender. On 22 August, the day before this ultimatum expired, *S90* was off the base covering the activities of the minelayer *Lauting* when she encountered the British destroyers. *Kennet*, the leader, opened fire and pursued. *S90* replied with her 50-mm weapons and hit the British ship twice, knocking out a gun, killing three men, and wounding seven. *S90* then cut inshore of a coastal island through uncharted waters. *Kennet* declined to follow and then broke off when Tsingtau's shore batteries opened fire. The British ship expended 136 rounds and one torpedo in her fruitless chase.[48]

Second Action off Tsingtau: 17 October, 0100
Conditions: Poor visibility
Missions: Japanese, blockade; Germans, raid
Japanese Force: CM *Takaschio*★.
German Force: TB *S90*.

Germany predictably refused the Japanese ultimatum. On 2 September the first contingent of a 50,000-man Japanese army landed and proceeded to lay siege to the German base. An Entente fleet remained

Map 2.7 Oceanic Waters

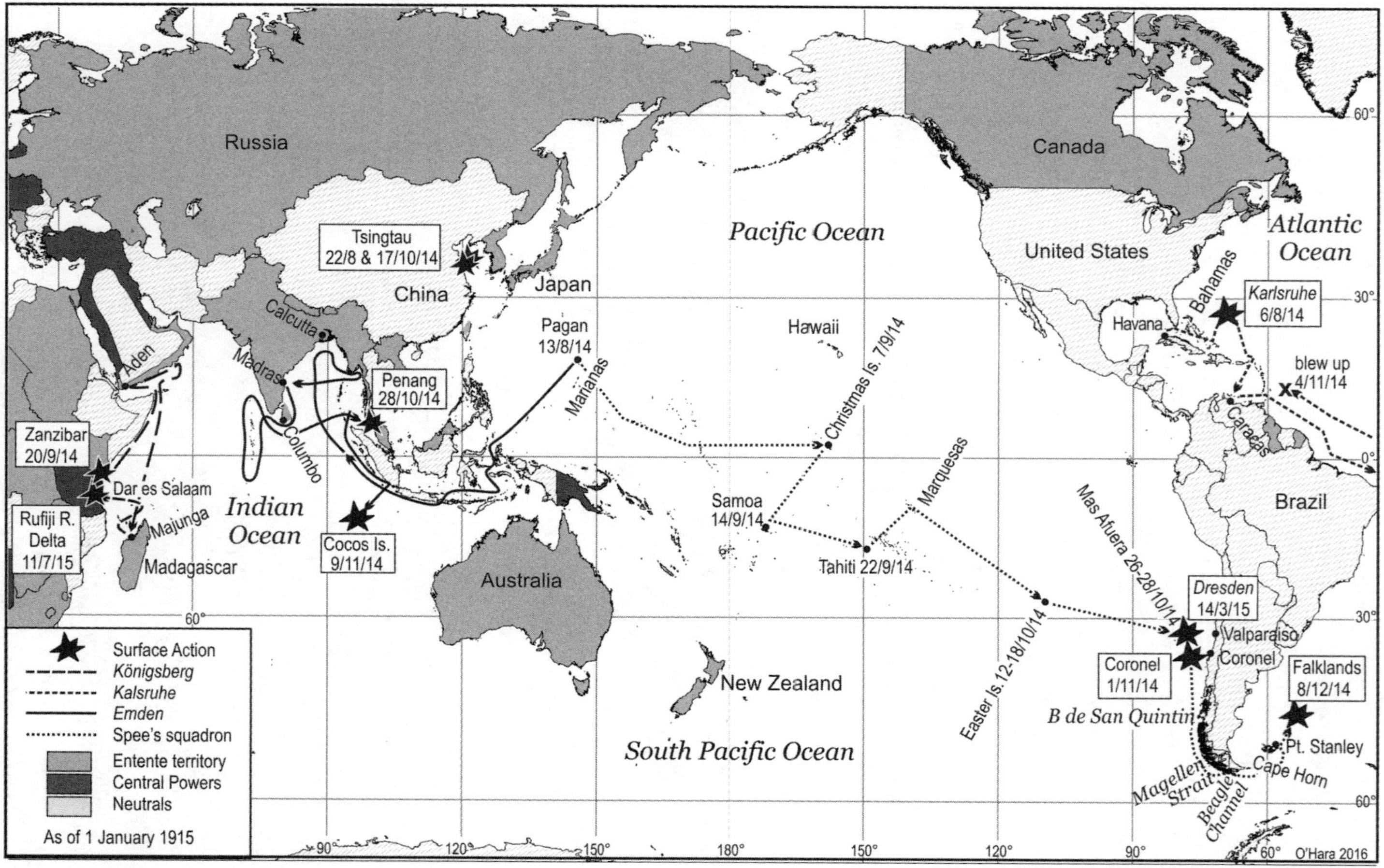
Russia
China
Japan
Tsingtau
22/8 & 17/10/14
Calcutta
Madras
Columbo
Penang
28/10/14
Cocos Is.
9/11/14
Aden
Zanzibar
20/9/14
Dar es Salaam
Rufiji R.
Delta
11/7/15
Majunga
Madagascar
Indian
Ocean
Australia
Pagan
13/8/14
Marianas
Pacific Ocean
Hawaii
Christmas Is. 7/9/14
Samoa
14/9/14
Tahiti 22/9/14
Marquesas
New Zealand
South Pacific Ocean
Easter Is. 12-18/10/14
Mas Afuera 26-28/10/14
Canada
United States
Atlantic
Ocean
Bahamas
Karlsruhe
6/8/14
Havana
blew up
4/11/14
Caracas
Brazil
Dresden
14/3/15
Valparaiso
Coronel
Coronel
1/11/14
B de San Quintin
Magellen Strait
Beagle Channel
Falklands
8/12/14
Pt. Stanley
Cape Horn
60°
30°
0°
30°
60°
90°
120°
150°
180°
150°
120°
90°
60°
60°
O'Hara 2016
Surface Action
Königsberg
Kalsruhe
Emden
Spee's squadron
Entente territory
Central Powers
Neutrals
As of 1 January 1915

offshore and contributed periodic bombardments. *Jaguar*, *S90*, and the Austro-Hungarian cruiser *Kaiserin Elisabeth* remained active but when the Japanese brought up siege artillery the German situation became untenable. In a desperate move *S90* sortied and on 17 October torpedoed the old Japanese cruiser-minelayer *Takaschio*, which exploded and sank with the loss of all but three of her 256 men. *S90* then evaded pursuit and ran herself aground on the Chinese coast. The other two warships scuttled on 2 November. The Japanese finally overcame the 4,600-man garrison on 7 November 1914.[49]

Karlsruhe *in the Caribbean: 6 August, 2015–2215*

Conditions: Moonlit night

Missions: British, interception; Germans, transit

British Force (Rear Admiral Christopher Cradock): CA *Suffolk*; CL *Bristol*.

German Force (Frigate Captain Erich Köhler): CL *Karlsruhe*.

Karlsruhe was one of Germany's newest and largest light cruisers. The outbreak of war found her in the Caribbean to relieve *Dresden*. The British West Indies Squadron, under Rear Admiral Christopher Cradock, attempted to monitor the movements of both these ships but lost them on 4 August. In fact, *Karlsruhe* met the liner *Kronprinz Wilhelm* on 6 August to transfer a pair of 88-mm guns and ammunition so the liner could serve as a merchant cruiser. This transfer was in process 270 miles east of the Bahamas when the armored cruiser *Suffolk*, with Cradock himself on board, surprised the German ships. They scattered while *Suffolk* chased *Karlsruhe* and called for the nearby *Bristol* to join. *Suffolk* lost the German vessel with the fall of darkness, but at 2015 *Bristol* spotted *Karlsruhe* in the moonlight six miles off her port bow. She closed to seven thousand yards and opened fire. *Karlsruhe* replied but neither ship hit the other. The German turned away and, being a faster steamer, lost her pursuer within two hours.[50]

Karlsruhe went on to operate off the Brazilian coast where, in company with a pair of supply ships, she captured sixteen British steamers. On 4 November 1914, however, she blew up with great loss of life while under way. The British did not learn of this event until March 1915 and continued in the intervening months to search for her.

Battle of Zanzibar: 20 September, 0510–0550
Conditions: Clear and calm

Missions: British, none; Germans, raid

British Force (Commander John Ingles): CP *Pegasus* *.

German Force (Frigate Captain Max Looff): CL *Königsberg*.

In August 1914 the light cruiser *Königsberg* at Dar es Salaam in Tangan-
yika was Germany's major East African naval asset. She cleared harbor
just before the outbreak of hostilities to avoid being trapped by the British and on 6 August claimed the first German prize in the war against
commerce, the steamer *City of Winchester* off Aden. After that her luck
turned sour. She appeared at Aden only to find an empty harbor and then
at Majunga, Madagascar, with the same results. Nonetheless, *Königsberg*
caused the Admiralty to order shipping to avoid the approaches to the
Red Sea and to form convoys escorted by two warships, one of which
had to be superior to the cruiser.[51]

In mid-September *Königsberg* began using the Rufiji River delta south
of Dar es Salaam as an improvised secret base. There she received intelligence that the British protected cruiser *Pegasus* was cleaning her boilers
in the anchorage at Zanzibar. *Königsberg* got under way and arrived at
Zanzibar at dawn on 20 September. She first disabled the tug *Helmuth*,
which had been stationed as a guardship, and then at 0510 surprised
the anchored cruiser by opening fire from nine thousand yards. As one
British participant remembered, "Our men dashed to their stations, but
shells were falling fast and did fearful execution." *Pegasus* replied briefly
but the German scored four hits on the British cruiser's waterline and
many more on her upper works, disabling three guns. As *Königsberg*
closed to within six thousand yards Captain Ingles struck his colors.
When the crew started to abandon ship *Königsberg* turned and steamed
away. *Pegasus* lost thirty-one men killed and fifty-five wounded, more
than a third of her complement. Attempts to beach the ship failed and
she capsized at 1430.[52]

Königsberg returned to her hideout, but the light cruisers *Chatham*,
Dartmouth, and *Weymouth* located her there on 28 October, thanks in
part to intelligence from a captured German steamer. Unable to cross
the bar to get at their enemy, or to target her so far upstream, the British

were forced to resort to a blockade. An attempt in December to bomb *Königsberg* from aircraft failed and the year ended in a standoff with one light cruiser occupying three.

Vice Admiral Maximilian Spee, commander of Germany's East Asia Squadron. Victor in the Battle of Coronel, he lost his life in the Battle of the Falklands five weeks later. (Library of Congress)

On 13 August Vice Admiral Spee departed Pagan in the Marianas to conduct cruiser warfare along the American coast, where he would be best able to obtain coal and least likely to encounter units of Japan's powerful navy. He detached *Emden*, the newest and fastest of his light cruisers, to stir up trouble in the Indian Ocean, while his auxiliary cruisers headed for Australian waters.

Emden appeared on the trade route between Calcutta and Columbo on 10 September. In five days, she sank six merchantmen and captured two. The British history complained: "That she should have slipped through the net which [Vice] Admiral [Martyn] Jerram had spread and suddenly appeared far up in the Bay of Bengal was beyond all calculation. No part of the Eastern seas was regarded as more secure."[53] On 22 September *Emden* bombarded Madras, India. Between 25 September and 19 October she sank nine steamers and captured two to serve as colliers. In response British, French, Japanese, and Russian warships steamed into the eastern Indian Ocean to hunt the elusive raider. Although she had some close calls, it was a big ocean and *Emden* confounded her enemies by staying on the move. At the end of October she transited the Indian Ocean to Penang, Malaya, base to one of the hunter-groups.

Battle of Penang: 28 October, 0515–1000

Conditions: Clear and calm

Missions: Entente, none; Germans, raid

Entente Forces: RU CP *Zhemchug*★; FR TGB *D'Iberville*; TB *Pistolet, Fronde, Mousquet*★.

German Force (Frigate Captain Karl Müller): CL *Emden*.

The Russian protected cruiser *Zhemchug* had just returned from a fruit-less search of the Andaman and Nicobar Islands and was cleaning her boilers in the northern part of the channel between Penang and the mainland. The French torpedo gunboat *D'Iberville* was also in port over-hauling machinery, along with the torpedo boats *Pistolet* and *Fronde*, the first with cold boilers and the second at one hour notice. The torpedo boat *Mousquet* was patrolling north of the anchorage. *Emden*, disguised with dark gray paint and a dummy funnel to resemble a British light cruiser, steamed unchallenged into the North Channel at 0515 on 28 October. She approached to within five hundred yards of *Zhemchug*, hoisted her colors and, as her executive officer recounted, "at a distance of 200 meters our first torpedo flew out of the starboard broadside tube, and at the same time our broadside guns opened up into the forecastle of the *Zhemtchug* where the crew was asleep." The torpedo exploded in the Russian's engine room. "One could plainly see the tremor that ran through the ship when she was struck." *Emden* then crept past at slow speed, guns blazing. "One could look clear through the ship through the large holes in her sides. One after another the projectiles kept on hitting." The Russian crew manned a few 4.7-inch guns and replied with a dozen rounds after *Emden* was already past. The German ship circled back and, concerned about taking damage from the cruiser's larger weapons, launched another torpedo. This detonated *Zhemchug*'s magazine. A large cloud of yellowish smoke enveloped the ship and when it dissipated, *Zhemchug* was gone. Ninety one men died and 106 were wounded.[54]

After this success Müller intended to attack *D'Iberville* (which initially mistook *Emden* for a British cruiser), when a lookout reported a torpedo boat entering the harbor. Hurrying north he opened fire briefly until identifying the craft as an unarmed patrol launch. Continuing, *Emden* stopped a steamer but before completing the capture she sighted a warship on the northern horizon. This was *Mousquet*. *Emden* attacked the small ship and scored a boiler hit at 4,500 yards with her third salvo. "A large cloud of black coal dust and white steam covered the entire after part of the ship." *Mousquet* returned fire with her 65-mm gun, and launched a torpedo, but all in vain. She sank after a ten-minute action. At 0635, as *Emden* rescued thirty-six survivors, *Pistolet* got under way and maintained contact until 1000, when an engine malfunction forced her to abandon the chase. *Fronde* left port but never caught up.[55]

This little raid magnified the German cruiser's already fearsome reputation and delayed the sailing of large troop convoys from New Zealand and Australia to the Middle East—a delay that ironically proved *Emden*'s undoing.

Battle of Cocos Island: 9 November, 0940–1120

Conditions: Clear

Missions: Australians, interception; Germans, raid

Australian Force (Captain John Glossop): CL *Sydney*[#].

German Force (Frigate Captain Karl Müller): CL *Emden*★.

After Penang *Emden* coaled from one of her captured ships and made for Cocos Island to attack the British cable station there. By coincidence, the thirty-five-ship strong Australian troop convoy, escorted by the cruisers *Melbourne*, *Sydney*, and the Japanese semi-battlecruiser *Ibuki*, had departed Australian waters on 1 November, after being delayed by *Emden*'s excursions, and was just fifty miles north of Cocos at the time.

When the disguised *Emden* steamed into the anchorage on 9 November the station was not fooled and broadcast an SOS before being jammed. The cruiser launched two boats with forty-four men to destroy the installations. However, the Australian convoy's commander received the alert and at 0700 dispatched *Sydney* to investigate. She sighted the island at 0915, and shortly thereafter, funnel smoke.

Emden's men had just finished their demolitions when the recall sounded. Lookouts had spotted the approaching cruiser but it was already too late to retrieve the landing party. *Emden* weighed and proceeded immediately to sea.[56]

The Australian ship had heavier guns and greater speed—1 knot more in theory, but 4 in practice due to *Emden's* lack of maintenance. The action opened at 0940 from 9,500 yards. The German ship fired first, immediately straddled, and hit with her second salvo. She quickly knocked out both of the Australian's fire control positions, but only damage to *Sydney's* engines could have saved *Emden* and the Australian cruiser's 2-inch belt kept the German ship's 38-pound shells out of her vitals. *Sydney* started hitting with her 100-pound rounds on the twelfth broadside. "Then a heavy salvo landed on the *Emden's* stern. . . . Fire broke out under the poop. For about 15 minutes flames shot 20 to 25 meters in the air out of the after end of the ship."[57] After ten minutes *Emden* lost her rangefinder and her gunnery rapidly diminished in accuracy and volume. Several times she tried to close to torpedo range, but *Sydney* always altered away. After an hour of combat Captain Glossop described *Emden's* situation thus: "First the foremost funnel of her went, secondly the foremast, and she was badly on fire aft, then the second funnel went, and lastly the third funnel." Finally, with damage and casualties mounting the German steered for North Keeling Island and grounded there at 1120. *Sydney* rescued 201 Germans but 115 died. The Australian received ten hits and suffered four killed and twelve wounded but her damage was "surprisingly small."[58]

Emden captured or sank sixteen Entente merchantmen grossing 70,825 tons. Even worse, her two-month foray delayed sailings from Bombay, Calcutta, Aden, and Singapore and seriously dislocated trade throughout the Middle and Far East.

If *Emden's* depredations caused a sensation, it was nothing compared to the threat presented by Spee's squadron of two armored and two light cruisers. The vice admiral departed the Marianas on 13 August accompanied by eight supply ships loaded with 19,000 tons of coal. This auxiliary fleet was necessary because each armored cruiser required a hundred tons of coal a day at cruising speed and five hundred tons at high speeds. Their bunkers carried two thousand tons while the light

cruisers held thirteen hundred tons. Thus, Spee began his voyage with
only enough extra coal on hand to resupply his ships twice: eight days
at high speeds or forty days at most economical speeds. This was little
considering the vast spaces and lack of bases that confronted the German admiral.[59]

The main squadron proceeded in a generally southeasterly direction,
stopping at Christmas Island on 7–9 September, Samoa on 14 September, and Tahiti on 22 September. At Tahiti Spee expected to capture coal
and perhaps destroy some shipping. In fact, when his squadron appeared
the French immediately fired the island's six-thousand-ton coal stock-
pile. The only warship present, the seven-hundred-ton gunboat *Zélée*,
had landed her weapons for use in a shore battery. The frustrated Germans sank this insignificant target and briefly bombarded the batteries,
expending a precious forty-six 21-cm and thirty-five 15-cm shells. They
then headed for the Marquesas, where they replenished their bunkers
from a collier. Spee next stopped at Easter Island between 12 and 19
October, where he met *Leipzig* and a collier. The squadron arrived at the
Juan Fernández group well off the Chilean coast on 26 October where
it depleted the holds of another collier. On 31 October Spee departed
these isolated islands heading south. On that day he received word of a
British cruiser at Coronel.

Symbolic of the war's global dimensions, the commander of the British force
Spee was about to encounter, Rear Admiral Cradock, had started the war on
the opposite hemisphere and a different ocean commanding the West Indies
Station. The nature of the developing surface threat drew Cradock south and
on 14 September the Admiralty instructed him to make the Falklands his coaling base and to counter a possible move by Spee toward the Atlantic.

The Admiralty gave Cradock two armored cruisers, *Good Hope* and
Monmouth, the modern light cruiser *Glasgow*, and an armed merchant
cruiser, *Otranto*, with the predreadnought *Canopus* en route. On 7
October Cradock learned Spee was bound for Easter Island which,
though not in his neighborhood, was surely on the way. He sent *Monmouth*, *Glasgow*, and *Otranto* into the Pacific while he waited for *Canopus* at Port Stanley. The predreadnought arrived on 18 October. *Good
Hope* departed Port Stanley on 22 October and *Canopus* followed the
next day.

Map 2.8 Battle of Coronel: 1 November 1914

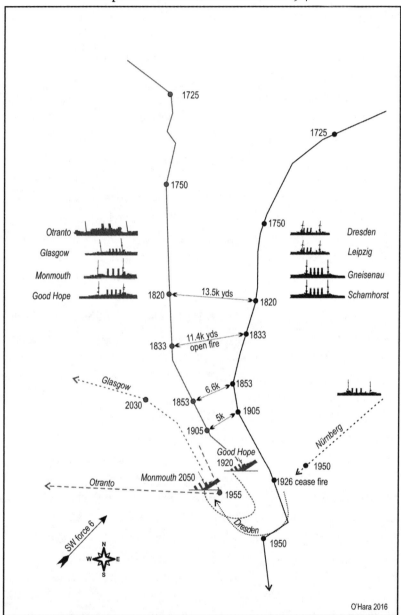

The long-range communications between Cradock and the Admiralty bred misunderstandings. It was not the Admiralty's intention that Cradock engage Spee with inferior forces and on the morning of 30

October, when *Good Hope* and *Monmouth* left Vallenar roads in southern Chile to sweep north, Cradock showed no signs of intending to do so. The rear admiral met *Canopus* arriving at the anchorage and left there a letter for the battleship's captain that stated that he thought *Leipzig* was somewhere close. Cradock declared his intention to return and instructed *Canopus* to keep steam up in case she was needed.

Battle of Coronel: 1 November 1611–2100

Conditions: Clear, heavy seas

Missions: British, interception; Germans, interception

British Force (Rear Admiral Christopher Cradock†): CA *Good Hope*★, *Monmouth*★; CL *Glasgow*#; AMC *Otranto*.

German Force (Vice Admiral Maximilian Spee): CA *Scharnhorst*+, *Gneisenau*+; CL *Nürnberg, Leipzig, Dresden*.

Glasgow had put into Coronel, a small port in south-central Chile, to relay signals. There she intercepted transmissions between *Leipzig* (through which Spee was routing all his radio communications) and a German supply ship. Upon being notified that an enemy light cruiser appeared to be in the vicinity Cradock collected *Otranto* and ordered *Glasgow* to join him at noon on 1 November so his whole force could sweep north to find the enemy. Spee, meanwhile, had received intelligence the day before that *Glasgow* was at Coronel and thus, like Cradock, he was looking to snap up an isolated cruiser. The mid-spring day was clear but the south-easterly wind was rising and there was a heavy sea.

At 1556 *Glasgow* sighted smoke broad on her starboard bow and hauled out to investigate. At 1611 the light cruiser made the signal that enemy ships were in sight and, with *Monmouth* and *Otranto* following, came about to join *Good Hope* approaching from the south. *Scharnhorst*, at the head of the German formation, saw smoke at 1617. Spee altered to starboard and ordered his squadron to concentrate as he sought to identify the source.

At 1642 *Good Hope* was heading east-southeast and the rest of the British force had joined her by 1717. Instead of the solitary light cruiser he was expecting, Cradock apparently realized that he had encountered Spee's armored cruisers. Nonetheless he did not attempt to avoid action or even order *Otranto* away, despite the fact that she was just a large, slow target. Instead, he established a line of battle in order: *Good Hope*, *Monmouth*, *Glasgow*, and *Otranto*. Five hundred yards separated each ship. He then steered southeast at 12 knots, altering to a southerly course as Spee gradually closed from the east, *Scharnhorst* leading *Gneisenau*, *Leipzig* and *Dresden* farther behind, while *Nürnberg*, which had been proceeding independently along the coast, was out of sight. By 1720 the two columns were on converging courses with the Germans slightly ahead. The British had the weather gauge and the advantage of light with the sun low in the afternoon sky to the west. Cradock turned to head south-southwest and then at 1754 called for top speed. Three minutes later he signaled his intention to attack. Spee, however, maneuvered to maintain range. He planned to open fire at sunset when the afterglow of the setting sun would silhouette the British ships. Cradock may have anticipated that the moon, which was almost full and due to rise in the east at 1800, would restore his advantage, but scattered rain showers on the eastern horizon at first masked the moonrise. In any case, the British admiral steered a steady course. *Otranto*, too slow to keep station, began to lag.

By 1820 slowly converging courses had reduced the range to 13,500 yards. *Scharnhorst* was slightly ahead of *Good Hope*. *Gneisenau* followed 720 yards behind with *Leipzig* 900 yards behind her and *Dresden* 1,700 yards behind *Leipzig*. Spee rang up 16 knots and turned slightly toward the enemy. Cradock held steady as the sun dipped below the horizon. At 1833 it was completely gone and Spee opened fire. The range between the flagships was 11,400 yards. Cradock replied almost immediately. This was near the limit of his 6-inch guns and those located on the main decks of both British armored cruisers were hard, if not impossible, to work in the heavy seas. The German 15-cm weapons had similar problems; the gun crews operated with water to their knees. According to Spee's report, "Observation and rangefinding work was most difficult, the seas sweeping over the forecastles and conning towers, and preventing the use of some guns on the middle decks."[60] He stated that *Good Hope* initially fired only her 9.2-inch pieces at a rate of one round every fifty seconds. *Monmouth*, however, fired six gun broadsides and initially her salvoes were rapid and well grouped. *Glasgow* aimed her two 6-inch

pieces at *Leipzig*. *Dresden* took *Otranto* under fire at 1836. Almost immediately the merchant cruiser dropped out of line and sought refuge on
Glasgow's unengaged side.

Scharnhorst landed a 21-cm round on *Good Hope* with her third salvo.
This struck between the forward turret and forecastle and ignited a large
fire. It may have also disabled the turret. *Good Hope*'s crew appeared
to bring the blaze under control but minutes later *Scharnhorst* blasted
her again in almost the same location and afterwards the fire raged
unchecked. At 1838 *Good Hope* turned 22.5 degrees toward the enemy,
presumably to increase the effectiveness of her 6-inch weapons.

Monmouth also received punishing damage from the first. One of
Gneisenau's early salvos exploded on the cruiser's forecastle and apparently ignited the fore turret's ready charges. The resultant explosion
blew the turret overboard and ignited a large fire. In return four 6-inch
shells struck *Gneisenau*. One temporarily jammed the aft main battery
turret and another started a small fire. Otherwise, the damage was insignificant. At 1838, just five minutes into the action, *Monmouth* staggered
out of line, forcing *Glasgow* to veer away to avoid coming between her
and the enemy.

By 1853 the range had dropped to 6,600 yards. *Scharnhorst* was pounding
Good Hope and Cradock's flagship was burning fiercely. She had failed to
hit *Scharnhorst* even once but continued to steadily close. At 1907 the range
was down to 4,400 yards and Spee, whose ships were now showing a little
better in the moonlight, assumed the British flagship intended a torpedo
attack. At 1920, however, *Good Hope* blew up in a tremendous explosion. An
officer on board *Glasgow* later wrote: "It was instantaneous from an internal
explosion in which very large pieces of debris, funnels, etc. were blown
about 200 feet up into the air; she was then only about half a mile from us
on our port bow and evidently not under control as a result of previous
damage."[61] There were no survivors. By this time *Monmouth* was burning
and her guns were nearly all silent. She continued south until 1935 when
she began a broad turn to starboard to put her stern to the sea. The German
armored cruisers briefly engaged *Glasgow* but she made a poor target in the
dark. They ceased fire at 1926 but not before *Glasgow* landed a pair of 4-inch
rounds on *Scharnhorst* causing minor damage and no casualties. These were
the only hits the German flagship suffered.

At 1937 Spee ordered his light cruisers to attack with torpedoes. *Leipzig* and *Dresden* swung north to comply as *Nürnberg*, coming in from the northeast, finally reached the battle zone. At 2050 she found *Monmouth* and pumped 135 rounds into the listing wreck which then capsized and sank with all hands. *Glasgow* and *Otranto* escaped separately. The British light cruiser had been the target of over five hundred rounds, mostly 10.5-cm, of which five hit. One waterline blow caused some flooding, but only four men were wounded.

Scharnhorst fired 422 21-cm and 215 15-cm rounds, almost all at *Good Hope*. *Gneisenau* expended 244 21-cm and 198 15-cm rounds; collectively this was roughly half their total supply. Berlin trumpeted the battle as a great victory and the first British defeat at sea in a hundred years. Spee summed it up nicely when he wrote: "We have at least contributed something to the glory of our arms—although it might not mean much on the whole in view of the enormous number of English ships."[62]

In the subsequent historiography the principal question has always been not how the battle was fought, but why it was fought. As for the why, a series of assumptions fed by poorly worded signals had led Cradock to believe that the Admiralty had ordered him to fight and that it believed he had sufficient force to do so. As for how, according to *Glasgow's* captain, "[Cradock] had no clear plan or doctrine in his head but was always inclined to act on the impulse of the moment . . . [he] was constitutionally incapable of refusing or even postponing action if there was the smallest chance of success."[63] In fact, Cradock's only combat experience was on land. Cradock and the Royal Navy went to war with a broadly understood doctrine that was subject to personal interpretation. Once committed to action the admiral fought in a rigid line of battle, even using a ship unsuited for such a formation. He kept a steady course, doing nothing to adjust his tactics after the action quickly turned against him except to close range. It was a profoundly ineffective performance and one, apparently, that surprised the participants. One of *Glasgow's* officers later wrote: "When we got formed up in sight of [the] enemy we all thought he [Cradock] would leave the *Otranto* and dash straight in to about 5,000 [yards], so as to give the 6-in. guns a chance. He had to do it at once, as if he put it off till sunset, we were bound to be in a hopeless position whereas if he managed it before [the] sun went down we had them at a disadvantage."[64]

Glasgow fled south and warned *Canopus*. Together they rounded Cape Horn and arrived at Port Stanley on 8 November. *Otranto*, meanwhile, sailed two hundred miles into the Pacific before turning south and making for the Falklands. Spee put into Valparaiso to the acclaim of the large German community and accepted the service of 180 volunteers from the dozens of German merchant ships sheltering there.

The Admiralty first heard of Coronel on 4 November from German sources, and once the full extent of the defeat became known the British reaction demonstrated the impact of an isolated naval squadron, even one with almost half its ammunition expended and a hand-to-mouth supply of precious coal. In case Spee suddenly debouched from the newly opened Panama Canal (through which the United States had declared it would limit passage to three belligerent warships at a time), one French and three British armored cruisers waited in the West Indies. At Halifax, Nova Scotia, the battlecruiser *Princess Royal* joined a predreadnought and more armored cruisers. In the South Atlantic battlecruisers *Invincible* and *Inflexible* and armored cruisers *Carnarvon*, *Cornwell*, and *Defence* were on their way to join the survivors of Coronel. In case Spee lunged toward South Africa the Admiralty gathered a predreadnought, the powerful armored cruiser *Minotaur*, and three cruisers. *Defence*, sister to *Minotaur*, would join them once relieved by the battlecruisers. A predreadnought, two large armored cruisers and two more cruisers guarded West African waters. The battlecruiser *Australia* along with Japanese and British cruisers collected around the Channel Islands off Southern California. All this was in addition to Japanese squadrons in the Pacific and powerful British and other Entente forces in the Indian Ocean. Spee, of course, did not know the details of the forces seeking him, but he sensed their magnitude, as demonstrated on 3 November when he declined the gift of flowers from an admirer in Valparaiso saying they would be better suited for his grave.

On 15 November the German squadron completed coaling from its rendezvous at Más Afuera, the outermost of the Juan Fernández Islands, and headed south. The cruisers coaled yet again well down the Chilean coast in the glacier-fed Bahia de San Quintin. Spee, accompanied by three supply ships, coaled a final time in the Beagle Channel after fortuitously capturing a British vessel loaded with 2,800 tons of best Welsh steaming coal. Berlin ultimately wanted the squadron to return home but gave Spee freedom to decide how to accomplish that feat and whether to conduct cruiser warfare along the way. On 6 December, the day his ships completed coaling, the German admiral resolved to destroy the wireless station at Port Stanley in the Falkland Islands, against the advice of all but one of his captains. He believed the port was empty and assigned *Gneisenau* and *Nürnberg* to conduct the raid while the other three warships waited fifteen miles offshore.

Battle of the Falklands: 8 December 1914, 0919–2130

Conditions: Clear, deteriorating later

Missions: British, none; Germans, raid

British Force (Vice Admiral Doveton Sturdee): BC *Invincible*#, *Inflexible*+; CA *Carnarvon*, *Cornwall*#, *Kent*#; CL *Glasgow*#, *Bristol*; AMC *Macedonia*.

German Force (Vice Admiral Maximilian Spee†): CA *Gneisenau*★, *Scharnhorst*★; CL *Nürnberg*★, *Dresden*, *Leipzig*★.

Had Spee arrived before 7 December, he would have found the islands defended only by *Canopus*, deliberately grounded near Port Stanley to cover the harbor entrance with her guns. The battleship had improvised a minefield and landed some 12-pounder guns and a marine contingent to join a 130-man strong home guard. This alone might have been enough to frustrate Spee's attack, but when he arrived at 0730 on the morning of 8 December he had to contend with the entire South Atlantic Squadron as well. *Macedonia* was on patrol outside the harbor, *Kent* was at a half hour notice; *Carnarvon*, *Glasgow*, and *Cornwall* had finished coaling, the battlecruisers had just started, and *Bristol* had her engines open for repairs. Sturdee's intention was to sail on the 9th and hunt for Spee, who he believed was still in the Pacific.

At 0915 *Gneisenau* and *Nürnberg* approached the harbor to bombard the wireless station. The British had already noted their smoke and had been raising steam for ninety minutes. As the German ships neared they could discern through the smog hanging above the port the masts of a cruiser (*Kent*) passing through the harbor channel. They increased speed to intercept her but at 0919 *Canopus* lobbed a salvo in their path. Her 12-inch shells fell two thousand yards short but the tall geysers they raised caused *Gneisenau*'s captain to veer 90 degrees away. After a few minutes *Gneisenau* turned back to engage *Kent* but then Spee signaled, "Do not accept action; concentrate on course E by N; proceed at high speed."[65]

Kent was the same class as *Monmouth* so by past experience *Gneisenau* should have made short work of her, but *Glasgow* was right behind *Kent* and *Carnarvon* behind *Glasgow*. The battlecruisers weighed at 1000. Spee did not know that capital ships were present but his orders to *Gneisenau* made sense. His best chance was to run as hard, as fast, and as soon as he could. Poor weather was his best ally and in that part of the world on a late spring day poor weather was to be expected. However 8 December had dawned clear with light, cold breezes and unlimited visibility. By 1030, *Carnarvon*, *Inflexible*, *Invincible*, and finally *Cornwall* had cleared the outer harbor. An officer on *Carnarvon* wrote: "A cloud of smoke right ahead showed the enemy funnel-down on the horizon. Full speed ahead we went, pounding through the blue sea, carelessly deployed in far flung array." Even *Bristol*, working to get her engines back together, weighed by 1032.[66]

The British squadron chased for two hours and twenty-five minutes before firing its first shots. During that period Sturdee dropped speed when he saw his ships were becoming scattered and increased it again when he was closing too slowly. Monstrous quantities of black smoke boiled from his battlecruisers' funnels.

By 1220 the rear German ship, *Leipzig*, was ten miles ahead of *Invincible*. *Inflexible* was on the flagship's starboard quarter while *Glasgow* was five miles off her port bow. *Kent* was off the port beam. *Carnarvon* and *Cornwall* were six miles astern. The Germans were fleeing in a rough line of bearing with, from northwest to southeast, *Nürnberg*, *Gneisenau*, *Scharnhorst*, *Dresden*, and *Leipzig*.

At 1220 Sturdee decided to press the action and fight without his armored cruisers, which plainly could not keep pace. He therefore rang up 26 knots. At 1255 *Inflexible*'s forward guns elevated to their maximum and began to fling ranging shots toward *Leipzig* 16,500 yards away. *Invincible* did the same two minutes later. Although no shells hit, this slow, long-range bombardment provoked a reaction from Spee. At 1320 he signaled his light cruisers to escape. Then, followed by *Gneisenau*, *Scharnhorst* turned east-northeast across the path of the onrushing battlecruisers. This maneuver provoked an equally radical response from the British as *Glasgow, Kent,* and *Cornwall* peeled off after the German light cruisers. In his battle instructions, delivered the evening before, Sturdee had covered this eventuality so the British reaction was automatic. *Invincible* meanwhile turned 80 degrees to port to parallel the German armored cruisers. Spee opened fire at 1330 from 13,700 yards. As *Kent* crossed the stern of the battlecruisers, her captain later wrote, "the German ships were firing salvo after salvo with marvelous rapidity and control. Flash after flash travelled down their sides from head to stern, all their 6-inch and 8-inch guns firing every salvo." At 1344 Spee scored the action's first hit: a blow on *Invincible* that struck the armored belt and "caused a severe tremor" all over the ship. In response, Sturdee edged away. By 1403 the range had crept up to 16,500 yards and the British, hampered by smoke, ceased fire. In this half hour the British fired 210 12-inch rounds at both armored cruisers and hit *Gneisenau* three times. The damage inflicted on *Scharnhorst* is unknown although the British claimed some success. At that same moment Spee took advantage of the smoke shrouding the battlecruisers and made a sharp turn south. As soon as he realized the Germans were running, Sturdee conformed and the chase was on again.[67]

At this time, away to the west, *Bristol* sighted smoke and turned to investigate. This belonged to the colliers *Santa Isabel* and *Baden*. *Bristol* and *Macedonia* eventually ran them down. *Bristol*'s captain, following his orders literally, had the crews removed and sank both despite their precious cargoes of coal and supplies. For this he was criticized by Admiralty staff. Spee had ordered a third collier to sail toward his flotilla to serve potentially as a hospital ship. The British never sighted her and she was eventually interned in Argentina.

At 1448 *Invincible* had closed to 15,000 yards and opened fire at *Scharnhorst*. *Inflexible* followed suit against *Gneisenau*. In response Spee turned to port to open his broadsides. The British battlecruisers turned as well

Map 2.9 Battle of the Falklands: 8 December 1914

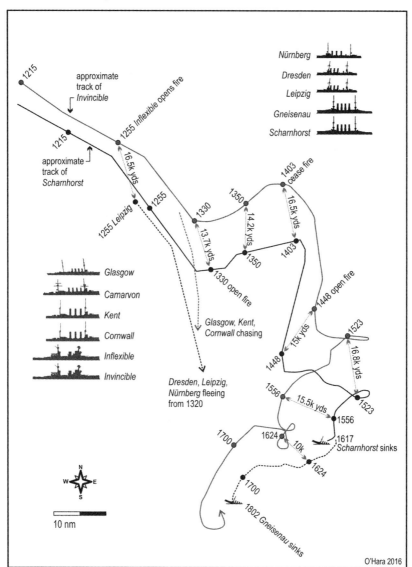

and once again salvos crossed the smoky sky as the ships settled on parallel courses. By 1500 the range had dropped to ten thousand yards and the German 15-cm guns were pumping rounds at the enemy. *Invincible* took several hits but *Scharnhorst* was burning forward and her gunfire had grown ragged. At 1515 *Invincible* made a 180-degree turn to escape the blinding effects of her own smoke. Meanwhile *Scharnhorst* sheered out of line, presumably due to steering gear damage, but by 1530 the Germans were back in line and had reversed course to stay in range of the British ships. Their speed had dropped to 18 knots and *Gneisenau* was listing so much her 15-cm weapons fell silent.

As Spee's armored cruisers were being pummeled the German light cruisers were to the southwest, steaming south by southeast through deteriorating weather at their highest speeds. By 1450 *Glasgow* was near enough to engage *Leipzig* with her forward 6-inch gun. The German cruiser, whose top speed was 21 knots, replied when the range was 11,000 yards. A cat-and-mouse game followed as *Glasgow's* fire provoked a response from *Leipzig*. Some hits were scored on each side while the other British cruisers slowly closed. By 1617 *Kent* and *Cornwall* were pitching shells at *Leipzig* as well. Up to this point the German vessels had remained together but now the three split up. *Dresden*, which was in the best condition, pulled away and was out of sight by 1700. *Kent* chased *Nürnberg* while *Cornwall* and *Glasgow* continued to persecute *Leipzig*.

Returning to the action between Spee and Sturdee, by 1535 *Scharnhorst* had steadied on a southwesterly heading roughly 12,000 yards from *Inflexible*, which was steering a parallel course. There is some confusion in this period as both battlecruisers reported they were firing on *Scharnhorst* although *Gneisenau* recorded hits from *Invincible* at 1532, 1536, 1548 (three), 1549, and 1605. By 1600 *Scharnhorst* was down by the bow, her funnels had been shot away, her guns were silent and she was burning fiercely from stem to stern. She made a signal to *Gneisenau* to escape as she turned again toward the British. By this time even the lagging *Carnarvon* was in range. She opened fire at 1615 from 11,000 yards, but within minutes *Scharnhorst* disappeared beneath the waves. The battle swept by and there were no survivors.

Gneisenau lasted nearly another two hours. The battlecruisers and *Carnarvon* maneuvered to get free fields of fire. It was now drizzling and the light was failing. Although "steam, fire and smoke were pouring from her everywhere," *Gneisenau* continued to fight and even hit *Invincible* again at 1715. Nevertheless, there could be only one result and shortly after 1800 the warship capsized and sank. The British plucked 177 survivors from the icy waters.[68]

By 1720 both *Glasgow* and *Cornwall* were comfortably in range of *Leipzig* and subjecting the light cruiser to a steady pounding. She fought back until she exhausted her ammunition at 1900. The British ships closed but not being certain that the German had surrendered, they reengaged at 1950 from very close range. *Leipzig* finally sank at 2123. Only eighteen men survived "in an exhausted and pitiable state. The others had succumbed to the intense cold of the water."[69]

Kent's chase of *Nürnberg* saw the German ship open fire first at 1700. The British captain described her shooting as "remarkably accurate." There were many near misses and she hit the cruiser once with the shell bursting on deck. *Kent*, due to a shortage of coal, was burning furniture and even her decking as she worked up to 25 knots. At 1745 *Nürnberg* suffered a burst boiler tube and the resulting loss of speed decided the action. *Kent* closed, ultimately to three thousand yards, and pounded the German ship. *Nürnberg* struck her colors at 1859 and sank at 1927. Only seven men survived. *Kent* had only two hundred tons of coal left when the action ended and was out of touch due to damage to her radio room.

The German armored cruisers each had 665 21-cm and 1,100 15-cm rounds. The light cruisers normally carried 1,860 10.5-cm rounds although they were short their full complement after Coronel.

Inflexible took three hits, *Invincible* twenty-two. She suffered some buckling of the bow armor and two compartments flooded. A 21-cm round penetrated the ship below the armor belt and flooded a bunker. *Glasgow* was hit twice, suffering damage to one boiler, and *Cornwall* eighteen times. She had no casualties but two port side bunkers flooded "producing a considerable list."[70] *Kent* took thirty-eight hits but these did no serious damage. The cruiser had four men killed and twelve wounded.

The British battlecruisers showed that they could hit at long ranges, but at such a low percentage Sturdee worried about running out of ammunition. German zigzagging tactics exacerbated the problem of poor accuracy. Germany gunnery, on the other hand, was good in both the Falkland and Coronel actions, but many hits at Falklands produced few results, unlike Coronel where a few hits on the British armored cruisers produced great results. The German ships were

Table 2.4 Battle of the Falklands: Ammunition Expenditure

Invincible	513 12-inch
Inflexible	661 12-inch
Carnarvon	85 7.5-inch; 60 6-inch
Cornwall	1,090 6-inch
Glasgow	316 6-inch; 889 4-inch
Kent	658 6-inch

incredibly difficult to sink. The speed difference between the British and German ships points up the difficulties of maintaining coal-fired boilers and triple-expansion piston engines in the face of long cruises, limited facilities for repair and overhaul, and mixed quality coal.[71]

The Falklands was one of the few true battles of annihilation fought in the First World War. At Coronel, visibility and sea conditions would have allowed Cradock to avoid battle. At the Falklands, Spee had no choice. At best, he might have fled headlong throughout the battle, hoping that a deterioration in weather would save him. The result of the Falklands battle accorded with pre-war concepts of faster ships running down slower prey. But such results would prove hard to duplicate in practice.

3

1915: No End in Sight

*It was not pleasant to have to run away. But the slightest damage in
the engine-room would have been enough to enable the battleship [sic]
to overtake us and deal with us at her leisure, for a broadside from the
Novara would have bounded off her like peas off a wall.*

—MIKLÓS HORTHY, MEMOIRS

Overview

The year 1915 would see trench warfare impose a stalemate on the
Western and Italian Fronts. In the east the Germans and Austrians
eliminated Russian gains in Galicia and conquered most of Lithuania and
Poland. Serbia finally fell to the Central Powers after Bulgaria entered the
war on their side in October. The Ottomans held their own against the
Russians on the Caucasus front and the Entente at Gallipoli. Sea power
allowed the British to conquer most of lower Mesopotamia.

At sea the year saw the elimination of the last German warships in the
great oceans—the light cruisers *Dresden* and *Königsberg*—in one-sided
surface actions. In less than eight months, the Royal Navy and its allies
had reduced the Central Powers to surface operations in the North, Baltic, Black, and Adriatic Seas—less than 1 percent of the world's saltwa-
ter surface area. Only submarines and raiders would regularly venture
beyond these restricted waters.

With its oceanic squadrons eliminated, Germany had only submarines
and a few auxiliary cruisers to impede the Entente's worldwide commercial trade. Being increasingly pressured by the British blockade, which
it naturally considered illegal, with its surface fleet unable to provide a

solution, and with no quick end to the war in sight, Germany declared British waters a war zone on 4 February 1915 and all enemy merchant shipping subject to attack. The results were devastating: by April German boats had sunk seventy-one merchant ships totaling 155,000 GRT.[1] Yet this success had a cost in that it limited Germany's ability to practice surface warfare. This was because doctrine assigned to submarines the missions of reconnaissance and attritional attacks against warships before a surface engagement. With only thirty-three operational boats at the beginning of the year, Germany could have an aggressive surface force or a submarine campaign against traffic, but not both.[2]

German battlecruisers would mount a raid at the beginning of 1915, only to be defeated in the Battle of Dogger Bank. After that setback, Kaiser Wilhelm replaced Admiral Ingenohl with Admiral Hugo Pohl. The kaiser permitted Pohl to undertake limited sorties without his express approval as long as appropriate caution was exercised and battle was joined only under favorable circumstances. Under such restraints and deprived of its submarine screen, the High Seas Fleet ventured from the Heligoland Bight on several occasions between March and October, but never farther than the edge of the Dogger Bank. Such peekaboo operations by Pohl, an admiral as risk adverse as the kaiser himself, had little chance of provoking a fleet engagement.

With the High Seas Fleet on such a short tether, the Grand Fleet's battle squadrons sailed two or three times a month, mostly in the upper half of the North Sea for exercises and sweeps. The Harwich Force guarded the waters to the south and the Dover Patrol strove to close the Dover Straits to the passage of German submarines. Both sides increased minelaying efforts.

In the Baltic a long winter kept Russian ships icebound in the Gulf of Finland until May. Although four dreadnoughts reinforced the Baltic Fleet during the year, these vessels were rushed into service and not fully operational. The Kaiserliche Marine, meanwhile, took advantage of the relative inactivity in the North Sea and committed elements of the High Seas Fleet to the Baltic. After a series of battles they forced passage into the Gulf of Riga in August, but with the army's advance toward Riga stalled, and nearly all the coastline under Russian control, the fleet quickly withdrew. Apart from defending the gulf, Russia's Baltic Fleet sowed mines and skirmished with enemy minelaying and scouting forces. Good intelligence allowed the Russians to intercept German formations at sea, albeit with lackluster results.

In the Black Sea the Russians focused on bombardment and anti-shipping missions. New dreadnoughts gave them sea superiority, although the introduction of German submarines later in the year made the Russians more cautious. Nonetheless, the combination of Russian sweeps and British submarine attacks in the Sea of Marmara inflicted grievous losses on the Ottoman merchant marine, which began the war with just 143 steamers of 70,000 GRT and 900 sailing vessels of 180,000 GRT.[3]

In the Mediterranean the Entente powers addressed the problem of stalemate on the Western Front by seeking to attack Constantinople. They believed this would drive the Ottomans from the war, influence Balkan neutrals, and open the Mediterranean–Black Sea supply route into Russia. They first conceived this action as a naval operation but eventually it became a major combined land-sea campaign focused on the Gallipoli peninsula.

Italy (or its pre-unification component states) had fought seven wars against Austria between 1820 and 1866. This cycle of conflict seemed to have ended in 1882 when Italy, Germany, and Austria-Hungary formed the Triple Alliance. Their partnership, however, did not stop Rome and Vienna from anticipating another round. In 1915 Italy's leaders succumbed to Entente enticements, polite blackmail, and the nation's desire to enhance its geopolitical position, and declared war on Austria-Hungary on 24 May.[4] Austrian naval missions against the Italians remained the same as against the French: protecting the Dalmatian coast and interfering with enemy traffic. The Italian high command, meanwhile, issued orders just before the declaration of war that designated the destruction of enemy naval forces as the navy's prime objective and made this the responsibility of the fleet's flotilla craft. The battle fleet would concentrate in the south to prevent Austrian forces from entering the Ionian or Tyrrhenian Seas (a task vastly facilitated by l'Armée Navale's presence south of the Otranto Strait) and not defend the east coast cities—an impossible task in any case given the lack of bases and the sheer number of potential targets.[5]

North Sea 1915

Admiral Ingenohl planned another battlecruiser foray in January 1915 to cover a minelaying sortie to the Firth of Forth. Bad weather forced a cancellation and when conditions finally improved Ingenohl sent Hipper's battlecruisers to the Dogger Bank to attack any enemy light forces encountered there. On the way back, they would seek out fishing trawlers, which each side suspected the other of using as a surreptitious scouting force.

Battle of Dogger Bank: 24 January, 0710–1300

Conditions: Clear, wind force 3–4

Missions: British, interception; Germans, raid

British Forces: Grand Fleet elements (Vice Admiral David Beatty): BC *Lion*[#], *Tiger*[+], *Princess Royal, New Zealand, Indomitable.* 1st LCS (Commodore William Goodenough): CL *Southampton, Birmingham, Nottingham, Lowestoft.* Harwich Force (Commodore Reginald Tyrwhitt): 10th DF: CL *Arethusa;* DD *Meteor*[#]*, Milne, Minos, Mentor, Mastiff, Morris.* 1st DF: CL *Aurora*[+]*,* DD *Acheron, Attack, Ariel, Hydra, Ferret, Forester, Defender, Druid, Hornet, Tigress, Sandfly, Jackal, Goshawk, Phoenix, Lapwing.* 3rd DF: CL *Undaunted,* DD *Lookout, Lysander, Landrail, Laurel, Liberty, Laertes, Lucifer, Laforey, Lawford, Lydiard, Louis, Legion, Lark, Miranda.*

German Forces (Rear Admiral Franz Hipper): BC *Seydlitz*[#]*, Moltke, Derfflinger*[+]*,* CA *Blücher*[*]; CL *Graudenz, Stralsund, Rostock, Kolberg*[+]*.* V TBF: *G12, V1, V4, V5, G11, G9, G7, G8, V2.* VIII TBF: *S178.* 15 TBHF: *V30, S33, S34, V29, S35.* 18 TBHF: *V181, V182, V185.*

Rear Admiral Hipper's force weighed anchor at 1745 on 23 January, planning to sweep the Dogger Bank at dawn on the 24th and return that afternoon. The rest of the High Seas Fleet remained at anchor. By this stage Room 40 was routinely intercepting and decoding German naval radio messages and learned of the mission before Hipper sailed. Consequently, Admiral Beatty's battlecruiser force deployed from Rosyth while three light cruisers and thirty-five destroyers sailed from Harwich to serve as anvil to Beatty's hammer. The Grand Fleet steamed from Scapa Flow in support.

The British judged matters nicely. At daybreak on the 24th *Aurora* of the Harwich Force sighted *Kolberg* to the east. At 0714 a sharp action between the cruisers ensued at eight thousand yards. *Aurora* hit *Kolberg* twice and shook the German light cruiser with two very near misses. In return *Kolberg* landed one shell on *Aurora,* although neither cruiser did any great harm to the other. The shooting had petered out by 0725.

Beatty's battlecruisers saw the gun flashes to the southeast while Hipper's big ships were northeast of *Kolberg.* Hipper had been leading his force northwest, unwittingly straight at the British battle line. In response to the light cruiser contract, the German commander turned southwest at 0718 and then at 0735 began bending course southeast in the direction of home. The British line with *Lion* at its head steamed south before turning southeast at 0736 to reach a position south and behind Hipper on a parallel course with the Germans to windward. *Lion* had the enemy in sight by 0750. Goodenough's 1st LCS also turned southeast, north of the main German formation.[6] They followed off the enemy's port quarter during the chase, twice being briefly engaged by the German line and by *Blücher* after she staggered out of line toward the end of the action. The cruisers used their position to spot for the battlecruisers. The Harwich Force vessels followed behind the Germans, with the faster M class destroyers pushing ahead to scout and report. *Meteor* led the "Ms" to within seven thousand yards of *Blücher* until the armored cruiser's fire forced their retreat at 0840.

The stage was thus set for the war's first engagement between post-1905 capital ships. Conditions favored the British. The seas were calm, visibility was unlimited, and the wind blew their funnel and gun smoke clear. Only flying spray inhibited British shooting. The full day remained for fighting and the outnumbered Germans were a long way from safety. Hipper signaled 23 knots at 0817 and the Germans never exceeded that speed. A 4-knot speed advantage allowed the British to close at a rate of eight thousand yards an hour. By 0820 both sides steadied on their new courses. Stokers were furiously shoveling coal, fire control parties were measuring and calculating, and the muzzles of the big guns rose to maximum elevation.[7]

Lion tried a ranging shot at 0852 but the distance of 22,000 yards was excessive. At 0905, with the range from *Lion* to *Blücher* (the trailing German ship) over 19,000 yards, the battlecruiser began to fire in earnest. Such distances, unheard of just a few years prior, reflected a new British belief that they had a gunnery advantage at long ranges. The Germans responded at 0909. Hampered by their own funnel smoke,

Map 3.1 Battle of Dogger Bank: 24 January 1915

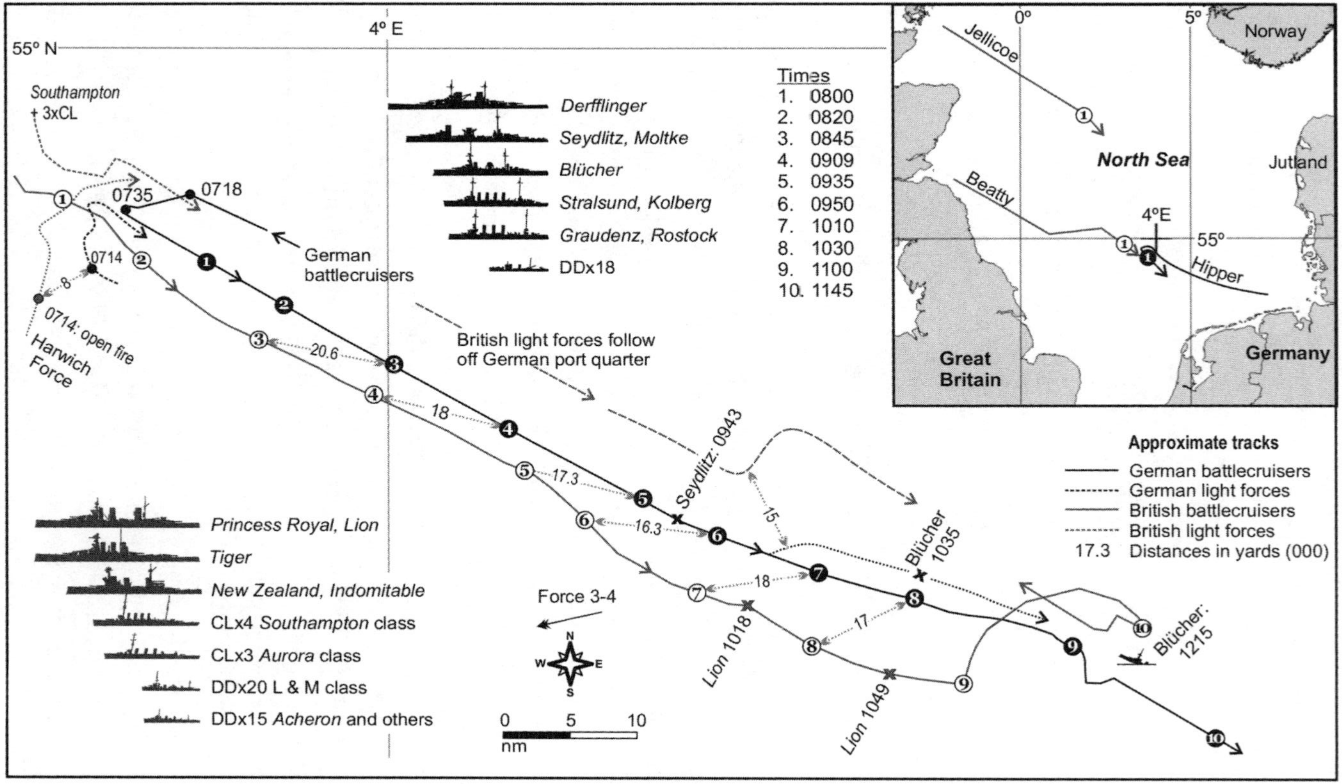

they concentrated on *Lion,* the most visible target. At 0912 *Blücher* took a blow to her forecastle in the action's first hit.

Over the next half hour *Lion* gradually worked within range of *Moltke, Derfflinger,* and finally, at 0935, *Seydlitz,* the leading German vessel. Beatty then ordered each ship to fire at its opposite number—*Lion* at *Seydlitz, Tiger* at *Moltke, Princess Royal* at *Derfflinger,* and *New Zealand* at *Blücher. Indomitable,* lagging behind, would engage when she could. On board the destroyer *Sandfly* one observer recalled, "about 10 a.m. the *Lion, Tiger, New Zealand,* and *Princess Royal* were all in action. It was very hard to see much from where we were, as our bridge was washing down, and one could not keep binoculars dry. As far as we could see our shots were straddling them all right, and theirs seemed to be all around our two leading ships, especially the *Tiger.*"[8] At 0943 a 13.5-inch shell struck *Seydlitz's* after barbette. A red-hot shell fragment penetrated the armor, ignited a cartridge, and sparked a massive conflagration. One of the ship's gunnery officers remembered: "I looked aft toward turrets C and D. It was an electrifying sight, the aft part of the ship was enveloped in a blue-red flash flame, that reached to the height of the mast tops."[9] Both aft turrets burned out, but prompt flooding of the magazines saved the battlecruiser from a catastrophic explosion. The whole time Hipper stood impassively on the flag bridge, chain-smoking. Meanwhile, Beatty opened the range in the belief that the German destroyers were about to attack, only to swing back to a roughly parallel course from 1000 on. He had previously ordered the Harwich Force to counter the German torpedo boats, but the battlecruisers were steaming so fast only the "M" class had any chance of overhauling them.

While *Seydlitz* was badly hurt, all was not well in the British formation. *Tiger* had misunderstood Beatty's order and engaged *Seydlitz* rather than *Moltke.* Being undistracted by enemy fire, *Moltke* made excellent practice on *Lion.* At 1018 two shells struck the British flagship and salt water infiltrated her port condenser. This ultimately forced her port turbine to shut down. Another blow at 1049 deprived the battlecruiser of electrical power. As an officer stationed in the forward transmitting station remembered, "A very heavy thump was felt [on] the port side, the whole ship lifted slightly and the lights went out." *Lion's* speed began to fall but *Blücher* was even worse off. At 1035 a pair of heavy rounds penetrated her armor deck and ignited powder charges in an ammunition tramway. This knocked out her two portside 21-cm gun turrets, destroyed communications throughout the ship, and cut the main steam pipe, reducing speed to 17 knots and causing the armored cruiser to haul out of line to port. At 1040 a 13.5-inch round dented but did not penetrate *Derfflinger*'s main belt above the waterline amidships. This caused minor flooding.[10]

As *Tiger* passed the slowing *Lion* the Germans hit her twice in succession. Her fighting effectiveness remained intact but a large fire amidships gave the impression of severe damage. Then, at 1054 Beatty "personally observed the wash of a [submarine] periscope" southeast of the British formation. Prewar the British had assumed the Germans would try to lure enemy ships into a submarine ambush, which seemed a quick way to improve the odds in any engagement. Thus, at 1100 Beatty ordered the battlecruisers to turn north, away from the perceived threat. By turning Beatty sacrificed distance he had taken nearly two hours to gain. Moreover, he believed he now faced the danger of mines being dropped behind the German formation—another presumptive German trick. Thus, he surrendered more distance by crossing the German wake. In fact, Beatty's eyes deceived him. Neither threat existed. What this maneuver did accomplish, however, was to frustrate a torpedo attack that Hipper had ordered at 1100 and it effectively cut off *Blücher* from any aid.[11]

The northerly course drew the British battlecruisers away from the three German battlecruisers, but closer to the faltering *Blücher*. Beatty wanted *Indomitable* to sink *Blücher* while the other battlecruisers continued the chase. He wanted to communicate two separate commands: that his ships should turn northeast and that they should then resume their attack on the German main body. Beatty's flag lieutenant had two signals hoisted: "Course N.E." and "Attack the enemy rear." He envisioned these orders as sequential—that the battlecruisers would turn northeast, go past the crippled *Blücher*, and then attack the rear of the German line. But because the signals seemed to be made executive at the same time, the effect was quite different. *Tiger*, *New Zealand*, and *Indomitable* all took in the signal (between 1108 and 1121) as "Attack the rear of the enemy bearing N.E." while *New Zealand* apparently missed the "Course N.E." flag hoist altogether and simply logged the signal as "Attack enemy rear." The enemy bearing northeast was *Blücher*, and so the British battlecruiser force concentrated on that hapless ship while *Seydlitz*, *Moltke*, and *Derf-flinger* escaped.

Rear Admiral Moore in *New Zealand*, commanding the 2nd BCS and ranking officer with *Lion* out of action, made no move to correct this situation. Beatty did not signal that Moore was in command, and Moore did not assume command on his own initiative until 1152. His next order, at 1158, brought the battlecruisers back west to assist *Lion*.

Although the entire British force pounded her, *Blücher* did not sink easily. One of the few survivors remembered: "If it was appalling below deck, it was more than appalling above. The *Blücher* was under the fire of so many ships. Even the little destroyers peppered her, although she managed to strike back with a hit on *Meteor*. 'It was one continuous explosion,' said a gunner. The ship heeled over as the broadsides struck her, then righted herself, rocking like a cradle." She sank at 1215 with the loss of 792 men, having absorbed up to a hundred shells and nine torpedoes.[12]

The other German ships escaped. The British hit *Seydlitz* three times and she was lucky to survive, while they hit *Derfflinger* once although several near misses caused some flooding. The Germans landed sixteen large shells on *Lion* and six on *Tiger*. *Lion*, *Tiger*, and *Indomitable* each absorbed a single 21-cm round. The British suffered fifteen killed and thirty-two wounded while the Germans lost 954 killed and 80 wounded. However, the British fired 1,150 large caliber rounds for only four hits (excluding *Blücher*) while the three German battlecruisers managed 22 hits from 959 rounds fired.

As the first clash of modern capital ships of similar class the British and Germans eagerly sought lessons from the battle. Beatty concluded that "rapidity of fire is essential. . . . The main object when opening fire must not be the straddle but to obtain a big volumn [*sic*] of fire . . . until hitting commences." *Lion*'s Captain A. E. M. Chatfield considered that his ship "fired much too slowly hampered by all the orders and restrictions on the subject."[13] The restrictions that frustrated Chatfield were those meant to reduce the risk of magazine explosions through the use of flash-tight doors, interlock systems, and limits on the number of powder charges in working areas. The British did not fully appreciate that their cordite propellant was already prone to explosions. Flouting these precautions made the problems that much more dangerous, as

Vice Admiral David Beatty as commander of 1st Battle Cruiser Squadron 1914. Young, handsome, and seen by some as the return of Nelson, he rose to the highest rank despite a mediocre record as a battle commander. (Library of Congress)

the battlecruiser force would discover to its sorrow at Jutland. The British also drew a host of conclusions regarding fire control. A postwar publication noted that "from a gunnery point of view the outstanding feature of this battle was that the British battle cruisers commenced to hit their opponents at 19,000 yards"; however, at such long range observations were unreliable, hits could "rarely be observed," and "'shorts' were the only guide to the fall of shot relative to the target."[14]

The ammunition fire on *Seydlitz* prompted the Kaiserliche Marine to limit the number of powder charges present before use. While this did not prevent turret fires altogether, the German precautions combined with more stable propellant reduced risk.[15]

Dogger Bank was popularly and properly hailed as a British victory although many were disappointed the German battlecruisers escaped. However, had the British battlecruisers chased more vigorously it is not clear they could have prevailed. *Lion* was out of the fight, *Indomitable* was occupied with *Blücher*, and *New Zealand* would have struggled to catch up. That would have left *Tiger* and *Princess Royal* to deal with *Derfflinger*, *Moltke*, and *Seydlitz*. By the time the chase ended, Beatty was closer to Wilhelmshaven and Ingenohl's dreadnoughts than he was to the Grand Fleet. A prompt pursuit could have easily allowed the Kaiserliche Marine to even the score. The Germans, meanwhile, had risked their most valuable ships for no apparent strategic reason. The kaiser sacked Admiral Ingenohl, who had failed to come to Hipper's support, and gave command of the High Seas Fleet to Admiral Pohl. Pohl quickly shifted to a submarine campaign against British traffic.[16]

Action off North Hinder Bank: 1 May, 1600–

Conditions: Clear

Missions: British, patrol; Germans, interception

British Force: DD *Laforey, Lawford, Leonidas, Lark.*

German Force (Lieutenant Captain Hermann Schoemann†):TB *A2**, *A6**.

The Entente powers countered Germany's occupation of the Belgian coast by deploying light forces to contain enemy naval activity. Although German surface forces were not numerous or aggressive at this point, the area's narrow and shoal-strewn waters made clashes inevitable. The first occurred in May 1915. Two German seaplanes had been scouting toward the Thames estuary. One went down with engine problems; the other spotted enemy trawlers patrolling off North Hinder Bank. The only two German torpedo boats in Flanders at the time, *A2* and *A6*, sortied to search for the downed plane's crew and attack the trawlers.

The torpedo boats found the trawlers at 1500. They quickly sank *Columbia* with a torpedo but missed with three others. After spending fifteen minutes riddling *Chirsit* and *Barbados* with 50-mm rounds, damaging the latter severely, they turned for home. Forty-five minutes later, however, they ran afoul of four Harwich Force destroyers that had been sweeping from Galloper Bank toward North Hinder in search of a submarine that had sunk the destroyer *Recruit* earlier that day. The Germans fled southeast trying to make Zeebrugge. The British vessels were faster but friendly minefields hampered their pursuit and they opened fire at the extreme range of eight thousand yards. By prodigiously expending ammunition (734 rounds in total), they managed to hit and eventually sink both boats. The Germans responded to this setback by dispatching a further five small torpedo boats to Zeebrugge before the end of May.[17]

Battle of Amrum Bank: 17 August, 2013–2057

Conditions: Clear

Missions: British, minelaying; Germans patrol

British Force (Captain S. Litchfield): ML *Princess Margaret;* DD *Morris, Manly, Matchless, Mentor*#, *Minos, Moorsom, Miranda.*

German Force (Corvette Captain Heinrich Schuur): II TBF: DD *B98, B109, B110, G103, G104.*

The Royal Navy mounted many minelaying expeditions into Heligoland Bight during the year. These rarely led to surface encounters. However, on the night of 17 August, five German destroyers were investigating a report of an enemy submarine and trawlers off Horns Reef; instead they found the minelayer *Princess Margaret* escorted by seven destroyers.

B98, the leader, spotted the British nine thousand yards to the west at 2013. *Princess Margaret* was steaming south, with *Morris, Manly,* and *Matchless* on her port quarter and *Mentor, Minos, Moorsom,* and *Miranda* following to starboard. *B98* fired one torpedo from long range, then closed to two thousand yards and uncorked two more. Belching funnel smoke blocked the views of the destroyers following and kept them from engaging.

Princess Margaret spotted the Germans at 2035 just as *B98* launched her second salvo. Loaded with mines, she immediately turned 90 degrees west, assuming her escort would deal with the enemy. *Morris* likewise saw *B98* but turned to follow the minelayer. *Mentor* noted the flashes of torpedoes being fired, but assumed *Princess Margaret* was the target. She was crossing the minelayer's wake when one of *B98's* torpedoes smacked her. The other Harwich destroyers followed *Princess Margaret* and failed to engage.

Concerned that stronger enemy forces were lurking nearby (the British covering force of four light cruisers was in fact more than a hundred miles away) and convinced they had sunk a cruiser and a destroyer, the German ships withdrew east. *Mentor* limped home, minus her bow.[18]

The Battle of Amrum Bank was the first North Sea night action. The Germans sighted the enemy first and fired first, establishing a pattern that would be repeated over the next three years. There were doctrinal and materiel reasons for this. As the weaker navy the Germans recognized they needed to embrace every opportunity to establish an advantage and night combat was just that. They were the first to develop starshell, a type of gun-fired flare that exploded beyond its target and illuminated and dazzled as it slowly descended. Their nighttime recognition system featured a complicated sequence of colored lights that was quick to use but difficult to mimic. They placed their searchlights high and gave them iris shutters so they could snap on with full intensity and go dark with equal speed. Of the British, on the other hand, one historian noted: "It was the policy of the Royal Navy, whenever possible, to avoid the risks and imponderables of night action and consequently it had adopted a 'head in the sand' approach to it." The British used a series of Morse flashes to identify friendly forces that the Germans merely repeated back when challenged. British search-lights were lower down and had no covers. They took time to come to full power and as one user complained: "When we switched off our search-lights we had to find tarpaulins to throw over them to hide the glowing carbons that stood out like full moons."[19] Finally, German binoculars were better than British ones, giving Kaiserliche Marine lookouts a sight advantage when it counted most.

The Germans stopped this British mining mission, but many went undetected. Although British mines had faulty triggers and so sank few ships, they were still the best antisubmarine weapon until 1917 and the barrages in the Bight had important effects beyond the damage they inflicted. Minesweeping slowed the pace of maneuver, which meant that the High Seas Fleet took longer to deploy and longer to return. Sweeping often resulted in a flurry of radio orders and reports that gave the British forewarning of impending enemy sorties. But only when the British adopted a German mine design in 1917 did their minefields become as effective as they should have been.[20]

Action off Ostend: 22 August, 2312–2325

Conditions: Bad visibility
Missions: French, raid; Germans, patrol
French Forces (Lieutenant F. L. Le Gall): TB *Branlebas, Oriflamme.*
German Forces (Senior Reserve Lieutenant Richard Gutermann): TB *A15*★.

The torpedo boat *A15* was patrolling off Flanders on the night of August 22 when she encountered two French torpedo boats arriving to cover a bombardment of Ostend by three monitors scheduled to take place at dawn. The French vessels were sailing parallel to the coast six miles offshore when they spotted a slow-moving silhouette two to three thousand yards north on a converging course. They turned to starboard and came to battle stations before challenging at 2312. *A15* responded with a round from her 50-mm gun. The French ships, each armed with one 67-mm and six 47-mm guns, answered in kind and their rapid volleys riddled *A15*. The German torpedo boat fled toward

Ostend as the coastal batteries there, alerted by the gunfire, started loft-
ing starshells over the combatants. *Oriflamme* closed to a thousand yards
and launched a single torpedo. This struck *A15* to starboard and sank
her at 2325. The French ships then withdrew. *A15* lost fifteen men.
Three other A-boats were in Ostend harbor and another three were
raiding merchant shipping off the Schelde Estuary, but neither group
could come to *A15*'s aid. The monitors conducted their bombardment
from 0530 to 0730 on 23 August.[21]

For the rest of 1915 the naval war in the North Sea featured mining,
patrols, and at least seven large British sweeps, but no surface engagements. Much to the disgruntlement of many German officers, the
High Seas Fleet was kept on a short leash. The German campaign of
unrestricted submarine warfare against mercantile traffic proved effective militarily—despite the small number of submarines available—
but a disaster politically. Pressure, particularly from the United States,
and incidents such as the sinking of passenger liner *Lusitania,* which
killed hundreds of civilians including 128 Americans, forced the German government to gradually reinstitute prize rules everywhere except
the Mediterranean (where there was much less danger of drowning U.S.
nationals). By year's end, Germany seemed to be at a naval impasse.

Baltic 1915

When the Baltic ice started to break up the Russians began plugging gaps
that time, weather, and the Germans had opened in the minefields off
Libau. This brought them into contact with German forces supporting
an advance up the Baltic coast.

Action off Libau: 7 May, 0205–0245

Conditions: Clear
Missions: Russians, minelaying; Germans, bombardment
Russian Force: CA *Admiral Makarov, Baian*; CP *Oleg, Bogatyr.*
German Forces: Cruiser Force (Corvette Captain Hans Carl Schlick):
    CL *München*[+]; DD *V181*. Destroyer Force: DD *V151, V153*.

Four Russian cruisers covered a minelaying force of eleven destroyers on a mission to the coast of Courland. *Novik* and six *Ukraina*-class destroyers sowed their deadly cargo south of Libau while four *Okhotniks*—minelaying specialists now—placed another field north of the city. All vessels had turned for home by 0200 on 7 May.

Meanwhile the IV Scouting Group with three light cruisers and sixteen destroyers had sailed at noon on 6 May in conjunction with a bombardment scheduled to support an army offensive. The German ships were just south of Libau and forty-five miles off the coast when at 2100 on 6 May they formed eight groups and deployed into a scouting line, steering north on a collision course with the Russian cruisers. Their ultimate goal was to control the waters between Gotland and Courland for several days. Consequently the cruisers' decks were loaded with coal. The weather was clear and the formations could occasionally see each other's smoke columns.

München and *V181,* which formed the second group from the right, detected smoke ahead at 0200 and steered to investigate. This belonged to the Russian cruisers, which likewise spotted the Germans and opened fire first at 0208 from just five thousand yards. Both forces turned west and then southeast, trading salvos the entire time. *München* found fire control difficult as "the distance was too great to employ searchlights, and it was too dark for optical instruments."[22]

München's executive officer was stationed below and experienced the battle by its sounds. "The guns began firing although not firing rapidly enough to be directed against torpedo boats. The loud explosion of shells around our ship could be distinctly heard through the thin sheets of side plating. Soon these explosions became more numerous and seemed to be coming from larger caliber guns, and at last it was such a hail of explosions that it was impossible to distinguish one from another. It was a very disagreeable situation." *München* launched torpedoes at 0230, but *V181,* judging the range excessive, tucked in on the cruiser's unengaged side. As the Russian barrage intensified, *München* zigzagged away and opened the range to almost ten thousand yards. Wrapped in funnel smoke and unable to spot a target, she ceased fire at 0235. The Russians continued toward the coast. When *München*'s executive officer came on deck he was "agreeably surprised not to find many hits, dead or wounded. . . . The whole deck was wet from the splash of enemy fire which had surrounded our

ship and there were innumerable shell splinters, but luckily, there was not
a single hit."[23]

V151 and *V153*, the group east of *München*, were drawn by the gunfire and crossed ahead of the Russian cruisers. Then at 0242 *Admiral
Makarov* suddenly emerged from the smoke on their port quarter 11,000
yards away. As Russian gunfire erupted the destroyers spun to the southwest. The cruisers continued southeast and the two groups lost contact.
The Germans concentrated and the IV Scouting Group headed south
"as quickly as possible to repel in company [with a force of German
armored cruisers] the threatened attack upon Libau."[24] At 0430 the Russians reversed course and sailed away before the Germans could concentrate. Libau fell that day while the newly laid Russian minefield claimed
V107 the next day.[25]

Action off Windau: 28 June, 1540–2000

Conditions: Clear and calm

Missions: Russians, patrol; Germans, minesweeping

Russian Forces: 6th DD Div: *Steregushchii, Zabaikalets, Voiskovoi,
   Ukraina, Turkmenets-Stavropolskii, Strashnyi, Kazanets.* 5th DD
   Div: *Gaidamak, Ussuriets, Vsadnik, Amurets, Emir Bukharskii, Finn,
   Moskvitianin, Dobrovolets.*

German Forces (Commodore Hans Karpf): CL *Augsburg, Lübeck;* TB *S130.*

After taking Libau, German troops advanced up the coast toward
Windau. At the army's request the navy dispatched the antique coastal
defense ship *Beowulf* to bombard the port. Six minesweepers were clearing a path for *Beowulf* through a newly sown field south of Windau
when one struck a mine at 1540 and started to sink. Within minutes
projectiles began to splash around the sweepers from a source unseen.
Augsburg advanced to investigate and at 1600 spotted a forest of masts off
Lyser Ort, ten miles past Windau. These belonged to the 6th Destroyer
Division. Trying to cut them off, Captain Karpf ordered *Lübeck* to head
for Irben Strait from the northwest while *Augsburg* and *Beowulf* continued up the coast behind the sweepers. *Augsburg* flung a few salvos
toward the Russians and they retired toward Irben Strait. At 1700 *Lübeck*
was nearing Irben Strait when, off her starboard bow, she encountered

Novik, returning from a scouting mission. *Lübeck* attempted to engage but the speedy destroyer easily dodged past the cruiser and by 1845 had entered the gulf.

Lübeck continued and at 1920, she spotted many enemy vessels along the coast and turned toward them. In fact, she had found 5th and 6th Destroyer Divisions. The fifteen warships engaged the German cruiser with thirty 4-inch guns at ranges from 14,000 down to 11,000 yards. *Lübeck* returned fire but her consort, *S130*, armed with only 50-mm weapons, was completely outranged and kept to the cruiser's unengaged side. *Lübeck* found herself "at a disadvantage not only as regards number of guns and the mobility of her adversaries, but also in the difficulty of picking out the targets and the lack of objects for obtaining the range: the gray-green boats melted into the wooded background and their smoke drifted straight towards *Lübeck*."[26] Nonetheless, the action continued until 2000 when the arrival of *Augsburg* and dusk prompted the Russians to withdraw through Irben Strait. Again, neither side inflicted significant damage on the other (*Lübeck*'s crew found a four-inch hole punched in the ship's ensign) but the Germans commented: "The Russian destroyers showed themselves to be worthy antagonists from a gunnery point of view; the spread of the salvoes was slight, the fire control of several boats in combination, apparently directed by flag signals, worked surprisingly well." *Beowulf* bombarded Windau from 2030 to 2055, delivering thirteen 24-cm rounds with unknown results.[27]

Battle of Gotland: 2 July, 0630–1021

   Conditions: Calm, periodic fog

   Missions: Russians, interception; Germans, transit

   Russian Force (Rear Admiral M. K. Bakhirev): CA *Riurik*#, *Admiral Makarov*+, *Baian*+, CP *Oleg*, *Bogatyr*.

   German Forces (Commodore Hans Karpf): Minelaying force: CM *Albatross**; CL *Augsburg*; DD *G135*, *S142*, *S141*. Support Force (Frigate Captain Hans Gygas): CA *Roon*+; CL *Lübeck*+.

In late June Russian naval intelligence reported that the Germans were going to withdraw some units from the Baltic. The Russian command ordered the Baltic Fleet's new commander, Vice Admiral V. A. Kanin, to exploit this apparent opportunity so he reluctantly dispatched Rear Admiral Bakhirev with a force of five cruisers and the 6th Destroyer Division led by *Novik* to bombard Memel. The cruisers sailed at 0100 on 1 July but heavy fog delayed the destroyers and Bakhirev canceled 6th Division's participation. *Novik* continued alone and joined at 1200. At 1700 the Russians ran into more fog and when changing course to the south the formation's rear vessels, *Riurik* and *Novik*, each became separated. The conditions caused Bakhirev to postpone the bombardment from the evening of 1 July to dawn of 2 July.

Russian intelligence was good, but it missed the fact that the Kaiserliche Marine had sent *Albatross*, *Augsburg*, and three destroyers north to lay mines near Bogskär Island northeast of Gotland. Two cruisers and four destroyers supported the minelayer force. Russian intelligence learned of this operation when it intercepted Commodore Karpf's transmission reporting that he had completed his mission and giving his current position. When Bakhirev received this information at 0400 on 2 July, he decided to steer north to intercept the returning Germans.

At 0630 the four Russian cruisers (minus *Riurik*) and *Augsburg*, leading the minelaying squadron, sighted each other's smoke. The support group was absent because just a half hour before Karpf had ordered them to proceed to Libau independently. The Russians believed they were facing a pair of light cruisers and turned 90 degrees from north to west to put the enemy on their starboard broadside. The Germans conformed. At 0632 *Admiral Makarov* targeted *Augsburg* with an 8-inch salvo from 8,900 yards. Visibility was variable, especially to the south. The Russians could clearly see their targets but the Germans could discern gun flashes only.

From 0635 to 0700 the two columns ran west. The Germans made frequent small course alterations to confuse the Russian aim and *Augsburg* sprayed oil on her fires to produce thick black smoke. A member of the minelayer's crew observed that "[Russian gunnery] was lively, however, very irregular.... The individual salvos lay short or wide, and at first hits were not obtained, so that the enemy fire made a wretched impression."[28]

The leader of the three small destroyers ordered an attack despite the boats being armed with old, short-ranged torpedoes, but they were still too far away when, at 0653, Karpf elected to save *Augsburg* and the destroyers by turning southeast across the head of the Russian column

Map 3.2 Battle of Gotland: 2 July 1915

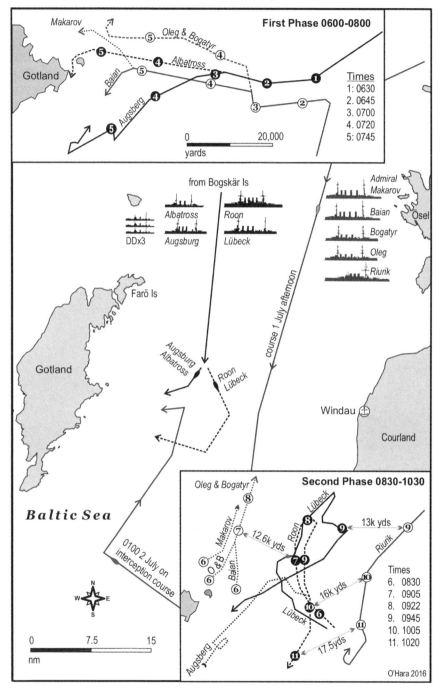

while *Albatross*, which had a top speed of only 20 knots, continued toward Gotland and the presumed safety of Swedish territorial waters seventeen miles ahead. At 0700 Rear Admiral Bakhirev responded by releasing his ships to operate independently. *Oleg* and *Bogatyr* continued after *Albatross*. The armored cruisers chased *Augsburg* but soon lost her in the mist and smoke. She had vanished by 0720.

The Russians first hit *Albatross* at 0720 and, with the range now down to 7,500 yards, more strikes quickly followed. According to a Russian history the cruisers "literally honeycombed their opponent."[29] *Albatross* reached Swedish waters around 0745 and ceased fire after expending five hundred 88-mm rounds and hitting *Admiral Makarov* once. Ignoring the niceties of international law, the Russians pummeled the German vessel until 0807. At 0812, steering by her engines and listing heavily to port, the minelayer beached herself to avoid capsizing. Six 8-inch and twenty 6-inch shells had

The German cruiser minelayer *Albatross* beached off Gotland following the July 1915 Battle of Gotland. (Wiki Public Domain)

hit, killing twenty-seven men and wounding fifty-five. *Albatross* remained interned for the duration and was scrapped postwar.

After finishing *Albatross* Bakhirev steered for the Gulf of Finland. At the start of the battle he had ordered *Riurik* to join him, but she remained out of sight, whereabouts unknown. Moreover, Bakhirev's ships had expended nearly three thousand rounds; *Admiral Makarov* was down to one-third her supply. As the Russian cruisers turned north the *Augsburg* group did the same, maintaining a safe distance. Meanwhile, Karpf had radioed *Roon* and *Lübeck* and they were steaming hard to reach the scene.

The Russians had formed a rough column in order of *Bogatyr*, *Oleg*, *Admiral Makarov*, and *Baian* when *Lübeck* and then *Roon* appeared to their southeast. At 0905 the German armored cruiser engaged *Baian* from 12,600 yards. *Baian* replied and hit *Roon* almost immediately, damaging a radio antenna. *Roon* tagged *Baian* once amidships inflicting light damage and wounding two men. *Oleg* and *Lübeck* also dueled at ranges of 14,000 yards or more but *Lübeck's* shells all fell short.

This ineffectual long-range exchange had lasted twenty minutes when at 0922 *Roon's* Captain Gygas turned away to starboard, worried that the Russians were luring him toward a more powerful foe. For his part Bakhirev was content to let the Germans disappear into the haze as his ammunition situation was now even worse. In fact, *Admiral Makarov* had deliberately held fire to conserve her supply. *Roon* discharged seventy-six 21-cm rounds for one hit while *Baian* hit once from forty rounds fired. Misty conditions, long ranges, and evasive maneuvering made for difficult shooting.

The German withdrawal sparked the day's final action. As *Lübeck* turned south, she spotted smoke to the west. It was *Riurik* arriving at last. *Lübeck* misidentified the large cruiser and closed, making a recognition signal. At 0945, with the range at 13,000 yards, *Lübeck* realized her mistake and came about whereupon *Riurik* opened fire. *Lübeck* shot back with considerable success, considering the range, hitting the Russian ship ten times. The light rounds caused only superficial damage except for one shell that forced the evacuation of a 10-inch turret while gases from the impact were vented. *Riurik's* 10-inch rounds straddled and caused some splinter damage, but her 8-inch guns fired short.

Roon, with *Augsburg* and her destroyers, appeared while this exchange was under way. At 1001 *Roon* lofted a 21-cm salvo from 16,000 yards.

The battle then continued in a southerly direction with the armored cruisers trading long-range broadsides, although *Riurik* also flung a few rounds toward *Augsburg.* The only hit was a heavy blow on *Riurik's* aft conning tower. Captain Gygas, commenting on this exchange, noted that "the observation during both battle phases was extraordinarily difficult, through uncertain weather and through the numerous short shots of the enemy. The fire of *Riurik* at the beginning had the impression of very precise measurement, but later became inexact with great ammunition expenditure."[30]

At 1021 *Roon* ceased fire. The final range was 17,500 yards. Karpf, concerned that the other Russian cruisers might reappear, turned his force to starboard. At the same time a false submarine report caused *Riurik* to veer away in the opposite direction and she lost sight of the enemy. *Riurik* expended 46 10-inch, 102 8-inch, and 163 4.7-inch shells. *Roon* fired 110 21-cm and four 15-cm rounds in both engagements. *Riurik* suffered fifteen wounded and one death; splinters lightly damaged *Roon.*

The day was a Russian victory, but a disappointing one. *Roon* should have been in a precarious position, but the first four Russians fought conservatively while poor visibility and a false submarine report frustrated *Riurik.* The Russian cruisers missed destroyer support. *Novik* alone would have sufficed to finish *Albatross.* The Russians had one consolation, however. The armored cruisers *Prinz Heinrich* and *Prinz Adalbert* had sailed from Danzig to support the returning force and perhaps salvage *Albatross.* At 1357 a torpedo fired by the British submarine *E9* struck *Prinz Adalbert* and damaged her severely.[31]

Destroyer Skirmish off Irben Strait: 17 July
Conditions: Clear
Missions: Russians, interception; Germans, minelaying
Russian Force: 6th DD Div: *Ukraina*–class DDx4.
German Force (Captain Lieutenant Konrad Zander): DD *V181, V183.*

As German troops drove toward the head of the Courland Peninsula Russian and German flotillas clashed more frequently. On 17 July, four *Ukraina*–class destroyers sallied from Irben Strait to harass *V181* and *V183* as they laid a dummy minefield to the south. The Russians opened a "remarkably well directed fire" at a range of nine to ten thousand yards, beyond the range of the German 88-mm guns. Zander tried to lure his harassers south toward *Bremen*, *V99*, and two other destroyers, but the Russians ducked back into the strait.[32]

On 18 July the Germans captured Windau and soon occupied Irben Strait's southern shores. To facilitate the army's continued advance, the Kaiserliche Marine decided to break into the Gulf of Riga. Concerned that the Russians might deploy their new dreadnoughts the Germans transferred to the Baltic eight dreadnoughts, three battlecruisers, five light cruisers, thirty-two flotilla craft, and thirteen minesweepers. This was in addition to a reinforced Baltic squadron of seven predreadnoughts, two armored and four light cruisers, twenty-four flotilla craft, a minelayer, and fourteen minesweepers. Forewarned of German plans by radio intelligence, the Russians positioned twenty-one fleet destroyers and sixteen small destroyers in the gulf, slipped the predreadnought *Slava* through Irben Strait during the night of 30/31 July, and thickened the minefields blocking the strait. The Russians did not want to incur heavy losses defending an advanced position like Irben Strait, but nonetheless resolved to resist the German offensive as best they could within those limits.

First Battle of Irben Strait: 8 August, 0545–1400

Conditions: Clear and calm

Missions: Russians, positional defense; Germans, minesweeping

Russian Force (Captain 1st Rank P. L. Trukachev): OBB *Slava*[+] (Captain 1st Rank S. S. Viazemskii); DD *Sibirskii Strelok*, *General Kondratenko*, *Okhotnik*, *Pogranichnik*, *Strashnyi*, *Ukraina*–class DDx3; GB *Khrabryi*, *Groziashchii*.

German Forces (Rear Admiral Hermann Alberts): OBB *Elsass*, *Braunschweig*; CL *Bremen*, *Thetis*[#]. II MS Div: MSx14. Neufahrwasser Aux MS Div: Aux MSx9. Swinemunde Aux MS Div: Motor MSx12. X TBF: DD *S144*[#], others.[33]

The German effort began at 0350 on 8 August when minesweepers began working in the middle of Irben Strait. They were escorted by *Thetis* with *Elsass*, *Braunschweig*, and *Bremen* supporting from outside the gulf. *Strashnyi* saw them coming at 0500 and raised the alarm. The

Germans had penetrated the outer barrage when at 0510 the sweeper *T52* struck a mine astern and sank within a quarter hour. Twenty minutes later a mine damaged *Thetis*, even though she was carefully following a pair of sweepers.

Shortly thereafter four destroyers led by *Sibirskii Strelok* appeared; soon, "bombs and projectiles [were] pitching at times right amongst the minesweeping boats."[34] The battleships responded and drove the Russians out of range. However, observing that salvos could be timed and were tightly grouped, Captain Trukachev ordered his flotilla to "sail toward the enemy with a signal flag ordering a 'four point turn to Starboard together' flying. As soon as the flames and smoke from a German battleship's salvo was observed, the Senior Officer ordered 'Down signal!' and the destroyers turned and headed away from the fall of enemy shots." This allowed them to approach the sweepers, discharge a few salvos, and then retreat.[35] They repeated this process of advance, fire, and retreat ten times during the morning, until *Bremen* finally worked in close enough behind the minesweepers to drive them off. Although the Russian guns could not reach to the battleships, they were still at risk as demonstrated at 0707 when *S144*, one of their screening destroyers, struck a mine.

While the destroyers danced, *Khrabryi* and *Groziashchii* appeared from Arensburg. They pitched into the north flank of the German forces and became immediate targets for the battleships, repeatedly disappearing behind walls of shell splashes. Certain that they would be overwhelmed, Trukachev ordered them to retire. This they did, miraculously undamaged.

The sweeping slowly continued. Then at 1030 the Germans spotted a large smoke cloud on the northern horizon. This signified the arrival of *Slava* accompanied by some small destroyers from the 9th Division. The German predreadnoughts engaged *Slava* at 17,500 yards and after only six salvos the Russian battleship turned away. Captain Viazemskii had overestimated the range as more than 20,000 yards and wanted to conserve ammunition and not reveal the limited reach of his guns. *Slava* remained on the edge of the mined area under occasional fire. The Germans did not hit her, but on several occasions close misses showered her with splinters.

The Germans had originally estimated it would take three hours to clear a channel. In fact, a narrow gap in the first line of mines was not opened until 1115. Then shortly after 1300 the sweepers encountered a second barrage. At 1332 *T58* blew up on one of these mines. The depth of the barrier, the slow progress sweeping, the exposure to submarine attack, and dwindling coal supplies caused the overall German commander, Vice Admiral Ehrhard Schmidt, to call it a day. After the Germans withdrew *Slava* and the Russian destroyers retired to Arensburg.[36]

Zerel Reveille: 10 August, 0350–0410

Conditions: Calm, some mist

Missions: Russians, patrol; Germans, raid/bombardment

Russian Force DD *Novik, Strashnyi, Voiskovoi, Sibirskii Strelok*[+], *Pogranichnik*, DDx16.

German Force (Captain Wilhelm Krosigk): CA *Roon, Prinz Heinrich*, CL *Bremen, Lübeck*.

On the morning of 10 August the Germans dispatched *Roon* and *Prinz Heinrich* screened by *Bremen, Lübeck*, and ten destroyers to bombard Zerel on the Irben Strait's north shore. Some Russian destroyers had spent the night laying more mines before anchoring east of Zerel. The German cruisers opened fire on them at 0350 firing 14,000 yards over the low-laying peninsula. *Novik's* first officer recalled: "[W]e were awakened by loud firing and the hissing and bursting of shells. I ran on deck to find out what was going on. The 'Novik' had already weighed anchor, and the other destroyers quickly followed, a whole shower of shells meanwhile falling down from somewhere." [37] In fact, the Russians received warning of the bombardment because shore lookouts had spotted the smoke and most ships were just getting under way. One 15-cm shell hit *Sibirskii Strelok* above the waterline on the starboard side and damaged the rudder control, causing her to circle. She had just repaired this casualty when another 15-cm round ricocheted off the aft gun's shield. This ignited the ready ammunition and caused another steering failure. After the action *Sibirskii Strelok* had to retire to Revel for repairs. The other destroyers escaped unscathed. The Germans ceased fire at 0430 having expended sixty-five 21-cm and two hundred 15-cm rounds.[38]

The large Russian destroyer *Novik*. She was the first of a series of fast, heavily armed destroyers that did excellent service in the Baltic and Black Seas. *Novik* herself participated in six surface engagements and sank a large German destroyer. (Wiki Public Domain)

Action off Utö: 10 August, 0524–0618

Conditions: Clear

Missions: Russians, none; Germans, bombardment

Russian Force: CA *Gromoboi*; TB *Porazhaiushchii*.

German Force (Captain Max Hahn): BC *Von der Tann*[+]; CL *Kolberg*; DD *S31*, *G197*, *V28*.

While *Roon* and *Prinz Heinrich* bombarded Zerel, *Kolberg* and *V28* headed north to attack Utö Island. Radio intercepts had forewarned the Russians of the bombardment and allowed them to set up an ambush by two submarines and order the ships off the island to withdraw. These consisted of old torpedo boat *Porazhaiushchii*, a couple of cutters, and *Gromoboi*. At 0500 *Kolberg* spotted the torpedo boat and the two cutters (reported as two destroyers). As the German cruiser approached, the submarine *Kaiman* started stalking her but was unable to obtain an attack position. At 0524 *Kolberg* opened fire from 11,000 yards. Three minutes later she spotted *Gromoboi* withdrawing as ordered and reported the cruiser. When he received this news Vice Admiral Hipper ordered *Von der Tann* escorted by *S31* and *G197* to advance. At 0556, *Von der Tann* engaged *Gromoboi*, firing over the island from 16,500 yards, while peppering the smaller Russian vessels with her 15-cm guns. At 0601 Utö's 6-inch shore battery entered the fray. One shell pierced *Von der Tann's* funnel mantle and caused light damage. The battlecruiser turned her guns against the battery and silenced it before targeting *Gromoboi* once again from nearly 20,000 yards. A submarine report from *Kolberg*, shallow water, and a suspected Russian minefield prevented the Germans from closing and the action fizzled out by 0618 after *Von der Tann* had expended sixty-two 28- and eighty 15-cm rounds.[39]

Patrol Action in Irben Strait: 14 August, morning

Conditions: Clear

Missions: Russians, patrol; Germans, patrol

Russian Force: DD *Novik, Okhotnik, General Kondratenko*.

German Force (Corvette Captain Ernst Tegtmeyer): DD *V191, G193, G194*.

Still determined to force Irben Strait, Vice Admiral Schmidt maintained a pair of light cruisers and destroyers west of the Sworbe Peninsula to prevent the Russians from laying new minefields and to "keep the enemy on tenterhooks by means of short bombardments."[40]

On the evening of 13 August *Pillau* fired 14,000 yards over the peninsula at a group of Russian vessels, targeting the tops of their masts. Then *V27* and *S31* advanced to provoke an action. They opened fire just short of nine thousand yards and claimed hits, but the Russians withdrew without replying.

The next night *Novik* was being relieved after a patrol when she spotted *V191, G193*, and *G194* seven miles away. She engaged, as did the destroyers coming to relieve her, *Okhotnik* and *General Kondratenko*. A long-range eight-minute fray followed, ultimately ending with no damage to either side. Such engagements were typical of the low-level bickering that went on between the opposing light forces while Germans organized their next push into the strait.[41]

Second Battle of Irben Strait: 16 August, dawn–1700

Conditions: Misty

Missions: Russians, patrol; Germans, minesweeping

Russian Force: OBB *Slava*.

German Force (Vice Admiral Ehrhard Schmidt): BB *Nassau, Posen*; CL *Bremen*.

The Germans launched another major effort against the strait on 16 August. This time Schmidt allotted five days to the minesweeping effort. Instead of predreadnoughts, the dreadnoughts *Nassau* and *Posen* would cover the sweepers. In addition the admiral detailed four light cruisers, thirty-three flotilla craft, and various auxiliaries to enter the gulf while another three battlecruisers, six dreadnoughts, two predreadnoughts, five cruisers, and thirty-two destroyers stood by in case the Baltic Fleet intervened. Due to the operation's scheduled length, a portion of Schmidt's force was always absent refueling.

Radio intelligence forewarned the Russians and they concentrated at Arensburg on the evening of 15 August. Predictably, the Germans suffered losses going in with *T46* being mined and sunk at 0130 on 16 August. With dawn *Khrabryi* and *Groziashchii* tried to disrupt minesweeping efforts in the northern part of the strait while *Slava* approached the southern area and nine destroyers (three of the *General Kondratenko* class, three *Dobrovolets*, and three *Ukrainas*) ranged along the entire position. *Slava* deliberately induced a list to increase the reach of her guns and shelled the minesweepers, forcing their retreat. The German dreadnoughts responded. *Slava*, "shuddering from near-misses," zigzagged to confuse the enemy's "methodical four-gun salvoes." The Russian battleship turned away and then, inducing a list on the other side, returned for another go at the sweepers. She also briefly dueled with *Bremen* before *Nassau* and *Posen* closed once again and drove her off. At 1700 the Germans terminated their sweeping, having cleared a large portion of the southern minefields. They withdrew to night positions, intending to resume the action the next day, while Russian forces retired to Arensburg.[42]

Raid on Slava: *16 August, 1955–2010; 17 August, 0110–0113, 0415–0432*

Conditions: Poor visibility

Missions: Russians, patrol; Germans, raid

Russian Forces: DD *General Kondratenko*, *Okhotnik*, then DD *Ukraina*, *Voiskovoi*[+], then DD *Novik*[+] (Captain 2nd Rank M. A. Berens).

German Forces: DD *V99*★, *V100*[+].

While *Nassau* and *Posen* had kept *Slava* at a distance, she remained a threat. The Germans responded by sending *V99* and *V100* into the gulf at 1820 in an attempt to torpedo the predreadnought. The patrol destroyers *General Kondratenko* and *Okhotnik* discovered the raiders at dusk (1955). They fought a fifteen-minute action at 6,500 yards before *V99* and *V100* broke contact by feigning retreat. The German vessels then doubled back and pressed on toward Moon Sound, searching for their target. They were on a fool's errand; *Slava* was anchored at Arensburg safely behind protective nets. At 0110 as the raiders returned toward Irben Strait they crossed paths with *Ukraina* and *Voiskovoi*. Searchlights flared, guns flamed, and torpedoes smacked the water in a three-minute action fought at ranges under a thousand yards. The Germans slightly damaged *Voiskovoi* before the ships lost contact.

V99 and *V100* then had to loiter until there was enough light to navigate the mine barriers. They had just turned for home when, at 0415, they sighted a single destroyer astern and came about to engage. This was *Novik*, which had already spotted the Germans. She came to port and opened fire from 9,400 yards. The Germans assumed a parallel course and replied but *Novik* quickly outmatched them. In a seventeen-minute fight the veteran ship fired 233 4-inch shells, decimating *V99*'s gun crews and starting fires. As *V99* sheered away to escape, she fouled an antisubmarine net fitted with explosive charges. By the end of the fight, Captain Berens reported "the lead destroyer [*V99*], which had been burning in two places the whole while, began to settle badly by the stern, firing colored rockets." *V100*, damaged only by splinters, made smoke and under this cover towed her stricken partner from the scene. Three destroyers from the Russian 5th Division appeared at the end of the action but did not engage. *V99* eventually had to beach herself west of Pissen on the Courland coast and was a total loss. The Germans lost twenty-three men and had thirty-nine wounded. Two ricochets slightly damaged *Novik* and wounded two men.[43]

Battleship Action in the Gulf of Riga: 17 August, 0620–0800

Conditions: Variable visibility
Missions: Russians, patrol; Germans, minesweeping
Russian Force: OBB *Slava*#.
German Force (Vice Admiral Ehrhard Schmidt): BB *Posen*, *Nassau*.

At 0620 *Posen* succored the force towing *V99*, which by this time included *V108*, *S31*, and *S34*, by dropping salvos among the Russian destroyers to the north; meanwhile, the minesweepers advanced to continue their work. Shortly after 0700 *Slava* emerged from her anchorage. Fog blanketed the German zone and the minesweepers as well. *Slava* could not see *Posen* and *Nassau* on the western horizon but she was in sunlight and clearly visible to them. The German dreadnoughts closed and opened fire at 0740 from nearly 18,000 yards. Three 28-cm shells quickly tore into the Russian pre-dreadnought and another near missed *Novik*, which was standing nearby. One round exploded in the officer's cabin flat, igniting a fire; the second punched through the 8-inch armor belt aft, just above the waterline, and damaged the steering control. It also started a fire that required the flooding of a 6-inch magazine. The third round lightly damaged the spar deck. *Slava* withdrew to make emergency repairs. Several hours later as the Germans continued to advance Captain Trukachev ordered all Russian forces to withdraw to Moon Sound. Even without active opposition the German minesweepers required another full day to clear the strait. Schmidt finally led his forces into the Gulf of Riga on the morning of 19 August.[44]

Battle of Kiuno Island: 19 August, 1930–2040

Conditions: Misty

Missions: Russians, transit; Germans, sweep

Russian Forces: GB *Sivuch*★ (Captain 2nd Rank P. N. Cherkasov), *Koreets*# (Captain 2nd Rank I. K. Fediaevskii); DDx7.

German Forces (Vice Admiral Ehrhard Schmidt): CL *Pillau*, *Augsburg*+; DD *V29*, *V100*. *Posen* Group: BB *Posen*; DD *S178*, *V185*, *S176*, *S179*.

On the fourth day of operations, mist hung over the Gulf of Riga. Most Russian ships had withdrawn into Moon Sound behind shore batteries and newly laid minefields. At 0745 the Germans began their advance into the gulf just as news arrived that the British submarine *E1* had torpedoed the battlecruiser *Moltke*. Although the damage was relatively minor Hipper ordered a withdrawal. Schmidt, however, decided to spend the day exploiting the hard-won success before evacuating the gulf.

Minesweepers observed *Novik* attempting to lay a barrage off Arensburg but *Pillau* forced her to retreat with her mines still on board. The

German cruisers then fanned out in search of prey. *Augsburg* and a pair of destroyers headed for Pernau. Other cruisers scouted Ösel's bays and the straits between Runö and the mainland while three ships from VIII TBF and minelayer *Deutschland*, preceded by sweepers, went to lay a minefield south of Moon Island. Seven enemy destroyers confronted this force but at 1747 *Pillau* drove them off with little difficulty. Most of the German raiders found little to attack. The only targets left in the gulf were the gunboats *Sivuch* and *Koreets* and some small merchant vessels. The gunboats had been laying mines off Riga. The need to replenish their coal bunkers delayed their retreat and not until that afternoon did they depart for the safety of Moon Sound. During their voyage the gunboats received reports of an enemy force near Pernau and approaching Moon Sound.

At 1930 *Augsburg*, *V29*, and *V100* were steaming south returning from their foray to Pernau, where they had sunk a small steamer. South of Kiuno Island they spotted two silhouettes to the northwest "distorted by mirage." The cruiser swung around the stern of the sighting and, when they failed to respond to her challenge, fired two salvos. *Augsburg* then came to full speed. In the dark and distance she mistook the gunboats for destroyers. The Russian ships fled at their best speed which was just 12 knots. *Koreets* was eight hundred yards astern and two hundred yards to starboard of *Sivuch*. *Augsburg* noted that "they were steaming slowly in spite of making a great deal of smoke."[45] By 1950 *Augsburg* was abeam of *Sivuch*. She switched on her searchlight and opened fire from 4,500 yards. She hit *Koreets* with one shell that exploded in the sick bay and broke a secondary steam pipe and another that passed through without exploding. By now *Augsburg*'s captain realized his opponents were gunboats, not destroyers, but believed they were armed with 8-inch guns. He ordered *V29* and *V100* to attack the gunboats with torpedoes but his order was misunderstood as the destroyer captains still thought they were engaging destroyers and did not see any gunboats. Thus, they turned toward the enemy, a maneuver that fouled *Augsburg*'s guns. The light cruiser sheered away and ceased fire. At the same time a shell struck her forecastle and disabled her forward searchlight, wounding seven men.

As the destroyers closed *V29* engaged *Sivuch* while *V100* took on *Koreets*. To the north *Posen* and *Nassau*, which were covering the Moon

Sound mining operation, saw the searchlights and heard the gunfire and were sailing to investigate. At 2010 *Sivuch*, having been hit several times, reversed course to dodge a torpedo fired by *V29*. *Koreets* swerved to avoid a collision and headed north northeast toward Kiuno Island. *Sivuch* fell in four thousand yards behind. *Augsburg* swung east to follow, firing furiously but failing to hit as she was closing so fast her gunners could not compensate for the rate of change. *Augsburg* made a loop to port to bring her aft light to bear and picked up *Sivuch* again. As *Koreets* vanished in the dark *Augsburg* and her destroyers closed to within six hundred yards of *Sivuch*, blasting her with gunfire.

At 2012 *Posen* joined the battle but, worried about hitting friendly vessels, only fired a few salvos. Then her searchlight "caught sight . . . of a ship, to all appearances *Slava*, 1000m ahead. . . . To bring her broadside to bear, *Posen* turned back to her old course, lost sight of the target whilst doing so and when firing was resumed, it was not certain whether a second ship was not now being fired at. The latter was in any case destroyed in a few minutes."[46] *Sivuch*'s second in command recorded that he lost consciousness in the concussion of a 28-cm blast. When he awoke the forward 4.7-inch gun had disappeared. *Posen*'s escort then launched torpedoes, one of which detonated on the fiercely burning vessel. *Sivuch* capsized at 2040. The Germans rescued fifty survivors, of whom twenty-seven were wounded, but *Koreets* escaped in the confusion. Her crew scuttled her the next day hearing that the Germans had landed at Pernau and believing the ship was in imminent danger.[47]

The Kaiserliche Marine evacuated the Gulf of Riga the day after this sweep. With the offshore islands and most of the mainland shore still under enemy control and with enemy submarines prowling the gulf itself, there was little sense in trying to remain. The bulk of the German navy had been used in an operation that cost the Russians two small gunboats sunk and an old battleship and a destroyer damaged. In return, the Germans lost three destroyers (*S31* was mined and sunk on the night of 20 August), three minesweepers, a light cruiser, a destroyer mined and damaged, and a battlecruiser damaged by torpedo. The Admiralstab concluded that the operation was a failure because it did not accomplish its major objectives, "the effective blocking of Moon Sound for a considerable time and the destruction of *Slava*."[48]

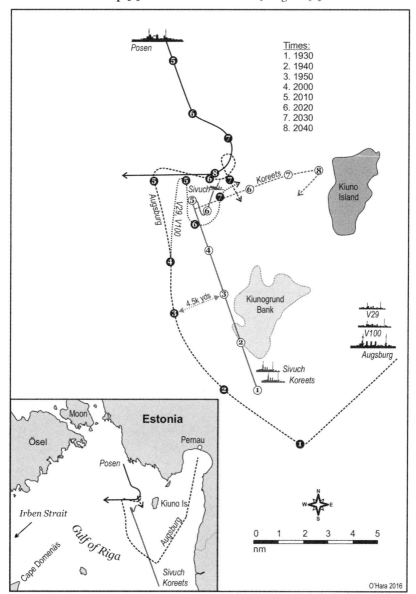

Map 3.3 Battle of Kiuno Island: 19 August 1915

This was the year's last surface engagement in the Baltic. Within the gulf the Russian navy played an active role supporting the army with the guns of *Slava*, destroyers, and gunboats and even conducting a battalion-sized landing south of Windau on 22 October, supported by *Slava* and flotilla craft. The Russians also took their first actions against the important maritime traffic between Sweden and Germany with some success, including a cruiser sweep into the Gulf of Bothnia in late October and the sinking of a number of merchantmen. The British submarine *E8* sank the armored cruiser *Prinz Adalbert* with the loss of 672 men on 23 October. In November with the advent of longer nights the Germans and Russians both undertook major mining operations. Finally, on the night of 19 November the Russians attacked the German patrol line off Windau with seven destroyers and sank the auxiliary patrol ship *Norburg*. A German force consisting of *Lübeck, Augsburg, Bremen*, and eight destroyers arrived too late to intervene. During the year the Germans lost an armored cruiser, two light cruisers, seven flotilla craft, a submarine, nine minesweepers, and twenty-six merchant vessels in the Baltic. The Russians lost two gunboats, a submarine, two minelayers, three minesweepers, and five merchantmen.[49]

Black Sea 1915

The British-built protected cruiser *Hamidieh* was the most useful large unit of the prewar Ottoman fleet. She, torpedo gunboat *Berk*, and *Midilli* set out to escort a convoy carrying coast defense guns to Zonguldak in the first days of January. *Berk* was mined and heavily damaged off the Bosporus, but *Midilli* continued east and *Hamidieh* followed a day later. She was west of Sinope at noon on 4 January, when she saw a smoke cloud to starboard. It proved to be protected cruiser *Pamiat Merkuriia* and four destroyers.

Pursuit of Hamidieh: *4 January, 1245–1600*
  Conditions: Clear
  Missions: Russians, sweep; Ottomans, transit
  Russian Force: CP *Pamiat Merkuriia;* DD *Gnevnyi, Derzkii*[+], *Bespokoinyi, Pronzitelnyi*.
  Ottoman Force (Corvette Captain Egon Kottwitz): CP *Hamidieh*[+].

Outgunned by the Russian cruiser and slower than the destroyers, *Hamidieh* was in a bad situation. She turned and ran west as *Pamiat Merkuriia* closed the range to 12,000 yards and opened fire at 1245. The four destroyers, whose long-barreled 4-inch weapons were the longest ranged destroyer guns then in service, soon joined in. The five

Russians bombarded the Ottoman cruiser until 1400, firing five hundred rounds while *Hamidieh* replied with eighty 6-inch shells from her stern gun. The Russians scored a 6-inch hit on her armored deck astern while near misses or splinters opened underwater seams and caused minor flooding. *Hamidieh* slightly damaged *Derzkii* in return. After they ceased fire the Russians trailed the Ottoman vessel for another two hours before turning northwest and disappearing in a rain squall. *Hamidieh* might ultimately have been faster than *Merkuriia*, but the failure of the Russian destroyers to close must have been a deliberate choice to avoid her 6-inch guns. Pressing her good fortune, *Hamidieh* reversed course and steamed into the northeastern Black Sea to meet *Midilli*.[50]

Action off Yalta: 6 January, 1915–2000

Conditions: Poor visibility

Missions: Russians, interception; Ottomans, raid

Russian Force: OBB *Evstafii*[+], *Ioann Zlatoust*, *Panteleimon*, *Tri Sviatitelia*, *Rostislav*; CP *Pamiat Merkuriia*; DDx7.

Ottoman Force (Frigate Captain Kettner): CL *Midilli*; CP *Hamidieh*[+].

The Russian forces had returned to Sevastopol after the 4 January engagement but steamed out again upon learning that *Midilli* was bombarding the Tuapse area southwest of Novorossisk.

The Russian force of five battleships, a cruiser, and seven destroyers encountered *Midilli* and *Hamidieh* after dark on 6 January, a hundred miles south of the Kerch Strait. Surprise was mutual. There was a flurry of gunfire and the Russians launched a few torpedoes as *Midilli* and *Hamidieh* fled in different directions and quickly vanished in the darkness. The Ottomans hit and damaged one of *Evstafii*'s 12-inch guns while a Russian shell knocked out *Hamidieh*'s searchlight.[51]

This action was part of an emerging pattern in which the Russians outgunned the Ottoman forces but the Ottoman ships outran their opponents. The Russians grappled with this issue throughout the Black Sea naval war. In another example they intercepted *Midilli* and *Hamidieh* east of Sinope on 27 January. A cruiser chased *Hamidieh* for more than six hours, but despite her tenacity could not draw into range.[52]

The Russians vigorously harassed traffic along the Anatolian coast and to the capital. On 7 March the Black Sea Fleet bombarded Zonguldak and Eregli and sank eight merchant vessels. On 28 March, in support of the Entente offensive against Gallipoli, the fleet demonstrated off the Bosporus, bombarding the lighthouses at the entrance to the straits and sinking a small steamer. The fleet shelled Eregli the next day after fog forced cancellation of the scheduled repeat bombardment, and Zonguldak and Kozlu on the 30th, sinking a dozen small vessels.[53]

Raid on Odessa: 3 April, dawn to after dark

Conditions: Deteriorating

Missions: Russians, interception; Ottomans, raid

Russian Force (Admiral A. A. Ebergard): OBB *Evstafii, Ioann Zlatoust, Panteleimon, Tri Sviatitelia, Rostislav*; CP *Pamiat Merkuriia, Kagul*; DS *Almaz*; DD *Gnevnyi, Pronzitelnyi*[+]*, Derzkii, Kapitan Saken*; TB *Zhutkii, Zhivuchii, Zvonkii, Zorkii, Zavidnyi, Zavetnyi*.

Ottoman Force (Captain Richard Ackermann): BC *Yavuz*; CL *Midilli*.

On 3 April an Ottoman squadron debouched from the Bosporus to attack Russian troop transports sheltering in Odessa—part of the force gathering to seize Constantinople should Entente efforts at Gallipoli succeed. *Yavuz* (still not completely repaired from her mine damage) and *Midilli* covered a raiding force consisting of cruisers *Hamidieh* and *Medjidieh*, destroyers *Muavenet* and *Jadhigar*, and torpedo boats *Tasoz* and *Samsun*.

Russia's massive minelaying efforts (nearly 4,400 mines laid in 1914) again paid off when *Medjidieh* struck a mine and sank in shallow water well short of Odessa. Vice Admiral Souchon canceled the operation, but a seaplane spotted *Yavuz* and *Midilli* off Sevastopol where *Yavuz* had sunk the steamer *Vostochnaya Zvezda* (945 GRT) at 0920 with eight 15-cm rounds. Meanwhile, the Russian fleet had been getting under way since 0600. *Pamiat Merkuriia, Gnevnyi, Pronzitelnyi*, and *Derzkii*, which had left harbor first, pushed ahead and established contact at 1015. *Yavuz* fired one extreme-range salvo at *Pamiat Merkuriia* that fell well short. When the Russians reversed course toward their approaching battleships *Yavuz* and *Midilli* turned their

Map 3.4 Attacks on Ottoman "Coal" Coast 1914–1916

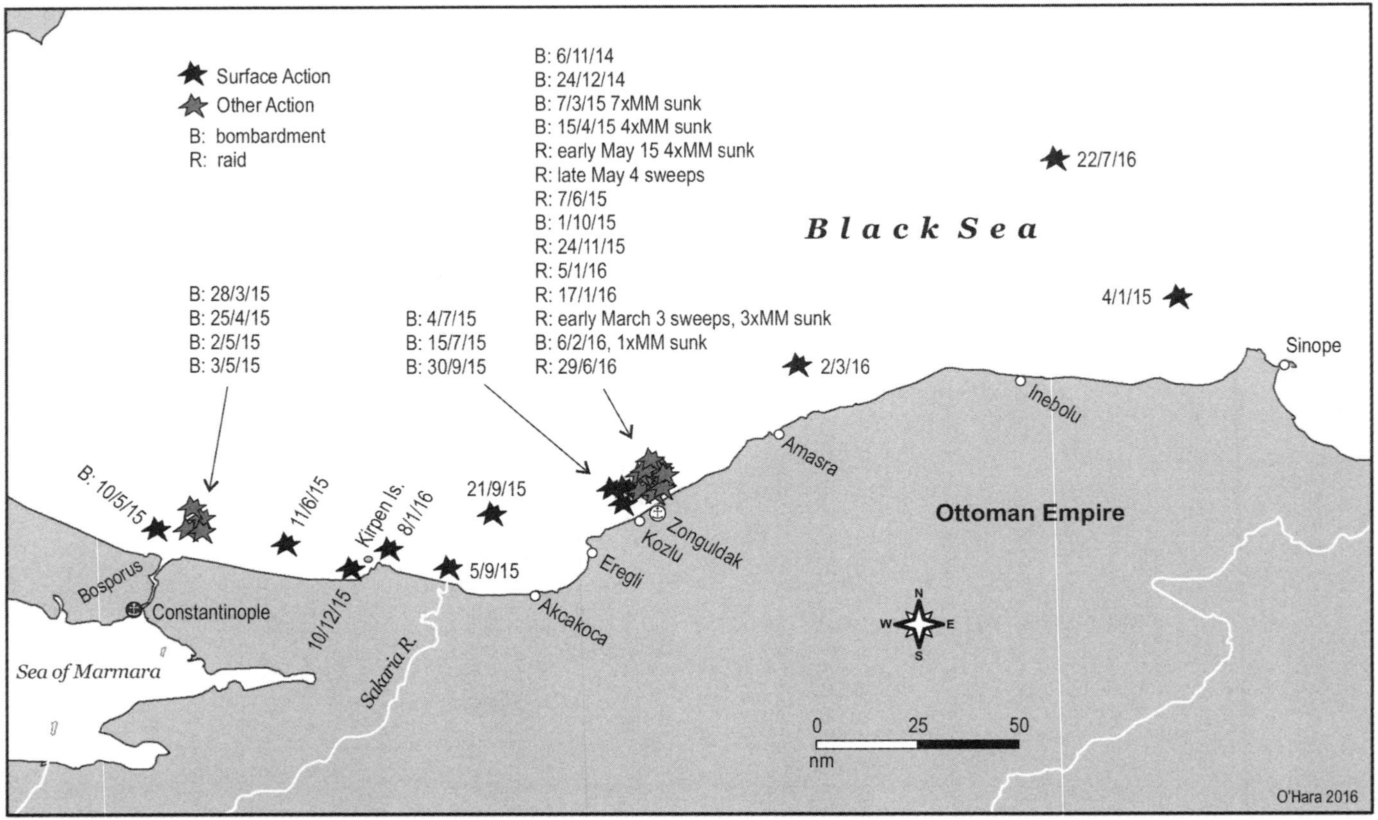

Surface Action
Other Action
B: bombardment
R: raid

B: 6/11/14
B: 24/12/14
B: 7/3/15 7xMM sunk
B: 15/4/15 4xMM sunk
R: early May 15 4xMM sunk
R: late May 4 sweeps
R: 7/6/15
B: 1/10/15
R: 24/11/15
R: 5/1/16
R: 17/1/16
R: early March 3 sweeps, 3xMM sunk
B: 6/2/16, 1xMM sunk
R: 29/6/16

B: 4/7/15
B: 15/7/15
B: 30/9/15

B: 28/3/15
B: 25/4/15
B: 2/5/15
B: 3/5/15

B: 10/5/15

O'Hara 2016

Black Sea

Ottoman Empire

Sinope

Inebolu

22/7/16

4/1/15

2/3/16

Amasra

Zonguldak
Kozlu

Eregli

Akcakoca

21/9/15

5/9/15

Kirpen Is.
8/1/16

Sakaria R.

10/12/15

11/6/15

Constantinople

Bosporus

Sea of Marmara

N
W   E
S

0   25   50
nm

prows for home. The Russians then followed. By 1115 they were in sight of the Ottomans and slowly closed the range to 26,000 yards, but could get no closer. *Yavuz* emitted "huge volumes of smoke during the whole period, probably using Turkish coal."[54] Because of the mine damage her best speed was 22 knots. At 1330 the Russian battleships briefly fired at *Midilli*, but the range was too great. At 1600 Admiral Ebergard ordered his destroyers forward. The smaller warships struggled to maintain high speeds in the deteriorating weather but the large and fast ships of the 1st Division— *Gnevnyi*, *Pronzitelnyi*, and *Derzkii*—forged ahead. After sunset *Gnevnyi* had passed *Midilli* and was drawing abreast of *Yavuz* when *Midilli* snapped on her searchlights, turned toward the destroyer, and opened fire. The range was less than four thousand yards. *Yavuz* joined in with her secondary batteries. *Gnevnyi* launched six torpedoes whereupon both Ottoman warships turned sharply away and vanished in the dark. The Ottomans holed one of *Pronzitelnyi*'s funnels and all three destroyers suffered minor defects from maintaining high speed in heavy weather. The main Russian fleet turned back to Sevastopol at 2300 after the destroyer attack failed.

Yavuz and *Midilli* joined the raiding force on the morning of 4 April and steamed back through the Bosporus. The Russians consoled themselves by salvaging *Medjidieh* and, in a repeat of the *Magdeburg* incident, recovered a code and signal book on board that naval intelligence subsequently found very useful. For their part German commanders noted that *Midilli* required heavier guns than her 10.5-cm pieces to deal with the big Russian destroyers.[55]

Battle off the Bosporus Forts: 10 May, 0700–0812

Conditions: Clear

Missions: Russians, bombardment; Ottomans, interception

Russian Forces (Admiral A. A. Ebergard): Screening Force: OBB *Evstafii*, *Zlatoust*, *Rostislav*, Z-class TBx6. Bombardment Force: OBB *Tri Sviatitelia*, *Panteleimon*; CVS *Imperator Aleksandr I*, *Almaz*; ML *Kseniia*; MS *Sviatoi Nikolai*; DD *Derzkii*, *Bespokoinyi*.

Ottoman Force (Captain Ackermann): BC *Yavuz*[#], DD *Numene*.

Entente forces landed at Gallipoli on 25 April and struggled from the first to maintain their beachheads. To support their allies, *Tri Sviatitelia* and *Panteleimon* bombarded the Bosporus forts on that day, expending 132 12-inch rounds. They bombarded again on 2 May (166 heavy shells) and on 3 May *Rostislav* and *Kagul* joined *Tri Sviatitelia* in a repeat performance. On 8 May the fleet sortied to hit the coal ports and then the Bosporus forts. On 9 May *Pamiat Merkuriia* sank two steamers and twenty-seven sailing vessels off the coast while destroyers dispatched a third steamer and Russian raiders landed at Eregli. *Yavuz* departed the Bosporus at 1300 to drive off the intruders. Meanwhile, Russians were deploying eastwards. *Panteleimon* and *Tri Sviatitelia* would bombard the forts, while *Evstafii*, *Ioann Zlatoust*, *Rostislav*, and six torpedo boats covered. The two protected cruisers patrolled the area. Supporting the bombardment force were two seaplane carriers, a minelayer, two minesweepers, and two destroyers.

At 0515 on 10 May the Ottoman destroyer *Numene* on patrol outside the Bosporus spotted enemy battleships. She radioed several reports over the next ninety minutes and even engaged the minesweepers until *Panteleimon* and *Tri Sviatitelia* chased her away. When *Yavuz* received the reports Captain Ackermann saw an opportunity to defeat the enemy battleships in detail so he came about and steamed to intervene. However, *Pamiat Merkuriia* spotted the battlecruiser at 0700 and her report led Admiral Ebergard to cancel the bombardment and concentrate his capital ships.

As *Yavuz* came into sight the Russians were steering northwest in order *Evstafii*, *Zlatoust*, and *Rostislav*. The two other battleships were four thousand yards behind and could not initially participate. *Yavuz* approached from the northeast at top speed. *Evstafii* and *Ioann Zlatoust* opened centralized fire at 0753 from 18,800 yards whereupon *Yavuz* came 90 degrees to starboard to a slightly converging course and replied.

Yavuz's fire was rapid and spotters reported the target surrounded by splashes; nevertheless, the Russians hit first at 0800 when a 12-inch HE round struck the battlecruiser's forecastle and penetrated two decks before exploding. *Panteleimon* closed enough to open fire at 0805 and claimed a hit with her second salvo fired from 20,000 yards. Actually a very near miss, the shell knocked out a secondary mount and dented *Yavuz*'s armored belt below the waterline, causing some flooding. Shortly after 0806, now under fire from four battleships and with the range to *Evstafii* down to 14,600 yards, *Yavuz* turned east-northeast and rapidly drew away. The last shots were fired at 0812 from 22,000 yards. The Russians pursued but *Yavuz* looped around and easily escaped into the Bosporus. The Russian ships expended 169 12-inch rounds and 36 8-inch while *Yavuz* fired 124 28-cm shells. Once again, the Russians brought superior combat power to bear on the *Yavuz*, damaging their target twice. *Yavuz* had used her superior speed to engage under reasonably favorable terms but failed to inflict any damage and thus used the same speed advantage to run when the battle turned against her. The German official history called the engagement a lost opportunity.[56]

In early June two German submarines arrived at Constantinople. After a fleet operation against Zonguldak, Kozlu, and Eregli on 7 June the Russian command decided there were not enough flotilla craft to screen the slow battleships against this new danger and so, pending the completion of the dreadnoughts expected later that year, relied on the powerful *Bespokoinyi*–class destroyers to harass commerce, especially between Zonguldak and the Bosporus. Typically operating in groups of two to four, the *Bespokoinyi*s had the right mix of armament, speed, and range for these crucial missions, which were slowly strangling Constantinople's supply of coal. As early as April 1915 Souchon "complained he had to avoid 'useless' sorties into the Black Sea because of the necessity to economize on fuel."[57] By mid-May the Ottomans had lost about a third of their shipping; the Russians made four more sweeps during the last half of May that depleted the Ottoman merchant fleet still further. The Ottoman coal authority had started the war with twenty-two colliers. By September nine remained. Only the opening of a direct overland supply route after Bulgaria's entry into the war in October averted a major energy crisis.[58]

Action West of Kirpen Island: 11 June, 0200–

Conditions: Poor visibility
Missions: Russians, sweep; Ottomans, interception
Russian Force: DD *Gnevnyi*[#], *Derzkii*.
Ottoman Force (Frigate Captain Leberecht Klitzing): CL *Midilli*[+].

The Russian destroyers did not always have things their own way. On 10 June, *Gnevnyi* and *Derzkii* sank three vessels at Zonguldak. They then headed west seeking more prey and were thirty miles off the Bosporus when at 0200 on 11 June they spotted a fast-moving vessel. *Derzkii* turned onto an opposite course and attempted a torpedo attack. When she failed to attain a good firing position, she switched on her searchlight and revealed *Midilli*, which was hunting the two destroyers. The cruiser counter-illuminated *Gnevnyi* and both *Midilli* and *Derzkii* immediately opened fire.

As *Gvnenyi* closed to launch torpedoes several of *Midilli*'s 10.5-cm shells slammed into the Russian destroyer from just two thousand yards; one sliced the main steam pipe and left her dead in the water. In return the Russian missed with five torpedoes. *Derzkii* landed two shells on *Midilli*, killing seven and wounding fifteen. *Midilli* broke off believing she had sunk *Gnevnyi*. In fact, *Derzkii* towed her crippled sister back to Sevastopol the next day.[59]

Despite the temporary loss of *Gnevnyi* and a setback on 4 July when the Ottoman destroyers *Gairet* and *Numene*, firing from behind a stone jetty, drove off a pair of destroyers, the Russians continued to target Zonguldak.[60]

Bombardment of Zonguldak: 15 July, 1653–1715

Conditions: Unknown

Missions: Russians, bombardment; Ottomans, transit/defense

Russian Force: DD *Pronzitelnyi, Bespokoinyi, Derzkii.*

Ottoman Force: DD *Numene*[+], *Muavenet, Jadhigar*[+].

Numene and *Muavenet* escorted three colliers into Zonguldak on the 12th, while *Jadhigar* had arrived with diesel oil for the submarine *UB7* on the 14th. On the 15th the Russians mounted another attack on the harbor. The destroyers took cover behind the jetty and waited for the enemy to approach. At 1653 the Russians opened fire from 11,000 yards. The Ottoman ships replied as the range dropped below ten thousand but the Russians seemed ready. In an accurate bombardment that lasted until 1715 they holed one of *Jadhigar*'s stacks, riddled *Numene* with splinters, and damaged a merchantman. These results led the Ottomans to conclude that it was too dangerous for their precious destroyers to try to defend Zonguldak against such attacks.[61]

Russian depredations on the collier route from Zonguldak prompted the Ottomans to sail these important vessels in escorted convoys. *Midilli*, the best unit for this work, was unavailable for several months after striking a mine off the Bosporus on 18 July. This forced a reluctant Souchon to press *Yavuz* into this service despite the danger from Russian submarines, two of which usually lurked off the Bosporus in a loose blockade. And even a strong escort was no guarantee of safety as demonstrated on 10 August when the submarine *Tyulen* torpedoed a collier in a convoy escorted by *Yavuz*, *Hamidieh*, and three destroyers.

Attack on the Hamidieh *Convoy: 5 September, night*
Conditions: Clear
Missions: Russian, interception; Ottomans, escort
Russian Force (Captain V. V. Trubetskoi): DD *Bystryi*, *Pronzitelnyi*.
Ottoman Force (Corvette Captain Kottwitz): CP *Hamidieh*; DD *Numene*, *Muavenet*; Colliers x3*.

An Ottoman squadron was escorting three colliers from Zonguldak to the Bosporus when Russian destroyers attacked between Kirpen and Eregli. At first the Russians stayed beyond range of the defender's 88-mm guns and, when both of *Hamidieh*'s 6-inch weapons malfunctioned after only thirty-four rounds, the escort retreated east under heavy fire. *Bystryi* and *Pronzitelnyi* then doubled back. The colliers, confronted by the Russian destroyers and submarine *Nerpa*, ran themselves aground and were finished off by gunfire with the loss of 10,780 tons of coal. *Yavuz* responded to the escort's calls for support, but was too late.[62]

After this action the Germans regarded *Hamidieh* as nearly useless, and considering the destroyers too vulnerable, restricted them to daylight antisubmarine duties. They reluctantly concluded that until *Midilli* was available again only *Yavuz* could effectively protect the colliers.[63]

Yavuz versus the Bespokoinyis: *21 September, 1413–1420*
Conditions: Clear
Missions: Russians, sweep; Ottomans, interception
Russian Forces: DD *Schastlivyi*, *Bespokoinyi*, *Pronzitelnyi*.
Ottoman Forces (Captain Ackermann): BC *Yavuz*.

Yavuz sortied again on 21 September to rescue three colliers from Russian destroyers reported off Zonguldak. At 1400 she spotted her prey. Much to Captain Ackermann's surprise the Russians headed straight toward him. At 1413 *Yavuz* turned to open her gun arcs and commenced fire at 17,000 yards. The destroyers' return fire fell well short as they spun about gushing smoke. The action was over by 1420. *Yavuz* expended twenty-six 28-cm rounds and nine 15-cm rounds and her diary noted that the Russians "maneuvered with great skill, which made shooting difficult."[64]

Yavuz continued in the trade protection role, steaming out of the Bosporus at least seven more times until 14 November, when two torpedoes from the Russian submarine *Morzh* narrowly missed and emphasized the risk this irreplaceable unit faced in doing a destroyer's work.[65] Bulgaria's October entry on the side of the Central Powers gave the Russians another enemy to worry about while opening an overland supply route to Constantinople. Nonetheless, the Russians continued to harass Ottoman traffic along the Anatolian coast, bombarding Zonguldak on 1 October and 24 November with the new dreadnought *Imperatritsa Mariia* providing a comfortable margin of superiority over *Yavuz*.

Gunboats off Kirpen Island: 10 December, morning

Conditions: unknown

Missions: Russians, interception; Ottomans, salvage

Russian Forces: DD *Derzkii, Gnevnyi, Bespokoinyi*.

Ottoman Forces (Captain Lieutenant Ellendt): GB *Ta köprü★, Yozgat★*.

On 29 November the German submarine *UC13* ran aground west of Kirpen Island in a storm. Constantinople sent a pair of gunboats to salvage material from her. They had worked through the night and started for the shelter of Kirpen harbor when three Russian destroyers appeared. The Russians pounded them for an hour, expending 370 4-inch shells. The gunboats tried to reply but were decisively outranged and finally ran aground to avoid sinking.[66]

Mediterranean 1915

Ottoman belligerence closed the route used by much of Russia's prewar trade and threatened the Suez Canal, which was vital to

Britain's imperial connections. Some in London argued that the best way to protect Suez was to strike directly at Constantinople. Italian neutrality had resulted in a "margin of predreadnoughts and cruisers ready for action and of no obvious value elsewhere." Initially the Entente armies declined to supply troops so the Admiralty asked the admiral on the scene whether he could force the Dardanelles with ships alone. His positive reply led the British War Council to order "a naval expedition in February to bombard and take the Gallipoli Peninsula with Constantinople as its objective." By mid-March Entente forces assigned to this objective totaled twelve British and four French predreadnoughts, the new superdreadnought *Queen Elizabeth*, the battlecruiser *Inflexible*, five cruisers (one French), sixteen destroyers, six French torpedo boats, ten submarines (four French), and twenty-one minesweeping trawlers.[67]

The attack commenced on 19 February. By 7 March, after several weather delays, most of the fixed guns of the outer defenses had been silenced and demolished by landing parties. However, mobile batteries proved impossible to locate much less neutralize and they made mine-sweeping "something of a [Victoria Cross] sort of job."[68]

Eighteen capital ships gathered for a major assault on 18 March. Once the forts were silenced, the minesweepers would begin working under the protection of their big guns. *Queen Elizabeth*, *Inflexible*, and four predreadnoughts opened the action. The batteries punished *Agamemnon* and *Inflexible*; after noon four French predreadnoughts advanced. They also came under heavy fire and several were significantly damaged. Nonetheless, by 1345 it seemed that Ottoman fire had slackened and minesweeping could begin. A fresh division of British predreadnoughts advanced to relieve the French but as *Bouvet* was withdrawing through the British line she struck a mine from an unknown barrage. The battle-ship sank in two minutes with 640 men drowned. Then, at 1605, *Inflexible* hit a mine and nearly foundered. At 1615 *Irresistible* suffered the same fate. Finally, *Ocean* was mined at 1805 when trying to pass a tow to *Irresistible*. Both battleships sank that night. Naturally, no mines were swept. The Entente forces thought they had wreaked great damage to the Ottoman defenses, but they were wrong. In any case, mines not guns were the main barrier and the fields remained intact.[69]

Map 3.5 Aegean and the Dardanelles

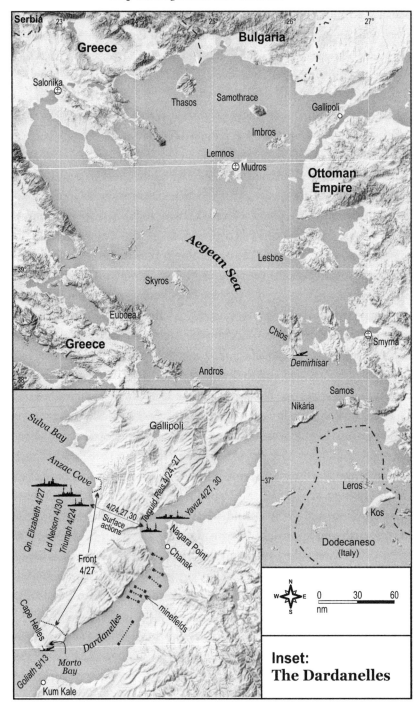

Serbia 23° 24° 25° 26° 27°

Greece

Bulgaria

Salonika

Thasos Samothrace

Gallipoli

Imbros

Lemnos

Mudros

Ottoman Empire

Aegean Sea

Lesbos

Skyros

Euboea

Greece

Chios

Smyrna

Demirhisar

Andros

Samos

Nikária

Leros

Kos

Dodecaneso
(Italy)

Inset:

Sulva Bay

Gallipoli

Anzac Cove

Qn. Elizabeth 4/27

Ld Nelson 4/30

Triumph 4/24

4/24,27,30
Surface
actions

Torgud Reis 4/24-27

Yavuz 4/27, 30

Nagara Point

Chanak

Front
4/27

Cape Helles

Dardanelles

minefields

Goliath 5/13

*Morto
Bay*

Kum Kale

N
W E
S

0   30   60
nm

Inset:
The Dardanelles

Bay to support French troops at Kereves Dere. Five destroyers screened the heavy ships. After dark the Ottoman destroyer *Muavenet,* guns landed to reduce her draft, moved down the strait to attack this anchorage. Taking advantage of fog and the dark night, she ghosted by *Beagle* and *Bulldog,* the nearest sentries, at a range she estimated to be less than a thousand yards and closed her target at 0100. *Goliath's* bridge personnel spotted a shape and flashed a challenge at 0115. *Muavenet* mimicked the signal, was challenged again, and then *Goliath* engaged. In reply *Muavenet* fired three torpedoes in quick succession. All three struck. An Ottoman officer wrote: "She began to roll on to her starboard side. The giant was burning! Dense smoke covered her entire length, a column of flame rising around her mainmast." The old battleship capsized with the loss of 570 men as *Muavenet* escaped unseen back up the strait.[74]

The appearance of *U21,* which had sailed all the way from Germany, further affected the campaign. She sank the battleships *Triumph* on 25 May and *Majestic* on the 27th but thereafter vigorous countermeasures prevented her from continuing to enjoy such success. Moreover, British submarines exacted some measure of revenge, sinking predreadnought *Heireddin Barbarossa* on 8 August.

Despite additional landings, the Entente forces were unable to break the deadlock on the peninsula. Finally, faced with winter storms, the overthrow of Serbian forces, and the opening of the direct rail line between Berlin and Constantinople with the prospects of a better supplied Ottoman army, the British War Council reluctantly ordered the evacuation of all beachheads, a process that was completed by 9 January 1916.

Adriatic 1915

The pace of the Franco-Austrian naval war slowed in December 1914. After an Austrian submarine torpedoed *Jean Bart* on 21 December 1914, the French moved their patrol line further south but continued to send single steamers escorted by destroyers to Antivari. Convoys arrived on 19 and 24 January 1915 and 3 and 5 February but on 24 February the French destroyer *Dague* struck a mine at the port. On 18 February and 10 April *Helgoland* and six destroyers scouted into the Strait of Otranto and established that, with the Dardanelles offensive under way, the French blockade of the strait was a loose affair. On the night of 1/2 March the

Map 3.6 Adriatic Sea

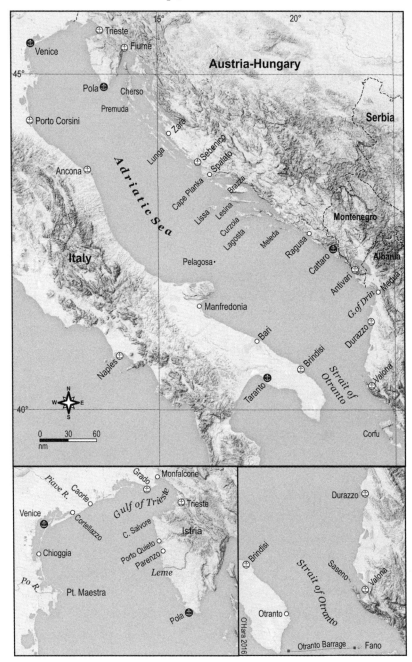

Map 3.7   Bombardment of Italian Coast: 24 May 1915

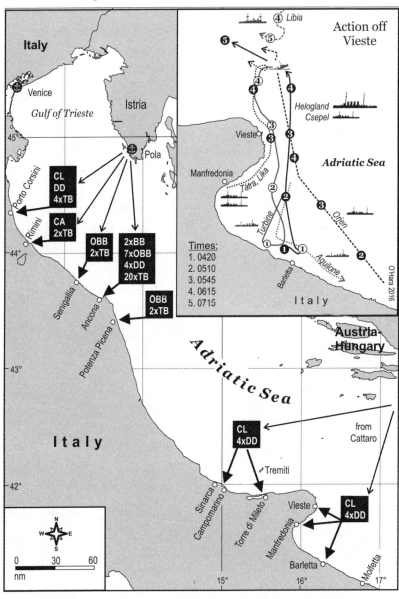

Austrian flotilla craft raided Antivari and the destroyer *Csikós* torpedoed the Montenegrin royal yacht *Rumija* (185 GRT) at anchor. Otherwise, the matter of Italy's entry to the war induced a wait–and–see attitude on all sides.[75]

Italian Declaration of War and Initial Austro-Hungarian Operations

The K.u.K. Kriegsmarine's Admiral Anton Haus anticipated Italian belligerence and planned an offensive action to punish Rome's perfidy. This involved the entire fleet attacking Italian east coast ports and cutting the coastal railway to delay Italy's mobilization. Italy's declaration came as expected at 1600 on 23 May. The Austrians had steam up and the battle fleet cleared Pola by 2000. Other squadrons were either at sea or sailed from Cattaro. The minor port of Ancona was the main objective of the I Division (dreadnoughts *Viribus Unitis* and *Tegetthof*, with the semi-dreadnought *Franz Ferdinand*); III Division (predreadnoughts *E. Karl*, *E. Friedrich*, and *E. Ferdinand Max*); and IV Division (predreadnoughts *Habsburg*, *Arpád*, and *Babenberg*) screened by four destroyers and twenty torpedo boats. Other targets, from north to south, included Porto Corsini (light cruiser *Novara*, a destroyer, and four torpedo boats); Rimini (armored cruiser *Sankt Georg* and two torpedo boats); Senigallia (the semi-dreadnought *Zrinyi* and two torpedo boats); Potenza Picena (semi-dreadnought *Radetzky* and two torpedo boats); Manfredonia, Vieste, and Barletta (light cruiser *Helgoland* and four destroyers); and Torre di Mileto, Tremiti, and Campomarino (light cruiser *Admiral Spaun* and four destroyers). Two light cruisers and two destroyers scouted the battle force's northern flank. These targets were all well beyond the intervention range of Italy's battle fleet at Taranto so there was no chance this large operation would incite the decisive battle Austrian prewar planning had envisioned. In fact, Rome expected the opening Austrian moves to be directed against Brindisi. The choice of targets came as a surprise, especially since, with the exception of Porto Corsini, they were all small commercial or fishing ports.[76]

Action off Vieste: 24 May, 0445–1719

    Conditions: Clear

    Missions: Italy, patrol; Austria, raid

    Italian Forces: First group: DD *Turbine*★ (Corvette Captain Luigi Bian-
        chi), *Aquilone*. Second group: CP *Libia*; AMC *Città di Siracusa*.

    Austrian Force: CL *Helgoland*+ (Captain Heinrich Seitz); DD *Csepel*+,
        Tátra+, *Orjen*, *Lika*.

There were Italian ships at sea on various missions related to the open-ing of hostilities but only one small surface action resulted. The small Ital-ian destroyers *Aquilone* and *Turbine* were scouting between Manfredonia

British light cruiser *Dublin* sailing past the Italian predreadnought *Benedetto Brin* at Brindisi, May 1915. (Aldo Fraccaroli Collection via Ufficio Storico Marina Militare)

and Vieste when, at 0100 on the 24th, they encountered four larger destroyers. The Italians believed they were friendly and the two columns passed in the dark. In fact, they were Austrian destroyers. *Turbine* and *Aquilone* then turned back toward Barletta but became separated when *Aquilone* veered away to investigate a possible sighting. Meanwhile *Orjen* joined *Helgoland* and screened the cruiser as she bombarded Barletta at 0400. Drawn by the gunfire, *Aquilone* appeared at 0438, saw an enemy cruiser, turned southeast, and escaped, chased on the way by some ineffective salvos. *Turbine* approached several minutes later and mistook *Helgoland* for a friendly vessel. A broadside from the cruiser corrected this misimpression whereupon *Turbine* fled north toward Vieste with *Helgoland* in pursuit. *Tátra* and *Csepel*, which had been attacking Manfredonia, approached on a parallel course at 0510 and opened fire at 0545. *Lika* and *Orjen* also joined the chase. The Italian destroyer hit *Tátra* and *Csepel* but these blows did little damage. The Austrian ships were faster and slowly closed. Finally a 66-mm round from *Lika* struck *Turbine*'s steam pipe causing an eruption of black smoke and steam. As her speed rapidly dropped *Tátra* and *Helgoland* also scored hits and *Turbine* was soon dead in the water and listing heavily to port. The crew abandoned ship at 0651 and she capsized shortly thereafter. The Austrians rescued thirty-five and torpedoed the wreck.

The Austrians were headed northwest when *Libia* and *Città di Siracusa* appeared from the west. They opened fire at 0710 from under ten thousand yards. The Austrian commander reported, "The enemy shooting was excellent. The first salvo fell a bit short below the railing and the second bracketed *Helgoland* and *Csepel*." During this engagement, which lasted from

0710 to 0719, a medium-caliber shell hit between *Helgoland*'s forward funnel and the command bridge. Another projectile exploded in *Csepel*'s wake. However, the slower Italian ships quickly fell out of effective range.[77]

The Habsburg fleet was back in port by noon on the 24th. Their massive naval operation made excellent headlines but the military impact was minor. It was the only time the Austrian dreadnoughts fired their big guns against enemy targets.[78]

Successes by Central Power submarines, including the torpedoing of the French armored cruiser *Léon Gambetta* on 27 April, the British light cruiser *Dublin* on 10 June, and the Italian armored cruisers *Amalfi* and *Garibaldi* on 7 and 18 July respectively, emphasized the danger of risking large warships in narrow waters. That did not stop light forces from conducting bombardments and counter-bombardments of minor targets (twenty-six by the Austrians and nineteen by the Italians). In July an Italian naval landing party occupied Pelagosa in the southern Adriatic. This provoked an Austrian counter-landing, which the defenders repulsed. But the fact that the Italians ended up withdrawing voluntarily proved the whole exercise had little point, and the fleets never met to contest possession of the barren islet.

Along the front lines to the north in the crowded waters of the Gulf of Trieste Italian and Austrian destroyers and torpedo boats laid mines and

French destroyer *Bisson*, 13 August 1915, just returned to Brindisi after sinking the Austrian submarine *U3*. (Aldo Fraccaroli Collection via Ufficio Storico Marina Militare)

patrolled but had no encounters. The Italians focused on naval gunfire support for their troops using pontoons and barges fitted with old guns from decommissioned warships. In addition Italian barges and small steamers delivered 61,900 tons of supplies directly to the front during the year. The K.u.K. Kriegsmarine concentrated on attacking targets along Italy's long and open coastline and made little effort to directly support their army or to ferry supplies to the front.

Two events occurred in October that changed the calculus of Adriatic operations. First, Bulgaria declared war and invaded Serbia. This led to Serbia's collapse and the ultimate evacuation of its army through Albanian ports. Second, German submarines, which had entered the Mediterranean in April, launched a campaign of unrestricted warfare. In the last three months of the year in the Mediterranean they sank seventy-five Entente merchantmen displacing 280,260 GRT.[79] With the Ottomans unable to supply diesel fuel, the German undersea campaign had to be based from Adriatic ports. This transformed the purpose of the Otranto patrol from stopping surface warships and blockade runners to disputing the passage of submarines.

When Italy entered the war it contributed flotilla craft to the Otranto patrol and in July 1915 the blockade was reorganized to shift more responsibilities to small craft and save wear and tear on valuable destroyers and torpedo boats. Nonetheless, in August the British Admiralty received complaints from Admiral, Malta that enemy submarines were passing through the straits at will. This led to a plan to stiffen the barrier by deploying drifters that would tow nets seeded with alarms. The first British drifters arrived at Taranto on 22 September and there were soon forty boats operating in groups of eight, with four groups constantly at sea.[80]

While the Entente navies stiffened the Otranto Barrage the Austrians raided south from Cattaro to interfere with the supply of Serbian armies and then with their evacuation. On 22 November *Helgoland* and six destroyers sank two small merchant vessels that were sailing independently. A group of four Italian destroyers failed to intercept the intruders. On 5 December Captain Miklós Horthy with *Novara* and seven flotilla craft hit San Giovanni di Medua and sank the motor vessel *Thira*, six motor schooners and, off Cape Planka, the French submarine *Fresnal*. Horthy claimed a bag of twenty-three vessels. "One ship blew up, a second caught fire, a third sank soundless. A sailing ship was burning with a weird yellow light." *Helgoland* and six destroyers hit Durazzo the next day and sank five motor schooners. The Entente powers scrambled to counter this new menace while Italy suspended traffic into Durazzo. The fourth raid in this series provoked a surface action.[81]

Battle of Durazzo: 29 December, 1320–1730

Conditions: Clear

Missions: Entente, interception; Austrians, raid

Entente Forces: First Force (Captain A. P. Addison, RN): BR CL *Dartmouth*; IT CL *Quarto*; FR DD *Casque, Bisson, Renaudin, Commandant Bory, Commandant Lucas.* Second Force (Rear Admiral Alfonso Belleni, RM): IT CL *Nino Bixio*+; BR CL *Weymouth*; IT DD *Abba, Nievo, Mosto, Pilo.*

Austrian Force (Captain Seitz): CL *Helgoland*#; DD *Balaton, Csepel*+, *Tátra, Triglav*★.

On 28 December 1915 Admiral Haus ordered forces at Cattaro to attack two Italian destroyers reported at Durazzo. *Helgoland* and five modern destroyers sailed from Cattaro that night to reach Durazzo at dawn on the 29th.

The Austrian flotilla encountered and rammed the French submarine *Monge* off Cattaro but at Durazzo they only found a small Greek steamer and two schooners. At 0730 the destroyers entered the bay (except for *Balaton*, which remained outside on submarine watch) and in twenty minutes sank the ships there. At 0800, however, a well-camouflaged 75-mm field battery opened up at point-blank range. As the destroyers swerved to avoid the gunfire *Lika* and *Triglav* blundered into mines in a newly laid Italian barrage. *Lika* sank and *Triglav* was crippled. When *Csepel* tried to pass a line to *Triglav* she fouled her screw, reducing her speed. Finally *Tátra* secured a tow to *Triglav* and the flotilla began the long journey north at 6 knots. British, French, and Italian warships were already at sea sailing to trap the Habsburg force. Realizing his peril, Seitz radioed for assistance. Armored cruiser *Kaiser Karl IV* with torpedo boats *70F, 71F, 80T,* and *81T* sailed from Cattaro at 1135 in response while an old battleship and two cruisers raised steam.

Lookout stations had reported the Austrians off Durazzo before 0700. Shortly after, one British and one Italian light cruiser and five French destroyers commanded by the British Captain A. P. Addison sailed from Brindisi. At 0900 Italian Rear Admiral Alfonso Belleni followed, leading two more light cruisers and four destroyers. By early afternoon the Austrians were just halfway home. The *Dartmouth* group had steered toward Cattaro and was thus to their north. When he heard of the enemy's troubles, Addison turned his tri-national force south and at 1320 lookouts sighted two columns of smoke. The first belonged to *Tátra* and *Triglav* and the other to *Helgoland, Balaton,* and *Csepel.* Seitz had already seen the enemy ships and at 1315 he ordered *Tátra* to drop *Triglav*'s tow (the crew had already been taken off). *Csepel*'s reduced speed, which she reported as 20 knots, made her especially vulnerable so she ducked south while *Helgoland* briefly steered toward the enemy. After *Tátra* joined his formation, Seitz turned southwest making 29 knots, 2 knots above *Helgoland*'s designed speed.

Addison immediately gave chase and at 1338 detached the French destroyers to sink *Triglav.* Five minutes later *Dartmouth*'s guns elevated to their maximum of 20 degrees and opened fire at 14,000 yards. *Helgoland* replied. She had the range as 12,000 yards but even at that her 10-cm shells splashed well short.

As the French squadron approached *Triglav, Casque*'s captain observed smoke from the derelict's funnel, which gave him the impression she was under way. He opened fire from 5,500 yards and was surprised the enemy did not reply. He finally decided *Triglav* was abandoned and sank her with gunfire. All this took time and by then the battle had moved far past his force. Although the French destroyers followed *Dartmouth* at full power, they could not catch up.

By 1400 *Helgoland* and two destroyers were steaming southwest. *Karl IV* was just thirty miles north of *Helgoland* and heading south but Addison's group was smack between them just six miles from *Helgoland. Csepel* was southeast of Seitz's force while Admiral Belleni and the powerful *Bixio* group was east of *Karl IV* and sailing south. *Dartmouth* chased on *Helgoland*'s starboard quarter, firing measured salvos and scoring the first hit at 1355. This blow killed one, injured seven, and forced Seitz to bend south to prevent the range from closing, rather than using his superior speed to work around ahead of the Entente ships. *Quarto,* a match for *Helgoland* in

Map 3.8 Battle of Durazzo: 29 December 1915

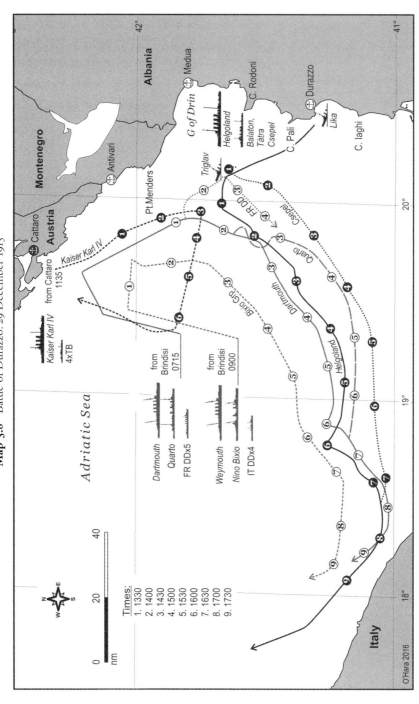

Times:
1. 1330
2. 1400
3. 1430
4. 1500
5. 1530
6. 1600
7. 1630
8. 1700
9. 1730

Adriatic Sea

Kaiser Karl IV
4xTB

from Brindisi 0715
Dartmouth
Quarto
FR DDx5

from Brindisi 0900
Weymouth
Nino Bixio
IT DDx4

Montenegro

Austria

Cattaro

Antivari

Pt.Menders

Albania

Medua

G of Drin

C. Rodoni

C. Pali

Durazzo

Lika

C. Iaghi

Helgoland

Balaton, Tátra
Csepel

Triglav

Kaiser Karl IV

from Cattaro 1135

FR DD

Csepel

Quarto

Dartmouth

Helgoland

Bixio Grp

Italy

O'Hara 2016

speed, had taken position directly in the Austrian flagship's wake, thinking to cut off *Csepel*, a movement that so worried Seitz he ordered a torpedo fired back at her at 1410. At the same time, however, Addison ordered the Italian vessel to take station off his port quarter. This caused *Quarto* to steer away, a movement that Seitz credited to his torpedo, noting in his report, "*Quarto* makes a big turn to port and loses position. At the same time *Csepel* is saved."[82] Minutes later Addison changed his mind; at 1430 he ordered *Quarto* to cut off *Csepel*. However, by this time *Csepel* had worked up to 26 knots and much valuable distance had been lost.

From 1430 to 1530 *Helgoland*, with the destroyers pacing her on her unengaged side, steamed at maximum speed slowly edging to starboard first to a westerly course and then to a little north of west under *Dartmouth*'s accurate but intermittent fire. Two shells hit at 1502. The *Bixio* group, meanwhile was north-northwest of *Dartmouth* and slowly closing on a converging course. The slow *Karl IV* group had turned west-north-west and was no longer a factor. *Csepel* continued to lag and *Quarto* opened fire on her at 1440 from 8,750 yards. She reported that the Habsburg destroyer began zigzagging. The ranges were long for the Italian ship in any case and up through 1508 she fired only twenty-three rounds. Seitz reported that the enemy fire was generally good and that the majority of rounds fell in the wakes of his ships. He also noted that many of *Dartmouth*'s rounds failed to explode when they hit the water.[83]

At 1550, with the sun dipping toward the western horizon, Admiral Belleni's group finally reached the running action and *Weymouth* engaged at extreme range. Their arrival put Seitz in a desperate position. He had managed to cross *Dartmouth*'s bow and was heading northwest but Belleni's arrival forced *Helgoland* to turn 90 degrees away back to the southwest. Now under the fire of four cruisers, *Helgoland* took a heavy hit amidships at 1626. She lost fire in two boilers and part of one funnel was blasted away. Seitz called it "the hardest moment of the fight."[84] Another round struck at 1645 on the waterline damaging the Austrian's armor belt. At the same time *Csepel*, having made up distance when *Helgoland* jogged north, fell in with the other destroyers. Seitz was running out of sea room with the Italian coast only twelve miles ahead but the sun was setting so at 1650 he once again veered to starboard. *Dartmouth* and *Quarto* were ten thousand yards astern and a little to the south while

Weymouth and *Bixio* were slightly farther away and to the north. At 1715 *Weymouth* opened fire again and pumped fourteen salvos at the Austrian ships now outlined in the sunset's glow. Seitz was still making 27 knots despite the accumulating damage.

As darkness descended *Abba* and *Nievo* approached but they were uncertain which forces were friendly and did not launch torpedoes. Belleni wrote: "[A]t 1730 the distance diminished rapidly, finally to 4,000 meters. Enemy shells were falling in our vicinity and one hit topside. The [*Helgoland*] profiting from the absolute darkness ceased fire and turned directly north. Her velocity permitted her to pass the bow of *Bixio*." Thus, despite the odds, and with great luck, Seitz had escaped. Ironically, *Tátra* suffered a machinery breakdown at 1845 that reduced her to 20 knots.[85]

The allies were rightfully frustrated by their failure to trap the Austrian raiders. Coordination between the various nationalities had been poor. An officer from *Weymouth* noted that communications was a particular problem, "this being done almost entirely by a system of Morse flag signaling. Signaling is consequently slow and unreliable and this on many occasions proved a serious handicap." On the Austrian side Haus sacked Seitz despite his escape. The commander of the cruiser force at Cattaro also incurred the fleet commander's wrath and he retired shortly thereafter. The loss of two modern destroyers was a serious blow because the Austrians had only four left: a reflection on how their prewar construction programs had failed to anticipate wartime needs.[86]

Non-European Waters 1915

In 1915 the last vestiges of Germany's overseas naval forces were mopped up in two one-sided surface actions.

Destruction of Dresden: *March 14, dawn*

Conditions: Clear
Missions: British, interception; Germans, none
British Force (Captain John Luce): CA *Kent*; CL *Glasgow*.
German Force (Captain Fritz Lüdecke): CL *Dresden*★.

Dresden, the only German ship to survive the Battle of the Falklands, took refuge in the desolate archipelago south of the Straits of Magellan.

During the last weeks of 1914 and into February 1915 a British force that included three cruisers explored the area and fruitlessly chased rumors. By March *Dresden*'s boilers were on their last legs. Consequently, she headed north to seek internment in the Chilean port of Talcahuano. The armored cruiser *Kent* sighted her on 8 March but could not get within gun range before nightfall. Then, acting on intelligence that a collier was to meet the German warship off the Juan Fernández Islands, *Glasgow*, *Kent*, and the AMC *Orama* concentrated there at dawn on 14 March and there *Glasgow* indeed found *Dresden*.

Although the German cruiser was anchored in a neutral port, *Glasgow* closed and opened fire at 8,400 yards. The second salvo hit as *Kent* came up and joined in with her 6-inch battery. After three minutes it appeared that *Dresden* had struck her colors, although according to Captain Lüdecke they were shot away. He sent a boat to the British force requesting a parley, but Captain Luce demanded unconditional surrender. The boat returned with this stipulation whereupon *Dresden*'s crew scuttled their ship by detonating her forward magazine.[87]

Destruction of Königsberg: *6 July, 0648–1530; 11 July, 1231–1400*

Conditions: Clear

Missions: British, interception; Germans, positional defense

British Force (Vice Admiral Herbert King-Hall): BMR *Mersey*[#], *Severn*[+].

German Force (Frigate Captain Max Looff): CL *Königsberg*[★].

At the start of the year *Königsberg* remained trapped up the Rufiji River in German East Africa, occupying British warships that could have been better employed elsewhere. Efforts to neutralize the light cruiser with aircraft failed twice and the 12-inch guns of *Goliath* proved unequal to the job. Finally, the Admiralty dispatched a pair of shallow-draft 6-inch gunned monitors, *Severn* and *Mersey*. It took them five weeks to make the voyage from Malta to East Africa where, on 3 June 1915, they joined the cruisers *Hyacinth*, *Weymouth*, *Pioneer*, and *Pyramus* under Vice Admiral Herbert King-Hall.

On 6 July, after preparations and repairs, the monitors, *Weymouth*, *Pyramus*, and three auxiliary minesweepers headed upstream. The monitors anchored 11,000 yards from their target and, using aerial spotting, started firing alternate two-gun salvos at 0648. *Königsberg* had spotters of

her own and she answered ten minutes later with four and five gun salvos that quickly found the range. As a postwar report expressed it, "so
good were the gunnery arrangements of the *Königsberg* that each monitor when under fire was straddled again and again by salvoes. The explanation of her having failed to get more hits than she did . . . does not lie
in any inferiority of skill, but almost entirely to the fact that the range . . .
if exceptionally great for a 6-in gun, was almost fabulous for a 4.1-in."[88]
When two rounds exploded alongside *Mersey* the ship began to slip her
mooring but at 0740 a shell struck the monitor's fore 6-inch gun shield
and killed four men. *Severn*, now, firing alone, landed four shells, knocking out one of the light cruiser's guns and wounding Captain Looff on
the bridge. Apparently having two ships in action had confused the corrections. However, by late morning the spotter aircraft had to leave and
the fire on both sides diminished in accuracy. The British retired at 1530
having expended 633 shells. Their guns required recalibration after the
shock of so much fire.

On 11 July *Severn* and *Mersey* were back. *Mersey* anchored near the original firing position while *Severn* continued upstream. The monitors fired
separately to facilitate spotting. This proved effective as *Severn* engaged
at 1231 from 9,500 yards after being straddled by the German ship and
absorbing some splinter damage. She then closed to 8,800 yards, hit with
her eighth salvo, and was soon hitting regularly. At 1252 a shell detonated
Königsberg's aft magazine. *Mersey* then took over, closing to eight thousand
yards and continued to hit. At 1400, with ammunition expended, Looff,
who had been wounded again, ordered his ship scuttled.[89]

The last surviving auxiliary cruisers, *Prinz Eitel Friedrich* and *Kronprinz*
Wilhelm, had sought internment in the United States in the spring. The
total shipping sunk by the light cruisers and raiders up through April
1915 was sixty-nine merchant vessels totaling 280,000 GRT. This was
half the total losses inflicted by all causes and, as the case of *Königsberg* so
clearly demonstrated, even an immobile raider caused disruptions and
subtracted from British naval strength.[90]

4

1916: In Search of a Solution

We collected the dead and wounded. The Captain, Lieutenant Com-
mander C. R. Onslow, was still alive but died a short time after. There
was not much left of the others on the bridge which was put in sacks.
—ABLE SEAMAN FRED KNIGHT, HMS *ONSLAUGHT*

Overview

The year 1916 was a time of deep frustration for the belligerents as they seemed caught in a conflict they could not end. The Germans at Verdun, the Italians in the battles of Isonzo, the British at the Somme, the Russians in Galicia—all fruitlessly sought victory in meat-grinder offensives that settled nothing. The Central Powers conquered Romania and the Russians most of Armenia but these were peripheral victories that brought the war itself no closer to a decision. The Entente blockade was beginning to affect the economies of the Central Powers but not to the extent where their ability to wage war suffered.

By the beginning of 1916 protests from neutrals forced the German government to restrict submarine attacks on merchant ships, thus evis-cerating the Kaiserliche Marine's undersea campaign. Admiral Rein-hard Scheer, who assumed command of the fleet from the terminally ill Admiral Pohl on 18 January 1916, wanted to use submarines against commerce, but if they had to operate with restrictions he preferred they support the High Seas Fleet instead. Scheer believed Pohl had been too passive; he planned to reinvigorate the naval war with raids by light forces and Zeppelins, bombardments of British coastal towns with the entire fleet in close support, offensive mining, and strikes against the British–Scandinavian trade routes. He quickly won the kaiser's approval for his program.[1]

Scheer's policies led to the massive Battle of Jutland in May. While the results of the battle did not dissuade Scheer from undertaking major fleet sorties in August and October, he concluded that a decisive victory over the Grand Fleet was unlikely and that only unrestricted submarine warfare could end the blockade of Germany and force Britain from the war.

Admiral Reinhard Scheer, commander of Germany's High Seas Fleet from January 1916. (Library of Congress)

Scheer's strategy kept his battleships concentrated in the North Sea; this, combined with the retirement of some old battleships and armored cruisers, left Germany's Baltic Squadron with fewer resources than in 1915. The navy's shift to the defensive in the Baltic was paralleled by the German army, which mostly kept to its trenches in the east as it began the Verdun offensive in the west. Meanwhile, the Russian fleet added new destroyers and submarines. With this and an early thaw, Russian warships reentered the Gulf of Riga in late April. The tsarist navy's greatest concern was to renew and extend its mine barriers and bolster its advanced mine/artillery positions. The navy also raided convoy routes from Sweden to Germany.

The sea superiority granted by its new dreadnoughts and large destroyers allowed Russia to dominate the Black Sea. In the first half of 1916 the Russian army attacked on the Caucasus front. The navy provided support including several small amphibious landings that were instrumental in advancing the front all the way to Trebizond by April. Later, after Romania's declaration of war, the Russians concentrated on laying mines off the Bosporus and the western coast of the Black Sea. These barrages greatly reduced the effectiveness of German submarines. The Russians also continued to interdict Ottoman traffic.

In the northern Adriatic, mines and submarines kept heavy ships port-bound while light forces patrolled aggressively and focused on harassment operations. In the south Montenegro's surrender in January 1916 rolled Entente observers and artillery back from the Austrians' southern base at Cattaro. Nonetheless, the Habsburg navy was unable to block the evacuation of the Serbian army and its subsequent transfer to Salonica, an effort that had begun in late 1915 and continued into 1916. The six reconstituted Serbian divisions thus rescued proved an important reinforcement to the front in Thessaly.

In the broader Mediterranean, the relative absence of neutral shipping allowed the Germans and Austrians to aggressively attack commerce, and their submarines based at Pola and Cattaro sank 944,766 GRT of shipping in the nine months from April to December, 51 percent of all ships sunk by German submarines worldwide.[7] Entente anti-submarine efforts included patrolled lanes and protected coastal routes but were ineffective. Thus, stiffening the Otranto Barrage became a priority for the Entente navies, while it became a more important target for the Austrians. The evacuation of Gallipoli, which the Entente completed on 9 February, also contributed to the focus of the Mediterranean naval war swinging back to the sea's central basin.

North Sea 1916

Admiral Scheer wanted to begin his new aggressive program with a destroyer raid in conjunction with a Zeppelin bombing attack on England. When bad weather and then a waxing moon forced cancellation of the Zeppelin component Scheer sent the destroyers on a night reconnaissance to the Dogger Bank. The battlecruisers provided distant support from the edge of the bight. The rest of the fleet remained in harbor with steam up.

The Dogger Bank Raid: 10 February, 2242–11 February, 0110

Conditions: Poor visibility

Missions: British, minesweeping; Germans, raid

British Force (Lieutenant-Commander Ronald C. Mayne): DS *Arabis★, Buttercup, Alyssum, Poppy.*

German Force (Corvette Captain Heinrich Schuur): II TBF: DD
   G101, G102, G104, B97, B111, B112, B109, B110, G103.

Twenty-five destroyers of the II, VI, and IX TBFs left the Jade in the late
afternoon of 10 February; however, fog delayed their passage through
the growing labyrinth of defensive minefields. Sailing in eight groups
across a twenty-five-mile front, they were north of Terschelling by 2108
with *Pillau, G42,* and *G85* behind in support. The night was particularly
dark and five of the groups had no contacts. II TBF, comprising the three
northernmost groups, had a more eventful time.

Room 40 deduced that an operation was in the works, but had little idea
of size or objective. The Admiralty ordered the Grand Fleet to sea on 9 February but then cancelled the sortie and put Jellicoe at two hours' notice the
following morning. By 2000 on 10 February, the Admiralty decided that
German light forces were going to raid the coast. In response it ordered
Beatty's battlecruisers to intercept the enemy on their return and dispatched
the Harwich Force to guard against a raid south of the Wash. It did not,
however, warn forces already at sea, fearing that such information broadcast to the many light units scattered across the North Sea would compro-
mise Room 40's sources. In the Admiralty's words: "Vessels at a distance from
their ports must take their chance."[3]

One such force was the newly formed Tenth Sloop Flotilla. It was out
sweeping a channel from Flamborough Head northeast toward Rosyth. At
dusk on the 10th Lieutenant-Commander Mayne detailed *Arabis* to spend
the night standing by a light buoy that marked the farthest point swept
while the others patrolled back and forth in the vicinity.

The sloops were heading toward the buoy when at 2230 the northernmost German group—the destroyers *G101, G102,* and *G104* commanded by Corvette Captain Heinrich Boest—spotted them and
came to a parallel course while trying to establish their identity. Boest
finally promoted the British sloops to *Arethusa*–class cruisers and his
ships launched three torpedoes at 2242 from less than two thousand
yards. However, an alert officer in *Buttercup* saw the flashes of the
launching charges and turned away. *Alyssum* and *Poppy* followed and
all torpedoes missed. Spotting the tracks, Mayne concluded an enemy
submarine was about.

Arabis, standing by the lighted buoy, next attracted Boest's attention. The German warships pumped out seven more torpedoes at her, starting at 2245, but despite a range of less than a thousand yards they all missed. Boest turned his force southeast and again encountered the other sloops at close range. His force fired and missed with two more torpedoes shortly after 2253. The three German destroyers then hauled back around to the northeast and reengaged *Arabis* at 2312 with two torpedoes and a barrage from their twelve 88-mm guns. *Arabis* replied with her two old 4.7-inch pieces. Her radio antenna and steering gear were shot away, but she was not otherwise harmed in the eight-minute action. Boest disappeared to the southeast; *Arabis* began repairs and returned to her station by the buoy.

Boest had radioed a sighting report and this brought a second destroyer formation to the scene: *B97*, *B111*, and *B112*, commanded by Corvette Captain Schuur. Schuur's group encountered to port the three sloops coming southwest. *B97* fired two torpedoes as the lines passed on opposite courses; the two destroyers following misidentified the sloops as destroyers, overestimated the range, and failed to fire. Schuur then turned east to rendezvous with Boest and the third group of II TBF ships (*B109*, *B110*, and *G103*, led by Corvette Captain Adolf Dithmar).

The three groups united at 0009 and returned to the light buoy. They attacked *Arabis* at 0102 with all weapons and hit with two torpedoes. This finally sent the ship to the bottom. The Germans rescued survivors under the light of starshell and then turned for home.

The Harwich Force stayed south in accordance with orders and never came within 120 miles of the action. On her return to port the cruiser *Arethusa* detonated a mine outside the harbor entrance laid by a submarine the night before. She beached and was a total loss. Beatty and Jellicoe sortied, but too late to catch the retiring Germans.

Although Scheer could claim a success for his first offensive sortie, it was a deeply unsatisfying one. His destroyer commanders consistently misidentified their targets and fired at least eighteen torpedoes at close ranges against slow targets for just two hits. They struggled to coordinate their forces and distinguish friend from foe. This confusion led to delays in attacking, and may have had some of II TBF dodging friendly torpedoes. The Germans would address these issues—particularly the matter of coordination—and the same trio of commanders would do much better in subsequent nocturnal engagements in the Dover Strait.

The British faced a difficult problem: concentrating their patrol forces enough to defeat an enemy foray, yet dispersing them enough to defend large areas. Room 40 could only help so much, as it was better able to predict when units of the High Seas Fleet were going to sea than what they would do once out. Direction finding of German radio transmissions could also help, but was dependent on the Germans broadcasting when under way and gave imprecise locations. The relative infrequency of the German raids posed its own problem, as patrols repeatedly assumed the raiders were friendly ships or single enemy submarines. Even when a ship or formation definitely spotted enemy raiders, poor communications frequently meant this information went nowhere.[4]

Action off the North Hinder Lightship: 20 March, 0756–0830

Conditions: Clear

Missions: British, raid; Germans, interception

British Forces (Commander W. deM. Egerton): DD *Lance*#, *Lookout*, *Lucifer*, *Linnet*.

German Forces: Flanders DDHF: DD *V47*+, *V68*#, *V69*.

Throughout 1916 Germany sent submarines, destroyers, and torpedo boats to its Flanders bases, allowing the naval forces there to assume a more aggressive posture. On 20 March, in an attempt to neutralize this growing threat, the Dover Patrol's Vice Admiral Bacon dispatched four minelayers escorted by two Harwich Force destroyer divisions to lay a series of barrages to shield the approaches to the Thames and the Straits of Dover. Seaplane carriers *Riviera* and *Vindex*, escorted by destroyers, would launch aircraft to attack the German seaplane base in Zeebrugge harbor while fifty land-based bombers attacked a nearby airfield.

The operation was delayed when one of the minelayers ran aground. Just before 0800 the 9th DF's *Lance*, *Lookout*, *Lucifer*, and *Linnet* were loitering five miles west of the North Hinder Lightship waiting for the minelaying to begin. A German reconnaissance seaplane out of Zeebrugge had already reported them at 0600 as two enemy destroyers apparently hunting a submarine. *V47*, *V68*, and *V69* sortied in response.

Map 4.1 Flanders Coast: 1916

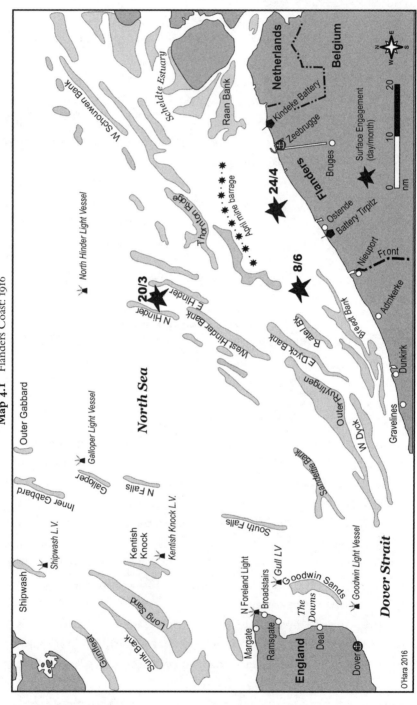

They spotted the intruders at 0738 and opened fire eighteen min-utes later.[5] The first notice the British had of the Germans was the splash of shellfire. *Lance* and *Linnet* came about to roughly parallel the enemy as *Lookout* and *Lucifer*, which had separated from their two sis-ters, sped to join the action. The Germans hit *Lance* but the action turned at 0825 when *Lookout* and *Lucifer* joined the fighting. Shortly thereafter a shell disabled *V68*'s forward gun. More German shells hit *Lance* but a round punched into *V47*'s bow in return. With that the Germans turned toward the Belgian coast. Commander Egerton "saw no advantages of continuing the action under these conditions," and turned for Harwich. His ship, *Lance*, had taken five direct hits and been damaged "somewhat severely." The rest of the British operation went as planned. The minelayers laid three fields and the bombers claimed they inflicted "considerable damage."[6]

The Hoyer Raid: 25 March, 2215–

Conditions: Poor visibility, heavy seas

Missions: British, transit; Germans, interception

British Force (Commodore Reginald Tyrwhitt): CL *Cleopatra*[+], *Undaunted*[#], *Penelope*, *Conquest*.

German Force (Captain Lieutenant Otto Paul): DD *G193*, *G194*★.

The British, frustrated by the impunity with which Zeppelins bombed southeast England, adopted the quixotic notion of using seaplanes to attack the large airships in their storage sheds. The planes needed to be launched within fifty miles of their target. They required weather calm enough to be lifted from their carriers onto the water without dam-age, but windy enough to permit take off with their bomb loads. If the planes could find the target they had only a few small bombs, crudely aimed, with which to hit it. Then, upon their return, they required good visibility over the carriers or they might miss their rendezvous, obliging the carriers and their escorts to search for them in close proximity to an alerted enemy. In short, conditions had to be perfect and even then suc-cess was unlikely.

Nonetheless, in June 1915 Commodore Tyrwhitt enthusiastically embraced a proposal to bomb Zeppelin sheds reported at Hoyer. Tyrwhitt completed his plans that November, but it took until the latter part of March 1916 for the weather to cooperate. Five light cruisers, two flotilla leaders, and sixteen destroyers were allocated to escort seaplane carrier *Vindex* across the mouth of Heligoland Bight to within forty miles of Hoyer. *Vindex* would lift seven seaplanes into the water, retrieve them after they had bombed the sheds, and withdraw with a small escort while the rest of the force covered their retreat across the bight. The battlecruisers would loiter to the north in case the Germans responded with capital ships.

Tyrwhitt left Harwich at 0400 on 24 March, while Beatty put out from the Firth of Forth with his battlecruisers and 1st DF (flotilla leader *Botha* and eleven *Acasta*-class destroyers) two hours later. Tyrwhitt arrived at the takeoff point in the northern bight at 0430 on the 25th. Five seaplanes struggled into the air at 0530. Two arrived over target to find that it was not a Zeppelin base. One pushed on and found the real base at Tondern a few miles east only to have its bomb release malfunction.

Two aircraft returned in deteriorating weather. *Vindex* recovered them at 0700 after which Tyrwhitt detached both flotilla leaders and half his destroyers to search for the three missing planes. At 0840 they found instead a German patrol: the armed trawlers *Otto Rudolf* and *Braunschweig*. The destroyers sank both within a half hour, but *Laverock* rammed *Medusa* while maneuvering through German smoke. *Laverock* suffered little harm but *Medusa* was holed in the engine room, dead in the water, and slowly settling. *Lightfoot* started towing her west at 12 knots as German seaplanes buzzed the formation.

The British were within a hundred miles of the main German base. Worse, the High Seas Fleet was in a position to respond. Its battlecruisers had just returned from the Baltic and were refueling, while a battleship squadron was off the Jade and the rest of the heavy ships were on three-hour notice for sea. Admiral Scheer learned of the raid at 0845. By 1245 he had ordered the battlecruisers, a light cruiser group, four torpedo boat flotillas, and a battleship squadron to head north toward Tyrwhitt. He directed another light cruiser group and two more torpedo boat flotillas supported by battleships to probe west after he received a false report of destroyers in that direction. Scheer's ships left on their assignments in a scramble, but the northern force with its five battleships and four battlecruisers was more than enough to crush Tyrwhitt and probably Beatty as well.

Fortunately for Tyrwhitt, Room 40 was listening in on the German radio traffic and at 1228 advised him to withdraw immediately. At 1820 the Admiralty reported strong forces in chase but at 1940 *Medusa*'s towline parted in rising seas. At this point the 1st DF, running low on fuel after a long high-speed run, had to turn for home. Without his destroyers, Beatty had to be cautious as his battlecruisers were in an area exposed to submarine and destroyer attacks.

Taking stock of the deteriorating situation, Tyrwhitt ordered *Medusa* sunk at 2015; at 2105 he decided that the rising seas would prevent her crew from being taken off and instead instructed she be left to drift with no lights in the hope that he could return for her the next day. In an example of order-counterorder-disorder, Tyrwhitt's second signal reached the destroyers escorting *Medusa* just after they had removed her crew. They set her adrift unmanned while Tyrwhitt turned north to elude pursuit.

At 1915 the Germans divided seventeen destroyers from the I and VI TBF into five groups and sent them northwest in a scouting line backed by *Regensburg*, *G195*, *G37*, and the five light cruisers of IV Scouting Group. The scouts were headed through the same area as Tyrwhitt's force but by 2110 the seas were so heavy the flotilla craft could no longer use their weapons. They were ordered to turn about.

G192, *G196*, *G193*, and *G194* formed the southernmost segment of the scouting line. When the withdrawal order came only *G193* and *G194* heard it. While *G192* and *G196* pounded on, the other two put about directly into the path of Tyrwhitt's cruisers. At 2215 *Cleopatra* spotted coal sparks off her port bow and *G193* saw the cruisers to starboard. Both ships maneuvered violently. *Cleopatra* and *G193* missed each other but the cruiser smashed through *G194* and was then rammed astern by *Undaunted*.

Cleopatra was slightly damaged but *G194* sank and water flooded *Undaunted*'s forward compartments. She shored up the foremost watertight bulkhead, but could only make 6 knots in the pounding head sea without risking the bulkhead's collapse.

Although the British had another cripple on their hands, heavy seas defeated the German pursuit. After midnight the weather was so violent even the heavy ships could only work their guns to leeward. With that, Scheer finally abandoned the chase.

Medusa became a Flying Dutchman, sighted occasionally over the next few days. A Dutch trawler captain finally snared the derelict on 3 April. He tried to bring her to Terschelling for salvage but she foundered on a sandbank off the harbor. The toll for the British was one destroyer lost, a light cruiser badly damaged, and a light cruiser and destroyer lightly damaged against a German destroyer and two trawlers sunk. Had the weather been better, British losses could have been far worse.[7]

The Belgian Barrage: 24 April, 1445–1655

Conditions: Clear

Missions: British, patrol; Germans, interception

British Forces: BM *Prince Eugene, General Wolfe*; DD *Medea*[#] (Commander G. L. D. Gibbs), *Melpomene*[#], *Murray*[+], *Milne*.

German Force: Flanders DDHF: DD *V67, V68, V47*.

On 24 April the Dover Patrol began another major operation as drifters and minelayers started laying the first of what was to be eighteen miles of deep minefields and moored, mine-studded nets parallel to the Belgian coast.

Minecraft being hidden by a smokescreen. This was a common scene in the waters of Heligoland Bight and off the shores of Flanders. (Library of Congress)

At 1445 *V67*, *V68*, and *V47* attacked the drifters attending the nets. The Harwich Force destroyers *Medea*, *Melpomene*, and *Murray* saw the enemy from nine thousand yards and set off through a gap in the nets to intervene. In response, the Germans turned west-southwest down the coast. Fifteen minutes later, with the range at 7,500 yards, they opened fire. On board *Murray* the captain saw "orange flashes rippling down their sides." The initial salvos fell short, but the second group "splashed into the sea all around us, projectiles seeming to whir and to whine in all directions." The range fell to five thousand yards over forty minutes of firing. "The sea seemed to be vomiting spray fountains almost as if some giant was flinging handful after handful of huge pebbles into a pond. It seemed surprising that we were not hit." At 1540, in a Parthian shot, one of the last 10.5-cm rounds fired by the Zeebrugge flotilla punctured *Melpomene*'s hull below the waterline and her engine room began to flood. With this, and being within five miles of the German-occupied coast, the British ships came about.[8]

As the destroyers turned stern to shore, "at least five miles of the coast started to wink in and out with red gun flashes." These signified German shore batteries opening an intense barrage.[9] The destroyers made smoke, but a 15-cm shell punched through *Murray* without exploding. Worse, *Melpomene*'s flooding finally reached the point where she lost all power. *Milne*, which had been hunting a submarine and had just rejoined the force, came alongside to pass a towline only to have it entangle a propeller shaft. *Medea* then closed on *Melpemene*'s other side while *Murray* went ahead to locate a gap in the nets.

The German destroyers observed the British situation and at 1630 renewed their attack. *Murray* covered the others with smoke while dueling with the Germans at ranges from eight down to five thousand yards. *Medea* joined *Murray* as *Milne* and *Melpomene* struggled toward the nets. The Germans shot well: three hits moderately damaged *Medea* before the 12-inch guns of the monitors *Prince Eugene* and *General Wolfe* rumbled into action at 1655. When giant geysers began splashing nearby the Germans disengaged. Admiralty staff noted that the Germans fired faster and that their 10.5-cm guns outranged British 4-inch weapons.[10]

The Lowestoft Raid: 25 April, 0430–0456
Conditions: Clear
Missions: British, interception; Germans, bombardment

British Forces (Commodore Reginald Tyrwhitt): Harwich Force: CL
   Cleopatra, Conquest#, Penelope. 9th DF: DL *Lightfoot*; DD *Terma-*
   gant, Manly, Meteor, Mastiff, Mansfield, Matchless, Mentor. 10th DF:
   DL *Nimrod*; DD *Loyal, Laertes#, Linnet, Lochinvar, Legion, Lassoo,*
   Lysander, Miranda.
German Forces (Rear Admiral Friedrich Bödicker): BC *Lützow, Derf-*
   flinger, Moltke, Von der Tann. II Scouting Group (Commodore
   Ludwig Reuter): CL *Frankfurt, Pillau, Elbing, Wiesbaden, Regens-*
   *burg, Rostock.*VI TBF: DD *G41, V44, S49, V43, G86, G87, V69, V45,*
   V46, S50, G37. IX TBF: DD *V28, V27, V26, S36, S51, S52, V30, S34,*
   S33, V29, S35.

Admiral Scheer undertook a major fleet operation in late April to support
the Irish Rebellion and in the perennial German hope of isolating and
destroying a portion of the British fleet. He planned a battlecruiser bombardment of Lowestoft and Yarmouth while the High Seas Fleet trailed
seventy miles behind. The fleet cleared the Jade by 1400 on 24 April but
did not get far before *Seydlitz*, the battlecruiser force's flagship, struck a
mine. This forced Rear Admiral Bödicker, temporarily replacing an ill
Vice Admiral Hipper, to transfer to *Lützow* while *Seydlitz* turned back.

Room 40 got indications of a German operation but the Admiralty
initially considered the evidence ambiguous and only ordered the fleet
to two hours' notice at 1550. The decryptions regarding *Seydlitz's* plight
finally prompted an alert. The delay meant that the Grand Fleet and Battlecruiser Force did not sail until 1905 on the 24th—too late to intercept, as it turned out.

The Harwich Force also got away late, sailing shortly after midnight on
24 April with three light cruisers and two destroyer flotillas. Shortly before
departure Tyrwhitt received an Admiralty signal giving a position and course
for Bödicker's battlecruisers that pointed to a coastal bombardment. Tyrwhitt's original orders sent him northeast to act as bait for a British submarine ambush. He deduced from the signal that his best chance of intercepting
the Germans was to steam directly up the coast, so that is what he did.

At 0350, just before dawn with the moon still in the sky on what
would be a fine clear day, Harwich Force scouts spotted the light cruisers
of II Scouting Group and their train of destroyers ten miles to the north.

Shortly thereafter the German battlecruisers emerged into view from behind the screen. Tyrwhitt reversed course and tried to lure the Germans south, but Bödicker stuck to his mission. The battlecruisers shelled Lowestoft for six minutes starting at 0411, expending thirty-four 30.5-cm and seventy-seven 15-cm rounds. *Lützow* sank an armed patrol boat with a 15-cm salvo at 0432. They then targeted Yarmouth but ceased fire after a few rounds when they heard gunfire to the south.

The Harwich Force had continued south until 0415 when gun-thunder made Tyrwhitt realize the Germans were conducting a bombardment. He turned west and then ran due north along the coast. The German light cruisers had been covering Bödicker to the southeast. The British spotted *Rostock* and *Elbing* and engaged at 0430 from 14,000 yards. According to the report of *Conquest*, "about 28 rounds were fired, but no hits were observed; owing to the poor light a good many shots were not spotted."[11] The two Germans held fire and turned to concentrate with the rest of II Scouting Group. Then, once all six German light cruisers had united and the battlecruisers—still out of sight to the north—were headed southeast, they replied. The range was long, visibility poor, and neither side hit.

That changed when Bödicker's heavies hove into sight at 0445. Tyrwhitt immediately spun around to the south as *Lützow* and *Derfflinger* engaged, "firing," as Tyrwhitt reported "rapidly and with much precision." Over seven minutes from 0449 to 0456 they shot sixty 30.5-cm rounds at ranges from 13,800 to 15,300 yards. *Von der Tann* and *Moltke* contributed several dozen 28-cm rounds. Two shells struck *Conquest* at 0451, bursting in the upper ammunition lobby, and three more ricocheted into the flagship cutting through the central funnel, hitting the main mast, and striking in almost the same place as the direct hits. "A considerable fire broke out on the main deck and on the upper deck . . . the 6-in cordite charges in two ready cases on the after superstructure caught fire and burned with a fierce flame until expended . . . the lobby was completely wrecked and all the men in it killed instantaneously." Fortunately the ship's speed was largely unaffected. The battlecruisers also targeted the British destroyers with their 15-cm batteries, hitting *Laertes* and destroying a boiler. Tyrwhitt ordered the destroyers to scatter and make smoke. At 0500, with the British on the run and largely invisible in the smoke, Bödicker turned for home.[12]

German destroyer *V150*. German flotilla craft had low profiles consistent with their
intended role as torpedo attack craft. This class was the first to have turbines and an
88-mm weapon mounted on the forecastle. (Wiki Public Domain)

Once the smoke cleared and Tyrwhitt realized the Germans were withdrawing he steamed to regain touch. He had the German smoke cloud in
sight when, at 0845, the Admiralty ordered him back to base. With no British capital ships in position to intercept, there was no point in continuing.
But any ship in the North Sea was always at some risk; *UB29* torpedoed and
damaged *Penelope* on her way home. *Conquest* did not return to service until
August while *Penelope* was back with the Harwich Force in September.[13]

Battle of Jutland: 31 May, 1530–1 June, 0240
Conditions: Variable
Missions: British, interception; Germans, interception
British Forces: Grand Fleet (Admiral John Jellicoe): BBx28, BCx9,
    CAx8, CLx26, DLx5, DDx73, MLx1, CVSx1.
German Forces: High Seas Fleet (Admiral Reinhard Scheer): BBx16,
    BCx5, OBBx6, CLx11, DDx61.

This study presents a bare outline of the Battle of Jutland; interested
readers will find a number of comprehensive accounts listed in the
bibliography.

As a part of Admiral Scheer's more aggressive policy the High Seas Fleet sortied in full strength once again at the end of May, still hoping to trap a portion of the Grand Fleet. This time, however, Room 40 provided enough information for the Grand Fleet to sail before the Germans even weighed anchor. The opposing battlecruiser forces made contact at 1530 on 31 May. Vice Admiral Beatty confronted Vice Admiral Hipper's five battlecruisers with six battlecruisers and four *Queen Elizabeth*–class superdreadnoughts, although the battleships were initially out of range. Hipper ran south, leading Beatty toward the German main body. Despite being outnumbered, the Germans shot more effectively and faster in better light conditions than their foe. They sank two British battlecruisers, *Indefatigable* at 1602 and *Queen Mary* at 1626, with hits that caused catastrophic explosions, and inflicted heavy damage on Beatty's flagship, *Lion*, while losing no ships of their own. Mutual destroyer attacks at 1630 cost each side two destroyers. A British destroyer torpedoed *Seydlitz* but this blow caused relatively light damage.

By 1638, Beatty's screen had Admiral Scheer's main force in sight. Beatty wheeled his ships around and ran north, with Beatty now leading Hipper and Scheer toward the Grand Fleet. A combination of improving visibility conditions for the British and the shooting of the *Queen Elizabeth*s resulted in mounting damage to *Lützow*, *Von der Tann*, *Derfflinger*, and *Seydlitz* as the formations churned north. At 1736 light cruisers from Hipper's screen ran into cruisers of the 3rd BCS, on the way to reinforce Beatty, with the result that *Chester* was heavily damaged and *Wiesbaden* disabled. A torpedo attack on the 3rd BCS by two German destroyer flotillas resulted in only the loss of a British destroyer.

As Beatty, Hipper, and Scheer converged, Admiral Jellicoe needed to decide how to deploy the Grand Fleet's battleships from their cruising formation of six four-ship columns into a single battle line. Despite inadequate information, Jellicoe made the right decision and placed the Grand Fleet across the head of the High Seas Fleet in a direction that gave his forces good gunnery conditions while denying them to the enemy.

The Grand Fleet's battle line opened fire at 1817 and shooting becoming general along the line by 1830. Nonetheless, the Germans scored some successes after 1800: they hit *Warspite* thirteen times when she lost steering control and turned in two involuntary circles within range of the advancing German line, and they savaged a formation of armored cruisers, sinking *Defender* with all hands and crippling *Warrior* and *Black Prince*. Still, Scheer was in a desperate situation. By 1830 the German ships were being punished but could see little but a line of gun flashes in the mist ahead. The 3rd BCS, ahead and to the south of the main battle line was shooting with particular effectiveness against the German battlecruisers until *Derfflinger* hit flagship *Invincible* at 1832. She became the third British battlecruiser to explode catastrophically. At 1833 Scheer ordered a "battle turn away," a difficult maneuver in which all battleships in the German line individually reversed course. The Germans did this successfully, removing themselves from immediate danger. When Jellicoe realized Scheer had turned, he set course south to cut the Germans off from their bases.

At 1855 Scheer, for reasons that are not clear, turned his force north once more. He quickly encountered the Grand Fleet, but under conditions even worse than before. During this phase, the British scored thirty-seven large-caliber hits, pounding *Derfflinger*, *Lützow*, and *Grosser Kurfürst*, while the Germans landed only two hits on *Colossus*. At 1910 Scheer ordered another battle turn away.

As the High Seas Fleet reversed course German destroyers launched a mass torpedo attack. Jellicoe ordered the British battle line to turn away from the torpedoes and this ended contact between the main fleets. Beatty had a brief engagement with Hipper before nightfall, but a general night battleship action had no part in Jellicoe's plans. The British admiral intended to block what he considered Scheer's most likely route back to base with the aim of renewing the battle the following day. Scheer erased the consequences of some of his questionable decisions and outguessed Jellicoe, cutting behind the British line to make directly for Horns Reef. Room 40 gave Jellicoe Scheer's course, but prior miscues led Jellicoe to doubt the information, while the Admiralty failed to forward to the admiral all the intelligence it possessed.

Admiral Jellicoe positioned the bulk of his flotillas to protect the rear of the fleet's main body from nocturnal attack. The High Seas Fleet swung through these units as it cut from west to east behind the Grand Fleet. The first contact came at 2150 and a series of actions resulted that ultimately involved five light cruisers, three flotilla leaders, and thirty-eight destroyers on the British side and twelve dreadnoughts, four predreadnoughts, seven light cruisers, and eight destroyers for the Germans, lasting until 0240 on 1 June. Many of the German destroyers had expended their torpedoes in the day's fighting and few were in position to make contact with the Grand Fleet, now cruising ahead and to the east of the Germans. The powerful II TBF was out of the fight entirely, hauling its torpedoes home via the Skaggerrak. British flotilla tactics and training emphasized defense against enemy torpedo attacks on the battle line, while German tactics and training were geared to the delivery of those attacks. Now the roles were reversed.

In the course of the night the British sank predreadnought *Pommern* with all hands, as well as three light cruisers; they lost one flotilla leader, four destroyers, and the damaged armored cruiser *Black Prince* when she blundered into the German battle line and was quickly annihilated. Most importantly, these engagements neither deflected Scheer from his course to Horns Reef nor gave Jellicoe useful information about the location of the German battleships. British battleships at the rear of the Grand Fleet's formation saw the gunfire and glimpsed the High Seas Fleet, but not one reported their contacts. The few sighting reports made by the British light forces were not received by the flagship. Scheer was home and safe by the morning of 1 June.

In summary, the Grand Fleet lost three battlecruisers and three armored cruisers (*Warrior* foundering on the morning of 1 June), a flotilla leader, *Tipperary*, and seven destroyers: *Ardent, Fortune, Nestor, Nomad, Shark, Sparrowhawk,* and *Turbulent.* Four dreadnoughts, three battlecruisers, three light cruisers, one flotilla leader, and nine destroyers received enough damage to require time in dock. The High Seas Fleet lost *Lützow, Pommern,* the light cruisers *Elbing, Frauenlob, Rostock,* and *Wiesbaden* and five destroyers: *S35, V4, V27, V29,* and *V48.* They suffered significant damage to four battlecruisers, five dreadnoughts, one predreadnought, five light cruisers, and five destroyers.

After the battle was over, the Grand Fleet remained overwhelmingly superior in strength but the High Seas Fleet was still potent. If anything, the battle showed the difficulty of converting superiority at sea into decisive victory. Jellicoe's conduct of the battle was conservative and the major criticism leveled against him boils down to a charge that he failed to seize several opportunities to win a decisive victory. This assumes that these opportunities actually existed, and while they seem apparent in hindsight, they were not so obvious at the time, given the poor visibility and poor information upon which Jellicoe based his decisions. There was, however, one thing Jellicoe knew for certain— he did not need to gamble. This informed all of Jellicoe's choices. He himself emphasized "the necessity for *not leaving anything to chance in a fleet action.*"[14] [Emphasis in original.]

The observed ineffectiveness of British armor-piercing shells led to frantic attempts to improve them. The Germans fired faster (twenty seconds on the average between rounds versus thirty for the British) and more accurately (3.39 percent hit rate versus 2.75 for the British). Even more troubling for the British was the loss of three battlecruisers to magazine explosions—likely due to unstable propellant combined with lax safety procedures in the battlecruisers and perhaps in the Grand Fleet as a whole. Jutland also highlighted the British inferiority at night combat.[15]

The High Seas Fleet would sortie again in August and October 1916, but only the August operation, a sweep to the English coast and a planned bombardment of Sunderland, created any chance for a general action. In the event, although Jellicoe got good warning of the German operation, a minefield scare and a picket line of German submarines delayed his progress. Scheer turned away from the Grand Fleet in the mistaken belief that he could fall on an isolated British force to the south. When this proved illusory, he turned for home without conducting the planned bombardment.

Action off Ostend: 8 June, 0525–0600

Conditions: Clear

Missions: British, patrol; Germans, interception

British Forces: BM *Lord Clive*; DD *Crusader*, Tribal–class DDx4.

German Forces: Flanders DDHF (Captain Lieutenant Georg Waitz): DD *V67*[#], *V68*, *V47*. II TBF (Frigate Captain Heinrich Schuur): DD *G101*, *G102*, *G104*, *B97*, *B111*, *B112*, *B109*, *B110*, *G103*.

In June Admiral Scheer decided to reinforce German forces in Flanders with the II TBF. Vice Admiral Ludwig Schröder, commander of

Marinekorps Flandern, planned to combine the flotilla's arrival with an ambush of Entente patrol forces off the Belgian coast. He sent *V67*, *V68*, and *V47* to sea on 8 June with orders to engage enemy destroyers and lure them north toward the arriving flotilla.

At first, things went as planned. At 0525 the Zeebrugge group spotted the Tribal-class destroyer *Crusader* and four others of the same type and engaged them at ten thousand yards. However, Frigate Captain Schuur, who had been loitering north of the fight's location, delayed II TBF's intervention by dodging southeast through a gap in the net barriers before heading southwest toward the enemy. Making matters worse, the Tribals did not obligingly run northeast into the trap but instead turned northwest at 0530 and southwest five minutes later. At 0552 the monitor *Lord Clive* joined the action from the west and hit *V67* in an oil tank between her boiler rooms, bringing her to a halt. As *V47* took her stricken sister in tow, II TBF finally arrived. The Zeebrugge detachment covered the area with smoke while the British Tribals broke contact and retreated north, a few having received minor damage. *V67* eventually returned to base under her own power, but that result was hardly the victory Schröder had planned. Moreover, the Admiralty now knew that II TBF was at Zeebrugge and reinforced the Dover Patrol accordingly.[16]

Action off the Hook of Holland: 23 July, 0015–0250

Conditions: Variable visibility, with squalls

Missions: British, patrol; Germans, minelaying

British Forces: North Hinder Force (Commodore Reginald Tyrwhitt): CL *Carysfort*; DD *Mentor*, *Manly*, *Mastiff*, *Mansfield*. Maas Force (Captain Percy Royds): CL *Canterbury*; DD *Melpomene*[+], *Morris*, *Matchless*, *Milne*.

German Force (Corvette Captain Dithmar): II TBF: DD *B97*, *B112*, *B109*, *B110*, *B111*, *G101*, *G103*, *G104*[+].

In June 1916 the British government concluded a trade deal with the Netherlands calculated to divert Dutch products to England rather than Germany. To protect this trade, the Harwich Force established regular patrols between Dutch and English ports. In turn, Marinekorps Flandern attempted to disrupt this traffic.[17]

Eight destroyers of II TBF left Zeebrugge on the night of 22 July to lay a small minefield by the North Hinder Light Vessel. *B111* carried the mines while the others covered. The Harwich Force was also out that night; *Carysfort* and four destroyers were patrolling by North Hinder Light Vessel near mid-crossing, and light cruiser *Canterbury* with four destroyers was off the Maas Light Vessel by the Dutch coast.

The North Hinder group spotted II TBF at 0015 on 23 July six thousand yards away. *Carysfort* closed to four thousand and opened fire just as *B111* was laying her mines. The attack surprised the Germans, but the dark night, smoke, and a providential rain squall allowed them to break contact. Captain Dithmar made no attempt to counterattack but instead steered for Zeebrugge. Anticipating this move, Tyrwhitt ordered the Maas Force to intercept.

Melpomene saw II TBF at 0145. At 0215 she opened fire from eight thousand yards. By that time *Melpomene* and *Morris* had separated from *Matchless* and *Milne*, which fell behind. *Melpomene* closed to three thousand yards before a combination of smoke from Dithmar's vessels and Royds' recall ended the action at 0250. The Germans hit *Melpomene* once, killing one man and wounding two, while a near miss wounded four of *G104*'s men. Two Dutch merchantmen ran onto *B111*'s minefield in the following days. II TBF returned to Wilhelmshaven at the end of July after slightly less than two months in Zeebrugge, having accomplished little.[18]

First Battle of Dover Strait: 26 October, 2035–27 October, 0020

Conditions: Clear, moonless

Missions: British, patrol; Germans, raid

British Forces (Vice Admiral Reginald Bacon): Patrol: DD *Flirt*★ (Lieutenant R. Kellett†). Dover Group (Commander H. Oliphant): DD *Viking, Mohawk*#, *Tartar, Nubian*★, *Cossack, Amazon*#. Dunkirk Group (Commander R. A. Hornell): DD *Laforey, Lucifer, Laurel, Liberty*. Downs Group (Lieutenant-Commander A. Scott): DD *Lawford, Lark*, L Class DDx2.

German Forces: Group Göhle (Corvette Captain Herbert Göhle): DD *V79, V80, S60, S51, S52, S36*. Group Tillessen (Corvette Captain Werner Tillessen): DD *V30, V28, V26, S34, S33*. Group Michelsen

(Commodore Andres Michelsen): DD *V71*, *V73*, *V81*, *G88*, *V67*, *V68*, *V47*. Group Hollmann (Corvette Captain Wilhelm Hollmann): DD *S53*, *S55*, *S54*, *G42*, *V70*, *G91*[+].

Scheer sent III and IX TBFs to Zeebrugge on 23 October. Vice Admiral Schröder planned to use them on the night of 26 October to raid the Dover Barrage and cross-Channel shipping lanes. The barrage, intended to keep enemy submarines from entering the Channel, had been started in September and was scheduled for completion in December. It consisted of a series of deep minefields and mined net barriers across the Dover Straits. Drifters, backed by a few larger ships, tended the nets and patrolled the barrier. On the night of the raid there were twenty-three drifters in four divisions: the 8th between Buoys 0A and 5A; the 10th between 5A and 10A; the 16th between 10A and 15A; and the 12th between 15A and 20A. Supporting them were the trawler *H. E. Stroud* near 4A and the yacht *Ombra* near 11A. The two support boats had light guns and wireless, while the drifters carried only rifles.[19]

The Admiralty knew one destroyer flotilla had transferred to Zeebrugge, but had no inkling of Schröder's plan. The Dover Patrol's Vice Admiral Bacon was more concerned about a German raid on shipping in the Downs or a German landing on the Belgian coast than a foray against the barrage, and his dispositions reflected those concerns.

Learning from experience, Schröder deployed his raiders in four widely separated formations each of five to seven destroyers so that any vessel they sighted could be safely considered unfriendly. Groups Göhle and Tillessen would pass through the barrage first and strike into the English Channel. Groups Michelsen and Hollmann would follow thirty minutes later and roll up the barrage patrol line.[20]

The Germans left port at 1930 on 26 October. It was a clear, moonless night. The English Channel groups slipped through the barrage slightly behind schedule. Group Tillessen glided by the elderly destroyer *Flirt* at 2035; *Flirt* challenged but when the Germans repeated her signal she let them pass and broadcast no warning. Group Göhle kept to the English side of the Channel and after 2200 accosted the transport *The Queen* (1,676 GRT). Göhle sent over a boarding party and gave the crew three minutes to abandon ship. His ships then opened fire

Map 4.2 Battle in the Dover Strait: 27 October 1916

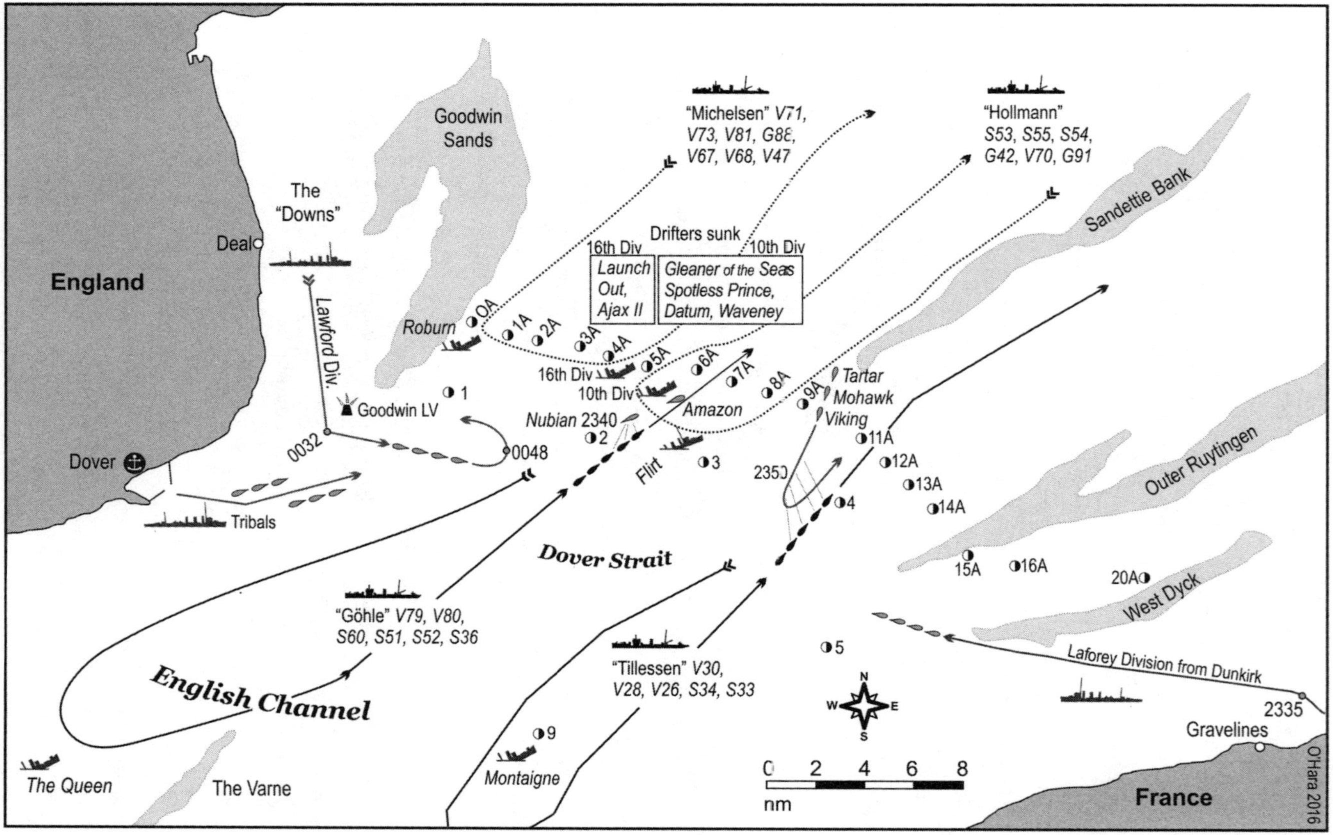

O'Hara 2016

France

Gravelines

2335

Laforey Division from Dunkirk

West Dyck

20A

Outer Ruytingen

16A

15A

14A

13A

12A

11A

"Hollmann" S53, S54, S54, S55, S55, G42, V70, G91

Sandettie Bank

"Michelsen" V71, V73, V81, G8E, V67, V68, V47

Drifters sunk

6th Div	10th Div
Launch Out, Ajax II	Gleaner of the Sea, Spotless Prince, Datum, Waveney

10th Div

Amazon

Tartar
Mohawk
Viking

16

8A

7A

6A

5A

4A

3A

2A

1A

0A

16th Div

Nubian 2340

2

Flirt

3

4

2350

5

"Tillessen" V30, V28, V26, S34, S33

Dover Strait

Montaigne

9

N W E S

0 2 4 6 8
nm

Goodwin Sands

Roburn

1

0048

Goodwin LV

The "Downs"

Lawford Div.

Deal

0032

Tribals

Dover ✠

"Göhle" V79, V80, S60, S51, S52, S36

England

English Channel

The Varne

The Queen

and *S60* torpedoed the transport, which sank six hours later. Group Tillessen cruised along the French shore sinking the French auxiliary patrol trawler *Montaigne* (226 GRT) and severely damaging the fishery protection boat *Albatros I*. Group Michelsen encountered the 10th Drifter Division southwest of Buoy 6A at 2110. After circling around the group, the German destroyers illuminated and opened fire, quickly dispatching *Datum*, *Gleaner of the Sea*, and *Spotless Prince*, and leaving *Waveney* in flames. Only the leader, *Paradox*, escaped.

From her position to the east *Ombra* saw the gunfire. She broadcast a warning at 2120 and tried to shepherd the drifters of the 16th Division away from danger. *Flirt* arrived upon the scene at 2130 and turned on her searchlight to reveal *Waveney* "enveloped in smoke and steam and much shattered by shell fire." She lowered a boat to rescue survivors. Captain Kellett saw destroyers nearby and assumed they were French vessels. In fact it was Group Hollmann. As soon as *Flirt's* boat was away the Germans opened fire at point-blank range and sank the destroyer with all hands, save the six men in her whaler. Group Hollmann continued northwest and struck the 16th Drifter Division, destroying *Launch Out* and *Ajax II*. At 2210 Group Michelsen, which had swept west along the line of buoys, encountered boats of the 8th Drifter Division about a mile and a half southwest of the barrage's western end. This group sank *Roburn* and damaged one other drifter but did not linger as they were close to British bases, and plans required them to be away before the two English Channel groups returned. Their only damage was a bent stem on *G91*, caused when she rammed *Roburn*.[21]

Ombra's warning sparked several responses. At 2150 Bacon ordered the six Tribal–class destroyers at Dover to intervene. However, it took time to leave the congested harbor and the ships sailed as they were able. *Viking*, *Mohawk*, and *Tartar* left by the western entrance and headed east at 25 knots. *Nubian*, *Cossack*, and *Amazon* exited by the eastern entrance at 2222 and steered toward the sound of gunfire. *Nubian* worked up to 30 knots but *Cossack*, which was older and slower, fell behind and lost touch. Four L class destroyers in the Downs, headed by *Lawford*, and another four at Dunkirk, led by *Laforey*, also sailed. The *Laforey* group received its orders at 2155 but the *Lawford* group did not get started until after midnight because it believed the initial alert referred to an airship raid. The Tribals arrived at their destination near *Flirt*'s sinking point at various times and then, not finding any enemy vessels, turned southwest.

Nubian was steering west-southwest intending to intercept the enemy destroyers reported to have attacked *The Queen* but this group, Group Göhle in fact, sailing northeast, sighted her first. Then, at 2340 when *Nubian* spotted the Germans, she misidentified the dark silhouettes as belonging to the *Lawford* group. She maneuvered to avoid a collision and flashed a challenge. The Germans answered with gunfire, riddling the British destroyer's port side as they ran past. *Nubian* swung to port trying to ram the last ship in the German column but as she was turning a torpedo smacked her under the bridge. The oil tanks ignited and a large fire engulfed the ship's forward section. *Nubian*'s wreck eventually drifted ashore. Her stern section was later attached to the bow section of her sister *Zulu*, which lost her stern on a mine, to make a new ship, *Zubian*.

Minutes later Group Göhle encountered *Amazon*, which had been following *Nubian* at a distance. Just like *Nubian* she mistook the Germans for friendly L Class destroyers; when they started shooting the British captain believed it was friendly fire and signaled the challenge. The German column steamed past, blasting *Amazon* and disabling her aft gun. An *Amazon* crewman stationed in the after magazine described the scene: "Suddenly there was an explosion, as the enemy got a direct hit on the gun platform above, hitting a case of cartridges which had just been passed up, setting fire to the gun platform, killing or wounding the gun crew, and scattering blazing cordite into the magazine flat below. . . . I shouted 'magazine flat on fire' and heard a lone voice from one of the gun's crew say 'put it out you silly bugger.'"[22] Another German round exploded in the after boiler room and disabled two boilers. The Germans also hit *H. E. Stroud,* which was nearby, killing her skipper. Group Göhle continued past the barrier near Buoy 6A and returned home undamaged.

At 2350 as Group Tillessen was approaching Buoy 12A, they sighted *Viking, Mohawk,* and *Tartar* off the port bow on an opposite course. For the third time the British challenged and the Germans, passing rapidly up the British column's port side, fired. A shell struck *Mohawk* and jammed her helm. She skewed out of line to port obstructing

Viking, which was in the process of coming about to bring her for-ward-mounted 6-inch gun to bear. The British ships fired only a few ineffectual rounds before the Germans disappeared to the north, pass-ing the barrier near Buoy 11A. *Viking* chased for a half hour before giving it up as a bad job.

The German raid accounted for one transport, one patrol boat, seven drifters, and two destroyers sunk or beached, and damage to two drifters and two destroyers. It is not surprising that individual vessels patrolling the barrage had been ineffective, as they were deployed to deal with soli-tary submarines. More concerning were the failures of the reserve forces intended to defend against raiders. They met the enemy three times and were worsted three times.[23]

This action was hardly the first occasion British night recognition sys-tems had proven deficient. The Germans used colored lights on their masts for night identification, while the British still relied on flashing blinkers to challenge and reply. The latter system took time and invited ambiguous results. It would continue to bedevil British night operations, where the Germans would consistently demonstrate better skills in tell-ing friend from foe.[24]

Raid on Dutch Shipping: 2 November, 0700–

Conditions: Clear

Missions: British, interception; Germans, raid

British Forces (Commodore Reginald Tyrwhitt): CL *Cleopatra, Con-quest, Centaur, Aurora, Penelope, Undaunted.*

German Forces (Corvette Captain Hollmann): IX TBF: DD *V79, V80, S60, S51, S52, S36.*

Pleased with the results of its first raid, Marinekorps Flandern planned a second operation for the end of October. III TBF and Flanders DDHF would reprise their role of attacking the barrage's patrol line, while IX TBF would strike for Margate and the Downs, where Entente shipping typically collected for the night. The weather however did not cooper-ate, forcing a delay until 1 November. When an intercepted radio mes-sage alerted the British to the impending danger they promptly recalled the Dover and Nore auxiliary patrols, directed transport ships in the

Channel to make for the closest harbor, and began to concentrate forces. The Germans in turn eavesdropped on the British messages generated by the intercepted German radio traffic. This, plus reports of strong enemy forces at Gravelines, prompted Marinekorps Flandern to cancel the participation of III TBF and Flanders DDHF, instead sending IX TBF to raid the Netherlands–England shipping lanes by Schouwen Bank. The British, however, intercepted the changes to the German plan and sent six Harwich Force light cruisers to cut the raiders off from their base at Zeebrugge. This ended the intelligence pas de deux, with both sides sticking to their changed plans.

IX TBF captured three Dutch steamers but the Harwich cruisers came across one of them and retook it from its German prize crew. The British cruisers then encountered six German destroyers in pursuit of another steamer at 0700 on 2 November. They chased, with *Centaur* and the Germans trading salvos at ten thousand yards. Neither side hurt the other; the destroyers made smoke and broke successfully for Zeebrugge while the British returned to Harwich.[25]

The Germans mounted two more raids before the end of the year, damaging drifter *Acceptable* on the night of 23/24 November and sinking armed trawler *Narval* on 26 November.[26] Marinekorps Flandern conducted these harassment operations without serious loss, but without the hoped-for harvest of sunk and captured merchant ships and patrol vessels. While the Germans could claim to have outfought the British, these operations only caused brief disruptions. They did, however, force the British to maintain strong forces in the area.

Baltic 1916
Action off Norrköping Bay: 13 June, 2328–14 June, 0015
Conditions: Clear
Missions: Russians, interception; Germans, transit
Russian Forces: Cover Force (Vice Admiral Trukachev): CA *Riurik*; PC *Oleg*, *Bogatyr*; DD *Voiskovoi*, *Turkmenets-Stavropolskii*, *Kazanets*, *Steregushchii*, *Strashnyi*, *Donskoi Kazak*, *Zabaikalets*. Attack Force (Rear Admiral A.V. Kolchak): DD *Novik*, *Pobeditel*, *Grom*.
German Forces (Reserve Captain Lieutenant Karl Hoffmann): AMC *Hermann**; AMT *William Jurgens*; PBx2; MMx9.

Responding to intelligence that the Germans would be convoying a large quantity of iron ore from Sweden, Vice Admiral Trukachev left the Finnish skerries at 1330 in command of three cruisers escorted by seven destroyers. Rear Admiral Kolchak followed a half hour later with three large destroyers. Kolchak was to close the Swedish coast and seek the convoy while Trukachev covered.

Kolchak's force sighted a smoke cloud at 2315 on 13 June off Norrköping Bay seventy miles south of Stockholm. This was one of several points along the coast where navigational hazards forced vessels out beyond the three-mile limit of territorial waters and exposed them to attack. The destroyers approached and sighted a group of vessels. Because they were burning lights, the Russians fired warning shots to see whether the ships were Swedish or German. In response *Hermann*, armed with four 10.5-cm guns, fired a rocket that sent the nine ore carriers of the convoy running for Swedish waters, while armed trawler *William Jurgens* and two smaller patrol vessels began laying smoke. The Russians concluded they had found prey and opened fire at 2338. They concentrated on *Hermann*, which had been at the convoy's rear, and which they first misidentified as a cruiser. This caused Kolchak to delay closing range. By the time *Grom* finally torpedoed and sank *Hermann* the convoy and the smaller escorts had escaped, forcing the frustrated Russians to turn for home at 0015 on 14 June.[27]

Action off Landsort: 30 June, 0010–0245

Conditions: Clear but occasional squalls

Missions: Russians, interception; Germans, patrol

Russian Forces: Cover Force (Vice Admiral A. P. Kurosh): AC *Gromoboi*; PC *Diana*; DD *Okhotnik, General Kondratenko, Emir Bukharskii, Dobrovolets, Moskvitianin*. Strike Force (Captain P. V. Vilken): DD *Pobeditel, Grom, Orfei*.

German Force (Captain Lieutenant Diether Röder Diersburg): 15 TBHF: DD *V183, V185, V181, V184, V182*. 20 TBHF: *S56*, DDx2.

After learning that another German convoy was scheduled to depart Stockholm, the Russians mounted a similar operation with a cover force of two cruisers and five destroyers and a strike force of three destroyers.

Map 4.3 Convoy Attacks: June 1916

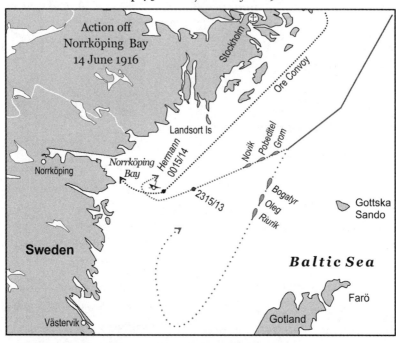

Action off
Norrköping Bay
14 June 1916

Stockholm

Ore Convoy

Landsort Is

Novik

Pobeditel

Grom

Norrköping

*Norrköping
Bay*

Hermann
0015/14

Norrköping

2315/13

Bogatyr

Oleg

Riurik

Gottska
Sando

Sweden

Baltic Sea

Västervik

Farö

Gotland

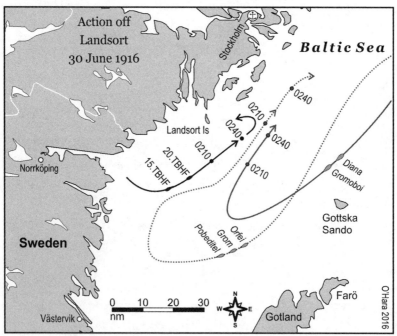

Action off
Landsort
30 June 1916

Stockholm

Baltic Sea

0240

0210

0240

0210

Landsort Is

0240

0210

Norrköping

20.TBHF

0210

15.TBHF

Diana

Gromoboi

Gottska
Sando

Sweden

Orfei

Grom

Pobeditel

Farö

Västervik

0   10   20   30
nm

N
W   E
S

Gotland

O'Hara 2016

When the Russians were under way they received word that fog had delayed the Germans but Kurosh decided to proceed anyway. At 2003 on 29 June the Russian submarine *Bars* spotted German destroyers patrolling the area earmarked for Vilken's sweep. She attacked unsuccessfully and then radioed a warning. Vilken's force had already turned toward the Swedish coast at 1935, intending to sweep north from Västervik toward Landsort. Just after midnight the Russian and German flotillas spotted each other at ranges reported variously as eight thousand yards or four thousand meters. Whatever the distance, the Germans opened fire and the outnumbered Russian destroyers ducked into a rain squall.

After losing contact the Germans headed east. At 0115, having steamed thirty miles, they saw smoke on the eastern horizon. This belonged to the Russian cover force, which was sailing northeast. The Germans were behind the enemy ships, at a long range for torpedoes, and faced unfavorable visibility to the east. The German commander, Röder, tried to move up abreast, but the coal-fired boats of 15 TBHF could only be pushed so hard before their stacks began to shoot sparks and gouts of dark smoke. With dawn breaking at 0210, the destroyers were running out of time to reach a good launching position. Röder authorized attacks by individual ships, but none of the seven torpedoes launched before 0210 hit a target.

Fortunately for the Germans, the Russians were also struggling with a problem. They had spotted the Germans, but Kurosh worried they might be friendly vessels. *S56* and the other two oil-fired ships of the 20 TBHF had probably forged ahead during the pursuit and the Russian admiral may have wanted to confirm they were not Vilken's destroyers.

By 0240 Röder judged that his ships had reached the best firing position they were likely to achieve. He ordered a mass torpedo attack and the flotilla unleashed a dozen weapons at ranges as close as five thousand yards. At the same time, Vilken radioed that he was ahead of the cruisers, allowing Kurosh to open fire. The German destroyers made smoke and turned away, zigzagging frantically. They succeeded in evading the Russian shells, but no torpedoes hit either. The Russians never found the German convoy.[28]

The most successful Russian effort against German shipping occurred on 11 July when the destroyers *Vnushitelnyi* and *Bditelnyi* captured the German steamers *Worms* (4,428 GRT) and *Lissabon* (2,781 GRT) in Swedish territorial waters. Vigorous Swedish protests caused the Russians to suspend such raids, as they could ill afford to be cut off from Swedish imports.

On 12 September the cruiser *Strassburg* and gunboat *Khrabryi* briefly clashed. A small Kaiserliche Marine force had advanced into the Irben Strait in hopes of drawing battleship *Slava* into a submarine/torpedo plane ambush. The trap was sprung with *Slava* being attacked by the torpedo planes and cruiser *Diana* by *U31*, but neither the planes nor the submarine scored. The surface action resulted in no significant damage to *Strassburg* or *Khrabryi*.[29]

The Germans mounted their largest surface operation of the year on 10 November when X TBF, with eleven destroyers, raided into the Gulf of Finland to attack shipping and bombard Baltic Port. *V75* and *S57* were mined and sunk on the way in. After shelling an empty harbor the force turned for home and ran into more mines, losing *G90*, *V72*, *V76*, *S58*, and *S59*. This disastrous operation demonstrated that the Russian defenses of the Gulf of Finland were formidable indeed.[30]

Black Sea 1916
As 1916 began action in the Black Sea continued to revolve around the coal traffic from Zonguldak to Constantinople.

Action off Kirpen Island: 8 January, 0823–1010
Conditions: Clear
Missions: Russians, interception; Ottomans, transit
Russian Forces: DD *Pronzitelnyi*, *Leitenant Shestakov*. Support Group: BB *Imperatritsa Ekaterina Velikaia*; PC *Pamiat Merkuriia*; DD *Derzkii*, *Gnevnyi*.
Ottoman Force (Captain Ackermann): BC *Yavuz*.

On 7 January *Yavuz* sailed to meet the collier *Carmen*, which was in transit to the capital. However, previously alerted by intelligence, *Pronzitelnyi* and *Leitenant Shestakov* ambushed *Carmen* off Kirpen Island at 0310 on 8 January, where *Pronzitelnyi* sank her with torpedoes. Learning from *Carmen*'s rescued crewmen that *Yavuz* was en route, the destroyers sailed east along the coast with a support group in the offing built around the dreadnought *Imperatritsa Ekaterina*. This new battleship had received her baptism of fire just the day before when two Russian destroyers mistakenly discharged seven torpedoes at her group. Lookouts spotted the flashes and *Ekaterina* turned sharply toward the attackers while flashing recognition signals. "By great good fortune . . . the torpedoes passed by the side."[31]

Captain Ackermann learned of *Carmen's* fate several hours after her sinking and turned back to Constantinople. However, the Russian destroyers sighted *Yavuz's* smoke at 0810 and radioed the support group. *Yavuz* spotted their smoke in turn at 0823 and came about to follow as the destroyers lured her northeast toward *Ekaterina*. At 0915 *Yavuz* saw more smoke to the northeast and the dreadnought hove into view twenty-five minutes later. The Russian battleship opened fire from 19,000 yards. *Yavuz* turned away and replied. The battlecruiser had one salvo near miss her target and six more fall in the vicinity but the rest were short. *Ekaterina's* fire, on the other hand, helped by *Leitenant Shestakov's* radio corrections, blanketed *Yavuz* with waterspouts and shell fragments, but turret defects slowed her rate of fire. *Yavuz's* nominal speed advantage was partially negated by loose propeller shafts, a foul bottom, and the need to zigzag to frustrate the accurate Russian shooting. Gradually, however, the range opened to 25,000 yards and at 1010 *Ekaterina*, low on fuel, broke off. *Yavuz* expended twenty-two rounds while the Russian ship fired ninety-seven. *Yavuz* had had a close call. Admiral Souchon advised the Ottoman command that the new Russian dreadnoughts made the transportation of coal by sea extremely dangerous. This led to calls for coal shipments from Germany (now possible with the fall of Serbia) and the dispatch of more German submarines to counter the Russian blockade.[32]

Actions off Amasra: 2 March, 1820 and 3 March, 0740

Conditions: Clear

Missions: Russians, sweep; Ottomans, sweep/transport

Russian Forces: First action: DD *Pronzitelnyi, Bespokoinyi*. Second action: DD *Gnevnyi, Schastlivyi*.

Ottoman Force (Corvette Captain Wolfram Knorr): CL *Midilli*.

By early 1916 Russian raids had reduced the Ottoman merchant fleet to a mosquito flotilla of wooden sailing vessels that could not handle heavy or cumbersome cargo or, more importantly, urgent goods. Warships had to fill the void. With the Russian offensive driving toward Trebizond, *Midilli* weighed anchor on 27 February to deliver a machine-gun company and munitions to the threatened city. On the way, she was to drop off diesel fuel and lubricating oil to Sinope for German submarines operating from there. Then she was to swing north on an antishipping mission before returning to Sinope to load food for the capital.

On the 28th, while en route to Sinope, *Midilli* received a series of messages regarding the depredations of two Russian destroyers that were sweeping west toward her destination. By the time *Midilli* anchored in Sinope, Captain Knorr knew the Russians were near. He stayed in harbor for only thirteen minutes, leaving at 1743. Burdened with troops and munitions, Knorr was not looking for a fight, especially at night when the enemy would be best able to deploy torpedoes and *Midilli* least able to use her guns; thus, he jogged west before swinging back east.

At 1820 *Midilli* encountered the enemy destroyers anyway, spotting them eight thousand yards away. The Russians saw the cruiser as well and closed range. At 1843, Knorr turned *Midilli* away in anticipation of a torpedo attack. When his lookouts reported torpedo tracks astern, he turned the ship again and lost the destroyers in the darkness. *Pronzitelnyi* had in fact been ready to launch five torpedoes, but *Midilli* disappeared before she could fire.

The cruiser proceeded to Trebizond, where she discharged the troops and munitions in just eighteen minutes. She then swept north to Tuaspe before heading back across the middle of the Black Sea. She made a swing down toward Sinope, but reports of storms in the area warned her off. Turning west again, she cruised uneventfully until 0720 on 2 March when smoke appeared on the western horizon. It was *Gnevnyi* and *Schastlivyi,* which had been sent to Sinope to support the 28 February attack on the cruiser. They had remained in the area to harass traffic. *Midilli* sighted the ships themselves at 0740.

An exchange of recognition signals left the tsarist ships uncertain of the cruiser's identity. *Midilli* came to 26.5 knots to close, but the Russian destroyers kept their distance. *Midilli* finally tried a couple of shots from her new 15-cm bow gun, only to see them fall short. The destroyers made off to the north; the cruiser broke off the pursuit.

The Russian destroyers failed to damage *Midilli* at night, when conditions favored them. She failed to damage them in daylight, when conditions favored her. This reflected the general situation in the Black Sea, where the Russian destroyers preyed on commercial traffic without much to fear from the Ottoman navy while the Ottomans (and their German officers) accepted the risks inherent in using irreplaceable ships for routine missions.[33]

Action off Novorossisk: 4 April, 0455–1000

Conditions: Clear

Missions: Russians, transit; Ottomans, transit

Russian Forces: BB *Imperatritsa Ekaterina Velikaia*; PC *Kagul*; DD *Gromkii, Bystryi, Pospeshnyi.*

Ottoman Forces (Corvette Captain Knorr): CL *Midilli*[+].

April 4th found *Midilli* returning from another transport mission to Trebizond. She had dropped troops, munitions, and weapons at the port on 3 April then steamed out to bombard Russian positions and sweep up the Caucasus coast looking for enemy shipping.

At dawn on 4 April she had just passed the longitude of Novorossisk on her return to the Bosporus when she sighted *Imperatritsa Ekaterina* and her screen to the south steaming on an opposite course. The darkened northern horizon shielded her from enemy view, but the growing light made that condition temporary. Edging further north would bring her closer to the enemy base at Sevastopol. Captain Knorr resolved to keep heading west but to be ready to increase speed should the Russians turn to follow.

The range closed to 11,000 yards and then began to open as the ships passed each other. However, a destroyer signaled *Midilli's* presence at 0436, and the Russian formation reversed course to the north. In response, *Midilli* increased speed. *Ekaterina*, concerned that *Midilli* might be a Russian ship, challenged at 0455. By that time Knorr estimated the range as 22,000 yards. He ordered his signal officer, a young lieutenant named Karl Dönitz, to signal "Pleasant journey" to the Russians as *Midilli* slowly drew away. In an episode that entered the Kaiserliche Marine's folklore, Dönitz added the postscript, "Kiss my arse."

Ekaterina answered the insult with a 12-inch volley. Her second salvo ventilated *Midilli*'s stern with splinters. The Russians had the range as 18,400 yards and given the accuracy of the battleship's fire, they were certainly closer to the mark than the Germans. Fortunately for *Midilli*, she had enough speed in hand to pull away even while zigzagging. *Ekaterina* chased until 1000, but *Midilli* survived both her captain's overestimation of the range and the impudence of her farewell message.[34]

The Russians missed another chance at *Yavuz* and *Midilli* on 6 and 7 July. The two ships were on missions to support an Ottoman counteroffensive at Trebizond. The Black Sea Fleet had both its operational dreadnoughts at sea, searching, but a German submarine warned of the Russian presence and the Ottoman warships slipped back to the Bosporus along the Bulgarian shore.[35]

Action off Inebolu: 22 July, 1355–1755

Conditions: Clear, with rain squalls later
Missions: Russians, interception; Ottomans, minelaying
Russian Forces: BB *Imperatritsa Mariia*; DD *Schastlivyi*, DDx4.
Ottoman Forces (Corvette Captain Knorr): *Midilli*[+].

Fresh from dock with a refurbished power plant and armament increased to eight 15-cm weapons, *Midilli* sailed for Novorossisk to lay a field of sixty-five mines. At 1305, while still fifty miles short of Sinope, she sighted smoke clouds to the north. Captain Knorr, suspecting he had encountered an enemy unit headed for Trebizond, altered south and then southwest. He had in fact stumbled upon *Imperatritsa Mariia* and five destroyers. The Russian squadron had left Sevastopol at 0830 that morning upon learning that *Midilli* had sailed.

Schastlivyi sighted *Midilli* at 1330 and in response Knorr dumped nine mines to free the firing arcs of his aft gun. The cruiser and destroyer dueled at 16,000 yards from 1355 to 1405 until *Schastlivyi*, finding that *Midilli*'s enhanced armament made her a formidable adversary, turned away. *Mariia* then appeared. *Midilli* fled south making funnel and chemical smoke using new smoke generators fitted while in dock. *Mariia* engaged at 1415 at a range of 22,800 yards. She shot well, when she could see her target through the smoke, with shells landing short but in line. *Midilli* weaved back to the southwest. *Mariia* lofted four more salvos at 1445 from 19,000 yards. Her final shots came from 21,800 yards and scored two near misses that wounded seven men on board the Ottoman cruiser. By 1552 *Midilli* had run out of chemical smoke and her boilers were fouling. She emerged into the clear to see that *Mariia* was now about 27,000 yards back, comfortably out of range. However, three destroyers were off her starboard quarter to her north. The cruiser dropped eight more mines in an attempt to discourage pursuit, but the Russians pounded on.

The Russian commander had ordered his destroyers to attack in pairs from each side of the cruiser. At 1630 one tried to cross *Midilli*'s wake, closing to 16,000 yards. *Midilli* fired fifteen shots from her aft 15-cm gun, which forced the destroyer to sheer off. At 1755 another destroyer appeared from behind *Mariia* and closed rapidly. Anticipating a torpedo attack, Knorr jettisoned six more mines to further clear his gun arcs. The attack, however, never materialized as *Midilli* entered a rain squall and shook the pursuit in the rain and gathering dark.

Midilli had escaped again. *Ekaterina* had already demonstrated the potent armament of the new Russian battleships. This engagement with *Mariia* also showed the impressive sustained speed of the new ships. The Germans resolved not to let *Midilli* go to sea again without making sure that all aspects of her power plant—and particularly the oil sprayers that increased the output of her boilers—were in top shape.[36]

Spurred by its new commander, Vice Admiral Kolchak down from the Baltic Fleet, the Black Sea Fleet began a mine offensive against the Bosporus in July and mounted minelaying operations every month for the rest of the year. This and an ongoing coal shortage in Constantinople kept the large Ottoman warships mostly port-bound. The Russian offensive against enemy shipping was also successful. By the end of the year the Ottomans had only two colliers still in service.[37] The Russians had accomplished their major objectives at sea, while the Ottomans struggled to maintain a minimal level of operations.

Adriatic 1916

Action in the southern Adriatic began early in the year, as the Austrians advanced through Serbia and Montenegro driving the remnants of their enemy before them. The evacuation of the Serbian army, conducted during the height of winter, involved forty-five Italian, twenty-five French, and eleven British steamers. On 22 January departures from San Giovanni di Medua ended and Durazzo, twenty-five miles south, became the last available evacuation port. The Austrians tried to interdict this traffic with mines, aircraft, submarines, and surface raids.

First Aborted Raid on Durazzo: 27 January, 1630–

Conditions: Unknown

Missions: Entente, patrol; Austrians, raid

Entente Forces: IT PC *Puglia*; FR DD *Bouclier*.

Austrian Forces (Captain Miklós Horthy): CL *Novara*; DD *Orjen*[+], *Csepel*[+].

On the 27th Austrian seaplanes reported that eight Entente merchantmen and five small warships crowded Durazzo harbor. The Austrian command at Cattaro dispatched Captain Horthy with the light cruiser *Novara* and the destroyers *Orjen* and *Csepel* to attack the port. En route, however, the two destroyers collided and both returned to base. Horthy continued but at 1630 during the return to Cattaro he encountered the protected cruiser *Puglia* and a French destroyer. *Puglia* only managed two salvos before the faster Austrian broke contact and continued north.[38]

Second Aborted Raid on Durazzo: 6 February, 1930–2100

Conditions: Clear and calm

Missions: Entente, patrol; Austrians, raid

Entente Forces: First Force (Captain G. W. Vivian, RN): BR CL *Liverpool*; IT DD *Bronzetti*. Second Force (Captain D. B. Crampton, RN): BR CL *Weymouth*; FR DD *Bouclier*.

Austrian Force (Captain Benno Millenkovich): CL *Helgoland*; DD *Wildfang*. 1 TBG: TB *74T*[#], *78T*, *80T*. 5 TBG: TB *83F*[+], *87F*, *88F*.

Having intelligence that loaded transports would be departing Durazzo that day, *Helgoland* and six torpedo boats sailed to attack them. The destroyer *Wildfang* proceeded separately to work inshore with two seaplanes and submarines.

Liverpool, accompanied by *Bronzetti*, intercepted *Wildfang* on her way south. The Austrian turned back toward Cattaro, staying out of reach of the cruiser's 6-inch guns. *Bronzetti*, however, pushed ahead and engaged at 1500. *Wildfang* returned fire but the range was extreme for both destroyers. *Bronzetti* broke off when *Wildfang* reached the cover of Cattaro's 17-cm batteries. The Entente ships returned to Brindisi while *Weymouth* and *Bouclier* replaced them on the patrol line.

These two vessels intercepted the *Helgoland* group thirty-five miles southwest of Cattaro at dusk, under a clear sky and calm conditions. *Weymouth* opened "a slow and deliberate fire at a range of seven thousand yards" while Captain Millenkovich ordered his torpedo boats to attack. The two torpedo boat groups crossed courses in their approach and *74T* and *83F* collided. Damage to *74T*'s machinery ended one attack, but the other group continued. *83F* launched two torpedoes at *Bouclier* from 1,500 meters, but both missed. *Helgoland* contributed little to the action, as first the torpedo boats fouled her range and then dense clouds of smoke prevented her from distinguishing friend from foe. The Austrians turned north with *Weymouth* and *Bouclier* following, but the Austrians had vanished in the dark by 2100.[39]

The evacuation ended on 9 February. In an effective demonstration of sea power, the Entente navies evacuated more than 260,000 troops, refugees, and prisoners of war from Albania, mostly to Corfu. Austrian hit-and-run raids by flotilla craft and the few submarines available failed to affect this movement, and the Habsburg command elected not to risk anything heavier. A greater effort may have been justified as the rescued Serbian troops formed the nucleus of six infantry divisions and made an important reinforcement to the Salonica front.[40]

The Regia Marina removed the last Italian troops from Durazzo on 26 February and the front eventually stabilized north of Valona. Austrian sweeps by three destroyers on 23 February, *Helgoland* and nine flotilla craft on 24 February, and *Helgoland* and six destroyers on the 26th did not interfere with the Italian movements. Because the land transportation of supplies into Albania was so difficult, the protection of maritime traffic into Durazzo became a major new responsibility of the Austrian navy for the remainder of the war. Merchant sailings from Cattaro to points south increased from nothing in 1915 to 370 in 1916, and 933 in 1917. This traffic was mainly carried out in barges and small vessels under the cover of darkness and generated several actions and encounters between surface forces.[41]

Chase of Orjen: 15 March, night

Conditions: Clear
Missions: Italians, patrol; Austrians, escort
Italian Force: DD *Animoso, Insidioso.*
Austrian Force: DD *Orjen.*

On the night of 15 March *Animoso* and *Insidioso* were scouting the Gulf of Drin when they encountered *Orjen.* The Italian ships chased her to Point Menders until 15-cm shore batteries forced them to turn away. In a brief exchange of fire neither side hit the other. Shortly thereafter, the Italian destroyers encountered a tug towing a barge. The tug quickly

The Austro-Hungarian destroyer *Tátra.* Austro-Hungarian destroyers were in high demand and short supply throughout the war. (Courtesy of Enrico Cernuschi Collection)

dropped her line and fled inshore while the destroyers sank the barge with twenty 76-mm rounds.[42]

The Italians repeatedly attempted to force enemy harbors using small, expendable units. The first such attack occurred on the night of 28 May 1916 when the torpedo boat *24OS* snuck into Trieste under the cover of bad weather and aimed two torpedoes at the steamer *Iskra*. These missed and exploded against the mole instead. The smaller MAS boats seemed better suited for the work, however, and provided proof of concept on the night of 6 June when *MAS5* and *7* penetrated Durazzo and sank the motor vessel *Lokrum* (924 GRT).

In the Northern Adriatic Italian and Austrian naval forces patrolled, laid (and swept) mines, supported air raids, escorted traffic, and conducted shore bombardments. Few surface actions occurred as the result of these activities and those that did were, as in the south, generally inconclusive chases.

Off Porto Corsini: 3 May, night

Conditions: No moon and overcast

Missions: Italians, minelaying; Austrians, raid

Italian Force: DL *Rossarol* (Frigate Captain Ettore Rota), *Pepe;* DD *Missori, Nullo.*

Austrian Force (Frigate Captain Heinrich Huber): DD *Velebit, Scharf-schütze, Pandur, Csikós*[+]; TB *76T, 92F, 93F, 98M, 99M, 100M.*

On 3 May an Italian force of two scouts and two destroyers set out from Venice to cover a minelaying mission by the destroyers *Zeffiro* and *Fuciliere* scheduled for that night off Sebenico. They were passing Point Maestra at 1430 when they saw smoke on the eastern horizon. The unit's commander, Frigate Captain Rota, turned his force to investigate while building speed to 28 knots. At 1450 three Austrian seaplanes attacked the Italian force with bombs and machine guns. *Pepe* suffered a steering failure, but this was quickly repaired and the Italians continued. Shortly after, they came in sight of ten Austrian flotilla craft that were at sea to support a seaplane raid on targets in Romagna. *Rossarol* and *Pepe* opened fire from ten thousand yards. The Austrians replied but their salvos fell well short whereas the Italians quickly straddled. The Austrians came about for Pola with the Italians in chase. During the exchange of gunfire *Csikós* suffered minor splinter damage. The distance was closing when, at 1550 with the coast of Istria in view, the Italian lookouts spotted what appeared to be an Austrian cruiser and two destroyers advancing to reinforce the enemy. Not willing to face superior guns so close to the main Austrian base, the Italians turned away. Austrian seaplanes attacked the Italians during their withdrawal but inflicted no damage.[43]

Action off Chioggia: 24 May, night
   Conditions: Dark with quarter moon
   Missions: Italians, patrol; Austrians, raid
   Italian Force (Lieutenant Vittorio Pertusio): TB *21OS*[+], *22OS*.
   Austrian Force (Frigate Captain Bogumil Nowotny): DD *Velebit, Scharfschütze, Dinara, Reka*; TB *89F, 92F, 98M, 99M, 100M, 75T*[#].

On 24 May, being the first anniversary of Italy's entry into the war, the Regia Marina augmented its patrols in case the Austrians tried to mark the occasion with special attacks. Two torpedo boats were about twenty miles off Chioggia when they sighted a silhouette in the dark. This was *75T*, rear unit in an Austrian formation that included four destroyers and six torpedo boats. The Austrians were loitering at slow speed awaiting the return of aircraft that were raiding Padua, west of Venice. The Italians closed and *21OS* launched a torpedo from just over two hundred yards. *75T* saw the flash and managed to avoid the weapon by turning toward *21OS*. Gunfire erupted as the two torpedo boats passed one another just a few dozen yards apart. As *21OS* tried to gain position to launch her other torpedo a 66-mm round struck her bow and ignited a fire, forcing the boat to decrease speed to prevent its spread. She turned away thinking to lure the Austrian over a nearby mine barrage but one of the Italian's 57-mm rounds had penetrated *75T*'s engine room and knocked out a turbine. *75T* thus withdrew toward the other units in her force. At the sound of gunfire these vessels had fired a series of long-range salvos in the general direction of their enemy and then withdrew at full speed, in accordance with their standing orders. *22OS* joined *21OS* to assist and the Italians lost track of their adversary in the dark. Later *99M* found *75T* and towed her home.[44]

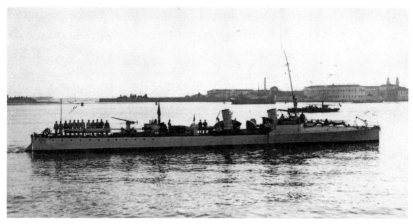

Italian torpedo boat *22OS* at Venice, 1916. These vessels and their Austro–Hungarian counterparts provided valuable service in the Adriatic's narrow waters. (Ufficio Storico Marina Militare)

Off San Giovanni di Medua: 16 June, night

Conditions: Clear

Missions: Italians, raid; Austrians, escort

Italian Force: DD *Pilo, Bronzetti, Mosto, Audace.*

Austrian Force (Corvette Captain Johannes Liechtenstein): DD *Wild-fang*[+], MMx2.

MAS boats did not have the range to cross the Adriatic and return so the Italians used destroyers to tow them to their destinations. On the night of 15 June a force was at sea to raid San Giovanni di Medua. Four destroyers brought two MAS boats to the port and then stood off as the small craft penetrated the anchorage. On this occasion the MAS boats did not find any targets and shore batteries opened up as they were departing. Meanwhile, *Wildfang*, which had been escorting two small merchantmen to Durazzo, came upon the covering force and shot sixty rounds at the destroyers. The Italian destroyers returned fire and hit *Wildfang* once, inflicting minor damage. When the MAS boats were clear the Italians turned for home. As a postscript to this action *MAS5* and *7* returned to Durazzo on the night of 25 June and sank the steamer *Sarajevo* (1,100 GRT).[45]

Once Austrian forces captured Durazzo, the main target of K.u.K. Kriegsmarine forays in the southern Adriatic became the Otranto mine barrage, especially after the barrier caused the 13 May loss of *U6* (the only verified casualty caused by the barrier during the entire war, although the total may have been as high as four submarines). *Novara* and *79T* probed the barrier on 3 April but had no contacts. On 31 May *Orjen* and *Balaton* with *77T*, *79T*, and *81T* sank the British drifter *Beneficient*. A 4 July raid by *Helgoland*, *Orjen*, *Tátra*, *Balaton*, *83F*, *85F*, and *87F* produced no fighting, although the Austrians thought that they saw three enemy destroyers rush by in the dark. Poor visibility also frustrated attempts to spot drifters on the barrage line.[46]

First Skirmish in Otranto Strait: 9 July, 0450–0715

Conditions: Clear

Missions: Italians, patrol; Austrians, raid

Italian Force (Corvette Captain R. Bernotti): DD *Impetuoso*, *Irrequieto*.

Austrian Force (Captain Miklós Horthy): CL *Novara*; TB *73F*, *54T*, *87F*.

The light cruiser *Novara* and three torpedo boats headed south on the night of 8 July. Early the next morning they encountered and sank the drifters *Spei* (82 GRT) and *Clavis* (87 GRT), and damaged *Bird* and *Ben Bui*. *Impetuoso* and *Irrequieto* were on the patrol line, having sortied from Brindisi in response to a report that some drifters had possibly snared a submarine in their nets. At 0435, they observed gun flashes and headed in that direction. The Italians spotted the Austrian raiders fifteen minutes later whereupon Horthy's force immediately turned north with the Italians in chase. *Irrequieto* had several boiler tubes that needed replacement and could not exceed 27 knots; this prevented the Italians from closing to effective range and at 0715 Bernotti came about in compliance with orders from Brindisi. The Italian captain took credit for disrupting the attack. The Austrians believed they were running from the scout cruiser *Quarto* and a pair of destroyers.[47]

Action off Cattaro: 2 August, 0919–1005

Conditions: Clear

Missions: Entente, interception; Austrians, transit

Entente Forces: Support Group (Frigate Captain Henri Frochot): FR DD *Commandant Bory*, *Bisson*; IT DD *Ardente*, *Impavido*. Valona Group: IT DD *Abba*, *Ardito*.

Austrian Forces: Bombardment Group (Corvette Captain Johannes Liechtenstein): DD *Wildfang*[+], *Warasdiner*[+]. Support Group (Frigate Captain Emil Konek): PC *Aspern*;TB *80T*, *85F*.

On 2 August *MAS6* slipped into Durazzo harbor and missed a steamship with two torpedoes. She then rejoined her support group of two French and two Italian destroyers.That same night *Wildfang* and *Warasdiner* were bombarding Molfetta, just up the coast from Bari. The *MAS6* group received news of the bombardment during its return and the destroyers bent course to intercept. *Ardito* and *Abba*, out of Valona, were at sea supporting a seaplane reconnaissance mission.They also headed toward the enemy. In Brindisi *Bixio* and *Liverpool* along with seven destroyers raised steam and put to sea as they were able.

The *Aspern* group, which had been on an antisubmarine mission by Cattaro, approached within signaling distance of the Austrian destroyers just before the Entente ships appeared on the horizon. *Abba* was first on the scene but the French units were close behind. *Commandant Bory* and *Abba* opened fire on *Wildfang* and *Warasdiner* at extreme range, and then turned southwest when *Aspern* joined the fight. The two sides exchanged heavy fire while steaming on parallel courses.The Entente ships hit *Wildfang* once while a near miss perforated *Warasdiner* with splinters. The Austrians then came about for Cattaro. The Entente destroyers continued to pursue but *Aspern*'s gunfire eventually forced them to give up the chase. The Entente cruiser group arrived too late to participate.[48]

Chase off Pola: 11 August, night
Conditions: Full moon
Missions: Italians, patrol; Austrians, raid
Italian Forces:TB *1PN*, *3PN*[+], *4PN*, *24OS*.
Austrian Forces:TB *91F*, *94F*, *98M*.

On the night of 11 August three K.u.K. Kriegsmarine torpedo boats were supporting an air raid against Campalto on the mainland near Venice when they encountered four Italian boats on patrol. The Austrians turned back to Pola while the Italians gave chase. In the minutes before the two forces lost sight, the Habsburg force damaged *3PN* slightly when a near miss showered the torpedo boat with splinters.[49]

Chase off Medua: 8 October, 1325
Conditions: Clear
Missions: Italians, patrol; Austrians, transit
Italian Force: DD *Bronzetti*, *Pilo*.
Austrian Force: TB *68F*.

Patrolling Italian destroyers surprised *68F*, which was transporting bombs and gasoline to the seaplane base at Durazzo. The torpedo boat dumped her dangerous cargo and ran for the shelter of Medua's 15-cm shore batteries. The Italians chased and opened fire at 6,500 yards but failed to inflict any damage.[50]

Second Skirmish in Otranto Strait: 22 December, 2140–2300
Conditions: Poor visibility
Missions: French, transit; Austrians, raid
French Force (Frigate Captain B. de Boisanger): DD *Casque*#, *Protet*, *Commandant Rivière*#, *Commandant Bory*, *Dehorter*, *Boutefeu*.
Austrian Force (Frigate Captain Bogumil Nowotny): DD *Scharfschütze*+, *Reka*+, *Dinara*+, *Velebit*.

On the night of 22 December four Habsburg destroyers headed south to raid the Otranto Barrage. At 2118 they reached their objective and sighted a drifter. *Scharfschütze* opened fire at 2130 but had time to damage only that one vessel when a French destroyer flotilla intervened. The French had been bound for Taranto to escort a convoy to Salonica the next day but detoured toward the sound of gunfire. Upon sighting the enemy Frigate Captain de Boisanger turned *Casque* in chase but the second ship in his column missed the signal and failed to conform. *Commandant Rivière*, the third ship, followed *Casque* but the others lost track of the leader. In a close range melee *Commandant Rivière* avoided a torpedo but at 2148 a 66-mm shell penetrated her aft boiler room, one of five hits she absorbed. The French hit *Scharfschütze* three times and *Reka* and *Dinara* twice, but none of these blows affected their speed.

The Austrians turned north and fired a torpedo back at *Casque*, which she evaded. *Casque* launched a torpedo of her own but this likewise missed. Then, at 2300 an Austrian shell penetrated into *Casque*'s forward boiler room cutting her speed to 23 knots. The French leader fell behind and eventually lost contact. After this the other French destroyers reunited with *Casque*. *Commandant Bory* recorded being bracketed by shells, without being able to identify the source.

Meanwhile, Vice Admiral Alfredo Acton at Brindisi had dispatched *Abba*, *Nievo*, and *Pilo* to the scene followed, once they had steam up, by *Gloucester*, *Impavido*, and *Irrequieto*. The first group of destroyers arrived at 0215. The rendezvous proved a bit too precise, however; in the dark *Abba* rammed *Casque* at 31 knots. Then *Boutefeu* piled into *Abba*. The ships were seriously damaged and had to be towed back to Brindisi. On the return to base the Entente force spotted and attacked the German submarine *UB36*, but without result. The Austrians returned safely having given a good account of themselves.

This action demonstrated three things: size was important but did not always triumph. The Austrian destroyers were half as large as the French vessels and their guns were smaller, but they scored "lucky" hits that enabled them to escape, whereas any vital hits by the French forces would have doomed them. Luckier still, *Dinara* took a dud to her boilers that could have slowed her had it exploded. This action also reaffirmed that fighting at night was dangerous and confusing. Breaking contact was far easier than maintaining it. Finally, the ability of the Entente forces to operate multinational forces in battle had advanced very little since the 29 December 1915 action off Durazzo.[51]

By the end of 1916, after twenty-nine months of war, the K.u.K. Kriegsmarine had lost one old cruiser, two destroyers, and four submarines. The cruiser and one of the destroyers had been sunk in surface actions. The losses suffered by the Entente navies were much greater: one dreadnought, two predreadnoughts, three armored cruisers, three auxiliary cruisers, five destroyers, two torpedo boats, and eleven submarines. Of these, one Italian destroyer was sunk in a surface engagement. Larger Austrian and Entente ships had limited operational relevance and surface activity centered around the defense of traffic, harassment raids, the support of ground forces (in the case of Italy), mine warfare, air missions, and the Otranto Barrage.

1917: The Struggle Continues

Opportunities of meeting the enemy have unfortunately been few and far between during the 3 ½ years of war, and those which have occurred have differed materially from one another and have demonstrated new points.
—VICE ADMIRAL BEATTY TO THE ADMIRALTY,
24 DECEMBER 1917

Overview

The year 1917 began at the start of a particularly harsh winter—known in Germany as the Turnip Winter. After twenty-nine months of war, millions were dead and the combatants were nearing exhaustion. The year would see the French army in mutiny and Russia torn apart by revolution. Blockade, poor harvests, and economic mismanagement would combine to create serious shortages of food and war material within the Central Powers. Despite a series of bloody offensives neither side could force a decision on the Western or Italo-Austrian fronts. Only driving Russia out of the war or bringing the United States in seemed to hold any promise of tipping the balance enough for one side to win a military victory over the other.

Major surface actions would be fought in the Baltic, North, and Adriatic Seas but submarine warfare was to have the greatest strategic impact. At the beginning of the year the Admiralstab pushed for a renewal of unrestricted submarine warfare. Naval staff projected that submarines would sink more than 600,000 GRT of shipping a month and that this would force Britain to the peace table in five months.[1] While Admiral Henning Holtzendorff, the chief of the Admiralstab, conceded that an unrestricted campaign might provoke the United States into declaring war, he argued that submarines would sink enough merchant shipping to keep American troops out of Europe. And once Great Britain sought peace, the United States would quickly follow suit.[2] Holtzendorff's confident predictions overrode the objections of Germany's civilian politicians and convinced the kaiser and General Staff.

Accordingly, Germany began unrestricted submarine warfare in February 1917. Allied and neutral shipping losses soared, but the gradual implementation of an oceanic convoy system, which began on a trial basis in May, soon reduced losses to a bearable rate.[3] The United States declared war on Germany on 6 April 1917. By the end of 1917 194,000 American troops had reached France, with almost 2 million more to follow.

German and British surface naval efforts in 1917 revolved around the submarine war. The Royal Navy redoubled efforts to deny German submarines passage of the Dover Straits, while Marinekorps Flandern did its best to blunt those efforts. Ten Marinekorps Flandern raids against the Dover Barrage sparked engagements between warships, while opposing patrols frequently skirmished. The absence of submarine support curtailed the activities of the High Seas Fleet and the diversion of destroyers to antisubmarine duties likewise affected the Grand Fleet's operations. Nevertheless, the Royal Navy continued an active program of minelaying and sweeps into the Heligoland Bight. These sweeps resulted in two significant actions, one being the war's last action involving capital ships on both sides. The Kaiserliche Marine in turn sent light forces to attack British trade in the North Sea.

Revolution swept Russia in March 1917 and profoundly altered that nation's military situation. Revolutionary sailors murdered the Baltic Fleet's commander, Vice Admiral A. I. Nepenin, on 17 March while the fleet was still icebound in Helsingfors. The new commander was little more than a figurehead of the sailors' Central Committee. The revolution reinforced Germany's decision to seek victory in the east. Moreover, the Admiralstab hoped that intensified operations in the Baltic would diminish unrest among the battleship crews, brought on by poor rations, harsh conditions, and inactivity.

Weather seemed to conspire with politics to slow the pace of Baltic operations, with pack ice persisting in the Gulf of Finland until mid-May. When navigation became possible both sides focused on minelaying and throughout the year the Russians laid 13,148 mines.[4] Major operations would not occur until October, when the Germans assaulted the Baltic Islands off the Gulf of Riga. Despite the revolutionary conditions, the Baltic Fleet would fight reasonably well against the Germans.

In the Black Sea the Russians started 1917 with plans for a large landing near the Bosporus but the revolution ended such ambitions. The Ottomans had their own problems. By mid-1917 delivery of coal into the capital was far below military and civilian requirements, despite daily rail shipments from Germany, while Russia's immense naval superiority and its intensive mining of the Black Sea's west coast made Ottoman maritime operations of any type hazardous. Turkish problems were compounded by defeats on land and severe food shortages.

In the Adriatic the K.u.K. Kriegsmarine had preserved its battle fleet by using flotilla craft to raid, defend its coastlines, and protect traffic. The increased emphasis on the submarine war sparked more Austrian attacks on the Otranto Barrage as the Austrians tried to facilitate the passage of German (and some Austrian) submarines into the Mediterranean. Military reverses and threatening famine would weaken the Habsburgs and, like the Germans, the crews of the larger ships were afflicted by revolutionary unrest.

The British, French, and Italian navies shared responsibilities in the southern Adriatic but poor coordination and command confusion marred the occasions when the three forces acted in concert. In the northern Adriatic the Regia Marina patrolled vigorously, working at keeping the enemy's heavy units in port and attacking them there. The opposing light forces fought half a dozen minor surface actions. Support for the army assumed heightened importance after an October 1917 Austro-German offensive ruptured the Isonzo front. Navy monitors played a role in blunting the enemy advance.

In the Mediterranean submarines continued to exact a toll. In the first six months of the year, before the general implementation of convoys,

German and Austrian submarines sank an average of 146,000 GRT of shipping a month, compared to 105,000 GRT a month over the last nine months of 1916.[5]

North Sea 1917

In 1917 the Kaiserliche Marine conducted many raids against Entente ports, shipping, or patrol forces. Twelve of these resulted in significant surface engagements. Active patrolling by Germany's Flanders flotillas and their Dover Patrol counterparts resulted in many additional small and poorly documented actions. Royal Navy sweeps into Heligoland Bight led to two more engagements, while the interception of a German flotilla coming to Flanders resulted in one.

Interception of the VI TBF: 23 January, 0245–0430

Conditions: Poor visibility

Missions: British, interception; Germans, transit

British Force: Harwich Force (Commodore Reginald Tyrwhitt): CL *Penelope, Undaunted, Cleopatra, Centaur, Aurora, Conquest*; DL *Nimrod*; DD *Moorsom, Mansfield, Manly, Matchless, Morris, Phoebe, Simoon★, Surprise, Starfish, Milne.*

German Force: VI TBF (Corvette Captain Max Schultz): DD *V69*[#], *V44, S49, G41*[#], *G87, G86, V43, S50*[#], *V46, V45, G37.*

Admiral Scheer sent VI TBF to Flanders in January 1917 to replace III TBF, which had returned in November 1916. Room 40 intercepted a radio transmission regarding the transfer so the British set an ambush with enough ships from the Harwich Force and the Dover Patrol to cover all routes the Germans might take. The Dover contingent took station by the Maas Light Vessel, while Commodore Tyrwhitt sent three light cruisers to the North Hinder Light Vessel, and another three forty miles farther east. *Nimrod* and ten destroyers gathered around the Schouwen Bank Light Vessel in two groups.

The German flotilla left the Ems on the afternoon of the 22nd. They were bound for Zeebrugge via Schouwen Bank, and the eastern cruiser group was directly in their path. Contact occurred at 0245 on the 23rd in bitterly cold weather when the columns swept past each other only two thousand yards apart. *Aurora* opened fire first followed by *Centaur* and *Conquest* and the Germans quickly replied. Lieutenant J. H. Bowen, in *Aurora*, later wrote: "I crossed to S1, the foremost 4-inch gun and at once saw, about 1,500 to 2,000 yards distant, three low, dark shapes, easily recognizable as destroyers, I could not with certainty say that they were hostile. The Captain had no doubt, for just as I had my glasses focused on the leading one, the tinkle of the fire-gongs sounded, immediately followed by the crash and blinding glare of our starboard broadside. I could see nothing for about half a minute, very nearly walking overboard as a result. . . . [The enemy] opened fire with their after guns. In their haste to be gone, they heaped on fuel . . . and four out of the six flamed at the funnels, giving our gunlayers a reasonable point of aim."[6]

V69, the lead German ship, launched two torpedoes and slewed away when a shell jammed her steering. She discharged a third torpedo and then *G41* rammed her. *G41* lost control, circled and rammed *V69* again. *S50* tried to fire torpedoes only to find her tubes frozen in place. She fell out of formation in the confusion caused by the collisions. *Conquest* dodged *V69*'s torpedoes while *Centaur*, with Tyrwhitt on the bridge, turned toward the enemy despite the close range. The skirmish was over by 0259 as the scattered formations lost touch. Tyrwhitt signaled that he was chasing the enemy northeastwards.

In fact, none of the German ships were headed northeast. The damaged *V69* steamed north, *S50* headed south, *G41* limped southeast at 8 knots toward the Dutch coast, and the other eight destroyers continued to Zeebrugge. *Penelope* ran her force in the direction of the gunfire, and was rewarded at 0340 by the sight of *V69* 1,400 yards ahead. After challenging and receiving no answer, *Penelope*, *Undaunted*, and *Cleopatra* illuminated and pummeled the solitary destroyer, hitting at least three times. They thought they sank her, but *V69* made the coast and eventually struggled back to Heligoland Bight.

At 0415 *S50* encountered *Simoon*, *Surprise*, *Starfish*, and *Milne* by the Schouwen Bank Light Vessel. *S50* and *Simoon* spotted each other at close range. *Simoon* tried to ram but missed. *S50* fired a torpedo that smashed into *Simoon*'s magazine and caused a spectacular explosion (Bowen saw "a huge flare over the southern horizon"), leaving a hulk to be sunk later.[7] *S50* made off to the northeast with *Surprise*, *Simoon*'s next astern, briefly following her. *Surprise*'s contribution proved negative because she fouled the range for *Nimrod* and the other destroyers as they flocked to the scene of the torpedoing from the east, and then nearly rammed *Nimrod* before recognizing her for a friend. *S50* escaped north; however, *Simoon* and *Nimrod*'s group had both hit her, inflicting casualties and damage and forcing her return to base.

The British had damaged three ships, but failed to sink a single vessel despite three times confronting the Germans with superior force. Poor visibility was a factor but there were also communication and control issues. For example, *Nimrod* abandoned her position to head north, partly due to Tyrwhitt's 0259 signal that the Germans were fleeing northeast. This left her patrol position uncovered and allowed the eight destroyers remaining in the German formation to slip by unchallenged.[8]

The German navy mounted twelve raids in 1917 that resulted in contact with major Entente units. Objectives included the Dover Barrage, shipping lanes, and bombardments of coastal towns. Merchant shipping was a worthwhile target, but bombardments had mainly propaganda value. The Germans believed that attacks on the barrage helped their submarines negotiate the gauntlet of patrols, nets, and minefields. What neither side realized—because both attributed unexplained submarine losses to the barriers—was how ineffective the barrage really was in sinking German submarines. In fact during this period the barrage's mines did more damage to friendly ships, accounting for only one enemy submarine (estimated) against British losses of a flotilla leader and three destroyers sunk and one patrol vessel damaged. By the summer, the Germans had analyzed their submarine losses and concluded that the barrage was largely a paper tiger. The British in turn retrieved a copy of the German analysis from a sunken submarine in October; the bad news they thus learned encouraged them to try other approaches to the submarine problem, such as constant illumination and the Zeebrugge Raid of 1918.[9]

Ostend and Zeebrugge had the obvious advantage of being close to the Downs and the Dutch shipping lanes, but they were cramped and awkward to use and could not accommodate cruisers or more than three destroyer flotillas. This meant that the raiders always risked being outgunned by British cruisers. Other factors also played an important role in the conduct of operations. Raids required the right weather conditions. Long nights were a must to cover the approach and withdrawal of the raiding forces. New moon periods were desirable because reduced visibility neutralized the potential British advantage in gun power and maximized the effectiveness of German torpedoes. Ideally, operations would be timed so that tidal conditions gave the intruders the greatest possible freedom of maneuver amidst the shallows of the straits and currents favored the raiders during their approach and withdrawal.

Raid of 25 February, 2235–2241

Conditions: Weather fine but overcast, dark with new moon.
Missions: British, patrol; Germans, raid
British Force: DD *Laverock*[+] (Lieutenant H. A. Binmore). Other patrols: DD *Lance, Landrail, Lochinvar, Laurel.*
German Forces: Group Tillessen (Corvette Captain Tillessen): DD *S49, V46, V45, G37, V44, G86.* DDx8 in two other groups.

Marinekorps Flandern mounted a major operation during the first new moon after VI TBF's arrival. Six destroyers, led by Corvette Captain Tillessen, targeted the Dover Barrage, with a bombardment of Dover if possible. Corvette Captain Conrad Albrecht, a future General Admiral, led five destroyers to raid shipping in the Downs and bombard Margate, while Captain Lieutenant Zander took three destroyers to cruise off the Maas Light Vessel on the Anglo-Dutch shipping lanes. These forces faced formidable defenses; following Admiralty recommendations, the drifters were now retiring at night and five destroyers patrolled singly on the barrage while two flotilla leaders and nine destroyers waited at Dover with steam up. Two light cruisers and four destroyers were anchored off Deal in the Downs and a monitor was stationed at each entrance to the Downs to protect the shipping that sheltered there at night.

The raid generated little action. At 2235, shortly after passing through the barrage near Buoy 11A, Tillessen's group encountered *Laverock* heading northeast on a reciprocal course. The Germans held steady on until, at a range of just four hundred yards, they opened fire and launched six torpedoes. *Laverock*, which had just spotted the enemy, replied and came hard to starboard, with one torpedo passing fifty yards astern. Another struck but only dented the destroyer's hull. *Laverock* then assumed the same southerly course as the Germans, following on their starboard quarter, which led Tillessen to assume he was facing a fresh group of enemy vessels. He turned northeast at 2241 and retired back through the barrage. *Laverock* lost contact in the darkness and returned to her original patrol line. Her only damage, apart from the dent, was a broken backstay. She claimed one hit but in fact the Germans were unharmed. When Tillessen intercepted *Laverock*'s contact report he assumed it would no longer be possible to bombard Dover and so returned to base.

The Albrecht group bombarded Margate and sent two destroyers to the northern entrance of the Downs, where they saw nothing. They had departed by 2320 when a response force from the Downs arrived. The Zander group likewise struck at empty seas, as an Anglo-Dutch convoy had just sailed two days previously. The supporting British forces responded to reports of the raiders but too late. As in past raids the British failed to make contact due to late notice, quick German withdrawals, and a dark night.[10]

Raid of 17 March, 2250–2315

Conditions: Calm and clear; moon last quarter

Missions: British, patrol; Germans, raid

British Forces: Barrage Patrol: DD *Paragon*★ (Lieutenant R. G. Bowyer†), *Laforey*, *Llewellyn*#, *Laertes*. Dover reserve: DL *Broke*; DD *Myngs*, *Lucifer*, *Linnet*, *Lochinvar*, *Morris*. Downs reserve: CL *Canterbury*; DL *Faulknor*; DD *Saracen*, *Viking*, *Mentor*, *Ambuscade*.

German Forces: Group Tillessen (Corvette Captain Tillessen): DD *S49*, *G86*, *G87*, *V43*, *V45*, *G37*, *V46*. Group Albrecht (Corvette Captain Albrecht): DD *V47*, *V67*, *V68*, *G95*, *G96*. Group Zander (Captain Lieutenant Zander): DD *S15*, *S18*, *S20*, *S24*.

Marinekorps Flandern's next operation called for Group Zander to attack shipping in the Downs and bombard coastal towns to the north. Group Tillessen would attack patrols in the western end of the Dover

Barrage, while Group Albrecht raided the barrage's eastern end. British defensive measures included four destroyers patrolling the barrage and a torpedo boat watching the northern entrance of the Downs. A light cruiser, a flotilla leader, and four destroyers were anchored off Deal while a destroyer leader and five destroyers waited at Dover. Two monitors guarded Ramsgate.

The Germans left port between 1800 and 2000 on 17 March. Tillessen's ships crossed the barrage near Buoy 11A at 2235—farther east than planned and near to where Albrecht's group was to transit at 2250. They then spotted *Paragon* approaching from the southwest. At 2250 *Paragon* began to challenge unidentified vessels steaming across her bow. Before the signal was completed, however, one of three torpedoes launched by *S49* and *G86* from less than five hundred yards struck the British ship's engine room. German guns also opened fire and scored several quick hits. *Paragon* got off only a few rounds in reply before she broke in two and sank. The suddenness and violence of the German assault was apparent in one survivor's testimony: "The first I knew about it was when the alarm bell rang and I rushed on deck with my lifebelt in my hand and before I could get to my action station I got blown down. The shell struck in the after oil tank and I was blown into the side of the ship, and before I could rise a torpedo blew me clean over the side. On coming up I saw the ship was going under. The enemy was not more than 100 yards away."[11] In the confusion, *V43*, *V45*, *G37*, and *V46* lost touch with Tillessen's leading ships. To avoid being taken for the enemy, the four promptly withdrew.

To the north the patrol destroyers *Laforey* and *Llewellyn* saw the explosions and made their separate ways toward the scene. *Laforey* arrived at 2259 to find survivors clinging to scattered wreckage amid large patches of burning oil. She switched on her searchlight and prepared to lower a boat. *S49*, *G86*, and *G87* had been steering toward the barrage but when they saw searchlights behind them they came about to investigate. Almost simultaneously *Llewellyn* appeared from the opposite direction and challenged *Laforey*. Learning of the sinking, her captain reported, "I stopped my engines and switched on my searchlight. About 10 seconds afterwards I was struck by a torpedo on the port side."[12] In fact, *S49* and

G87 each launched a torpedo at 2315. One hit *Llewellyn* in the stem, crippling her. Never seeing the enemy destroyers, the British assumed a submarine had delivered the blow. *Laforey* abandoned her rescue efforts and set out at full speed to hunt the culprit. The Germans had a close call when Albrecht's group came onto the scene just as Tillessen was setting up to torpedo *Llewellyn*. The German night recognition system functioned well, however, and they avoided a friendly fire incident.

The swiftness of the German strike, the fact that *Paragon* was unable to make an enemy report, and that *Laforey* mistakenly reported a submarine attack confused the British response. Vice Admiral Bacon dispatched two antisubmarine vessels to hunt the reported U-boat and then recalled them when reports that Margate was being bombarded reached him at 0045 and *Laforey* reported at 0058 that the two survivors she rescued before embarking on her antisubmarine hunt stated that destroyers had sunk *Paragon*.

At 0030 Zander's group crossed the line of drifters guarding the Downs' northern entrance. The drifter *Paramount* spotted them and lofted a flare. Zander's ships perforated the small vessel with 88-mm rounds, but she doused her lights and escaped into the darkness. She later beached to avoid sinking. *TB4* reported the German ships at 0045 when they briefly bombarded Ramsgate and Broadstairs. The Zander group finished by torpedoing the steamer *Greypoint* (888 GRT), which had failed to make the sanctuary of the Downs due to a machinery breakdown. The German raiders then returned to base unmolested.

The Kaiserliche Marine did well on this raid, sinking a destroyer and a steamer and badly damaging another destroyer and a drifter. The Royal Navy had several failures. Of the patrol vessels just *Paragon* managed to engage the enemy, and only briefly before being overwhelmed. Poor reporting kept the reserve forces from intervening in time. Prodded by the Admiralty, Bacon reappraised the practice of scattering patrolling destroyers individually behind the barrage and began to concentrate patrols to increase firepower at the point of attack and allow ships to attack without challenging.[13]

These new dispositions did not stop another German raid on March 29/30, which was aimed at Lowestoft farther to the north and which resulted in the sinking of merchantman *Mascota* (1,097 GRT). Monitor *Havelock* saw the German attack, but judged the range excessive and the light too poor to engage.[14] The raiding went both ways, as demonstrated on 8 April when four British motor torpedo boats torpedoed and sank *G88* off Zeebrugge.[15]

Raid South of Goodwin Sands: 21 April, 0045–0115

Conditions: Calm and clear, very dark with new moon

Missions: British, patrol; Germans, raid

British Forces: West Barrage Patrol (Commander A. M. Peck): DL *Swift*[#], *Broke*[#]. East Barrage Patrol: DDx4. Reserve: DDx6

German Forces: Group Gautier (Corvette Captain Theophil Gautier): *V71*, *V73*, *V81*, *S53*, *G85*★, *G42*★. DDx9 in two other groups.

On 20 April the Germans conducted an operation that nearly mirrored their 17 March foray. Group Zander's three destroyers would raid the Downs from the north while Group Albrecht would attack in the east and then bombard Calais. Group Gautier would break through the western Dover Barrage and shell Dover. British dispositions featured one significant change: instead of individual destroyers patrolling behind the barrage, a four-destroyer formation protected the barrage's eastern end while flotilla leaders *Swift* and *Broke* guarded the western end.

Albrecht's force penetrated the barrage unseen, flung three hundred rounds at Calais from 1110 to 1115, and retired without contact. The Zander group cruised south almost to the Gull Light Vessel but saw only a small sailing ship. The Gautier Group likewise slipped through the barrage, damaged the armed trawler *Sabreur* patrolling off Dover, pumped 350 rounds into the Dover area over the course of seven minutes, and at 1132 headed for home. They would have escaped cleanly but Gautier decided to double back and scout the southern part of the Downs. His formation turned west at 0018 on 21 April and back east at 0036 having seen nothing. This jog put them on an interception course with *Swift* and *Broke* approaching from the east.

The Germans were steaming in two groups of three ships each. At 0045 the British flotilla leaders, heading southwest at 12 knots, saw *V71*,

V73, and *V81* ahead and to port. The Germans claimed to have got in the first salvo while the British commander's report states that "[b]oth sides were in readiness and fire was opened almost simultaneously."[16] *Swift* came hard to starboard in an attempt to ram. Instead, she shot between the first and second ships in the enemy column, absorbing hits that disabled her wireless and flooded the stoker's mess deck. *Swift* and *V81* each launched a torpedo but missed. *Broke* flung a torpedo at *V73* and then opened fire. Almost immediately a German shell struck a box of cordite on *Broke*'s bridge and flames flared up. As the first German trio vanished to port the second group appeared to starboard. Again the British ships put their helms hard over and fired torpedoes, one or two of which ran true and clobbered *G85*. The destroyer came skidding to a stop, burning heavily. Then *Broke* rammed *G42*. *Broke*'s captain wrote: "I hit her at full speed almost at right angles abreast after funnel, port side, and she literally tore her side out and bent my stem to port."[17] During the two minutes the ships were locked together German sailors reportedly tried to storm *Broke*'s forecastle. After she pulled free *Broke* fired another torpedo and attempted to ram *S53*. *Swift* then crossed *Broke*'s bow. After the British leaders exchanged recognition signals, *Swift* set off pursuing the first group east. *S53* lingered to pummel *Broke* at close range. Burning brightly, the British leader made a hard-to-miss target and *S53*'s barrage disabled all but one of *Broke*'s forward guns, started more fires, and severed her main steam pipe. *S53* tried to fire a torpedo, but her own muzzle blasts blew the torpedo officer to the deck as he attempted to launch the weapon. She then disappeared north, leaving *Broke* drifting near the fiercely burning *G85*. The two wrecks exchanged gunfire and *Broke* torpedoed her immobile opponent for good measure.

At 0115 *Mentor* from the Dover group arrived on the scene to find *Broke* wallowing in the swells near the hulks of *G85* and *G42*. *Broke* was towed back to Dover the next morning. She was hit eight times, suffering twenty-one men killed and thirty-six wounded, while *Swift* had one killed and four wounded. Both were several weeks in dock. *G85* and *G42* sank with the loss of seventy-two crewmen. While the British reserve forces were again too late to play a role, the new tactic of concentrating patrols had made the Germans pay a price.[18]

Encounter off Dunkirk: 25 April, 0140–0148

Conditions: Dark, new moon rise 0300

Missions: French, patrol; Germans, raid/bombardment

French Force: TB *Étendard*★ (Lieutenant Pierre Mazaré†); AMT *Nelly*, *Notre Dame de Lourdes*#.

German Force (Captain Lieutenant Kurt Assmann): TB *A39*, *A40*, *A42*, *A45*.

Marinekorps Flandern's coastal torpedo boats also engaged in offensive operations. Four improved A26-type boats sallied on the evening of 24 April to bombard Dunkirk, repeating a raid they had made on 25/26 March. They fired 350 rounds into the town in a seven-minute bombardment that started at 0115 on 25 April. As they withdrew along the coast, they encountered *Étendard* and a pair of trawlers patrolling to the east. *Étendard* sent up a signal rocket and opened fire but she had just one 67-mm and six 47-mm weapons pitted against eight 88-mm guns. Several German shells struck the French vessel before, at 0148, *A39* walloped her with a torpedo that detonated *Étendard*'s magazine. She exploded with a column of fire that billowed a hundred yards into the sky. Seventy-five crewmen and all officers died. The Germans also shot up trawler *Notre Dame de Lourdes* as they passed. The monitor *Lord Clive* and destroyer *Greyhound* saw *Étendard*'s demise and tried to cut off the enemy retreat. The monitor also lobbed a few rounds, but in the poor visibility she made no hits before the German torpedo boats vanished into the night.[19]

The next German raid, on April 26/27, followed the established three-formation pattern. Six destroyers sortied to North Foreland, three steamed to the Kentish Knock Light Vessel and five cruised between the Shipwash and North Hinder Light Vessels. Only the North Foreland group, *V71*, *V73*, *V81*, *S15*, *S20*, and *S24*, saw action, bombarding Margate, Broadstairs, and Ramsgate at ranges of seven to nine thousand yards. *Marshal Ney* saw their starshells and fired some 6-inch rounds in response, but they must have landed far off, as the German official history reports there was no response to the bombardment.[20]

Raid of 10 May, 0358–0550

Conditions: Sunrise at 0417, calm and clear but with glare

Missions: British, patrol; Germans, raid

British Forces: Main Force (Commodore Reginald Tyrwhitt): CL *Centaur*, *Carysfort*, *Conquest*; DD *Stork*⁺, *Redoubt*, *Sybille*, *North Star*. *Lightfoot's* Detachment (Commander W. deM. Egerton): DL *Lightfoot*, DDx4.

German Forces (Corvette Captain Adolf Kahle): III TBF: DD *S53*, *V71*, *V73*, *V81*, *S54*, *S55*, *G91*, *V70*. 1 Flanders DDHF: DD *V67*, *G95*, *V68*, *G96*. 2 Flanders DDHF: DD *S15*, *S20*, *S24*, *S18*.

Acting on intelligence that merchantmen would be sailing between the Netherlands and England on the night of 9/10 May, Marinekorps Flandern dispatched twelve destroyers to attack these targets plus another four destroyers and eight A26-class boats to scout and screen. After they arrived near the North Hinder Light Vessel south of the anticipated route, *S53*, *V71*, *V73*, *V81*, *S54*, and *S55* spread out into a line of two-ship groups and searched to the north. At 0358 instead of prey they encountered predators: three light cruisers and four destroyers of the Harwich Force. The Germans made smoke, consolidated, and retreated south toward the rest of their flotilla and the 1 Flanders DDHF. The agglomeration then continued south at top speed, dropping smoke floats and spewing funnel smoke as the British cruisers chased.

The shooting started at 0405 at 13,000 yards. The British straddled with their fourth salvo, but the Germans bracketed *Centaur* in turn even as the range opened to 14,000 yards. After the Germans "effaced themselves by a most efficient smoke screen" Tyrwhitt ordered his destroyers to pursue at top speed.[21] Gun blast interference delayed the signal and the destroyers were slow to respond when the flags did go up. *Stork*, in the lead, started her charge at 0430, becoming separated from the rest of her division.

By 0502 the fleeing Germans were beyond range of the cruisers' guns and they ceased fire. *Centaur* had expended 235 rounds and *Conquest* 70. The Germans had joined the four destroyers of 2 Flanders DDHF but *Stork* and her division were still dogging them and Zeebrugge was miles to the east. Flotilla leader *Lightfoot*, at the head of a column of four destroyers, then appeared northeast of the Germans. *Lightfoot* fired a ranging shot but it fell short. When the Germans got within four miles of the Belgian coast they turned east for Zeebrugge. *Stork* took a parallel course and tried to close, but she and her division quickly attracted the attention of the destroyers and German shore batteries. *Lightfoot* ordered them away after 0533 and the gunnery died out by 0550. *Stork* suffered minor splinter damage and had one man wounded. The main action had lasted for more than an hour, but smoke, long range, poor visibility, and a stern chase had rendered the shooting ineffective.[22]

Raid of 17 May, 2250–

Conditions: Foggy

Missions: British, patrol; Germans, raid

British Force (Commander J. V. Creagh): DD *Sylph*[+], *Setter*[*], *Recruit*, *Minos*.

German Forces (Corvette Captain Kahle): III TBF and Flanders DDF (DDx16). Engaged: *V71*, *V81*, *S55*[#].

The III TBF and Flanders flotillas returned to the Dutch coast in the evening of 17 May. Twenty-five steamers were plying local shipping lanes that night, a potentially rich haul for the raiders. But while German timing was good, the weather was not; dense fog reduced the operation to a deadly game of blind man's bluff.

The destroyers divided into four search groups. *S53* and *V73*, leading one formation, sank the British merchantman *Cito* (819 GRT) fifteen miles southeast of the North Hinder Light Vessel. At 2250 the two trailing ships of the group (*V71* and *V81*) encountered, at the rear of a convoy, *Sylph*, *Setter*, *Recruit*, and *Minos* in visibility of less than a mile. *Sylph* initially thought the shapes emerging from the dark belonged to the convoy. Then the Germans opened a "heavy and very rapid fire," before vanishing in the murk.[23] *Sylph*, turning hard to starboard to avoid a collision, was unable to reply. The British formation lost cohesion and in casting about for the enemy *Sylph* made another contact and steered to ram. Too late she recognized *Setter* and at 2310 slammed into her flotilla mate's engine room. *Sylph* tried to tow *Setter* back to port, but her after stokehold bulkhead collapsed and at 0030 *Setter* foundered.

The other German forces made no contacts, except for a merchant-man that loomed up out of the fog and rammed *S55*, forcing her return to base. The action demonstrated once again the difficulties a defending force faced with bad visibility and friendly forces in the area. By keeping their raiding forces well separated, the Germans avoided most of these problems, and proved themselves better at distinguishing friend from foe when separate groups did close each other.[24]

Raid of 19 May, 2355–20 May, 0010

Conditions: moonless night

Missions: French, patrol; Germans, raid

French Force (Frigate Captain Vincent Guy): DD *Capitaine Mehl#*, *Enseign Roux, Magon, Bouclier#*.

German Force (Lieutenant Günther Lütjens): TB *A42, A39, A40, A43+, A45*.

As the nights grew shorter Marinekorps Flandern raided closer to Zeebrugge. On the dark night of 19 May, it sent five torpedo boats along the coast to Zuidcote Pass just short of Dunkirk. The ships saw nothing on their outward leg, but the leading group of *A42, A39*, and *A40* fell in with French destroyers on their return.

The Marine Nationale force had reached the western end of its patrol line and was reversing course. The first three ships had already come about when *Bouclier* at the column's end saw several ships passing to starboard also heading east. *Bouclier* hesitated, concerned they were British. The Germans had no doubts, especially since flares being fired from Nieuport silhouetted the French ships. They launched two torpedoes from six hundred yards before opening fire when the range had dropped to four hundred. Even under fire, the French continued to flash recognition lights. A flurry of 88-mm shells riddled *Bouclier's* bridge, slaughtering her commander and seven other men, wounding eleven, and causing her to circle at 25 knots with her rudder hard over. At the head of the French column it was not apparent what was happening astern. Blinkers continued flashing as the French tried to sort out their line, but the Germans mimicked these signals, adding to the confusion. By the time the destroyers had sorted friend from foe, all of the Germans, including the trailing *A43* and *A45*, had swept past. In the process the A-boats landed a shell in *Capitaine Mehl*'s boiler room, cutting her speed to 12 knots. The other French destroyers pursued, including *Bouclier*, now under the command of a sublieutenant who "climbed into a bridge so cluttered with corpses he could hardly set foot there." Separated from the formation by her gyrations, *Bouclier* straightened her course, ran up on *Magon*, and barely avoided a collision. The last German ship vanished from view after a fifteen-minute action. Some shell fragments did minor damage to *A43*. Tactically, the Germans demonstrated superb night-fighting skills, spotting the French first, launching torpedoes before opening fire, and uniting separate formations without confusion or a friendly fire incident.[25]

In addition to increased raiding activity, 1917 saw many skirmishes between German and Entente patrols off the Flanders coast. Most resulted from the unrestricted submarine campaign. This spurred the Entente to conduct more bombardments, lay more mine barrages, and patrol more vigorously, while conversely requiring Marinekorps Flandern to clear paths through the minefields and provide security for minesweepers and submarines.

Many actions were inconclusive because one side or the other did not want a fight. Entente forces were understandably leery of following the Germans into range of their coastal batteries, while the Germans were careful about venturing too far beyond this protection. Moreover, opposing forces often engaged across minefields or shoals that restricted their movements and limited the ability to exploit favorable opportunities.

Ratel Bank Action: 26 May, 1155–1230

Conditions: Clear

Missions: British, none; Germans, interception

British Force: BM *General Wolfe*, *M27*, *M24*; DD *Leven* (Lieutenant A. P. Melsom, RNR).

German Force: DD *S15*, *S20*, *S24*, *S18*.

British monitor *General Wolfe* was conducting an experimental shoot near Ratel Bank attended by a pair of small monitors and an old destroyer. At 1200 four destroyers of 2 Flanders DDHF ran in and launched a torpedo at *M24*, which missed a hundred yards ahead. *Leven* engaged at seven thousand yards and pursued, but the Germans had broken contact by 1230.[26]

Ostend Bombardment Action: 5 June, 0235–0315
Conditions: Mixed visibility
Missions: British, bombardment; Germans, patrol
British Force: Harwich Force (Commodore Reginald Tyrwhitt): CL *Centaur, Concord, Canterbury, Conquest*; DL *Lightfoot*; DD *Surprise, Truculent, Starfish, Recruit, Taurus, Sharpshooter, Satyr, Torrent.*
German Force (Captain Lieutenant Zander): *S15*[#], *S20*[★].

The Harwich Force was covering a bombardment of Ostend with four light cruisers, a flotilla leader, and eight destroyers when at 0227 *Lightfoot* spotted *S15* and *S20* to the south-southwest on a westerly course. The dawn's tricky light conditions and the glassy sea may have prevented the Germans from seeing the British force until they were well within range. *Lightfoot* challenged at 0233 and opened fire two minutes later.

Commodore Tyrwhitt in *Centaur* ordered the lead destroyers *Taurus, Sharpshooter, Satyr,* and *Torrent* to close as the cruisers opened fire over them. A 6-inch shell penetrated *S20*'s boiler room at 0250. *Satyr* and *Torrent* then approached to within two thousand yards of the stricken ship, smothering her with 4-inch shells. *S20* clearly being finished, *Taurus, Torrent,* and *Sharpshooter* pursued *S15* toward the coast, hitting her repeatedly. Tyrwhitt recalled them at 0257 after four more German destroyers and the Flanders shore batteries joined the action. *A39* and *A45* towed the heavily damaged *S15* into Zeebrugge, while *Satyr* sank the derelict *S20* at 0315.[27]

Barrage Actions of 25 July, 0500–1306
Conditions: Variable, hazy at the start
Missions: British, patrol; Germans, raid
British Force (Vice Admiral Reginald Bacon): First action: BM *Terror*, 10th DF: DL *Broke, Nimrod*; DD *Taurus, Teazer, Retriever, Springbok, Tempest,*

Skilful, Sceptre, Torrid. Second and third actions: DL *Faulknor*, DD
Milne, Tempest, Sceptre, Skilful, Torrid.

German Force: 6 TBHF (Captain Lieutenant Carl A. Claussen): DD
G91, S55, V70, S54.

On July 25, an Anglo-French armada of 102 vessels appeared off
Flanders to refresh the mines and nets along a section of the coastal
barrage near Thornton Ridge. *G91* and *S55* were on patrol and tried
to take advantage of the dawn haze to pick off some of the drifters
engaged in the effort. At 0512 *Nimrod*, followed by eight destroyers,
engaged the intruders from 9,700 yards. The British found it difficult to spot their fire and most ships only discharged a few rounds.
The Germans replied, straddling *Nimrod* as they fell back toward
their coastal batteries. Then *Terror* pitched in with her 15-inch guns.
Battery Tirpitz's four 28-cm guns, located west of Ostend, shelled
the monitor in turn. The action petered out at 0538 with both sides
unharmed.

Twelve miles of barrage had been laid by 0630 and most of the
British force had turned back to base but *Faulkner* and five destroyers continued to patrol the freshly laid barrier. German seaplanes
harassed them, and after a submarine scare they skirmished with all
four destroyers of 6 TBHF between 0750 and 0802 at ranges variously
reported as 13,000 to 8,000 yards. *Torrid* claimed (incorrectly) two
certain hits. The Germans headed toward the coast but the British did
not follow because of the shore batteries. At 1303 the Germans and
British exchanged fire again the Germans straddled *Skilful* with one
very near miss. The visibility was deteriorating, however, and although
the British had glimpses of enemy forces, the last at 1930, there was no
more combat. Reflecting the low intensity nature of these actions, few
rounds were expended: *Nimrod*, fifteen 4-inch; *Retriever*, four 4-inch;
Taurus, twelve 4-inch; *Teazer*, eight 4-inch; *Springbok*, none; *Sceptre*,
two 4-inch in the first combat and nineteen in the second; *Tempest*,
eight and twenty-four rounds; *Skilful*, thirteen and fifteen rounds; and
Torrid, sixty-four rounds in both actions. The British estimated that
the Germans fired forty rounds in the first action and around twenty
in the second.[28]

While Kaiserliche Marine raids were strictly hit-and-run affairs, the Royal Navy raided from a position of strength, often ready to escalate all the way up to a capital ship action. Given the German reluctance to take risks against potentially superior British forces, it was not remarkable that only two of the many Royal Navy forays into Heligoland Bight in 1917 generated actions.[29]

Encounter with Heligoland Minesweepers: 16 August 1917, 0935–1135

Conditions: Limited visibility, about eight thousand yards

Missions: British, patrol; Germans, minesweeping

British Force: CL *Centaur* (Commodore R. Tyrwhitt), *Conquest, Canterbury, Concord, Cleopatra, Aurora*; DL *Nimrod, Valkyrie*; DD *Surprise*[+], *Redgauntlet, Satyr, Thisbe, Torrent, Truculent, Retriever, Sybille*.

German Forces: 5 and 6 MSHF (Captain Lieutenant Hermann Glimpf): TB *A36*; MS *M65*[#], *M55, M53, M37*[+], *M4*[+], *M28, M29.*

On 16 August seven sweepers were forty miles north-northwest of Terschelling Island maintaining "Route Yellow," one of the major submarine transit lanes going west from Wilhelmshaven, when at 0935 *A36*, their buoy boat, spotted smoke to the south. This turned out to belong to the Harwich Force: six light cruisers, two leaders, and eight destroyers, which had been supporting a minelaying mission into Heligoland Bight. *A36* ran north making smoke and zigzagging while the nearest British destroyer, *Surprise*, opened fire at 0947 from six thousand yards. The British mistook *A36* for a destroyer and reported many hits and a large fire, although in fact the little torpedo boat escaped undamaged. Then lookouts on *Centaur* spotted *M28* to the east followed by six more minesweepers. The British pegged them as cruisers and turned their guns on them. The sweepers formed column and fled east, spewing smoke as they went. The Harwich cruisers chased, their progress delayed at 1001 when Tyrwhitt ordered a 90 degree turn to port following a report of a periscope sighting. After ten minutes the British reformed and continued after the sweepers. They hit *M65* at 1018, severing her main steam pipe, and *M4* and *M37* once. German fire lightly damaged *Surprise*. At 1023 Tyrwhitt turned away. Visibility was deteriorating and, unsure of his position, the commodore did not want to blunder into a German minefield known to be nearby. After another submarine scare the British continued on to port.

A support force of light cruisers *Frankfurt*, *Karlsruhe*, and three destroyers from 12 TBHF did not engage, because its commander, Frigate Captain F. Rebensburg, felt he lacked sufficient information about the situation. This hesitation cost him his job.[30]

The Mary Rose *Convoy: 17 October, 0600–0930*

Conditions: Clear with heavy swell

Missions: British, escort; Germans, interception

British Force (Lieutenant Commander C. L. Fox†): DD *Mary Rose*★, *Strongbow*★; AMT *Elise*, *P. Fannon*; BR MM *Benelench*, *City of Cork*, DA MM *Margrethe*★ (1,241 GRT), *Stella*★ (815 GRT), BE MM *Lonionier*, NO MM *Habil*★ (636 GRT), *Dagbjørg*★ (640 GRT), *Silja*★ (1,222 GRT), *Sørhaug*★ (1,007 GRT), *Kristine*★ (568 GRT), SW MM *Visbur*★ (902 GRT), *H. Wicander*★ (1,256 GRT).

German Force (Frigate Captain Max Leonhardi): CM *Brummer*⁺, *Bremse.*

Short summer nights halted the German raids, but they resumed in the fall. The Admiralstab dispatched the fast cruisers-minelayers *Bremse* and *Brummer* from Wilhelmshaven on 16 October to attack traffic between Great Britain and Norway. Although lightly armed they had long range and good speed due to a steam plant that was mainly oil-fired. They also resembled British light cruisers, a similarity the Germans enhanced with a Royal Navy gray paint job.

Room 40 warned that a German operation was under way but could give no indication of objective or composition. The Admiralty believed the intelligence portended a minelaying operation farther south and Admiral Beatty sent three capital ships, twenty-seven light cruisers, and fifty-four destroyers on a fruitless search for enemy forces.

The Admiralty did not halt the Britain–Norway convoys. Thus, two destroyers and two armed trawlers were escorting one Belgian, two British, and nine Scandinavian merchantmen as they shouldered their way into a heavy swell westward from Bergen. At dawn (0530) on 17 October the convoy was spread over ten miles of ocean with *Mary Rose* and two ships eight miles ahead of the rest of the formation and sixty-five miles east of the Shetland Islands. The other ten ships and the trawlers followed *Strongbow*. The convoy was dispersed because cargo had shifted in one vessel, which caused her to fall behind while two others, being faster, had pushed ahead.[31]

At 0600 *Strongbow* sighted ships approaching from the southeast and challenged. The German cruisers made a series of replies (with dim lights and then "poorly morsed" letters) as they rapidly closed range. *Strongbow*'s captain, called to the bridge, agreed with the watch officer that they resembled British County–class cruisers. Then at 0606, when just three thousand yards distant, there was a series of sharp cracks, smoke puffs appeared from their barrels, and geysers erupted just short of the destroyer. A round from the next salvo landed in *Strongbow*'s engine room and burst the main steam pipe. Smoke and steam enveloped the ship as she shuddered to a stop. The ship's lieutenant testified: "[S]econd salvo hitting forecastle and started fire on lower mess deck. Foremost gun was put out of action, most of the gun's crew being killed." This blast also wrecked the wireless and stopped the transmission of a contact report. *Strongbow* launched three torpedoes but the amidships gun discharged just one round, "unable to fire any more owing to the steam escaping from the Engine-Room." The aft gun jammed after fifteen rounds. Having quickly reduced their opponent to a bloody shambles the cruisers started chasing merchantmen.[32]

Meanwhile, on board *Mary Rose* men had seen the flashes and heard the fire and Lieutenant-Commander Fox immediately turned back and ordered his crew to action stations. As *Mary Rose* closed, lookouts reported four enemy light cruisers and four destroyers. Nonetheless, she came on and, according to the testimony of survivors, opened fire at 0630 from 7,800 yards. The Germans did not answer until the range was six thousand. *Brummer*'s report complimented the British destroyer's gunnery. "Fires quick salvos with good ranging on the bridge. Several straddling salvos and *Brummer* takes a hit on the forecastle that caused minimal splinter damage."[33] *Mary Rose*'s survivors, on the other hand, described the German fire as "quite bad with the majority of the shots short." When she was about 2,500 yards away *Mary Rose* started a 180-degree turn to starboard. She was preparing to launch torpedoes when a shell exploded in her engine room. As the destroyer lost way the Germans crossed to her starboard quarter and pummeled her with 101-pound rounds. One hit No. 3 Boiler and others silenced the forward and amidships guns. Two men fired a torpedo on their own initiative but at 0703 Fox ordered the ship abandoned.

Brummer closed to five hundred yards and deliberately fired three rounds into the hull; Mary Rose sank shortly thereafter. One survivor noted that "her side, when we were in the water, was one mass of holes." The trawler Elise made for Mary Rose's position. Her captain testified that "the last we saw of her was her bow sticking out of a cloud of smoke. When this went away, she had gone. We did not hear any explosion. We found no trace of Carley floats or boats. We picked up two Norwegian boats close to the spot. I asked them where the destroyer was. They replied 'English destroyer sank, Englishmen all drowned.'" In fact, one Carley float got away but although the survivors signaled with a cloth tied to a paddle, the trawler did not see them and returned to Strongbow, which was still afloat. Eighty-seven men died and ten survived. A lifeboat from Silja plucked the survivors from their raft in the forenoon and sailed back across the North Sea to make landfall north of Bergen after a forty-four hour voyage.[34]

With both destroyers neutralized the Germans methodically went from ship to ship shelling them and, in at least one case, firing torpedoes. They reported that many came to a halt and some even dropped boats even before they were fired upon. Two merchantmen tried to flee but Bremse chased them down. Elise returned to Strongbow, which provoked another attack at around 0820. One survivor remembered, "The cruiser came back a third time when the Trawler approached the ship. The cruiser opened fire at the ship and the motor boat and Carley floats which had drifted away to windward of the ship. There were very many small splashes around the boat which looked like shrapnel. . . . [T]he cruiser also raked us fore and aft with a pom-pom. Each time the cruiser left us, she steamed on to the convoy firing at the ships in turn."[35] Strongbow finally sank at 0930 after her captain ordered the engine and boiler rooms flooded. She lost forty-seven men; there were thirty-nine survivors, most being taken on board Elise. Brummer and Bremse ultimately accounted for nine merchantmen in addition to the two destroyers. The Germans believed they sank the entire convoy except for one trawler.

The Admiralty's inquiry into the disaster considered "the most remarkable point . . . is that although *Mary Rose* recognized the hostile character of the light-cruisers sighted she apparently made no attempt to communicate with her consort or to report the presence of enemy vessels to Lerwick by W/T." Staff considered it would have been better for the destroyer to stand off and report and observe rather than go charging in as she did.[36] In fact, *Mary Rose* did try to report, but the Germans successfully jammed her transmissions.

The Grand Fleet did not hear of the sinkings until that afternoon. The cruisers circled north before turning for home. They were south of Bergen by 1800 and off the Skagerrak by midnight, handily avoiding enemy patrols and having achieved a significant victory. In the propaganda backwash the British accused the Germans of atrocities, which the Germans denied, while a Swedish captain asserted that the Germans had not fired at men in the water and that the British had left Scandinavians to drown, preferring to rescue their own.[37]

Raid off Dunkirk: 19 October, 0030–0050

Conditions: Poor visibility
Missions: British, at anchor; Germans, bombardment
British Force: BM *Terror*★.
German Force (Captain Lieutenant Assmann): TB *A49, A50, A60, A61.*

On the night of 18/19 October Marinekorps Flandern dispatched seven torpedo boats to bombard the harbor and airfields at Dunkirk under the cover of a half-flotilla of destroyers. Targeting airfields reflected aviation's growing importance in naval warfare.

Shortly after leaving Zeebrugge *A48* and *A58* collided, forcing both ships to return together with *A59*, the third ship in *A58*'s formation. The other four continued to Dunkirk, arriving at 0026 and holding their fire as a group of Entente destroyers filed by six hundred yards off. They started the bombardment at 0030, with the forward mount on *A60* using starshells to illuminate.

The puny shells quickly stirred up a hornet's nest, with return fire coming from shore batteries, patrol boats, and at least one destroyer. Monitor *Terror* had been anchored offshore and at 0038 the torpedo boats sighted her and seized the opportunity to attack such a worthwhile target. All four launched their single torpedoes at a range of only three hundred yards for three hits—two forward and one about eighty feet back at the start of the bulge protection. With torpedoes expended and the defenses thoroughly aroused, the Germans withdrew, edging by two more Entente destroyers at 0050. The foremost fifty feet of the monitor's hull were blown away but thanks to good underwater protection and a tug she was able to reach shallow water before sinking. *Terror* was subsequently refloated and then spent ten weeks in dock. The Germans would have to wait for the Second World War to sink her permanently.[38]

Dunkirk Patrol: 27 October, 1501–1530

Conditions: Unknown

Missions: Entente, patrol; Germans, patrol

Entente Force: BR DL *Botha*; BR DD *Morris*; FR DD *Capitaine Mehl, Magon*.

German Force: 6 TBHF (Captain Lieutenant Claussen): DD *G91, S54, S55*.

On 27 October *Botha* and *Morris*, with the French destroyers *Capitaine Mehl* and *Magon*, were patrolling the barrage near Dunkirk when an estimated twenty-five German bombers attacked. The small ships maneuvered to avoid direct hits, although a near miss caused casualties on board *Magon*. Then, at 1501, 6 TBHF appeared and opened fire. For a half hour the two sides skirmished at ranges of from thirteen down to ten thousand yards before breaking contact. *Capitaine Mehl* claimed one hit on the German ships.[39]

The Erebus Operation: 28 October, 1535–1612

Conditions: Good

Missions: British, patrol; Germans, interception

British Force: DL *Botha*; DDx2.

German Force (Captain Lieutenant Friedrich Frorath): DD *G91, S55*.

The 15-inch monitors working with the Dover Patrol carried a big punch and outranged most German shore batteries. To attack them the Kaiserliche Marine developed a novel weapon: a wire-guided motorboat packed with 1,540 pounds of explosives. The boat was steered by a shore station that guided it based on observations from an aerial spotter. The Germans used this weapon on 6 September and 1 October, but in the first attempt the target destroyed the boat with gunfire and in the second Entente fighters drove off the observation plane. Marinekorps Flandern tried again on 28 October, and this time succeeded at 1323 in hitting monitor *Erebus* squarely amidships despite heavy defensive fire. Although the German observers thought that they saw fire and secondary explosions, the boat struck on the monitor's bulge, which absorbed much of the blow. Two crewmen were killed and fifteen injured.

G91 and *S55*, at sea to protect minesweepers, were sent to apply the coup de grâce but at 1650 British destroyers intervened. A twenty-two-minute engagement at long range followed. Neither side was damaged but the Germans were forced to turn back. *Erebus* returned to service on 21 November.[40]

Second Battle of Heligoland Bight: 17 November, 0700–1015

Conditions: Light winds with haze, foggy by 1000

Missions: British, raid; Germans, minesweeping

British Forces: Battle Cruiser Force (Vice Admiral William Pakenham): 1st CS (Vice Admiral T. D. W. Napier): CL *Courageous, Glorious*[+]; DD *Ursa, Nerissa, Urchin, Umpire*. 6th LCS (Rear Admiral Edwyn Alexander-Sinclair): CL *Cardiff*[#], *Ceres, Calypso*[#], *Caradoc*; DD *Valentine, Vimiera, Vanquisher, Vehement*. 1st LCS (Commodore Walter H. Cowan): CL *Caledon*[+], *Galatea, Royalist, Inconstant*; DD *Vendetta, Medway*. Close support engaged: BC *Repulse* (Rear Admiral Richard Phillimore).

German Forces: Support Group (Captain Max Grassoff): BB *Kaiserin, Kaiser*. II Scouting Group (Rear Admiral Ludwig Reuter): CL *Königsberg (ii)* [#], *Nürnberg (ii)*[+], *Frankfurt*[#], *Pillau*[#]. VII TBF: DD *S62, G87, G92, G93, V83, V43, V44, V45*. 4 MSHF: TB *A63, A68, A69, A74, A41, A52*. 6 MSHF: MS *M66, M7, T74, M53, M4, M3, M1*; TB *A36*. AMT *Fritz Reuter, Kehdingen*★.

The Germans began a major minesweeping operation seventy miles northwest of Heligoland Island on 17 November, deploying 4 MSHF

German trawler *Fritz Reuter* prewar. She is typical of the fishing trawlers pressed into war service and armed, in this case, with an 88-mm gun. (Courtesy of Peter Schenk Collection)

and 6 MSHF, a flotilla of minesweeping trawlers, a pair of barrier-breaker vessels, and two armed trawlers. II Scouting Group, with four light cruisers, and VII TBF, with eight destroyers, screened the sweepers. *Kaiserin* and *Kaiser* waited near Heligoland Island in case heavy support became required.

Admiral Beatty had been seeking opportunities to raid German minesweeping operations on the fringes of their defended area. A light cruiser foray into the Kattegat on 31 October sank an armed auxiliary and nine trawlers. After radio intercepts revealed the mid-November effort the Admiralty instructed Beatty to attack. The admiral deployed the 1st CS and two light cruiser squadrons with the 1st BCS (three battle cruisers with a light cruiser and eight destroyers) in close support. Six battleships loitered several hours to the north in distant support.

The proliferation of mine barrages had greatly changed the bight's geography since the August 1914 battle. Beatty's staff failed to distribute accurate information about these fields and commanders entered battle with substantially different understandings of where the dangerous areas were. This greatly affected the resulting action.

British forces sailed from Rosyth at 1630 on 16 October. At dawn on the 17th, "the sea was flat and there was an easterly breeze, and some haze and overcast sky."[41] Most of the German sweepers had just reached their starting point when, shortly after 0730, the British squadrons confronted them from the west. At 0737 *Courageous* loosed a salvo at *Pillau* off her starboard bow with her main battery and at a sweeper with her 4-inch guns. She put the range as 12,000 yards. *Glorious* followed, her guns aimed at *Nürnberg*. She made the range as ten thousand yards but her initial rounds dropped well short. *Cardiff* and the leading destroyers engaged the sweepers. From the bridge of *Courageous* it appeared that "[a]lmost immediately all enemy craft in sight seemed to scatter and make smoke screens from smoke pots and funnels. Submarines appeared to dive hurriedly and were not seen again." In fact, the minesweepers fled eastward as the destroyers laid smoke; only the trawler *Kehdingen*, acting as a navigation boat, was sunk during this phase by British destroyers as they swept by. After this the destroyers fell back to the disengaged side of the cruisers. *Umpire* from Napier's screen, for example, took station abaft the starboard beam of the 1st LCS at 0815 and spent the remainder of the action trailing the cruisers. Her captain complained that his helm jammed twice and that "it is not safe to manoeuvre at high speed."[42]

As the sweepers fled, *Pillau*, *Nürnberg*, and *Frankfurt* charged through the billowing smog to confront the British. "They were firing 5-gun salvoes with a spread of 200 to 300 yards, and straddling, [although] neither *Courageous* nor *Glorious* was actually hit." *Königsberg*, which had been searching for a tardy minesweeping detachment, joined them along with *G87*, *G92*, and *V45*. *V45* launched torpedoes at the British line at 0743 and 0746, but missed. *Ursa* (under the command of a future Admiral of the Fleet, Commander John C. Tovey) responded with a torpedo at 0800, which likewise missed.[43] After their attack Reuter's light cruisers reversed course and fled southeast in a line of bearing with *Königsberg* to starboard and farthest south and then *Frankfurt*, *Pillau*, and *Nürnberg* to port and farther north. Reuter wanted to lead the enemy away from the sweepers and toward *Kaiserin* and *Kaiser*, which he assumed would be charging to his aid.

Smoke sharply reduced the already spotty visibility. Although a 15-inch shell from *Courageous* drew blood smashing one of *Pillau*'s guns at 0755, the battlecruisers had to check fire after a few minutes as they steamed toward the smoke screen, uncertain what lay on the other side. At 0800 Napier plunged through the billowing wall, an action few commanders in the history of modern naval warfare would emulate (although he did prudently turn sharply south). Seven minutes later he emerged into the clear and spotted Reuter's cruisers bearing southeast. At the same time Admiral Pakenham in *Lion* ordered *Repulse* forward to support Napier.

Courageous and *Glorious* opened fire again at 0810. *Courageous* reported this was the only time during the battle she had a clear target and that "several salvoes fell very close to the ship on both sides. Small Zig Zaggs were carried out."[44] Meanwhile the light cruiser squadrons got into the fight with *Cardiff* engaging at 0812 and most of the others by 0820. *Vanquisher* and *Valentine* dashed forward to launch torpedoes, but found *Königsberg*'s fire too hot. Under intense pressure the German light cruisers spread a second smoke screen starting at 0830.

This smoke coincidentally marked the farthest point Napier believed free of mines based upon the outdated maps he carried. He could follow the Germans through the danger area if he could see their course, but the smoke blocked his view. He therefore turned *Courageous* and *Glorious* northeast at 0840 and checked fire. The commanders of the light cruiser squadrons also made a jog to the northeast, but not as sharp. These maneuvers put Napier on *Nürnberg*'s port quarter while the light cruiser squadrons remained to the south on

Map 5.1 Second Battle of Heligoland Bight: 17 November 1917

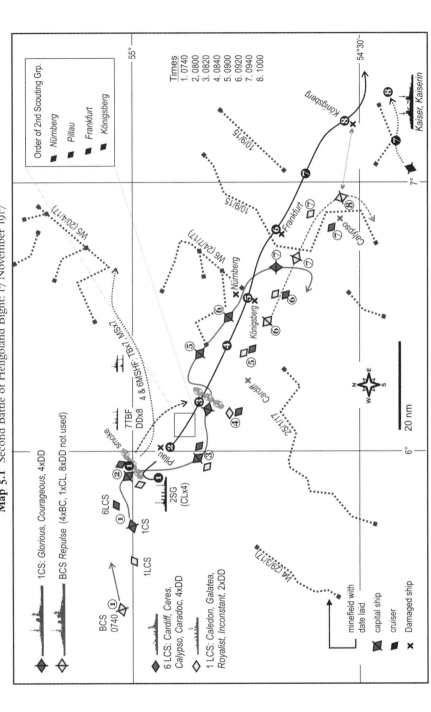

Königsberg's starboard quarter. They were much nearer and at 0850 and shortly thereafter three shells slammed into *Cardiff*: one started a fire forward, another hit above the aft control station, and a third struck the torpedo flat.

As the Germans found the range, Napier spotted the enemy and saw they were holding a southeast course. At 0852 he renewed the pursuit by steaming in their wake and disregarding an 0858 recall signal made by Admiral Pakenham in the belief that the opposing forces had lost contact.

At 0900 a near miss peppered *Nürnberg* with splinters and a light caliber shell struck *Königsberg*. This pressure caused the Germans to start laying fresh smoke at 0910. At 0912 Reuter ordered his destroyers to attack with torpedoes and over the next half hour *V45*, *V44*, *V43*, and *G92* and the light cruisers launched nine torpedoes to starboard toward the British light cruisers. One narrowly passed ahead of *Royalist* and another missed *Cardiff* by thirty yards but there were no hits.

As a result of the distance lost when crossing the second smoke screen, the shooting was poor for the 1st CS. At 0907 *Glorious* reported that "range of enemy appeared to be well over 30,000. Hulls were not visible, only column of smoke being seen from bridge."[45] At 0915 *Courageous* ceased fire. The distance between *Königsberg* and the nearest British cruiser, however, had dropped below ten thousand yards and continued to fall. *Repulse* was behind the light cruiser squadrons and steaming hard to catch up. At 0915 her weapons rumbled into action, firing five two-gun salvos over the 1st LCS, range 20,400 yards. Starting at 0920 three 6-inch rounds plunged into *Frankfurt* in rapid succession. One knocked out a gun and rangefinder and another hit the main mast.

Along with smoke and spotty visibility a fear of submarines inhibited the British attack. Lookouts on board *Glorious* reported torpedo tracks four times and periscopes thrice, although the captain rightfully regarded these sightings as doubtful. *Repulse* fired several times on what her lookouts believed were submarines or periscopes and she maneuvered to avoid imaginary torpedoes. Her captain complained that "it [was] necessary to pay more attention to this menace than was conducive to satisfactory gunnery results."[46]

By 0932, Napier reached what he considered the absolute edge of safe waters and started bending course to the south. For the next half hour *Courageous* and *Glorious* loitered on this stop line. Fog was thickening in the area and *Courageous* reported visibility of a thousand yards. Rear Admiral Phillimore on board *Repulse* had more accurate information about the minefields and pressed deeper into the bight with the light cruiser squadrons in company. At 0937 *Repulse* obtained a target and delivered five double salvos in just under four minutes. At 0940 a 15-cm round from *Pillau* or *Frankfurt* struck *Calypso*'s conning tower and killed everyone there. Splinters also sprayed the bridge and cut down many, including the captain.

At this point the *Kaiserin* leading *Kaiser* finally appeared from the southeast. The two dreadnoughts had a lot of distance to cover from Heligoland Island after learning II Scouting Group was in action with enemy battlecruisers. Moreover, the German senior officer, Captain Grassoff, believed (with reason) he would be facing a superior force and rather than rush headlong into battle (which might have cut off the British), he turned northeast on a converging course. Upon obtaining a distance glimpse of the enemy light cruisers he mistook them for the battlecruisers he expected because of their tripod masts. At 0941 *Kaiserin* opened fire at an estimated range of 17,500 yards. She fired two salvoes before the targets disappeared. As huge geysers erupted around the light cruisers, *Caledon* signaled *Repulse* that the enemy battle fleet was in sight. This report was punctuated by a 30.5-cm round that struck the light cruiser on the waterline (but did little damage). *Galatea* reported: "Battleships, Battle Cruisers and Light Cruisers," and at 1002 *Repulse* herself recorded the enemy battle fleet was visible bearing 160 degrees. At 1003 *Repulse* swung to starboard assuming a southwesterly course. As Phillimore rushed to break contact the battlecruiser's aft turret fired one salvo. This Parthian shot landed on *Königsberg* from 16,000 yards and ignited a serious fire in a coal bunker. By 1005 the action had died away. *Kaiserin* had fired eight salvoes in total and *Kaiser* only two. At 1040 fog rolled in and visibility dropped to nil, ensuring there would not be a vigorous pursuit even though the Germans had concentrated another four capital ships in the area by noon.[47]

Admiral Beatty and the Admiralty were unhappy with the operation's results although, given the minefields that severely cramped movement (and staff's failure to disseminate updated information on them), the calm, hazy weather that was ideally suited to the creation of smokescreens, and the proximity of heavy enemy units, their expectations were unrealistic. Beatty criticized Napier in particular for advancing too slowly in the early stages of the battle, even though Napier pursued at 25 knots—close to the maximum speed of the British light cruisers—and boldly plunged through two smoke screens. It might have been better to ask why the opportunity was not taken to savage the "infinitely more valuable minesweeping vessels." The British fired 3,170 4- and 6-inch rounds for just four hits. On the German side the Admiralstab considered that Reuter had protected the minesweepers effectively but that Grassoff had shown "a lack of resolution in the face of the enemy." Grassoff ended the war ashore in Austria while Reuter was rewarded with Hipper's old job as German battlecruiser commander.[48]

The Pellew Convoy: 12 December, 1205–1240

Conditions: Rough seas, high winds from the northwest, squalls
Missions: British, escort; Germans, interception
British Force (Lieutenant-Commander J. R. C. Cavendish): DD Pellew[#], Partridge*; AMT Commander Fullerton*, Livingston*, Lord Alverstone*, Tokio*. Convoy: BR MM Cordova* (2,284 GRT), NO MM Bollsta* (1,701 GRT), Maracaibo* (525 GRT), SW MM Bothnia* (1,723 GRT), Torleif* (846 GRT), NO MM Kong Magnus* (1,101 GRT).
German Force (Captain Lieutenant Hans Kolbe): 3 TBHF: DD G101, G103, G104, V100.

The High Seas Fleet mounted another antishipping operation to Dogger Bank on 12–13 November, but with little success. Undiscouraged, staff scheduled a third operation. This time, the raiders would be the eight big destroyers of the hardworking II TBF. Four would hunt along the English east coast while the other four swept the Anglo-Norwegian convoy route where Bremse and Brummer had enjoyed their success.

II TBF left base at 0245 on 11 December, taking a northern course through German and British minefields. The destroyers turned west at the Horns

Reef Light Vessel and reached the northwestern edge of Dogger Bank at 1600. There the flotilla split, with four destroyers heading north and four west to the English coast. Room 40 failed to detect the planned operation.

The English coast contingent chased a phantom convoy (incorrectly deduced from intercepted British radio signals) through the early morning hours of 12 December and almost met with a real one. *B112* torpedoed and sank a straggler from the convoy, while *B112* and *B97* together torpedoed and damaged another, and the group combined to sink one of a group of four trawlers.[49] They turned for home at 0440 and reached base without further adventure. The Admiralty was unaware of their presence as the stragglers made no signals and the trawlers reported a submarine attack.

The four destroyers that headed north zigzagged back and forth across the Anglo-Norwegian convoy route and at 1127, when ninety miles northeast of Stavanger, finally spotted smoke on the southern horizon. This came from a convoy of six steamers out of Lerwick bound for Bergen, being led through heavy seas by two destroyers and four armed trawlers spread around the convoy's perimeter. *Partridge* saw the strangers at 1145 but because of a defective signal light she was slow to challenge. The German ships used the delay to close range. When it dropped to roughly eight thousand yards Lieutenant-Commander Cavendish ordered the convoy to scatter and turned to confront the Germans. At 1205 *G101*, *G103*, and *V100* began firing at the British warships from six thousand yards while *G104*, speed limited by a condenser defect, chased merchantmen.

The fight quickly turned against the escorts. The Germans were aided by a northwest wind blowing spray over the British ships and by the fact that they outgunned them by a factor of three to one. At 1215 a shell exploded in *Partridge*'s engine room. This blow severed her main steam pipe, scalded everyone nearby to death, and brought her to a halt. Next a shell destroyed her aft gun. *V100* and *G103* launched torpedoes as *Partridge* lost way and one detonated forward. *V100* and *G103* closed to torpedo her again, whereupon two officers on board the sinking ship uncorked a torpedo at *V100*. This missed whereas the German ones did not, hastening *Partridge*'s end. There were only twenty-seven survivors.

Pellew fared little better. A German shell blasted her engine room and reduced her speed. She likely would have shared *Partridge*'s fate but a fortuitous rain squall hid her from view as she staggered south. Rather than chase her down, *G101*, *G103*, and *V100* joined *G104* in savaging the convoy. None of the steamers or trawler escort escaped the quick and efficient execution and by 1240 the German destroyers were shaping course for the Skagerrak.

The British destroyers had promptly reported the attack although without giving details. The message was received at noon by a squadron of two armored cruisers and four destroyers sixty miles west. The destroyers arrived at the scene in time to rescue survivors, but the Germans were far away by then. Three light cruisers and four destroyers patrolling farther south also missed the raiders.

Once again the Kaiserliche Marine had struck with apparent impunity. Without bigger escorts the Norwegian convoys would always be vulnerable to a well-handled raiding force. This action and the *Mary Rose* disaster helped precipitate Admiral Jellicoe's resignation as First Sea Lord while Admiral Beatty (now commanding the Grand Fleet) began sending a battleship division to cover this convoy route.[50]

Baltic 1917

By the second half of 1917 Russia seemed to be teetering on the brink of defeat. In September the German army took Riga and, looking for any means to make the new government sue for terms, allocated a reinforced division to capture the archipelago off the Gulf of Riga. The navy command was eager to cooperate, hoping action would quell rising unrest among the fleet's sailors. Thus, the Kaiserliche Marine committed massive forces to the operation: one battlecruiser, ten battleships, nine cruisers, fifty destroyers, six submarines, and many auxiliaries, all commanded by Vice Admiral Ehrhard Schmidt, who had led the 1915 Gulf of Riga offensive.

The German concept behind this operation, codenamed Albion, was simple. The navy would land the troops on the north coast of Ösel Island. Once ashore, they would prevent the garrison from escaping east to Moon Island and capture the heavy Russian shore batteries on the Zerel Peninsula. The ships would support the army with their guns and prevent the Russian navy from intervening. Once the army secured Zerel, the fleet would break through the Irben Strait mine barriers, steam into the gulf, and expel the Russian navy. At the same time, the troops would cross the gap between Ösel and Moon and round up any enemy troops remaining in the archipelago. The Russians would lose the gulf and much of the Estonian coast, and the Germans would be that much closer to Petrograd.

The Russians recognized the threat, but were uncertain of the schedule. They thickened the Irben Strait minefields and reinforced the batteries at Zerel and elsewhere throughout the archipelago. The fixed defenses were backed by a squadron commanded by Vice Admiral M. K. Bakhirev consisting of two old battleships, two armored cruisers, a light cruiser, three gunboats, twenty-three destroyers, and three submarines. Four regiments garrisoned the islands.[51]

Action in Soela Sound: 12 October, 0930–

Conditions: Clear

Missions: Russians, patrol; Germans, bombardment

Russian Force (Captain 1st Rank Postelnikov): DD *General Kondratenko, Pogranichnik.*

German Forces (Commodore Paul Heinrich): CL *Emden.* 2 Baltic ASWF: DD *T130*; TB *A31, A27, A29.*

The German assault troops landed on Ösel at Tagga Bay and Pokka early on 12 October, establishing beachheads against weak opposition. Naval operations in the invasion's immediate wake focused on Soela Sound and Kasser Wiek to the east. While the sound was too shallow for ships larger than destroyers, it provided passage for Russian flotilla craft to raid German beachheads, while the Germans could use it to threaten the Moon Island anchorages.

The first action in Soela Sound was instigated by a German bombardment of the radio station at Pamerort on Ösel's north coast. Three torpedo boats and an old destroyer entered the sound and were promptly confronted by *General Kondratenko* and *Pogranichnik.* The Russians opened fire at 0930 and forced the Germans to retreat. The light cruiser *Emden*, hovering off the sound's western entrance, entered the fray firing from 17,000 yards and drove the Russians back into Kasser Wiek.[52]

Action in Kasser Wiek: 12 October, 1400 to dusk

Conditions: Clear

Missions: Russians, patrol; Germans, raid

Russian Force (Rear Admiral G. K. Stark): GB *Groziashchii*[#]; DD *Desna, General Kondratenko, Pogranichnik, Raziashchii*.

German Forces: 13 TBHF (Captain Lieutenant Konrad Zander): DD *V82, S64, S61, S63, V47*. Baltic ASWF (Frigate Captain Otto Rosenberg): DD *T144*; TB *A32, A28, A30, A31, A27, A29*.

The Germans made their first determined thrust into Kasser Wiek on the afternoon of 12 October. The battleship *Bayern* pounded the 6-inch battery on Dagö while *Emden* ventured as far forward as shoal waters would permit. At 1430 the 13 TBHF and the ASW flotilla passed through Soela Sound. The Germans hoped the shallow drafts of the A-boats would give them more freedom to maneuver and allow them to support the lightly armed bicycle troops, who had pushed forward to seize the causeway between Ösel and Moon Islands.

Gunboat *Groziashchii* was patrolling Kasser Wiek supported by *General Kondratenko* and *Pogranichnik*. At 1426 *Groziashchii* opened fire from 14,000 yards on the approaching Germans. She straddled with her fourth salvo and forced the destroyers to make smoke and zigzag. The Germans then turned their broadsides to the enemy to force the gunboat back and continued their advance as *Groziashchii* retreated toward *General Kondratenko* and *Pogranichnik*. The antagonists repeated this pattern several times at ranges that varied between eight and thirteen thousand yards. The German shells hit *Groziashchii* three times toward the end of the action, by which time the destroyers *Desna* (flying the flag of Rear Admiral Stark) and *Raziashchii* had reinforced the embattled Russian squadron. *Desna* pumped out fifty-seven 4-inch shells from 12,800 yards. *Novik, Iziaslav, Zabiiaka*, and *Grom* also headed toward the fray but arrived too late to participate.

Map 5.2 Baltic Islands

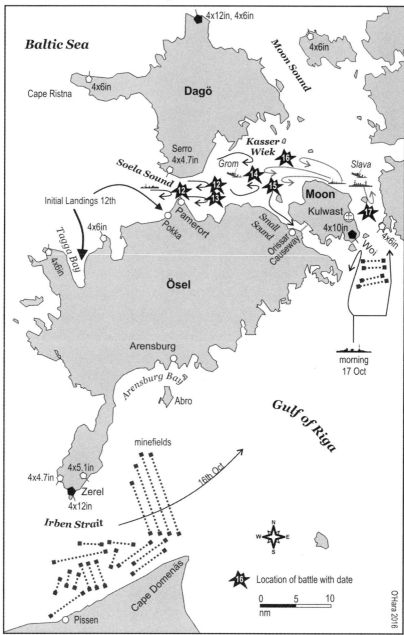

As their troops battling for the causeway did not require immediate
support, the Germans withdrew so as to exit Soela Sound before dark.
The Russians had successfully stood off the first probe with some

damage to *Groziashchii*, but the Germans had established that Soela Sound was not blocked by mines. They would be back.[53]

Actions in Kasser Wiek: 13 October, 0750–, 0930–, 1349–1355

Conditions: Variable visibility with rain

Missions: Russians, patrol; Germans, patrol

Russian Force (Rear Admiral G. I. Stark): GB *Khivinets*; DD *Novik*, *Grom*[+], *Raziashchii*, *Iziaslav*, *Samson*.

German Force (Commodore Heinrich): CL *Emden*; Baltic ASWF: DD *T144*; TB *A32*, *A28*, *A30*, *A31*, *A27*, *A29*.

The next day skirmishing in Kasser Wiek continued. *Novik*, *Grom*, and *Raziashchii* closed and engaged the ASW flotilla near Soela Sound at 0750. The Germans riposted by bringing *Emden* up to return fire from 15,000 yards. The Russians withdrew east, while the German boats shifted west. Other than some splinters, the only damage done was to *Grom*'s radio antenna.

After this action died away, *Emden* closed the sound and at 0930 engaged the newly arrived destroyers *Iziaslav* and *Samson*. This second engagement took the same course as the first. After a few rounds from the light cruiser the destroyers retired out of range.

Determined to dislodge *Emden* from the western end of the sound, Admiral Stark ordered *Khivinets* to advance. He believed *Khivinets*' 4.7-inch guns outranged *Emden*'s weapons by 1,600 yards. At 1349 *Khivinets* opened fire at extreme range but *Emden*'s reply straddled the gunboat forcing her to withdraw after only six minutes. Meanwhile, 13 TBHF had pulled back to take on ammunition (one boat ran aground when returning to Soela Sound and required docking), while the destroyers of 4 TBHF arrived to bolster German forces for another a break-in attempt on 14 October, this time with battleship support.

The Russians had kept Kasser Wiek and Soela Sound open as a sally port but German strength made them conclude the passage would be better sealed. They planned to sink a blockship and lay mines, but their plans went awry. The blockship ran aground before it reached position, while on minelayer *Pripiat* the sailor's committee aborted the operation because they considered it too dangerous. Combat on 14 October would again be ship against ship.[54]

Break-in to Kasser Wiek: 14 October, 1145–1600

Conditions: Good, then deteriorating visibility

Missions: Russians, patrol; Germans, raid

Russian Forces: 1st DD Div (Captain 2nd Rank G. S. Pilsudskii): DD *Grom*★, *Zabiiaka*#, *Pobeditel*+, *Konstantin*; GB *Khrabryi*+. Reinforcements (Rear Admiral G. K. Stark): GB *Khivinets*; DD *Novik, Samson, Steregushchii, Zabaikalets, Vsadnik, Amurets, Moskvitianin, Finn.*

German Forces (Commodore Heinrich): BB *Kaiser*; DD *V46, S50*; MS *T55, T62.* II TBF: DD *B98, G101*#, *G103*#, *G104, V100, B111, B109, B97, B110, B112.* 13 TBHF: DD *S61, S64, S63, V74.* Baltic AWSF: DD *T144*; TB *A32, A28, A30, A31, A27, A29.*

Kaiser arrived off Soela Sound early in the morning of 14 October. Schmidt planned to have her support a more determined effort to penetrate Kasser Wiek. The passage to her designated anchorage had to be searched for hazards so not until 1145 did *Kaiser* open fire on *Grom, Zabiiaka, Pobeditel*, and *Konstantin* anchored in western Kasser Wiek. The destroyers promptly got under way, gushing smoke to cover their withdrawal, but *Kaiser* landed a 30.5-cm shell on *Grom's* starboard turbine from 21,000 yards before they could get clear. *Grom* made it back into the inlet, but soon lost all power. Meanwhile, German light forces advanced. Ten destroyers of II TBF separated into two groups and headed toward Soela Sound's southern part. The 13 TBHF went north, and *T144* with six A-boats followed. The A-boats would turn south into Small Sound to support the German troops at the Ösel–Moon Island causeway. Even though *Kaiser* ceased her initial bombardment by 1208, the German vessels did not clear the tricky passage before 1320. *G101* never made it through the sound; she grounded and had to withdraw.

At 1330 the Germans debouched into Kasser Wiek, dueling with Russian destroyers at ranges from 12,000 yards. The two southern groups formed a line of battle while 13 TBHF supported with flanking fire from the north. During the action the Germans hit *Zabiiaka* on a gun mount, and *G103* was rocked by a near miss astern that caused flooding and forced her retreat. Rear Admiral Stark sent *Khrabryi*, just returning from a bombardment mission at Small Sound, to tow *Grom* clear of danger. The gunboat came alongside and began to drag the crippled ship eastward at 3 knots while the other destroyers struggled in the increasing winds to cover her with smoke.

Khrabryi had not gone far when, at 1340, the heavy wash of two destroyers rushing by at high speed snapped the tow. She tried to secure another line but *Grom*'s demoralized crew had had enough. When the gunboat approached some men leapt to her decks and others into the water. *V100* added to the pandemonium, smacking *Grom* astern at 1345 with a 10.5-cm shell and starting a fire. *Khrabryi* gave up the salvage attempt and the Russians withdrew east, making smoke and firing at both the enemy and the abandoned destroyer. The Germans replied, hitting *Pobeditel* once and *Khrabryi* twice. *B97* tried to tow *Grom* back to Soela Sound but the Russian vessel capsized before she had gone far. The Germans, however, captured current maps of the minefields from the wreck. These proved vital in subsequent operations.

As II TBF and 13 TBHF pressed eastward, the Russian commander called for reinforcements. At 1535 destroyers *Novik*, *Samson*, *Steregushchii*, *Zabaikalets*, *Vsadnik*, *Amurets*, *Moskvitianin*, and *Finn* plus gunboat *Khivinets* all entered the fight. Their fire along with deteriorating visibility stopped the German advance.

During the surface action the A-boats headed south along the Ösel coast to Orissar. This village dominated the causeway to Moon Island. The German troops there were hard-pressed; they had seized the causeway's western end on the day of the invasion but had since been pushed back. After sorting friend from foe, the A-boats shot up some Russian armored cars crossing to Ösel and landed some much-needed ammunition for the beleaguered troops. The A-boats returned from their support mission late in the day. The ships of 13 TBHF and II TBF then turned about and anchored in the western portion of Kasser Wiek.

The Kaiserliche Marine had sunk a Russian destroyer and damaged two others as well as a gunboat, but it had lost the services of two of its big destroyers, *G101* and *G103*. It had pushed the Russians far enough east to allow the A-boats to support the infantry ashore, but it did not break through to Moon Sound or even retain a hold on most of Kasser Wiek. More hard fighting lay ahead.[55]

Action in Kasser Wiek: 15 October, dawn to dusk

Conditions: Clear

Missions: Russians, patrol; Germans, raid

Russian Forces: OBB *Slava*; AC *Admiral Makarov*; GB *Khrabryi, Khivinets*. 5th DD Div: DD *Vsadnik, Moskvitianin*. Reinforcements: DD *Samson, Leitenant Ilin, Desna*; GB *Groziashchii*.

German Forces (Commodore Heinrich): DD *S50, V46*. II TBF: DD *B98*#, *G104, B109, V100, B110*#, *B111, B97, B112*#. 13 TBHF: DD *S61, S64, S63, V74*. Baltic ASWF: DD *T144*; TB *A32, A28, A30, A31, A27, A29*.

The Russians finally succeeded in mining Kasser Wiek during the night of 14/15 October and then assigned destroyers *Vsadnik* and *Moskvitianin* and gunboats *Khrabryi* and *Khivinets* to cover the new barrage.

The next morning eleven destroyers screened *T144* and the six A-boats as they deployed toward Small Sound to support the troops there. The larger ships weighed anchor at 0455 in three groups: half of II TBF to patrol north-south while the rest of the flotilla and 13 TBHF patrolled east-west lines. *V100, S50*, and *V46* formed a fourth covering group at 0800. The Germans came under fire from *Khrabryi* and *Khivinets* to the east, *Admiral Makarov* from the northeast, and *Slava* and three 10-inch guns of the Woi battery from beyond Moon Island. The A-boats advanced at 0530 and started shelling the Ösel–Moon causeway but withdrew when *Vsadnik* and *Moskvitianin* confronted them. They returned after an hour and resumed their task with such enthusiasm that *A29* and *A31* emptied their magazines. These two vessels returned through Soela Sound: *A29* to get more ammunition for the A-boats and *A31* to load munitions for delivery to the troops the following morning.

The other German and Russian warships dueled in Kasser Wiek throughout the day. The Russians sent in gunboat *Groziashchii* and destroyers *Samson* and *Leitenant Ilin* at midday and *Desna* in the afternoon. In contrast, the Germans weakened as the day progressed. *B98* lost her bows to a mine sown the night before and *B110* and *B112* ran aground at 1610 while maneuvering in the inlet. *B112* holed an oil bunker and damaged a propeller. *B98* survived her mining, but both she and *B112* were out of the battle.[56]

Last Push in Kasser Wiek: 16 October, 0830–1230

Conditions: Clear

Missions: Russians, patrol; Germans, transport

Russian Force (Vice Admiral M. K. Bakhirev): OBB *Slava*; CA *Admiral Makarov*; GB *Khivinets, Groziashchii*; DD *Vsadnik, Moskvitianin, Samson, Leitenant Ilin, Iziaslav, Avtroil#, Gavriil.*

German Forces (Commodore Heinrich): DD *S50, V46.* II TBF: DD *V100, G104, B109, B110, B97.* 13 TBHF: *S64, S61, S63, V74.* Baltic ASWF: DD *T144*; TB *A32, A28, A30, A31, A27, A29.*

On the morning of 16 October the fighting at the eastern end of Ösel reached a climax. Eleven destroyers protected the A-boats as they again sallied to support the troops. *Slava* and the Woi battery subjected these units to indirect fire. With their movements restricted by the minefield laid on 14 October in the middle of Kasser Wiek, two II TBF ships took forward positions while the rest anchored to the rear. At 0830 Russian patrol forces (*Khivinets, Groziashchii, Vsadnik, Moskvitianin, Samson,* and *Leitenant Ilin*) began to harass the picket ships but the engagement ended when the rest of the German squadron raised anchor and drove them off. At noon five minesweepers arrived and, supported by the eleven destroyers, cleared the field.

The appearance of German hospital ship *Viola* in Kasser Wiek sparked the day's most violent action. The Russians assumed she was a transport bringing troops to assault Moon Island. *Slava,* the Woi battery guns, and *Admiral Makarov* attacked her vigorously from long range while the patrol force, reinforced by destroyers *Iziaslav, Avtroil,* and *Gavriil,* intervened and engaged from 13,000 yards at 1214. The Germans responded when the range closed to 11,000 yards. In a fifteen-minute action the Germans hit *Avtroil* three times, perforating an oil bunker and inflicting casualties among her bridge personnel.

Admiral Schmidt considered a night torpedo attack on the Russian squadron in Moon Sound, but decided the potential rewards of an attack did not justify the risk. The Kaiserliche Marine and the Russian navy had committed many ships to a small area and battled each other to a standstill. The focus of naval operations would now shift to southern Moon Sound.[57]

The Battle of Moon Sound: 17 October, 0722–1040

Conditions: Clear

Missions: Russians, interception; Germans, raid

Russian Force (Vice Admiral M. K. Bakhirev): OBB *Slava*★, *Grazh-danin*#; AC *Baian*#; DD *Ukraina, Voiskovoi, Donskoi Kazak, Turk-menets-Stavropolskii, Silnyi, Storozhevoi, Dyelni, Dyeyatelni*.

German Forces (Vice Admiral Paul Behncke): BB *König, Kronprinz*; CL *Kolberg, Strassburg*. X TBF: DD *S56, T170, T169, T172, G175, T165, V78, V77, G89, S65, S66*. 3 MSHF: MS *T136, M67*+, *M68, M75, M76, M77*+, *T59, T65, T68, T82, T85*. 8 MSHF: MS *M64, M11, M31, M32, M39*; TB *A35*.

While the Russians and Germans were trading punches in Kasser Wiek, the main German naval effort went forward in Irben Strait. Minesweepers chewed a path through the extensive barrages while German troops advanced toward the 12-inch battery at Zerel. Zerel fell on 16 October and two dreadnoughts, two light cruisers, X TBF, 3 MSHF, and 8 MSHF, along with a dozen minesweeping motorboats, had penetrated the Irben Strait minefields by mid-afternoon. The sweepers remained crucial because there were additional fields south of Moon Sound. Nor was the gulf free of other perils, as the Germans discovered when British submarine *C27* missed *König* with two torpedoes and hit tender *Indianola* with one. Directed to attack the Russians at Moon Sound, the German ships anchored several miles south of its entrance while their commanders made plans for the next day.

Two roughly rectangular barrages guarded Moon Sound's southern approaches, stacked north and south. The Germans planned to send 3 MSHF eastward along the bottom edge of the southern minefield and then north between the mainland and the eastern edge of both barrages. The battleships would follow. The 8 MSHF and the motorboats would move north up the western edges of the minefields. *Kolberg* and *Strassburg* would follow and head for Small Sound.

The Russian picket destroyers, *Dyelni* and *Dyeyatelni,* saw the smoke clouds of the German ships at 0600 on the 17th. By 0700 Vice Admiral Bakhirev ordered battleships *Slava* and *Grazhdanin* (ex-*Tsesarevich*), the cruiser *Baian*, and six destroyers south to confront the threat. The battleship crews were initially reluctant to move, but finally followed Bakhirev in *Baian* when she steamed past signaling "follow the admiral." At the same time, *König* scattered the Russian pickets with a few 30.5-cm salvos so the minecraft could begin sweeping.

The Woi battery opened on the western group of minesweepers at 0722 but 8 MSHF continued its advance toward Small Sound. By 0805 *Grazhdanin* had reached southern Moon Sound and was firing at the western group of sweepers. *Slava* soon joined her; 8 MSHF and its escort of two destroyers tried to screen their activities with smoke.

König and *Kronprinz* had turned east at 0800 to follow the eastern minesweeper group. This brought them within *Slava's* range. Her four 12-inch guns and mountings had been modified and could reach to 23,000 yards, compared to *Grazhdanin's* maximum of 17,600 yards and the German battleships' 22,400 yards. *Slava* shifted her fire to the enemy's capital ships by 0812. They found her shells dropping within fifty yards while their return salvos splashed short. Vice Admiral Behncke decided to hold the battleships back until 3 MSHF had cleared more water. He therefore ordered the big ships to reverse course while the minesweepers continued cutting cables and exploding mines.

The sweeping proved slow and difficult. Soon the sweepers came close enough for the predreadnoughts to use their 6-inch weapons, and the shells raining down complicated an already dangerous job. Nonetheless, splinter damage to *M77* and *M67* was the only harm suffered. The sweepers turned the corner to the north by 0840. *Slava* switched back to the German battleships at 0900 but found the range excessive. Unfortunately *Slava's* final salvo disabled her forward turret. Reinforced by motor minesweepers at 0940, the sweeping force continued working north. At this point the larger Russian warships paused to feed their crews while the Germans kept coming. By 1004 the Russians were again in action, *Slava* with her stern to the enemy to deploy her aft guns. The battleships targeted the minesweepers, now less than 14,000 yards off.

Russian predreadnought *Slava* sinking in Moon Sound, October 1917, after bitterly contesting the German conquest of the Baltic Islands. (Wiki Public Domain)

Vice Admiral Behncke had been waiting for the sweepers to close the range. He now lunged north in their wake at high speed. *König* engaged *Slava* at 1013 while *Kronprinz* opened on *Grazhdanin* at 1017. At 1025 three projectiles from the same salvo slammed into *Slava*. One blasted a fifteen foot hole beneath the waterline and caused severe flooding forward and a 9-degree list to port. Several fires erupted and casualties littered *Slava's* decks. Over the next fifteen minutes *König* landed four more rounds on *Slava* while *Kronprinz* hit *Grazhdanin* twice. With this, Vice Admiral Bakhirev ordered his ships to withdraw. He brought up the rear in *Baian*, but not before *König* knocked her at 1036 with a particularly heavy blow that started fires, holed the double bottom, and forced the flooding of her forward 6-inch and 8-inch magazines. Russian return gunnery was ineffective. *König* and *Kronprinz* had decided the action by hitting ten times in twenty-six minutes at ranges of 18,000 yards or greater. But while they forced the Russians to withdraw, they could not pursue because of the mine danger and a net barrier discovered at the southern mouth of Moon Sound. The Russian ships were beyond range by 1040.

With *Slava* badly damaged and the German forces pressing on both land and sea, Bakhirev abandoned the Moon Island position. The Russians had dredged a channel north from Moon deep enough to give heavy vessels access to the Gulf of Finland, but not deep enough to accommodate *Slava* in her flooded state. Bakhirev intended that she block the channel's southern end, but the engine room personnel abandoned their stations prematurely and she grounded east of the channel mouth instead. *Slava* was blown up at 1158 and then torpedoed for good measure, although only one of the six torpedoes fired hit her and exploded.

While the main action went on south of Moon Sound, the forces in the Kasser Wiek remained relatively quiet, as the German ships resupplied during the morning. *V100* advanced to investigate the smoke cloud resulting from *Slava*'s scuttling, but gunboat *Khrabryi* and destroyer *Konstantin* quickly forced her back. A night torpedo attack by *S61*, *S64*, and *V74* (with *S50* as a marker boat) went adrift when *S64* hit a mine and ran aground. She was abandoned and the attack canceled.[58]

Last Gasp in Moon Sound: 18 October, 1310–1415

Conditions: Clear

Missions: Russians, minelaying; Germans, sweep

Russian Force: GB *Khivinets, Groziashchii, Khrabryi*; DD *Zabaikalets, Voiskovoi, General Kondratenko, Pogranichnik*; ML *Gruz, Minrep, Udarnik, Kapsiul.*

German Force: DD *V180, V184.*

Russian resistance in Moon Sound continued even after *Slava*'s destruction as light forces remained to lay minefields and evacuate personnel. At 1310 *V180* and *V184* ventured north to scout Moon Sound and ran into a buzz saw. First they exchanged fire with *Zabaikalets* and *Voiskovoi*, which were laying mines, and then *Khivinets*, the escort of the Moon Sound evacuation force. Finally they ran afoul of *General Kondratenko* and *Pogranichnik* and gunboats *Khrabryi* and *Groziashchii* covering other Russian activities. When the last force opened fire at 1415 the German duo decided enough was enough, made smoke, and headed south. While the Germans had considerable mopping-up to do, this was the last action in the Gulf of Riga.[59]

Albion was Germany's largest sustained naval effort of the war and the largest combined operation undertaken by the German military. They captured the Baltic Islands, but at considerable cost. While the navy lost only one destroyer, three minesweepers, and a few other minor vessels, battleships *Grosser Kürfurst* and *Bayern* hit mines during the operation and *Markgraf* shortly after its conclusion. *B98* and *B111* were mined as well; tender *Indianola* was torpedoed by *C27* and other ships were damaged through grounding. In return the Germans had sunk *Slava* and *Grom*. On occasion the Baltic Fleet's determination seemed shaky but overall Russian crews fought better than the troops ashore. The Bolshevik revolution was just weeks away and would bring in its train the end to all naval operations beyond those necessary to keep the fleet out of German clutches, but there was no way for the Germans to predict that when they launched Albion and at the time it was a logical, perhaps overdue, use of force.

Black Sea 1917
Battle off the Bosporus: 25 June, 1215–1715
Conditions: Clear
Missions: Russians, transit; Ottomans, transit
Russian Force: BB *Svobodnaia Rossiia*; DD *Schastlivyi, Gnevnyi*.
Ottoman Force (Corvette Captain Knorr): CL *Midilli*; TB *Basra*.

On 23 June *Midilli* navigated the hazards at the mouth of the Bosporus on a mission to lay a barrage off the mouths of the Danube and raid a radio station on nearby Fidonisi Island. She destroyed the station and when it went off the air the Russians investigated and learned that *Midilli* was at sea. By chance a Black Sea Fleet squadron consisting of dreadnought *Svobodnaia Rossiia,* (ex-*Imperatritsa Ekaterina*) and two destroyers was also under way, covering two mine groups detailed to thicken the Bosporus barrages. The battleship group was the farthest west and in the best position to intercept the Ottoman raider.

Rossiia spotted *Midilli*'s smoke to the west at 1210 and sent *Gnevnyi* to investigate. *Midilli* saw the destroyer five minutes later. The two warships traded ineffective salvos at long range (15,400 yards according to the Russians; 21,500 according to *Midilli*). Meanwhile, the battleship crept up on the Ottoman cruiser's port beam and the destroyers escorting the mine groups were ordered to cut *Midilli* off. At 1424 *Rossiia* judged the range to be 24,400 yards and opened fire with her forward turrets. Her shells splashed short whereupon *Midilli* increased to 25 knots, began

to make smoke, and edged away to the west. Realizing that *Gnevnyi*—
now tucked into *Midilli*'s wake—was directing *Rossiia*'s guns, the cruiser
tried to jam her radio transmissions and opened fire in a bid to blind the
destroyer with shell splashes. *Gnevnyi* zigged at 1435 only to zag back
and close range.

By this time, *Midilli* had pulled beyond *Rossiia*'s reach. The cruiser
slowed to 18 knots both to ease the strain on her overtaxed machinery and to draw *Gnevnyi* into gun range. At 1619 the Russian was close
enough. Three salvos quickly followed forcing *Gnevnyi* to make a 90- degree
turn. This rid *Midilli* of one tormentor, but her respite was only temporary. *Rossiia* had closed when *Midilli* slowed. In this the battleship was
inadvertently helped by the torpedo boat *Basra*, which joined *Midilli*
to escort her to the Bosporus. *Basra*'s top speed of 18 knots restricted
Midilli to that speed as well. By 1658, *Midilli* was again under destroyer
fire and three minutes later *Rossiia* joined in. Fortunately for *Midilli*, she
had almost reached the straits. The Russians broke off the action at 1715
when it became clear that *Bystryi*, *Derzkii*, and *Gromkii,* the destroyers
sent to cut *Midilli* off, had failed in their mission. The light cruiser had
survived another perilous encounter.[60]

As 1917 wore on the Black Sea Fleet slowly slid into revolutionary
impotence. The last tsarist commander of the fleet, Vice Admiral Kolchak, was ousted by sailors' and soldiers' councils just before this action.
Nonetheless, Russian destroyers continued to patrol the Anatolian coast
up to the end. The last surface engagement occurred shortly before the
Bolshevik takeover.

Attack off Iğneada: 29 October, 0600–0900

    Conditions: Unknown
    Missions: Russians, raid; Ottomans, escort
    Russian Force: DD *Bystryi*, *Pylkii*.
    Ottoman Force: TB *Hamidabad*★.

Hamidabad had escorted three motor minesweepers to Iğneada near the
Bulgarian frontier and was anchored there when the Russian destroyers
attacked at dawn, opening fire at just over three thousand yards. The torpedo boat was loaded with gasoline and the second Russian salvo caught

her astern. This ignited her cargo and she sank with eight men killed and six wounded. The destroyers also damaged two steamers and forced the minesweepers ashore. All were later salved. A battery of 88-mm guns engaged the Russians but its fire was ineffective. *Midilli* sortied when news of the attack arrived in Constantinople but far too late to catch the raiders.[61]

The effect *Yavuz* and *Midilli* had on the Black Sea naval war is debatable. Some authors have portrayed their addition to the Ottoman fleet as of high strategic value, but this assessment seems exaggerated.[62] The two ships may have made Constantinople's entry into the war on the side of the Central Powers more likely, but a strong pro-German party already exerted great influence, and the British government's preemptory takeover of the dreadnoughts ordered by the Porte guaranteed the ascendancy of the anti-Entente factions. The two ships did not influence the Gallipoli campaign, which was a victory for Ottoman minefields and land defenses. As to their effect against the Russians, the German official history lists eleven forays by the *Yavuz* into the Black Sea, twenty-one by *Midilli*, and seven in which the ships acted together. They did little to offset Russian operations in support of the army or against Ottoman maritime traffic. Perhaps the Russians could have more quickly overwhelmed Ottoman seaborne communications in the absence of the ex-German warships. In early 1915 their presence complicated Russian plans to undertake an amphibious assault against the Bosporus, although there were other more compelling reasons why this landing never occurred. The most that can be said is that *Yavuz* and *Midilli* contributed a bit more to the Central Powers by being based at Constantinople than at Pola or Wilhelmshaven. Overall, the activities of the Ottoman navy had little strategic relevance.

Adriatic 1917
During 1917 submarines created havoc in the Mediterranean, producing a crisis by April when fourteen German boats sank more than a quarter million tons of shipping. As a consequence in the Mediterranean just as in the North Sea much surface forces activity revolved around the submarine war, especially maintaining the Otranto Barrage as a barrier against the underwater menace or attacking it to facilitate the passage of submarines through it.

On the night of 11/12 March four Austrian destroyers swept the strait but failed to sink an unescorted French steamer they encountered. On the night of 21/22 April the Austrian torpedo boat *100M* sank the Italian steamer *Japigia* (1,269 GRT). On 11 May *Csikós* with *96F*, *78T*, and *93F* headed south. The Italian destroyers *Animoso*, *Ardito*, *Ardente*, *Abba*, and *Audace* intercepted them short of their objective and forced their retreat to Cattaro. There was no damage on either side.

Rear Admiral Alexander Hansa, commander of the Austrian Cruiser Flotilla, planned an elaborate reprise of the 11 May attack for the night of the 14/15th. The scout cruisers *Novara*, *Helgoland*, and *Saïda* would raid the trawler line while two destroyers attacked shipping along the Albanian coast. At the same time the German submarine *UC25* would lay mines off Brindisi and the Austrian subs *U4* and *U27* would lurk in ambush off Valona and Brindisi respectively.

Borea *Convoy Action: 15 May, 0324–0345*

Conditions: Calm, clear, new moon

Missions: Italians, escort; Austrians, raid

Italian Force: DD *Borea*★; MM *Carroccio*★ (1,657 GRT), *Verità*#, *Bersagliere*+ (993 GRT).

Austrian Force: (Frigate Captain Johannes Liechtenstein) DD *Csepel*, *Balaton*.

The Habsburg ships departed Cattaro after dark on the 14th. It was a tranquil night, three days short of the new moon. *Csepel* and *Balaton* had a quiet run south and reached station off Valona at 0230 on 15 May. Forty minutes later they sighted shapes in the darkness. The raiders approached from astern and at 0324 *Csepel*'s searchlight pinned *Borea* just as she was turning to investigate smoke off her starboard quarter. In a flurry of rapid salvos the Austrian's 10-cm guns hit four times; one shell severed the old destroyer's main steam pipe. A large fire erupted as *Borea* coasted to a stop and began to settle. *Balaton* targeted *Carroccio* and detonated the steamer's cargo of ammunition. Next, Austrian guns pounded *Verità* and left her in flames. A tug from Valona towed the ship to port the next day. *Balaton* fired a torpedo at *Bersagliere* but missed and this transport escaped with minor damage.

Map 5.3 Battle of Otranto Strait: 15 May 1917

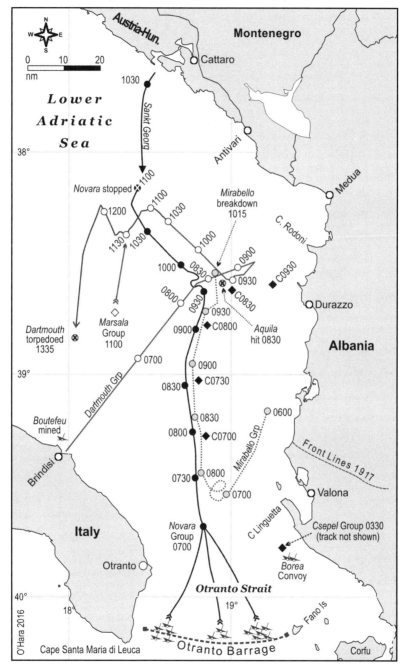

N
W · E
S

0 10 20
nm

Austria-Hun.

Montenegro

Cattaro

Lower Adriatic Sea

1030

Sankt Georg

38°

Antivari

Medua

1100

Novara stopped 1100

1200

1100

1030

Mirabello breakdown 1015

C. Rodoni

1130   1030

1000

0900

1000

0830

C0930

1000

0930

Durazzo

0800

0930   C0830

Albania

0930

Aquila hit 0830

Dartmouth torpedoed 1335

Marsala Group 1100

0900   C0800

Dartmouth Grp

0700

0900

39°

0830   C0730

0830

0600

Boutefeu mined

0800   C0700

Mirabello Grp

Brindisi

0730   0800

Front Lines 1917

0700

Valona

C Linguetta

Novara Group 0700

Csepel Group 0330 (track not shown)

Italy

Otranto

Borea Convoy

Otranto Strait

40°

18°

19°

Fano Is

O'Hara 2016   Cape Santa Maria di Leuca

Otranto Barrage

Corfu

The short, violent action lasted twenty minutes after which the raiders turned north at 25 knots. *Borea* sank shortly before dawn with eleven killed and twelve wounded. In the merchantmen five men died and nine were wounded. This well-conducted attack once again emphasized the importance of the first sighting and an effective first salvo. Only the presence of powerful enemy forces to the north kept Liechtenstein from lingering to finish the job.[63]

Battle of Otranto Strait: 15 May, 0710–1206

Conditions: Clear

Missions: Entente, interception; Austrians, raid

Entente Forces: Group 1: IT DL *Mirabello*; FR DD *Commandant Rivière*, *Cimeterre*[#], *Bisson*. Group 2 (Rear Admiral Alfredo Acton, RM): BR CL *Dartmouth*[#], *Bristol*; IT DL *Aquila*[#]; IT DD *Mosto*, *Pilo*, *Schiaffino*, *Acerbi*. Group 3: IT CL *Marsala*; IT DL *Racchia*; IT DD *Insidioso*, *Impavido*, *Indomito*.

Austrian Forces: Cruiser Group (Captain Miklós Horthy): CL *Helgoland*[+], *Saïda*[+], *Novara*[#]. Destroyer Group: *Csepel*, *Balaton*. Cattaro Group (Rear Admiral Alexander Hansa): CA *Sankt Georg*; DD *Tátra*, *Warasdiner*; TB *84F*, *88F*, *99M*, *100M*.

Horthy's cruisers reached the barrage at 0400. With masts cut down so as to resemble British cruisers, the ships passed through the line of drifters. There was at least one challenge, but the disguise seemed to work and no alarms were raised. They then doubled back, separated, and attacked from the south. Around 0500 *Helgoland* struck the western end of the forty-mile line, *Saïda* the middle, and *Novara* the east. Over the course of an hour they sank fourteen of the forty-seven drifters on patrol: *Admirable* (90 GRT), *Avondale* (80 GRT), *Coral Haven* (82 GRT), *Craignoon* (77 GRT), *Felicitas* (67 GRT), *Girl Gracie* (95 GRT), *Girl Rose* (86 GRT), *Helenora* (88 GRT), *Quarry Knowe* (98 GRT), *Selby* (75 GRT), *Serena* (86 GRT), *Taits* (93 GRT), *Transit* (83 GRT), and *Young Linnet* (93 GRT). They also damaged four others, three severely. Most crews obeyed megaphoned instructions to abandon ship. *Gowan Lee* resisted, but her 57-mm rounds merely bounced off *Novara*'s 20-mm armored belt. *Floandi* also fought back (and like

Gowan Lee survived damaged). The Austrians rescued seventy-two crewmen but fifty died.

At 0700 when Horthy's cruisers rendezvoused at a point midway between Otranto and Cape Linguetta there were already several Entente formations steaming to intercept. The Italian scout *Mirabello* and three French destroyers (a fourth, *Boutefeu* had dropped out due to condenser problems) were off Durazzo on the northern leg of their patrol when, at 0435, they received word of *Borea's* troubles. *Bristol* with *Mosto* and *Pilo* sortied from Brindisi shortly after 0500. Italian Rear Admiral Alfredo Acton in *Dartmouth*, accompanied by *Schiaffino* and *Acerbi*, followed at 0525. *Aquila* left port shortly thereafter. The scout cruiser *Marsala*, the scout *Racchia*, and more destroyers were raising steam. The armored cruiser *San Giorgio* and the light cruiser *Liverpool* were at six hours' notice due to coal shortages and this prevented their participation. The failure to have heavy support available would prove costly. By 0645 the seven ships that formed the *Dartmouth* group had concentrated and were sailing northeast at 24 knots in a ragged line abreast under Acton's command.

At 0700 the *Mirabello* group sighted Horthy's cruisers ten miles to the southwest and closed in line abreast. Their forward guns opened fire at 0710 from 9,300 yards and more but things went wrong from the beginning when *Cimeterre's* forward 100-mm gun exploded with its first shot. *Mirabello's* rounds dropped short while the Austrian return salvos were soon bracketing. After seven minutes *Mirabello* ordered a turn to starboard to form column and bring more guns to bear. Then she reported a submarine and torpedo tracks and made a complete circle to starboard to avoid this perceived danger. When the Entente group finally straightened out on a northerly course, Horthy had slipped past and was to their northwest.

Csepel and *Balaton* had hastened northward after sinking *Borea*. At 0735 they were twenty-five miles ahead of Horthy when they noted smoke to the northwest and bent course away from it. The smoke belonged to Acton's formation which, in turn, spotted the Austrians at 0745. They steamed on converging courses for a time, with neither side certain of the other's identity. At 0750 Acton ordered *Aquila* and the four destroyers to investigate and twenty minutes later to attack.

As the Italians moved out in line abreast with *Aquila* in the center, *Cse-pel* and *Balaton* ran toward Cape Rodoni. The brand-new *Aquila* was the fastest ship in the Regia Marina and she pulled ahead of her four smaller companions, opening fire at 0815 from 12,500 yards, deliver-ing a dozen 152-mm rounds as the range dropped to 10,500 yards. The report filed by Liechtenstein stated: "[W]hile the *Csepel* was hardly targeted, the *Balaton* was well covered by enemy salvos. Some shots fell close alongside *Balaton* at 0832." Nonetheless, *Csepel* hit first. At 0830 one of her 10-cm rounds exploded in *Aquila's* central boiler room, severing the main steam pipe and killing seven men. This blow deprived the large destroyer of power and she drifted to a stop. It was the second crippling blow *Csepel* had delivered that morning, this time at extreme range.[64]

Mosto and *Schiaffino* continued, approaching to nearly eight thousand yards, but their 76-mm rounds fell short. They turned away at 0905 when Durazzo's 15-cm shore battery started dropping rounds around them. At 0918 Acton ordered the small destroyers to rejoin his cruisers. Once the way was clear, *Csepel* and *Balaton* returned to Cattaro, evad-ing an attack by the French submarine *Bernouilli* along the way.

The action against the *Csepel* group had pulled Acton's force toward the Albanian coast, whilst astern the *Novara* group approached from the

Austro-Hungarian scout cruiser *Helgoland*. She and her two sisters were the most effective warships in the K.u.K. Kriegsmarine. (Ufficio Storico Marina Militare)

south. Wireless reports from *Csepel* and from aircraft radioed to Cattaro and rebroadcast to Horthy gave the Austrian commander a grasp of the general situation. He first spotted smoke off his starboard bow at 0845 and turned in that direction. At 0905 more smoke revealed Acton's formation. Forming a column in order *Novara, Saïda*, and *Helgoland*, he decided to distract the enemy from *Csepel* and *Balaton*, unaware they were already safe. He also radioed Cattaro to dispatch the armored cruiser *Sankt George* as quickly as possible. However, this would take several hours. The Austrians, like the Italians, had problems supplying their forward bases with enough coal and economized by keeping larger ships at partial readiness.

At 0910 Acton's lookouts spotted the enemy cruisers. The Italian admiral's first thought was for *Aquila*, which was helplessly wallowing in their exact route, and which was, at the moment, under attack by two Austrian seaplanes. Accordingly, he altered course to the southwest to cover *Aquila* rather than northwest to cut the enemy's line of retreat. At 0929 *Dartmouth* engaged *Novara* from nearly 11,000 yards. *Bristol* joined in a minute later, her target being *Saïda*. At this time *Aquila* was still closer to the Austrians and she contributed eight salvos starting from a distance of under ten thousand yards before the enemy steamed out of range. The Austrian cruisers replied almost immediately and began to generate heavy chemical and funnel smoke as they briefly bore to the southwest. Horthy explained: "I ordered the smoke-screen apparatus to be used, so that we should be able to draw in closer and thus be able to use our smaller-calibre guns and launch our torpedoes to greater effect. The enemy was certain to come nearer, as he would be convinced that we were refusing battle."[65]

The smoke forced *Dartmouth* and *Bristol* to fire blind, or at mast tops poking up out of the murk. As the battle moved past *Aquila, Acerbi*, and *Mosto* rejoined the British cruisers. *Schiaffino* eventually towed *Aquila* back to Brindisi under *Pilo's* escort.

The Austrians meanwhile had swung north. Trying to maneuver at high speed in the thick, artificial fog, *Novara* and *Helgoland* almost collided and as they avoided each other *Saïda* nearly piled into *Helgoland*. When Horthy finally reformed his column *Saïda* was astern. These gyrations allowed the *Mirabello* group to close range and the Italian warship started pitching 4-inch rounds at the Austrian column at 0940. *Saïda* quickly replied from 8,750 yards. Horthy reported that "the destroyers that had followed us from the south had approached so I expected a torpedo attack on their part and this forced me to once again steer to the northwest." At the same time a pair of Italian seaplanes bombed the Austrians from an elevation of four thousand feet and missed by about a hundred.[66]

When Horthy's formation emerged from the smoke Acton's cruisers were a little over five thousand yards to starboard. The two columns steamed north-northwest on parallel courses and at 0945 began exchanging rapid salvos. At 0950, as a pair of Austrian seaplanes bombed and machine-gunned *Dartmouth*, *Bristol* hit *Helgoland* between the forward funnel and the bridge. Five minutes later a shell struck *Novara*'s chart room. Both *Bristol* and *Mirabello* claimed credit for this strike. However, with a foul bottom and due for docking, *Bristol* could not keep the pace. *Acerbi* moved forward and assumed second place in the column.

Around 1000 several 10-cm rounds struck *Dartmouth*. One pierced the upper deck and exploded on the after mess deck, killing three men and igniting a small, quickly extinguished fire. Another hit the waterline but failed to detonate and only flooded a small compartment, while a third round burst on the deck near the aft gun but caused little damage. At 1004 a shell hit *Helgoland* forward and ignited a small fire that was quickly quenched. Two others splashed very near. *Dartmouth* scored at 1010 with a blow to the base of *Novara*'s bridge superstructure. This caused significant damage and splinters wounded Horthy, forcing him to temporarily surrender command.

By 1015 *Bristol* trailed *Dartmouth* by six thousand yards and had to cease fire. At the same time *Mirabello* had to shut down her boilers because salt water had contaminated the fuel supply. As *Mirabello* lost way an Austrian aircraft dropped two bombs that near missed. *Bisson* turned aside at 1015 to rescue the crew of an Italian seaplane that had been dogfighting with the Austrians and ditched because of engine trouble. *Commandant Rivière* and *Cimeterre* continued on for a time but were too slow to keep up and so returned to screen *Mirabello* while her crew worked to fix her machinery. At 1100 *Mirabello* got her engines going and the group headed north, but at 1145 *Commandant Rivière* suffered a machinery breakdown. The *Mirabello* group then returned to Brindisi with *Commandant Rivière* in tow.

The Austrian ships were running at 29 knots while *Bristol* was capable of only 24. With *Mirabello* stopped and *Bristol* out of range, *Dartmouth* was the only Entente ship actively in the fight. By 1024 the distance between *Dartmouth* and *Novara* had increased to nearly 11,000 yards. Shells were flying back and forth. *Dartmouth's* gunnery officer wrote: "I could see the hits on her side quite distinctly, and almost every salvo when we were straddling I saw a cloud of grey smoke appear on her deck which I think must have been shell bursting inside."[67] *Dartmouth's* fire was not as effective as her gunners imagined but at 1035 a round from her last salvo detonated in *Novara's* aft turbine room killing eleven men. This was a serious blow that eventually took half of her boilers off line. By 1045 *Novara* was making no more than 20 knots and ten minutes later, only 5. Masking *Novara's* troubles was the fact that machinery problems were slowing *Saïda*, the rear ship, as well.

Fortunately for the Austrians, the situation was not apparent to Acton. The three scout cruisers had concentrated their guns on *Dartmouth* and at 1045 the Italian admiral ordered *Dartmouth* to reduce speed to 23 knots, and then at 1050 to 20 to let *Bristol* catch up. Because *Bristol's* rate of closing was relatively high she was better able to appreciate that *Saïda* had lost speed. She opened fire once again and at 1050 one of her shells punched through *Saïda's* bow leaving an impressive-looking hole but not affecting the ship's combat effectiveness. *Novara* finally came to a stop at 1100.

At 1058 *Dartmouth* resumed fire against *Novara* from 13,000 yards. Acton, however, still believed that the Austrians were too fast for him to trap their entire force. He wrote: "At 1100 I came to port to cut the tail [ship] of the enemy formation (*Saïda*) by closing the distance to 7,500 meters and opening an intense fire on her supported by *Bristol* which had joined me. I believed that *Dartmouth's* salvos seriously damaged the enemy."[68] He did not perceive that *Novara* was dead in the water, perhaps distracted by the enemy aircraft that were attacking *Dartmouth* repeatedly with bombs, machine guns, and by a shell that plunged through *Dartmouth's* forecastle deck at around 1100 and exploded, killing three men. The captain ordered the forward magazine flooded, but, as there

Modern Italian "three stacker" destroyer *Impavido*. (Ufficio Storico Marina Militare)

was no fire, this action was canceled after only a few inches of water poured in. Then, at 1104 Acton issued the unfortunate order for *Dartmouth* to turn south and join the *Marsala* group, which had left Brindisi at 0835. As the Entente forces concentrated, *Sankt Georg,* two destroyers, and four torpedo boats were steaming hard to Horthy's rescue.

At 1115 *Saïda* began the process of passing a tow to *Novara* while *Helgoland* cloaked the proceedings with smoke. Meanwhile, *Acerbi*, having misread the signal to withdraw, attacked independently, coming to within 8,200 yards and opening what the Austrians described as a "furious" fire.[69] However, the destroyer was unsupported and the combined gunnery of the three cruisers kept her at a distance. At 1125 the *Marsala* group joined Acton and the Entente force, thus reinforced, turned north once again. *Racchia*, accompanied by *Impavido,* pushed out ahead of the slower cruisers. At the same time the Austrians saw the welcome sight of smoke to the north which signaled *Sankt Georg*'s impending arrival. At 1130 *Helgoland* engaged *Racchia* from 12,000 yards. *Racchia* returned fire before turning east. *Impavido* continued alone and closed to 6,500 yards before turning away.

At 1206 Acton reached the apex of his turn north. The smoke of the *Sankt Georg* group was plainly visible. Believing he was outgunned, the admiral decided to return to Brindisi. His force had been under constant air attack, he was only forty miles from the main Austrian base and twice that from Brindisi, with at least three crippled ships to his rear. He was 19,000 yards south of *Novara* and 31,000 south of *Sankt Georg. Novara* was not under tow until nearly 1230 by which time *Sankt Georg* was in contact.[70]

On the return home the submarine *UC25* torpedoed *Dartmouth*. She was severely damaged but managed to make Brindisi. *Boutefeu* then hit one of *UC25*'s mines and sank.

Reflecting the extended and intense nature of the action, the Austrian ships expended large quantities of ammunition: *Novara*—675 10-cm; *Saïda*—832 10-cm; *Helgoland*—1,052 10-cm, 6; *Csepel*—127 10-cm, 78 7-cm, 2 torpedoes; *Balaton*—85 10-cm, 60 7-cm, 2 torpedoes.

In the Battle of Otranto Strait the Austrians won a clear success. The raid was deadly and they extracted their valuable scout cruisers from what seemed an impossible situation; including the efforts of their submarines, they inflicted more damage; and they accomplished their short-term strategic goal inasmuch as the barrage was not maintained at night for a month while the Entente navies arranged to augment the escorts. The Entente failure had several causes. Poor communications once again resulted in uncoordinated actions, such as solitary attacks, and a failure to apply the force available effectively. Rear Admiral Acton fought the battle with an eye toward avoiding damage rather than inflicting it, as if he possessed the inferior force rather than the reverse. Finally, the Austrians were lucky. They shot well and Entente forces suffered a number of inconvenient mechanical failures—a symptom of the hard use and constant patrolling these warships were put through in being ready, at any time, to react to enemy initiatives.

Despite the success, the K.u.K. Kriegsmarine concluded that the danger to its irreplaceable light cruisers inherent in such actions was too great, and it did not mount another raid into the Otranto Strait until 20 September when four destroyers went south and saw nothing. On 18 October a foray by *Helgoland* and six destroyers likewise failed to locate any targets. On their return *Helgoland* avoided submarine and bombing attacks. The Italo-British-Franco reaction force of three light cruisers, four scouts, and eleven destroyers never got more than a distant view of the enemy's smoke. Bad weather frustrated Austrian raids on 12 November and 22 November. On 13 December three Austrian destroyers believed they encountered four Entente destroyers. They fired torpedoes and turned for home. If the target had indeed been destroyers, the attack went unreported.[71]

Encounter in Leme Channel: 24 September, night

Conditions: Clear
Missions: Italians, raid; Austrians, raid
Italian Force: TB *9PN, 10PN, 11PN, 12PN.*
Austrian Force: TB *95F*, TBx3.

On the night of 24 September off the Leme Channel in central Istria four Austrian torpedo boats led by *95F* encountered four Italian torpedo boats at sea to support an air raid. The Austrians abandoned their mission and immediately turned south. The two sides briefly exchanged fire at 7,500 yards before the Italians lost their enemy in the dark. The Italians sent three destroyers to sweep the area but they found nothing.[72]

Action off the Po Delta: September 29, 0045–September 30, 2355

Conditions: Night, new moon
Missions: Italians, raid; Austrians, raid
Italian Force (Rear Admiral Mario Casanuova Jererinch): DL *Sparviero*[#];
    DD *Abba, Orsini*[+]*, Acerbi, Stocco, Audace, Ardente, Ardito.*
Austrian Force (Corvette Captain G. Grundorf): DD *Turul*[+]*, Velebit*[#]*,
    Huszár*[+]*, Streiter;* TB *90F, 94F*[+]*, 98M, 99M.*

At 1630 on 29 September an Italian squadron consisting of the scout *Sparviero* and seven destroyers departed Venice with the dual roles of supporting an air attack on Pola and interfering with an Austrian operation that intelligence indicated was forthcoming. In fact, four Habsburg destroyers and four torpedo boats were off the coast to support a raid against Ferrara airport by five naval flying boats. It was a dark night with a new moon rising at 0020.

The Austrian air strike destroyed the Italian airship *M8*, after which the warships turned southeast for home at full speed. The Italian squadron heard of the raid at 2045 and, forming two columns, headed toward a point off the Po River delta hoping to intercept the Austrians. At 2203 *Sparviero* duly sighted the enemy formation off the starboard bow from four thousand yards. The Austrians likewise saw the Italians and both sides opened fire almost simultaneously while the second Italian column, *Ardito*, *Acerbi*, and *Stocco*, turned to close range.

The initial Italian salvos were long but the Austrians hit *Sparviero* five times and *Orsini*, right behind her, once. Such accuracy discouraged Rear Admiral Casanuova from closing. Fighting on a parallel course, however, Italian gunfire began to register, landing a shell on *Huszár* and another on *Velebit*, the last ship in the Austrian column, while near-missing *Turul*. *Huszár* and *Turul* were lightly damaged but *Velebit* caught fire and lost steering control. *Acerbi* launched a torpedo at 2209 from two thousand yards and another at 2214, but both missed.

By 2230 both sides had lost contact. The Italians headed north and reformed into a single line as the Austrians split into several groups and *Streiter* took *Velebit* in tow. *Sparviero* briefly sighted one of these formations at 2245 and opened fire hitting *94F*, which suffered one casualty. After this Casanuova turned away in compliance with orders to avoid the mined waters of the Istrian coast.

As with the Battle of Otranto Straits, the combat's intensity can be judged by the ammunition expended: *Sparviero*, 115 rounds of 6-inch; *Audace*, *Ardente*, and *Ardito* collectively 35 of 4.7-inch; 291 of 4-inch by *Orsini*, *Stocco*, and *Abba*; and 187 of 3-inch by *Sparviero* and *Ardente*: 628 rounds in total during the short engagement.[73]

First Action off Cortellazzo: 14 November, dawn
Conditions: Variable
Missions: Italians, transit; Austrians, patrol
Italian Force: DD *Animoso*, *Ardente*, *Audace*, *Abba*.
Austrian Force: TB *84F*, *92F*, *94F*, *99M*, *100M*.

One of the Italian's navy's primary missions in the fall of 1917, especially after the Central Powers cracked the Italian front lines in the Caporetto offensive of late October, was to support the army by bringing in supplies, conducting shore bombardments, protecting specialized bombardment craft such as gun-mounted pontoons, and keeping the Austrians from doing the same. On the night of 13 November the four Italian destroyers expended eight hundred 4-inch shells bombarding a column of enemy troops near the mouth of the Piave River. As they were withdrawing at dawn they encountered five Austrian torpedo boats that were charting Italian minefields. The Italians opened fire, joined by a nearby coastal battery. The Austrians replied, shooting two hundred rounds as they escaped across a known minefield. The Italian ships drew up to four feet more of water than the Austrians and thus declined to follow through waters filled with submerged mines. So ended the action.[74]

Second Action off Cortellazzo: 16 November, 1230–

Conditions: Clear

Missions: Italians, interception; Austrians, bombardment

Italian Force (Commander Costanzo Ciano): DD *Orsini, Acerbi, Animoso, Stocco, Ardente, Abba, Audace.*

Austrian Force (Captain Alexander Mahovitsch-Ridolfi): OBB *Wien*[#], *Budapest*[#]; TB *Tb6, Tb9, 84F, 92F, 94F, 98M, 99M, 100M*; MS *Tb23, 27, 30, 61T, 65F, 66F.*

The critical war situation and the need to maintain the Austro-German land advance beyond the Piave River finally convinced the Austrians to use heavy warships to support the imperial army's flank. On 15 November naval command dispatched from Trieste two old coastal battleships preceded by six minesweeping torpedo boats and escorted by eight torpedo boats. The objective was to open the coastal road for the army's further advance and destroy the Italian 6-inch battery at Cortellazzo.

The Austrians opened fire at 1035 from 11,000 yards but the bombardment failed to silence the battery. In return, the battery struck *Wien* with seven shells that bounced off her armored hull and hit *Budapest* once below the waterline. At 1230 the Italian destroyers approached the Austrian squadron and tried to lure it toward three MAS boats that were waiting in ambush. When the Austrians declined to bite and resumed their bombardment, *MAS13* and *15* attacked anyway, using as cover the enormous quantities of smoke produced by the Austrian guns. They launched four torpedoes from a thousand yards, but all missed. The Italian destroyer flotilla reengaged as the old battleships *Saint Bon* and *Emanuele Filiberto*, which had sailed from Venice to support them, were reaching the area. Captain Mahovitsch-Ridolfi, informed of their approach by aerial spotters, elected to withdraw. He was relieved a few days later. This was another instance where the potential of great rewards would have justified the K.u.K. Kriegsmarine risking their dreadnoughts to at least cover the bombardment force.

Wien only survived another three weeks. *MAS9* and *13* snuck into Trieste harbor on the night of 9/10 December. *MAS13*'s attack against *Budapest* was unsuccessful but *MAS9*, under Lieutenant Commander Luigi Rizzo, hit *Wien* with two torpedoes. She capsized and sank in five minutes with the loss of forty-six men.[75]

On 19 December, in a final effort to break through the Italian lines along the coast, the K.u.K. Kriegsmarine sent another strong bombardment force out from Trieste. This consisted of the old battleships *Budapest* and *Arpád*, the cruiser *Admiral Spaun*, six destroyers, ten modern torpedo boats, and ten elderly torpedo boats to sweep for mines. However, weather did not cooperate. There was dense fog that day forcing the Austrians to fire blind, and Italian surface forces that sortied, including *Saint Bon* and *Emanuele Filiberto*, could not locate the enemy. The mission was a failure.

6

1918: Winding Down

But we suffered the bitterest disappointment at the hands of the crews of the Fleet. Thanks to an unscrupulous agitation which had been fermenting for a long time, the idea had taken root in their minds that they were to be uselessly sacrificed.

—ADMIRAL SCHEER, *HIGH SEA FLEET*

Overview

The war's ultimate resolution remained in doubt for much of 1918. The collapse of Russia allowed German and Austro-Hungarian forces to occupy most of western Russia and the Ukraine but this victory came too late. A grand German offensive failed to win a decision in France before the arrival of large-scale American reinforcements. After that, Entente pressure against the Germans on the Western Front was relentless and ultimately decisive. The Italians held on in front of Venice and eventually counterattacked. The Entente blockade had been in effect for more than three years and by 1918 its impact finally became decisive. As one historian expressed it, "Blockade was a blunt and indiscriminate instrument, similar to unrestricted aerial bombing in the following war. But its designers had gauged correctly: Imperial Germany did not have the resources of management, ruthlessness, and legitimacy to contain discontent. Its emperor, generals, and statesmen had rashly launched into war, and the war had called their bluff. When they failed, as principals, to prevail, the people discarded them as agents."[1] The effects of blockade were even more dire for the Austro-Hungarian and Ottoman Empires.

The Bolshevik revolution ended most naval action in the Black and Baltic Seas, while 1918 operations in the North Sea and Adriatic focused on minelaying and the submarine war. The humble minesweeper had joined the battleship as an arbiter of naval power. Little could be done without their daily attention to the underwater menaces that, in the tens of thousands, choked littoral waters. Thus, they worked continuously, weather permitting, always subject to attack, venturing ever farther from shore as the deadly fields grew much like the trench systems on land. Germany had started the war with thirty sweepers. By the armistice the Kaiserliche Marine deployed 394 sweepers including auxiliaries; the British minesweeping service consisted of 726 vessels of all types. During the war the British laid more than 128,000 mines, the Americans 57,600, the Russians 52,000, the Germans 43,000, and the Austrians 6,000; Italy, the Ottomans, and all other powers accounted for another 23,200 mines. Losses to mines were staggering. The British alone lost 46 warships, 225 auxiliaries, 214 minesweepers, and 260 merchant vessels totaling 670,000 GRT. Even more ships were damaged.[2]

The submarine war remained important. When the war started submarines were expected to support the surface fleet; by 1918 the roles were, in many respects, reversed. While unrestricted submarine warfare had not driven Britain to the peace table as the Admiralstab had predicted, the Germans continued their campaign into 1918. The Kaiserliche Marine devoted much effort to maintaining open lanes through minefields, thus aiding submarines transiting the Heligoland Bight and Dover Strait, while the Royal Navy defended against submarines with static barriers, roving patrols, and escorted convoys. Submarine and antisubmarine warfare similarly occupied navies in the Adriatic and Mediterranean.

The unglamorous work of convoy escort was, in fact, the best use of the Entente's smaller warships in the face of the submarine threat. It took the various navies years to consent to this practice but convoys quickly proved far better at defending traffic than offensive patrols or barrages. Germany started 1917 with 149 serviceable submarines. These sank 6.235 million tons of merchant shipping, while seventy boats were lost to all causes (sixty-three to enemy action). This was an average of 520,000 GRT a month sunk and 89,000 GRT sunk per submarine lost. In 1918, with convoying in full swing, Germany started the year with 164 submarines.

In ten months the Germans lost eighty-six boats and sank an average of 274,000 GRT a month (32,000 GRT sunk per submarine lost). By these measurements the Entente powers had clearly reduced the effectiveness of German submarines in 1918.[3] The implementation of convoying was not the only reason for this turnaround. The development of depth charges and hydrophones gave surface ships more tools to fight submarines, aircraft were a greater factor in patrolling and defending coastal waters, and the Entente forces were getting better intelligence of U-boat movements and developing more effective tactics. The massive barrages and barriers, while not particularly effective in killing submarines, at least forced boats to take longer in transit and reduced their time on patrol.

Social discontent also directly affected naval operations in the closing stages of the war. This had taken root in the German and Austrian fleets in 1917 and before war's end rendered offensive action by their great ships impractical.[4] Under these conditions, the number and scale of surface battles diminished in 1918. The Germans and Austrians each launched their battle fleets on one operation that year; both ended in failure. *Yavuz* and *Midilli* emerged to fight a surface engagement in the Mediterranean, in a raid with little strategic value. All other actions were skirmishes between light forces.

North Sea 1918

The Royal Navy's major North Sea effort in 1918 was an attack on Zeebrugge on the night of 22/23 April. In this effort to block the harbor the raiders scuttled two of the three blockships in their intended positions, but even that success was fleeting as the Germans quickly cleared a channel around the wreckage. The raid boosted British morale, as it seemed to show that the Royal Navy was prepared to mount daring and perilous operations, while the raid's strategic failure only became widely known postwar. A second raid against Ostend, mounted on 10/11 May, failed entirely.

Clover Bank *Action: 23 January, 1055–1125*

Conditions: Misty, smooth seas, light southwest winds
Missions: British, patrol; Germans, minesweeping
British Force: BM *M26* (Commander A. A. Mellin); drifter *Clover Bank*.
German Force: DD *V67*, *G95*, *V68*, *G96*.

Germany continued to undertake offensive naval operations. On 14 January destroyers bombarded Great Yarmouth. A typical skirmish off the Flanders coast occurred at 1055 on 23 January when four German destroyers covering a group of minesweepers surprised the British drifter *Clover Bank* tending nets off the Belgian coast and her escort, the monitor *M26*. *Clover Bank* was five hundred yards ahead of the monitor and both were steering north-northeast when enemy shells began dropping around them. The source was a German destroyer five thousand yards dead ahead. The British ships reversed course immediately and fled at their best speed of 10 knots, with *Clover Bank* leading. *M26* was unable to spot the enemy for twelve minutes but *Clover Bank* returned fire with her 57-mm gun, even claiming two hits (from six rounds fired). She also dropped two smoke floats, one of which malfunctioned.

At 1107 *M26*, which had been zigzagging in a westerly direction, finally located a target eight thousand yards off her port quarter. At first her 3-inch gun fired at maximum range then at 1112 the 7.5-inch gun went into action and discharged nine rounds over eight minutes (with several misfires) before the enemy turned southeast and disappeared. By this time the destroyers *Marksman* and *Melpomene* were in sight. Both had sailed to the sound of gunfire but never sighted the enemy. Neither side hit the other.[5]

On the night of 14/15 February seven German destroyers of II TBF surprised the British patrol lines and sank seven drifters (including *Clover Bank*) and the trawler *James Pond*, and badly damaged the paddle minesweeper *Newbury*, five drifters, and another trawler. Three of the German raiders passed only four hundred yards astern of a column of four British destroyers (*Termagant*, *Melpomene*, *Zubian*, and *Amazon*, on patrol duty by the eastern barrage) but held fire due to being slowed by a leaky condenser in *G103*. *Amazon*, the rear ship, challenged the Germans without reply but took them for friendly vessels because they did not fire on her and showed dim stern lights. A court-martial and improved recognition procedures followed, but this was the last time German destroyers encountered a Channel patrol.[6]

German destroyers had used Flanders bases to conduct fifteen raids in the twenty months from 8 June 1916, when II TBF first moved south, to 16 February 1918. In these raids they sank four destroyers, three merchantmen, two trawlers, and thirteen drifters, and damaged two destroyers, two destroyer leaders, eight drifters, three trawlers, and a fisheries protection vessel. They also captured two steamers. The Germans lost five destroyers: three destroyers in surface actions and two to mines. Another four destroyers were damaged. The losses inflicted, however, were not the greatest impact of these raids. The Dover Patrol and the Harwich Force together employed sixty-eight destroyers—more than a fifth of the total in home waters. Although the need for destroyers shot up after April 1917 when the Admiralty finally implemented Atlantic convoys, the British felt unable to reduce significantly the number guarding the straits. It was here that the German policy of aggressive raiding from Flanders made its greatest contribution to Germany's war effort—there were occasions, for example, when the Grand Fleet had to restrict its operations for lack of sufficient destroyers to screen the battleships while convoys went begging for effective escorts.[7]

Raid off Dunkirk: 21 March, 0435–0456

Conditions: Poor visibility

Missions: British, interception; Germans, bombardment

Entente Force (Commander R. L'E. Rede, RN): BR DL *Botha*#; BR DD *Morris*; FR DD *Bouclier, Capitaine Mehl, Magon.*

German Forces (Corvette Captain Assmann): Marker Force: TB *A19*★, *A7*★. Bombardment Force: TB *A59, A61, A49, A43, A48.*

Marinekorps Flandern's last raid to generate a surface engagement occurred on 21 March when seven destroyers and eight torpedo boats sailed to bombard targets from Dunkirk to Adinkerke in support of the first great Kaiserschlacht offensive.

Group Assmann included two *A1*–class torpedo boats serving as marker vessels for five *A26*–class boats bombarding Dunkirk. Alerted by gunfire, the monitor *Terror* fired starshells over the enemy force at 0355. The British flotilla leader *Botha* with destroyers *Morris, Bouclier, Capitaine Mehl,* and *Magon* already had steam up and sortied from Dunkirk steering toward the gunfire. At 0435 they found the raiders with *A7* and *A19* at the rear of the German formation.

Each side pumped shells at the other from 1,300 yards while the Germans also laid smoke. The exchange lasted ten minutes before a German shell landed in one of *Botha*'s stokeholds, slowing her. As the leader lost speed she launched two torpedoes at the bombardment group without effect and then rammed *A19*, splitting her in two. *Botha* missed on the same maneuver with *A7*, but raked the torpedo boat with her aft guns. At this point, with *Botha* and *A7* cloaked by the German smoke screen, *Bouclier* weighed in by sinking *A7* with gunfire but *Capitaine Mehl* mistook *Botha* for the enemy and put a torpedo into her after boiler room, an unsurprising mistake given the smoke, radical course changes, and the fact that *Botha*'s electrical circuit for her fighting lights had been shot out. *Botha* survived and *Morris* later towed her into port. The firing died away by 0456 as the other torpedo boats disappeared into the dark.[8]

Action off Terschelling Bank: 20 April, 1615–1659

Conditions: Clear
Missions: British, interception; Germans, transit
British Force: DD *Thruster, Starfish, Satyr, Sturgeon*[#], *Tetrarch*.
German Force (Corvette Captain Gautier): DD *V81, V73, S55, G91*.

In April 1918, the Admiralstab ordered four destroyers of III TBF to Flanders. Accompanied by sweepers, they left Heligoland on the morning of 19 April along the southern route through the German and British minefields. The journey proved slow going and by that evening, after three unsuccessful attempts to navigate the barrages, it was clear they could not make Zeebrugge before dawn. Gautier therefore decided to temporarily abandon the mission.

The German force came about, but their troubles were just beginning. First *M95* hit two mines and quickly sank and then the same fate befell *M39* and *M64*. With that, the remaining ships anchored and waited for more minesweepers from the Ems. The additional sweepers arrived after daylight on 20 April and started the arduous task of clearing a channel toward the anchored ships. However, they were still at work when, at 1615, German lookouts spotted smoke to the west-southwest. This heralded the arrival of five Harwich Force destroyers. They had sailed in company with

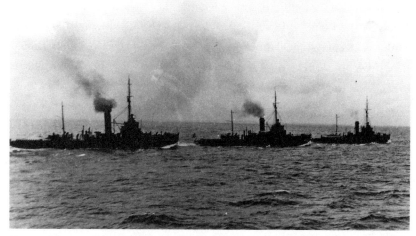

German M-type minesweepers in line abreast. The Germans built capable minesweepers that filled a variety of roles. (Courtesy of Peter Schenk Collection)

the light cruisers *Coventry* and *Cleopatra* at 1000 on the 20th with orders to destroy enemy minesweepers that might be working on minefield A.36. They were supported at a distance by another five C-class cruisers and twelve destroyers.

After spotting the enemy, Corvette Captain Gautier ordered his destroyers to get under way; he then turned south and engaged the British destroyers on a reciprocal course at ranges of eight to ten thousand yards while the minesweepers generated smoke and retreated east. The opposing forces steamed past each other at least twice as Gautier tried to shield the sweepers. Neither side attempted to close the range and the battle ended by 1659. Although the British claimed one hit, the German force denied any damage. One of the 312 shells they fired hit *Sturgeon* in the engine room and she required a tow back to base.[9]

This action highlighted the claustrophobic impact of minefields by this point in the war. Coastal waters were clotted with British fields, German fields, and drifting mines; movement had become slow and dangerous.

The High Seas Fleet's last combat sortie into the North Sea occurred on 23 April when it sailed to strike the Norwegian convoy routes. Scheer diligently maintained radio silence and was lucky in steaming right past a British submarine whose commander assumed that the Germans were

British, but faulty intelligence negated these successes. The Germans got the convoy sailing dates wrong, giving them nothing to attack on the day their dreadnoughts appeared off the Norwegian coast. The sortie nearly ended in disaster when *Moltke* suffered a cascading series of engineering mishaps that started with the loss of one of her propellers and ended with two engine rooms flooded and the battlecruiser dead in the water. *Moltke* started back to harbor on the end of a towline. Radio transmissions reporting her problems alerted the Grand Fleet of the German operation, but it steamed too late to intercept. *Moltke* restored some power but then, forty miles off Heligoland, the British submarine *E42* torpedoed her. The battlecruiser was lucky to survive.[10]

Flanders Patrol Action: 27 June, 1755–1815

Conditions: Good visibility, rough seas, and fresh northeasterly wind
Missions: British, patrol; Germans, minesweeping
British Force (Commander A. B. Cunningham): DD *Termagant, Meteor, Nugent, Milne*⁺.
German Forces: 5 TBHF: DD *V71, V81, V83*. 1 Flanders TBHF: TB *A46, A9, A8, A16, A12*.

On 27 June five A-class torpedo boats were sweeping mines off the Flanders coast screened by *V71, V81*, and *V83*. At the same time *Termagant* followed by *Meteor, Nugent*, and *Milne* were patrolling the net barrage in the vicinity of the monitors *Terror, M23*, and *M21*. The British destroyers spotted smoke close inshore and, steaming to investigate, saw A-boats firing on British seaplanes. They engaged the A-boats whereupon the three destroyers of the 5 TBHF intervened. Beginning at 1755 the two groups fought across the net barrier, exchanging fire at ranges that started at six miles and dropped to four. The rough conditions made the small warships unstable gun platforms. The British commander, Andrew Cunningham, a future Admiral of the Fleet, later wrote: "I have never seen anything to equal the wretched shooting of the *Termagant* and our three others. The German commander helped us all he could by forming his nine [*sic*] boats in line abreast at right angles to our line; but even so we could not hit them. Nor did they hit us, though their salvoes certainly appeared to be better controlled than ours." By 1815, the

British ships were running low on ammunition so they fired four torpedoes and turned away under cover of smoke, hoping to draw the Germans into range of the monitors. The Germans, however, ignored the
bait. The only damage either side suffered was a hit on *Milne*'s motor
boat that wounded four men.[11]

Other than a series of actions by small motor torpedo boats of each
side, surface warfare off the Flanders coast was over. Under increasing
pressure from coastal bombardments, air raids, and the advance of the
Allied armies, the Germans evacuated their Flanders bases at the end
of September. They extracted eleven destroyers, thirteen torpedo boats,
and seven submarines, but were forced to scuttle, sink, or abandon five
destroyers, twelve torpedo boats, and three submarines. The Harwich
Force patrolled vigorously hoping to disrupt the German withdrawal,
but weather and a lack of specific intelligence frustrated its efforts.[12]

In late October Admiral Scheer, now head of the Admiralstab, ordered
a sortie by eighteen battleships and five battlecruisers, the first fleet
operation since April. He intended to provoke an action off the Thames
Estuary against the Anglo-American fleet of thirty-five battleships and
eleven battlecruisers. Morale had been deteriorating for over a year, with
serious unrest among the big ships first occurring in the summer of
1917. When the fleet concentrated to carry out the orders, the battleship crews, convinced that they were being sacrificed in an effort to
sabotage armistice negotiations then under way, became insubordinate.
Confronted by this revolt Vice Admiral Hipper, fleet commander since
August, canceled the operation on 30 October, the day before it was to
begin. This failed to quell unrest and a full-blown mutiny broke out on
3 November in Kiel. The sailors of the High Seas Fleet thus contributed
to the end of the war not by winning a decisive victory but by refusing to fight.[13]

Adriatic 1918

Interception in the Otranto Strait: 22 April, 2115–23 April, 0010

Conditions: Calm and clear

Missions: Entente, patrol; Austrians, raid

Entente Forces: East Group: FR DD *Cimeterre*, BR DD *Alarm*. Center
    Group (Lieutenant Commander Henry Pridham-Wippell): BR

The British 1st Light Cruiser Squadron sailing in line ahead formation and executing an eight-point turn to port. (Courtesy of John Roberts Collection)

DD *Comet*, AU DD *Torrens*. West Group (Lieutenant Commander A. M. Roberts): BR DD *Jackal*[+], *Hornet*[#].

Austrian Force: DD *Triglav* (Frigate Captain Karl Herkner), *Csepel*, *Uzsok*, *Dukla*, *Lika*.

Entente forces assigned to the Otranto Barrage increased as the war progressed and schemes to close the strait to German and Austrian submarines grew more elaborate. The British assembled submarines, trawlers with hydrophones, and destroyers in the hopes of finding and then destroying submarines in passage. The French and Italians believed that a permanent net barrier was the solution and, after assembling material and forces, they began constructing this obstruction in the third week of April. The Austrian command at Cattaro noted this activity and on the night of 22 April five destroyers sortied to disrupt enemy activities.

The weather was calm and clear with a moon four days short of full. Six Entente destroyers were patrolling in groups of two over a span of thirty miles in the center of the strait. The West Group was sailing west along their beat at 12 knots when at 2110 *Hornet* spotted vessels to the north. She and *Jackal* altered course to starboard, mistaking the contact for Italian transports. *Jackal* challenged at 2125 after noting large bow waves, which indicated the ships were moving at speed. The Austrians came east and shot back with gunfire at three thousand yards. *Jackal* and *Hornet* immediately replied and made smoke. They reversed course to the south hoping to lure the enemy farther from base, while to the east *Comet* and *Torrens* saw the gun flashes and at 2134 reported that enemy cruisers were attacking. In Brindisi several cruisers and destroyers started to raise steam.

Uzsok was pioneering the use of tracer shells to aid night spotting and Austrian gunnery once again found the mark quickly and effectively. Three rounds hit *Jackal*: one toppled her mainmast and wireless antenna, another exploded in the wardroom, and a third above the wardroom hatch. The rear destroyers targeted *Hornet* with effective salvos that ignited fires in her forward shell room and magazine. An explosion in the magazine killed or wounded many while a shell punched into the forebridge. *Hornet* lost steering control and started to circle, her siren howling. After fifteen minutes, the Austrians turned north and *Jackal* turned to pursue. Meanwhile, the other four destroyers had concentrated. They passed *Hornet* and at 2210 sighted *Jackal*. The chase continued for two hours until, just twenty miles short of Cattaro, the Entente destroyers were ordered back for fear of blundering into an enemy minefield.

Although the Austrians severely damaged one Entente destroyer and escaped unharmed, their attack failed to achieve its larger objective. In addition, the drifter crews appreciated that the raiders had been driven off before they could attack.[14]

Captain Miklós Horthy's success in the Battle of Otranto Straits made him Austria-Hungary's leading naval hero. On 27 February 1918, after a naval mutiny at Cattaro, Emperor Karl I promoted him to rear admiral and commander of the fleet, replacing Admiral Maximillian Njegovan and passing over eleven more senior officers. From the first Horthy planned to mount a fleet action against the Otranto Barrage—once morale was restored and training completed. His plan involved four dreadnoughts, three predreadnoughts, four light cruisers, thirteen destroyers, and thirty-two torpedo boats. The objective was for the heavy ships to cut off and destroy Entente formations that would certainly pursue the force raiding the barrier.

By June preparations were completed and the operation commenced. Horthy divided his forces into nine formations. One of the two dreadnought groups consisted of *Tegetthoff* and *Szent István* escorted by seven flotilla craft. These ships were passing Premuda on their way south just before dawn on 10 June when two Italian motor torpedo boats on routine patrol spotted them. According to a watch officer on *Szent István*, "every man was at his battle station [and] antisubmarine batteries were ready and had orders to fire immediately upon sighting a suspicious object." Nonetheless, the attack caught the ship by surprise. Each boat fired both of its torpedoes. *MAS21* missed *Tegetthoff* but *MAS15*, commanded by Lieutenant Commander Rizzo, scored with both weapons against *Szent István*. Progressive flooding eventually caused the battleship to capsize.[15]

This attack underscored the vulnerability of capital ships to cheap, expendable weapons but it also demonstrated the importance of experience and training. Although in commission for more than thirty months *Szent István* had been at sea only fifty-four days and had conducted just one real sortie. Her other voyages had lasted but forty-five minutes steaming to and from the protected Fasana Channel for firing exercises. Although Horthy had implemented an intense training program, the battleship's crew was inexperienced and lacked not only the ability to control damage effectively, but, like the escort, to spot the small boats that attacked in the dim predawn light. The Italian crews, on the other hand, were veterans. Lieutenant Commander Rizzo, who had sunk predreadnought *Wien* on 10 December 1917, became one of only two men in the war to sink two battleships. With surprise lost, Horthy canceled the entire operation.[16]

Encounter off Caorle: 1 July, 0310–0330

Conditions: Some haze, light land breeze, moon in the east in its final quarter

Missions: Italians, patrol; Austrians, raid

Italian Forces (Commander Domenico Cavagnari): DD *Orsini*[#], *Missori*, *La Masa*, *Audace*, *Acerbi*, *Sirtori*, *Stocco*[#].

Austrian Forces: DD *Balaton*[+] (Frigate Captain Friedrich Luschin), *Csikós*[+]; TB *83F*[#], *88F*[+].

Captain Miklós Horthy, victor at the May 1917 Battle of Otranto Strait. He was Austria-Hungary's greatest naval hero and ended the war as fleet commander. (Wiki Public Domain)

On this night four Austrian ships were at sea supporting an air raid against Venice. By this point the flotilla craft on all sides were suffering from hard use. *83F* had bow damage and she and *Balaton* both were having boiler problems that limited the formation speed to 20 knots.

The Austrians encountered seven Italian destroyers off Caorle commanded by the future Italian chief of staff Commander Domenico Cavagnari on board *Orsini*. Conscious of the rarity and fleeting nature of night engagements, Cavagnari steered for the enemy and opened fire. Following their doctrine, the Austrians turned toward Pola at full speed. In an intense, close-range exchange *Balaton* fired a series of effective salvos. A 10-cm projectile holed *Orsini*'s forward funnel. Smoke was sucked into a boiler room causing a temporary loss of speed while *Stocco*, the next ship in line, absorbed three rounds and caught fire. In return, the Italians hit each of the K.u.K. destroyers once while three shells struck *83F* and *88F* took one. *Balaton* had two forward compartments flooded. The Austrian vessels split up and the torpedo boats launched torpedoes, all of which missed. The forces then vanished in the dark after seventeen minutes of combat. The Austrians fired 225 7-cm and 36 10-cm rounds. *Balaton* accounted for 120 of these shells in the action's opening minutes. *Stocco* required eight days in dock to repair her damages.[17]

Chase in the Gulf of Drin: 5 September, night
Conditions: Clear

Missions: Italians, patrol; Austrians, minesweeping

Italian forces: DL *Aquila, Nibbio*; DD *Sparviero*; TB *6PN, 12PN*.
Austrian Forces: TB *86F*[+] (Lieutenant Josef Farfoglia); MS *Tb19, Tb36*.

On 5 September *Sparviero* and two torpedo boats, covered by the scouts *Aquila* and *Nibbio*, were recovering a flying boat bought down by an engine defect. The Italian force sighted *86F* covering *Tb19* and *Tb36*, which were sweeping mines in the Gulf of Drin. The Italian warships engaged at a range of nine thousand yards, with *86F* replying when the range dropped to 5,500 yards. Although the Austrians were hampered by the slow speed of their minesweepers, the Italians managed only to damage *86F* before the Austrian vessels reached the cover of Medua's shore batteries.[18]

Bombardment of Durazzo: 2 October, dawn–1240

Conditions: Clear

Missions: Entente, raid/bombardment; Austrians, transit/defense

Entente Forces: Support Squadron: IT BB *Dante*; BR CL *Glasgow, Gloucester*; IT CL *Marsala*; IT DL *Aquila, Nibbio, Sparviero, Racchia, Riboty, Rossarol, Pepe, Poerio*; IT DD *Nievo, Schiaffino*; AU DD *Swan, Warrego*; BR DD *Acorn, Lapwing, Tribune, Shark, Badger, Fury*; US SC *SC 215, 128, 129, 225, 327, 96, 179, 338, 337, 130, 324*. Bombardment Squadron: IT CA *San Giorgio, San Marco, Pisa*; BR CL *Lowestoft, Dartmouth, Weymouth*[#]; BR DD *Nereide, Ruby, Nymphe, Cameleon, Acheron, Goshawk, Jackal, Tigress*; IT TB *8PN, 10PN, 11PN, 35PN, 36PN, 37PN, 38PN, 42PN, 67PN*. MAS Force: MAS *92, 97, 98, 102, 202, 210*.

Austrian Force: DD *Scharfschütze*[+] (Corvette Captain Heinrich Pauer), *Dinara*[+]; TB *Tb87*[+]; MM *Stambul* (3,817 GRT)★, *Graz*[+], *Hercegovina*[+].

On 14 September the Entente army on the Salonika front finally cracked the Bulgarian-German-Austrian-Ottoman lines. The French were worried that the Austrians might reinforce their armies through Durazzo and so proposed a naval action to prevent this, offering to do it themselves. Italy had never wanted a French fleet inside the Adriatic, desired one even less now that the war was clearly winding down and old rivalries were reasserting themselves, and so decided to undertake the bombardment with British help. Although the Austrian command ordered the port's evacuation on 28 September and Bulgaria signed an armistice two days later, the large operation went forward. On the day of the attack the Austrians had at Durazzo two destroyers, a torpedo boat, and three merchant vessels. Austrian submarines *U29* and *U31* were offshore.

The operation commenced with six MAS boats dashing into the open roads before dawn and launching torpedoes. Then came "repeated and persistent attacks by Italian and British aircraft." At noon three Italian armored cruisers made a forty-minute, 8-knot firing run from 13,000 yards with their 10-inch and 7.5-inch guns. Torpedo boats swept ahead of the cruisers and screened off each beam. Eleven American sub chasers maneuvered a thousand yards off each flank of the division—and incorrectly took credit for sinking both Austrian submarines. After the heavy cruisers finished the three British light cruisers moved in, firing from 11,000 yards. At this point *U31* torpedoed *Weymouth* and blew off her stern. The powerful force standing offshore in support, including the dreadnought *Dante*, saw no action. Neither did the eight British, French, and Italian submarines patrolling off Austrian bases in case the K.u.K. Kriegsmarine reacted.

The Austrian warships dodged salvos and escaped with light damage. The shelling sank *Stambul* and damaged the other two steamers. Harm to the facilities was minor; far less than claimed at the time. Italian cavalry occupied Durazzo on 14 October.[19]

Surface combat in the Adriatic was largely a product of accidental nocturnal encounters between light units engaged on other business, or interceptions and prolonged pursuits of raiders trying to return to the safety of their base. There were no cases where larger warships traded broadsides, or even where both sides accepted combat and tried to fight to a resolution. Generally, K.u.K. Kriegsmarine forces were the ones refusing combat; this was because the Habsburg navy could not replace warships larger than a destroyer and the need to preserve ships limited operations. In Italy's view there was no reason to risk its superior position. Both Austria-Hungary and Italy followed coherent naval strategies that recognized their geographic and material constraints, sometimes to the irritation of their allies. Their battle fleets got little use, but there was little for them to do in such narrow and mine-infested waters.

Mediterranean 1918
Battle of Imbros: 20 January, 0740–0930
Conditions: Thick mist in the morning, clearing
Missions: British, patrol; Ottomans, raid
British Force: BM *M28*★, *Raglan*★; DD *Lizard*, *Tigress*.
Ottoman Force (Vice Admiral Hubert Rebeur-Paschwitz): BC
  Yavuz#; CL *Midilli*★; DD *Numene*, *Muavenet*; TB *Samsun*, *Basra*.

After the *Goeben* and *Breslau* passed up the Dardanelles in August 1914, they did not return to the Aegean until 20 January 1918. The occasion was a planned raid of two Entente bases near the mouth of the Dardanelles, Kusu on the island of Imbros and Mudros on Lemnos. This was a project of the Ottoman fleet's new German commander, Vice Admiral Hubert Rebeur-Paschwitz. He secured enough coal for his ships (it was necessary for *Yavuz* to fill her bunkers at Zonguldak) and maintained secrecy by not sweeping the minefields outside the Dardanelles, which the British considered a prerequisite to any sortie.

The ships departed Constantinople after dark on 19 January accompanied by four escorts and entered the Aegean at 0555 the next morning. *Yavuz* struck her first mine just fifteen minutes later, but as the damage was minor Rebeur-Paschwitz pressed on. The ships turned north toward Kusu Bay while the escorts waited near the mouth of the Dardanelles.

A thick mist favored the Ottoman enterprise and at 0730 they neared their first destination undetected by lookout stations on Imbros. The destroyer *Lizard*, on patrol north-northwest of the harbor, and two drifters off the harbor sighted the enemy just before 0740. They sounded an alarm, which was hardly necessary as *Yavuz* opened fire on the lighthouse from only six thousand yards. *Midilli* sent *Lizard* running with a few salvos. The monitors *M28* and *Raglan* were anchored in the bay against the shore and at first held fire hoping the enemy would not spot them. However, this proved wishful thinking when both Ottoman ships targeted *Raglan*. The monitor's 14-inch guns fired at least one round, which fell near *Yavuz*, and her 6-inchers several more, but all missed while the raiders quickly found the range. *Midilli*'s fourth salvo destroyed *Raglan*'s spotting top, forcing her to fire under local control. More 15-cm shells from the light cruiser shredded the monitor's superstructure. Then a 28-cm round penetrated *Raglan*'s barbette and ignited a cordite fire. This forced the turret's evacuation. The Ottomans closed to four thousand yards and another shell detonated the monitor's 3-inch magazine. The crew abandoned ship and *Raglan* sank by the bow at 0815. *Midilli* turned her guns on *M28* and walloped her amidships with her second salvo, igniting an oil tank. The flames coming up through a hatch forced the crew to abandon the ship's 9.2-inch gun. Then at 0827 the fire reached the shell room and *M28* blew up in a massive explosion "that showered debris and human remains over a wide area."[20] *Raglan* suffered 127 casualties out of a crew of 220, while *M28* had only eight casualties from her crew of sixty-six despite the spectacular nature of her sinking.

When the gunfire started the destroyer *Tigress*, which had been patrolling to the west, headed toward Kusu along the shoreline. *Midilli* engaged her at 0820 when she came into sight, whereupon *Tigress* veered away and joined *Lizard* to shadow the enemy.

After this success Rebeur-Paschwitz turned toward Mudros. At that base raising steam were the predreadnought *Agamemnon*, the light cruisers *Lowestoft*, *Foresight*, and *Skirmisher*, the sloop *Heliotrope*, and the destroyers *Arno* and *Ribble* (the semi-dreadnought *Lord Nelson* was usually at Imbros but the base commander had used her to ferry him to a conference at Salonika). Several other warships were in dock or unavailable. However, the Ottoman vessels had gone only a short distance when, at 0830, *Midilli* struck a mine. *Yavuz* came up to pass a tow, but she touched off a mine herself at 0855 that caused more serious damage than the first. Then *Midilli* detonated four more mines in quick succession and rapidly began to settle. British airplanes were overhead by this time harassing the Ottomans. *Yavuz* managed to extract herself without further adventure and turned toward the Dardanelles, but struck yet another mine at 0948. The Ottoman escorts, meanwhile, came out to rescue *Midilli*'s crew but at 0930 *Lizard* and *Tigress* engaged and chased them back to the cover of shore batteries on Cape Helles. After *Yavuz* made the Dardanelles, a navigation error put her aground near Nagara Point in the narrows about a third of the

Map 6.1 Battle of Imbros: 20 January 1918

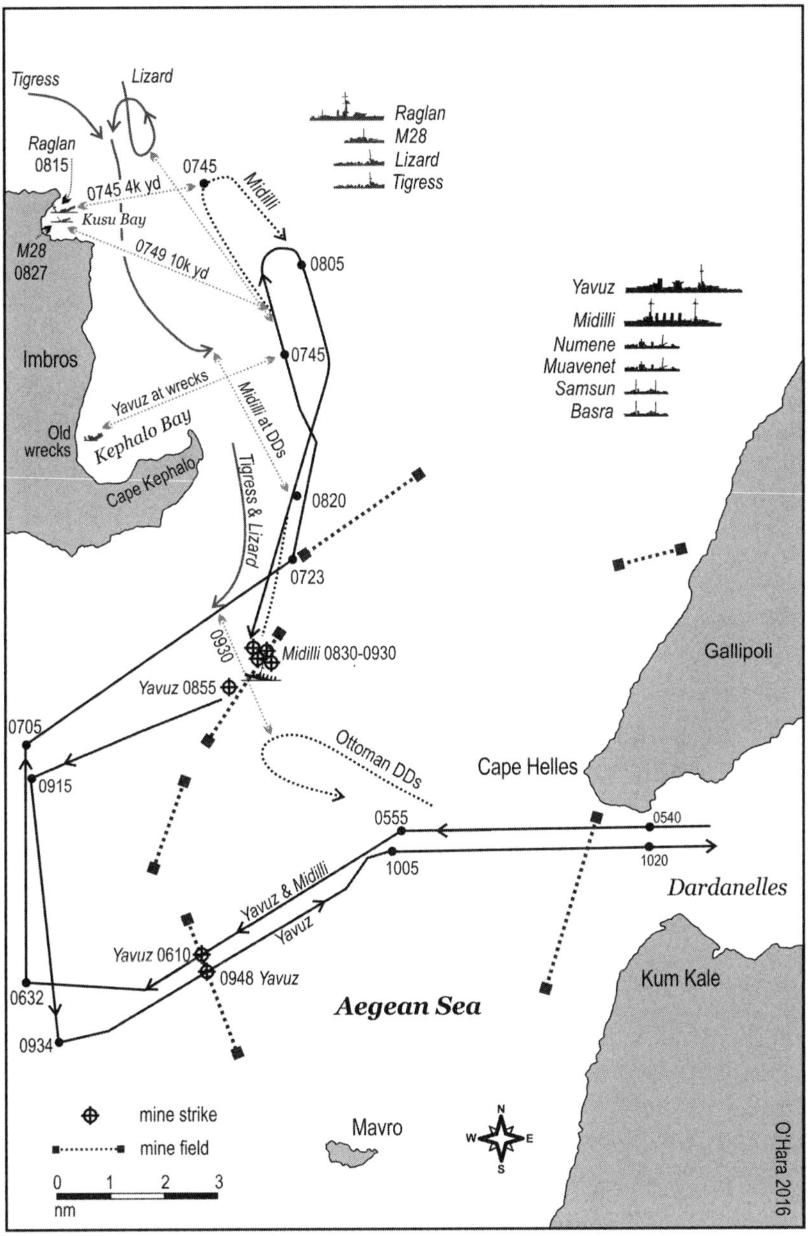

Tigress   Lizard

Raglan
0815

Raglan
M28
Lizard
Tigress

0745
0745 4k yd
Midilli
Kusu Bay
0749 10k yd
M28
0827

0805

0745

Imbros

Yavuz at wrecks

Old wrecks   Kephalo Bay
Cape Kephalo

Midilli at DDs
Tigress & Lizard

Yavuz
Midilli
Numene
Muavenet
Samsun
Basra

0820

0723

0930   Midilli 0830–0930
Yavuz 0855

0705

0915

Ottoman DDs

Gallipoli

Cape Helles

0555   0540
1005   1020

Dardanelles

Yavuz & Midilli
Yavuz

Yavuz 0610
0948 Yavuz

0632

0934

Kum Kale

Aegean Sea

⊕ mine strike
▪····▪ mine field

0 1 2 3
nm

Mavro

N W E S

O'Hara 2016

way up the strait. The British were unable to exploit this opportunity, despite launching "no less than 217 aeroplane bomb attacks." She was refloated on 27 January and towed to Constantinople, but she never fought again. Rebeur-Paschwitz accomplished in a morning what the Russians could not in three years.[21]

Baltic 1918

In the Baltic, the ice broke up early. On 25 February, in the interval of "no war, no peace" between the end of effective Russian resistance and the Treaty of Brest-Litovsk, the Germans captured Revel. The Russians saved most of their ships, including five cruisers, eight submarines, twelve minesweepers, and thirty-one auxiliaries, but they were forced to scuttle eleven submarines. In March the Germans conducted landings in the Åland Islands and then on the Finnish mainland, forcing the Russians to withdraw their fleet from Helsingfors to Kronstadt by 11 April. More than sixty warships and ninety-two other vessels escaped but eighty-five vessels were abandoned or scuttled, including seven British submarines. The German fleet threatening the port included the dreadnoughts *Westfalen*, *Posen*, and *Rheinland*. During this operation *Rheinland* ran aground and sustained heavy damage. She was towed back to Kiel on 27 July after a major salvage operation, but never returned to service.[22]

Black Sea 1918

The German-Bolshevik armistice that preceded the Treaty of Brest-Litovsk, signed on 3 March 1918, had called for all Russian warships in the Black Sea to be demilitarized in home ports. The Ukraine was to be an independent nation, but German and Austrian troops advanced through the region in March 1918 to secure its resources. The Germans occupied Odessa on 13 March and the shipbuilding center of Nikolayev on 17 March. Although the main fleet base at Sevastopol was allocated to Russia, the Germans occupied it on 14 May. Most of the Black Sea Fleet's more modern units, including two dreadnoughts and sixteen flotilla ships, sailed for Novorossisk but Germany captured the fleet's predreadnoughts, three cruisers, and many smaller ships. In January the Ottomans took advantage of the opportunity to send *Yavuz* to Sevastopol for docking. This was her first time in dry dock since the war began.

The fear that the Germans would supplement their fleet with captured Russian ships obsessed the Entente powers, although in retrospect this seems an almost impossible undertaking. The captured ships required a huge and specialized infrastructure to be effective and the Central Powers faced enormous difficulties in finding coal, oil, and sailors, all at a time when the Kaiserliche Marine was decommissioning surface ships to man U-boats and sharing its oil reserves with the army. Even though a majority of the crews of the Novorossisk contingent voted to return to Sevastopol and accept internment (motivated by German threats to continue their advance and promises to make good their pay), this did little to fulfill Berlin's pipe dream of a Black Sea fleet. Only the dreadnought *Volia*, three of the large destroyers, and two torpedo boats made it back to Sevastopol. In the Black Sea's final surface action of the war, the destroyer *Kerch*, with a pro-Soviet and anti-internment crew, torpedoed *Svobodnaia Rossiia* off Novorossisk on 19 June. Four weapons hit the dreadnought, the last one causing a massive explosion. She capsized and sank in minutes. The remaining destroyers scuttled.

Of the major warships only *Volia* entered German service and this was not until 15 October. "The German crew had great difficulty making her battle ready and working the unfamiliar equipment."[23] The 30 October armistice between the Ottoman Empire and the Entente powers exposed the German fantasy of operating a captured fleet on the Black Sea, and the first Entente warships arrived in Sevastopol in mid-November, in time to participate in the spreading Russian civil war.[24]

7

Summing Up

*The race is not always to the swift, nor the battle
to the strong, but that's the way to bet.*
—DAMON RUNYON, *RUNYON ON BROADWAY*

Sea power played a vital role in World War I and surface warfare was fundamental to its application. Ship to ship combat capability was not all that navies needed, and as the war progressed it had to be balanced against other capabilities, but it was essential to all functions. To borrow a phrase from Clausewitz, it was the "cash payment" of World War I sea power and as such the ultimate expression of naval warfare. This was true in every theater of war. In the North Sea the overwhelming surface warfare capability of the Grand Fleet—and the readiness to use that capability—reduced the German fleet to offensive impotence. In the Baltic, minefields, submarines, and shore batteries played significant roles but, as demonstrated at Irben Strait in 1915 and 1917, Russia needed the firepower of surface warships to defend its fixed positions. In the great oceans the British (with allied help) quickly hunted down all but two of the German warships at large and destroyed them in surface combat. In the Mediterranean Entente surface warfare superiority confined the K.u.K. Kriegsmarine to the Adriatic, while in the Black Sea it established and then maintained Russian dominance. Even during the war's last years, when submarines and minecraft grew in prominence, surface combat power remained critical to the successful use of these systems and to the defense against them. As the British admiralty staff expressed it, "It was only the support of the battleships which enabled the German minesweepers to carry out their tasks

294

undisturbed." And, "This latent power of the High Sea Fleet to hold our forces immobilized from other spheres of work adversely affected anti-submarine measures of every sort."[1]

The Numbers of the Surface War

This section examines how surface combat power was used and considers the effectiveness of its application. The basic demographics are as follows:

- Actions: 144
- Ships engaged: 2,250 (15.6/battle)
- Ships sunk: 118 (0.8/battle, 5.2 percent of ships engaged)
- Ships significantly damaged: 142 (1.0/battle, 6.3 percent of ships engaged)

Thus, the average First World War surface naval battle involved sixteen ships with nearly one ship sunk and one damaged per action.

After demographics come characteristics: was either side seeking battle; did either side have advance intelligence about the other; did both sides fight willingly; and finally, was the battle fought during the day or at night:

- Intentional: 87 (60 percent). At least one side sought combat upon contact;
- Intelligence: 64 (44 percent). At least one side had advance notice of the enemy;
- Non-consensual: 108 (75 percent). One side immediately tried to break contact or was forced into combat unwillingly;
- Night: 45 (31 percent). The action was fought at night.

The next consideration is why battles occurred:

- Attacking a specific objective, such as a harbor or a convoy: 17 (12 percent);
- As a consequence of a more general offensive action: a raid, bombardment, sweep, or reaction to an enemy mission: 59 (41 percent);
- As a consequence of an unexpected encounter: 68 (47 percent).

Finally, who won? This analysis assigns victory to the side that accomplished its mission while preventing its opponent from so doing. If both or neither side accomplished its mission, the side that inflicted the most damage is considered victorious.

- Entente Powers: 60 (42 percent);
- Central Powers: 58 (40 percent);
- No clear victor: 26 (18 percent).

Four salient facts emerge from the above.
- In the great majority of actions one side immediately tried to break contact or was fighting unwillingly;
- Nearly half the actions were unexpected;
- Relatively few actions resulted from attacks on specific targets;
- While actions could be large, relatively few ships were sunk or heavily damaged.

The significance of these facts can be best considered by putting them in context and that can be done by comparing ship-to-ship fights in World War I to those in the Russo-Japanese War and World War II. Broadly, all three wars applied the same surface warfare technologies: guns, torpedoes, and primarily optical fire control systems.

In looking at World War II naval engagements the authors have considered 161 ship-to-ship actions involving purpose-built warships greater than 500 tons displacement in which guns or torpedoes were fired.[2] The World War I actions include those involving ships as small as 100-ton torpedo boats. For the Russo-Japanese War, the authors have considered twenty-one actions for which reasonably reliable information exists, involving warships with displacements down to 50 tons.[3] For the numbers below, Jutland is treated as two battles: one encompassing the fighting during the day and the other the fighting in the following night, while Tsushima (the final battle of the Russo-Japanese War) is counted as a single action stretching over two days.

Three Wars: Basic Numbers

The basic numbers for the three wars are summarized in the following tables.

The average number of ships involved in an action shrank from one war to the next, as more combat power became concentrated in larger hulls. In both the Russo-Japanese War and World War II, combats were deadlier: 20 and 23 percent respectively of ships involved were either lost

Table 7.1 Basic Demographics of Surface Actions

Russo-Japanese War	Battles	Ships Engaged (average)*	Ships Sunk (average)**	Ships Damaged (average)***	Percent Sunk or Damaged
Day	11	387 (35.2)	37 (3.4)	55 (5.0)	24%
Night	10	214 (21.4)	6 (0.6)	23 (2.3)	14%
All	21	601 (28.6)	43 (2.0)	78 (3.7)	20%

World War I	Battles	Ships Engaged (average)*	Ships Sunk (average)	Ships Damaged (average)***	Percent Sunk or Damaged
Day	99	1716 (17.3)	87 (0.9)	101 (1.0)	11%
Night	45	534 (11.9)	31 (0.7)	41 (0.9)	13%
All	144	2250 (15.6)	118 (0.8)	142 (1.0)	12%

World War II	Battles	Ships Engaged (average)*	Ships Sunk (average)	Ships Damaged (average)***	Percent Sunk or Damaged
Day	69	956 (13.9)	102 (1.5)	88 (1.3)	20%
Night	92	1047 (11.4)	160 (1.7)	114 (1.2)	26%
All	161	2003 (12.4)	262 (1.6)	202 (1.3)	23%

* includes noncombatant vessels escorted by warships.
** includes ships captured.
*** refers to significantly damaged and interned ships.

or damaged compared to 12 percent in World War I actions. In World War I there were ninety-three actions with no ships sunk (65 percent) compared to eleven (52 percent) in the Russo-Japanese War and fifty-one (32 percent) in World War II. Thus, by the measure of ships sunk or damaged, World War I appears a less intense naval conflict than World War II or the Russo-Japanese War.

Comparing the Three Wars

The overall likelihood of a ship being sunk or damaged in a World War I surface engagement was roughly half that in World War II or the Russo-Japanese War. This does not mean, however, that surface combat in World War I was tentative or lacked intensity. The fact that World War I combat was more frequent and involved more ships suggests just the opposite. Then why the difference? Several possibilities suggest themselves:

- Did the Russo-Japanese War and World War II feature more battles in which one side overwhelmed the other, thus inflating loss ratios?
- Did improved material, tactics, or technology result in deadlier fights?
- Did combat experience make a difference?
- Did context and the missions of the forces involved influence intensity?
- Did each side's overall strategic situation influence the nature of combat?

With respect to the first point the 1905 Battle of Tsushima resulted in thirty-one ships sunk. This battle of annihilation inflated the Russo-Japanese War's loss ratio, but even excluding Tsushima the percentage of ships sunk or damaged in the Russo-Japanese War was still higher than in World War I (15 percent versus 12 percent). There was no comparable battle of annihilation in World War II. While surface combat between evenly matched forces was rare in all three wars, overall World War I battles were more unbalanced. However, such imbalance tended to reduce losses because the inferior force usually fled quickly and successfully.

Regarding material, tactics, and technology, offensive capabilities improved throughout the period, but so did defensive capabilities. Ships got larger and tougher, damage control procedures improved, and many of the offensive advances, especially in fire control, had the effect of moving battle ranges farther out and so blunting their effects— at least until radar fire direction and control became more sophisticated in the second half of World War II. The cruder technology of the Russo-Japanese War produced deadlier sea fights than did the more refined technology of World War I because battles were fought at closer ranges in the 1905 war.

Material, technological, and tactical improvements affected combat intensity most strongly in night actions. In the two earlier wars night actions were generally fleeting as ships rapidly lost contact with opponents and friends alike. In the 1904–1905 war ships damaged at night outnumbered ships sunk (or captured) by almost 4:1. In World War I, this ratio was 4:3 but in World War II it was 4:6; that is, more ships were sunk than damaged. Night actions were chaotic affairs even in the Second World War, but better weapons (particularly improved torpedoes and flashless powder), better detection and tracking (through night optics, pyrotechnics, efficient searchlights, night recognition procedures, and above all radar) and better command and control (through radio and particularly UHF voice radio) made World War II night actions more deadly.

Regarding experience, in the Russo-Japanese War combat experience was all on the side of the victorious Japanese, with many officers and men having fought against China ten years before. Senior officers of World War II were junior officers in World War I—many commanded destroyers in surface actions. Collectively, they possessed a body of experience they could apply in the 1939–1945 war and share as mentors for younger officers who had only known peace. If one accepts the premise that experience and education have any value at all, this pool of veterans would have enhanced the surface combat effectiveness of World War II navies.

An examination of the contexts in which actions took place shows marked differences between the three wars, as the table below shows.

In the Russo-Japanese War and World War II, one side was far more likely to have advance intelligence of the other before an engagement. Intelligence was better in World War II because aircraft were more efficient and the timeliness and quality of radio direction finding and signals intelligence was much improved; it was better in the Russo-Japanese War because of a close blockade of the main Russian base and (eventually) on-shore observation. Another key difference emerges from an examination of mission types. Attacks against specific targets predominated in the Russo-Japanese War and comprised 42 percent of World War II missions, but only 17 percent of World War I missions. This is significant as directed attacks against an opponent tied to defending a specific objective, such as a convoy, were most likely to force battle. Thus, because surface actions in the Russo-Japanese War and the Second World War were based on better intelligence and were more directed, they were deadlier.

Decisions whether to stand and fight or flee played an obvious role in combat losses. The table below presents the number of engagements in which one side ran either immediately or after a very brief fight.

Forces tied to the defense of convoys, harbors, or fortified positions usually (but not always) accepted battle, but in World War I these cases were rare and thus more often one side or the other attempted to flee from the outset or after a brief engagement. Moreover, the Austrian and Ottoman navies, fighting with irreplaceable warships, declined combat even in situations where they were superior. In World War II, on the other hand, there were seventy actions where the weaker side had to

Table 7.2 Surface Actions in Context—Three Wars

	Russo-Japanese War	World War I	World War II
At least one side had advance intelligence of the other	86%	44%	67%
Mission against a specific objective, such as a harbor, convoy or beachhead	62%	12%	42%
Neither side intended an encounter	5%	47%	17%

Table 7.3 Fight or Flee—Actions in Which One Side Quickly Tried to Break Contact

	Day	**Night**	**Total**
Russo-Japanese War	0 of 11 (0%)	0 of 10 (0%)	0 of 21 (0%)
World War I	53 of 99 (54%)	35 of 45 (78%)	88 of 144 (61%)
World War II	20 of 69 (29%)	22 of 92 (24%)	42 of 161 (26%)

fight to defend convoys, beachheads, or harbors. In the Russo-Japanese War both sides accepted combat in all actions. This increased the relative deadliness of these wars relative to World War I.

Each side's strategic situation affected combat intensity. For example, the Italian navy lost eleven flotilla craft in World War I, but eighty-five in World War II. Losses in surface combat rose proportionally: two of eleven in World War I and eighteen of eighty-five in the second conflict. Losses were so much greater in World War II because the Italians fought a campaign that required the Regia Marina to protect supply lines from Italy to Africa and the Balkans. This strategic imperative forced the Italians to accept combat even when their opponent had superior numbers and material, or at night where their opponent had an operational edge. This example can be expanded generally; navies in the Russo-Japanese War and World War II had more compelling reasons to fight, more strategic settings that led to fighting, and, in World War II, more tools, like radar and aerial reconnaissance, to force combat.

Contrasting the Russian navy in the Russo-Japanese War and the Japanese and German navies of World War II to the German, Austro-Hungarian, Italian, and Russian Baltic navies of World War I reveals another strategic difference that affected combat intensity. These World War I navies followed a strategy of maintaining a fleet in being. This was possible because the fleet could shelter from the enemy but still strike if necessary. Such a strategy minimized risk but still tied down enemy ships to counter the sheltered fleets. The benefits of such a strategy, however, proved largely illusory when the German, Austrian, and Russian Baltic fleets descended into mutiny by the war's end. The Russians in the Russo-Japanese War and the Germans and Japanese in World War II could not pursue this strategy. In the Russo-Japanese War, one Russian fleet came under the guns of a besieging army and another was forced to confront a superior opponent. In World War II, this strategy became irrelevant as the war progressed—first as it became clear there would be no negotiated peace and second as airpower gradually removed each fleet's safe havens. The best part of the Kaiserliche Marine steamed into internment at the end of World War I. Such a fate was unimaginable for the Kriegsmarine or the Imperial Japanese Navy.

To conclude, several factors reduced the deadliness of naval surface combat in the First World War. Unbalanced force ratios tended to decrease intensity rather than increase it. Advances in materiel, technology, and tactics were significant, particularly in night actions, but not enough to explain the leap in intensity between World War I and World War II and useless in explaining the greater deadliness of combat in the Russo-Japanese War. It is likely that experience and the thoughtful application of lessons learned enhanced a navy's effectiveness in surface combat. Intelligence affected combat intensity, and the large number of incidental or accidental actions fought in World War I reduced overall losses. Finally, the strategic background played a key role, driving missions and forcing combat to achieve mission goals while depriving defending navies of safe havens. The differences in naval surface combat in these three wars resulted from a combination of these factors.

Navy Scorecards

How comparatively effective were the navies of World War I in surface warfare? The tables which follow specify the number of ships each navy and its opponents brought to battle, the ratio of those forces, and modified force and effect ratios weighted by ship types. In the following tables the modified force ratio (MFR) is based on ship cost—more expensive ships are worth more. Where the modified ratio exceeds the base ratio, it indicates that the navy committed more potent ships than its opponents to surface combat. A smaller modified ratio means the opposite. The effect ratio (ER) is the chance of a ship harming an opponent divided by the chance of a ship being harmed itself. The ER is modified by extent of damage and ship cost, and so increases by the degree of harm inflicted and the size of the ships harmed. Comparing ER to MFR provides a rough measurement of a navy's effectiveness. An ER greater than the MFR is evidence that the force was outperforming its enemies in terms of inflicting losses and damage; an ER less than the MFR suggests the opposite.

The Entente

The main Entente navies all fought at least one action in company with allies. Actions under the individual navy headings are those fought by that navy alone; coalition actions are covered at the end of the section. Ship for ship, the Entente navies were less effective than their Central Powers opponents in both day and night actions.

United Kingdom: Royal Navy

Actions fought: 59 (44 day/15 night)

Victorious actions: 22 (37 percent)

Victories against superior forces: 6 (10 percent of total, 27 percent of victories)

Ships Lost: 50 (BCx3, OBBx1, CAx5, CLx2, DLx1, DDx15, BMx3, MSx1, AMTx4, MMx15)

Ships Sunk: 36 (BCx1, OBBx1, CAx3, CLx13, DDx14, TBx3, AMTx1)

The Royal Navy achieved its strategic goals of blockading the Central Powers, safeguarding the transport of troops and supplies to the fighting front, and protecting trade. A forbidding preponderance of surface combat power helped accomplish the first two goals and was key to the Royal Navy's dominance of the North Sea. The Kaiserliche Marine always had to face the prospect of superior enemy forces lurking just over the horizon. The combination of greater British numbers and conservative British leadership that was generally guided by the doctrine of force preservation decreased the overall intensity of combat.

The Royal Navy suffered its greatest surface defeat in the Battle of Coronel, but otherwise applied superior force to sweep German ships from oceanic waters. The British did not fare as well as their opponents in terms of damage inflicted versus damage taken, but compensated by bringing more ships to battle. In part the unfavorable effect ratio was a consequence of the Royal Navy's relative inferiority in night combat.

Table 7.4 Royal Navy Force Ratios

	Friendly Ships	Enemy Ships	Base Force Ratio	Modified Force Ratio	Effect Ratio
Day	503	379	1.33	1.33	0.97
Night	138	134	1.03	1.08*	0.45*
Overall	641	513	1.25	1.15	0.91

*excludes Jutland night action.

Imperial Russian Navy

  Actions Fought: 49 (38 day/11 night)

  Victorious actions: 21 (43 percent)

  Victories against superior forces: 5 (10 percent of total, 24 percent of victories)

  Ships Lost: 9 (OBBx1, DDx1, MLx1, GBx2, MMx4)

  Ships Sunk: 10 (CLx1, DDx1, CMx1, GBx2, AMCx1, TBx1, MMx3)

The Tsarist navy's efforts to protect defensive positions accounted for much of the surface combat in the Baltic. Offensive efforts were mixed and raids by surface forces produced limited success. That is understandable given that the Russians needed to maintain good relations with Sweden, which inhibited attacks against Germany's important trade with that country. Germany's potentially overwhelming surface power kept Russia from using its dreadnoughts aggressively in the Baltic.

In the Black Sea the fleet played an active role from the start and launched a full-blooded offensive once the first of its dreadnoughts entered service. Strategically, the Black Sea Fleet did all that was asked of it—strangling Ottoman trade, bombarding enemy positions, supporting the army, and carrying on an active offensive mining campaign—before finally succumbing to revolutionary pressures in late 1917.

Table 7.5 Imperial Russian Navy Force Ratios

	Friendly Ships	Enemy Ships	Base Force Ratio	Modified Force Ratio	Effect Ratio
Day	287	240	1.20	1.29	0.73
Night	63	38	1.66	3.73	1.04
Overall	350	278	1.26	1.48	0.77

In terms of tactical effectiveness, there were similarities and differences in Russian performance in the Baltic and Black Seas. In both theaters, losses were low. In the Black Sea, 163 Russian ships faced just 38 Ottoman ships in 21 actions. The high ratio and the slight results reflect the fact that many Black Sea actions featured the Russians pursuing an inferior, but faster, force: it was difficult to produce results in such a situation. Overall, Russian gunnery was generally less effective than German gunnery and Russian torpedoes performed poorly. However, the big Russian destroyers in both the Baltic and the Black Sea particularly impressed their opponents, and accounted for seven of the ten ships that the Russians sank.

Italy: Regia Marina

Actions Fought: 17 (8 day/9 night)

Victorious actions: 10 (59 percent)

Victories against superior forces: 3 (18 percent of total, 30 percent of victories)

Ships Lost: 3 (DDx2, MMx1)

Ships Sunk: 0

Table 7.6 Regia Marina Force Ratios

	Friendly Ships	Enemy Ships	Base Force Ratio	Modified Force Ratio	Effect Ratio
Day	31	52	0.60	0.63	0.00
Night	39	36	1.08	1.19	0.26
Overall	70	88	0.80	0.82	0.16

306 Chapter 7

The Regia Marina's objective was to dominate the Adriatic, support the army's maritime front, and maintain the bridgehead in Albania. Its battle fleet stood ready in the unlikely event the Austrian fleet tried to break out of the Adriatic, but the navy relied on flotilla craft, motor torpedo boats, submarines, and mines to assert sea control in a war of patrol and harassment. It also emphasized attacking enemy units in harbor using small or specialized craft. The Regia Marina generally accomplished its objectives, although it received substantial aid from its French and British allies in maintaining the blockade of the Otranto Strait.

An analysis of its actions shows that the Regia Marina won a high proportion of its battles through mission fulfillment, and not by inflicting losses on its opponents; only its motor torpedo boats sank any Austrian warships, including two battleships in surface combat, and these are not included in the Regia Marina ratios. A striking aspect of the Regia Marina's surface combat experience in World War I was that, despite nine of its seventeen actions being fought at night, the navy did not emphasize night-fighting by the time it entered World War II.

France: Marine Nationale
   Actions Fought: 5 (1 day/4 night)
   Victorious actions: 2 (40 percent)
   Victories against superior forces: 0
   Ships Lost: 1 (DDx1)
   Ships Sunk: 2 (CPx1, TBx1)

Table 7.7   Marine Nationale Force Ratios

	Friendly Ships	Enemy Ships	Base Force Ratio	Modified Force Ratio	Effect Ratio
Day	65	2	32.5	54	0.89
Night	15	14	1.07	1.33	0.32
Overall	80	16	5	16.35	0.69

Although overshadowed by the army, the French navy fought from Penang to the Adriatic to the Flanders coast. The main tasks of the Marine Nationale in the Mediterranean, its principal area of responsibility, were to safeguard the movement of troops and supplies from North Africa to the Métropole and to contain the Austrian fleet. Both tasks were substantially eased by Italy's neutrality and later declaration of war on the Austro-Hungarian Empire. The French navy also played a substantial role first in supplying the Serbian army through southern Adriatic ports and then in evacuating that army after Bulgaria's entry into the war. It struggled, however, to protect trade and transport in the Mediterranean from submarine attacks, and was late to adopt effective convoying. Those problems were overcome, but only through interallied efforts and relatively late in the war.

Like the Royal Navy, the Marine Nationale found night fighting hard to master and faced the familiar frustrations in the Adriatic of trying to run down or cut off Austrian raiding forces when acting as part of a hard-to-coordinate coalition force.

Coalition Actions

Actions Fought: 10 (5 day/5 night)
Victorious actions: 5 (50 percent)
Victories against superior forces: 0
Ships Lost: 2 (CPx1, TBx1)
Ships Sunk: 4 (DDx1, TBx2, MMx1)

Table 7.8 Coalition Action Force Ratios

	Friendly Ships	Enemy Ships	Base Force Ratio	Modified Force Ratio	Effect Ratio
Day	98	27	3.63	3.59	0.42
Night	25	28	0.89	1.16	2.62
Overall	123	55	2.24	2.64	0.61

The Entente navies fought ten engagements as coalition forces. The French featured most prominently, participating in nine of the ten actions. The British engaged in seven, while the Regia Marina fought in five and the Russians in one. The Entente navies found it particularly hard to coordinate their joint efforts in the face of the enemy, especially the British, French, and Italian forces guarding the Otranto Barrage. This led to missed opportunities and allowed the Austrians more success than they might otherwise have achieved. It was a problem that the Entente never satisfactorily resolved. Nonetheless, Entente navies managed to best their opponents in three of the night coalition actions fought.

Central Powers

Germany: Kaiserliche Marine

Actions Fought: 91 (64 day/27 night)

Victorious actions: 39 (43 percent)

Victories against superior forces: 14 (15 percent of total, 36 percent of victories)

Ships Lost: 41 (BCx1, OBBx1, CAx3, CLx13, DDx15, TBx5, CMx1, DSx1, AMTx1)

Ships Sunk: 54 (BCx3, OBBx1, CAx5, CLx4, DLx1, DDx17, BMx1, TBx1, GBx1, MSx1, AMTx4, MMx15)

Table 7.9 Kaiserliche Marine Force Ratios

	Friendly Ships	Enemy Ships	Base Force Ratio	Modified Force Ratio	Effect Ratio
Day	587	665	0.88	0.82	1.16
Night	186	191	0.97	0.66*	1.73*
Overall	773	856	0.90	0.89	1.16

*excludes Jutland night action.

Every German fleet commander recognized that a confrontation between the High Seas Fleet and the whole Grand Fleet would likely end in a German defeat. The Admiralstab pinned its hopes on two complementary strategies: whittling down the British strength with mines, submarines, and light forces, and catching a portion of the Grand Fleet with the High Seas Fleet's full strength. The first proved illusory and the second difficult to achieve, with reconnaissance never able to give the German admirals the absolute assurances they needed to commit to combat.

Tactically, the Kaiserliche Marine showed a qualitative surface warfare advantage over the British. The Germans also demonstrated a significant surface warfare advantage against the Russian navy, losing a minelayer, a destroyer, and an auxiliary escort ship while sinking an old battleship, a destroyer, and two gunboats in twenty-seven engagements. They were helped in this result by bringing more ships to combat than the Russians.

Despite its tactical superiority the German navy was unable to break the British blockade, interfere with British traffic to France, or cause any lasting disruption to British trade through cruiser warfare. Only in the Baltic did the Kaiserliche Marine achieve its strategic goals, cutting off Russian trade through the Skagerrak and guarding the coasts of East Prussia from a seaborne Russian invasion (helped by the fact the Russians intended no such invasion). By 1915 the Kaiserliche Marine had discovered that submarines were its most effective naval weapon against Entente trade. This weapon's unrestricted use brought Germany close to major success but it was ultimately defeated and, far worse, provoked the United States into declaring war against the Central Powers.

Austro-Hungarian Empire: K.u.K. Kriegsmarine
  Actions Fought: 26 (13 day/13 night)
  Victorious actions: 9 (35 percent)
  Victories against superior forces: 3 (12 percent of total, 33 percent of victories)
  Ships Lost: 3 (CPx1, DDx1, MMx1)
  Ships Sunk: 3 (DDx2, MMx1)

Table 7.10 K.u.K. Kriegsmarine Force Ratios

	Friendly Ships	Enemy Ships	Base Force Ratio	Modified Force Ratio	Effect Ratio
Day	80	189	0.42	0.24	0.71
Night	58	61	0.95	0.86	4.15
Overall	138	250	0.55	0.32	0.92

The Imperial and Royal Navy of the Austro-Hungarian empire spent much of its prewar construction budget on a squadron of modern dreadnoughts, but when war arrived it had no intention (or need) of risking them in a climactic battle. What the K.u.K. Kriegsmarine really needed were modern destroyers and light cruisers. Of these types there were never enough and because ships larger than destroyers were essentially irreplaceable, the balance between risk and reward was always the governing consideration in Austrian operations. The goal was always to hit and run, never to stand and fight, even when the odds favored fighting.

In the northern Adriatic Austrian flotilla craft were out many nights conducting bombardments, laying mines, or supporting aerial raids. Not until the war's final year did the navy attempt to support the Imperial and Royal Army directly. The battle fleet ventured out of port on only three occasions—on the war's first day to support *Goeben*, upon the Italian declaration of war, and in 1918 when it lost a dreadnought to a motor boat's torpedo. In general the navy met its limited goals but hard usage gradually diminished the capability of its flotillas.

In the south the navy did not disrupt the evacuation of Serbian troops from Albania, failing in a situation where a determined attempt to exercise sea power could have materially affected the war. The K.u.K. Kriegsmarine was able to raid Entente patrols along the Otranto Strait—the stated goal being to ease the passage of German submarines through the straits—but strategically, this activity was of minor consequence, as the Austrians realized.

The K.u.K. Kriegsmarine fought well in many of its surface actions, demonstrating an impressive ability in its night actions to hit first and hit effectively. However, this must be tempered by its loss of two battleships to Italian motor torpedo boats in night attacks. The sinking of dreadnought *Szent István* was a particularly stunning blow, erasing the generally credible results of the prior four years.

Ottoman Empire: Osmanli Donanmasi
  Actions Fought: 27 (22 day/5 night)
  Victorious actions: 10 (37 percent)

Victories against superior forces: 6 (22 percent of total, 60 percent of victories)
Ships Lost: 8 (CLx1, TBx2, GBx2, MMx3)
Ships Sunk: 9 (OBBx1, GBx1, BMx2, MLx1, MMx4)

Table 7.11 Osmanli Donanmasi Force Ratios

	Friendly Ships	Enemy Ships	Base Force Ratio	Modified Force Ratio	Effect Ratio
Day	43	152	0.28	0.47	0.51
Night	7	29	0.24	0.18	18.3
Overall	50	181	0.28	0.42	1.23

The Ottoman navy had two main strategic tasks: keeping the Dardanelles and Bosporus closed and the Black Sea open. With the help of shore batteries and mines it succeeded in the first task, but the second proved beyond its abilities even with the addition of *Yavuz* and *Midilli*. The navy's greatest day came on 18 March 1915, when a field of twenty mines laid by an auxiliary minelayer sank three Entente predreadnoughts in the Dardanelles. The Entente would lose six predreadnoughts before abandoning the Gallipoli campaign, and the Ottomans would lose one.

The Ottoman navy preserved some freedom of action in the Black Sea until the first of the Russian dreadnoughts came into service, but from that point (October 1915) the Ottomans and their German allies were reduced to a furtive existence. While the mere presence of the *Yavuz* acted as a brake on more ambitious Russian plans, the navy could not prevent the Black Sea Fleet from savaging maritime trade, bombarding troops, and covering amphibious assaults almost at will.

The Ottoman surface navy's greatest achievement came when the destroyer *Muavenet* sank the battleship *Goliath* at anchor. Russian predreadnoughts forced *Yavuz* to flee in both of the stand-up fights she attempted, and the remaining actions generally developed into one side pursuing the other unsuccessfully. On balance the Ottoman navy showed limited ability to fight effectively. Even *Yavuz* and *Midilli* with mostly German crews turned in lackluster performances. The Ottomans fared better in night actions, where they could surprise their opponents or break off the action quickly. The enormous night effect ratio of 18.3 is the result of the *Goliath* and Odessa harbor raids combined with the Russian Black Sea fleet's failure to inflict meaningful damage in any night engagement.

Lessons Learned

What lessons did navies take from World War I surface warfare? First and foremost, surface combat power was still regarded as the most essential capability of navies and so the battleship, despite having to be protected from other increasingly potent threats, retained its status as the highest expression of naval power. Surface torpedo attacks had been surprisingly ineffective and postwar efforts focused on improving both the weapons and the means of delivery. Navies increased the torpedo load per ship and worked to improve tactics for coordinated torpedo launches. Thought was also given to countering surface torpedo attacks, with some navies concluding that battleship secondary armaments were inadequate for the task and that reliance would have to be placed on screening units. Interwar navies would develop progressively larger destroyers with an emphasis on gun power as well as torpedoes. The torpedo boat—the third most prevalent surface combatant in the First World War—became an anomaly in the Second, perpetuated only by the artificial terms of arms treaties.

The impact of submarines on surface fleet operations was a major development of the First World War. Prewar, all navies regarded submarines as an integral arm of the battle fleet. In the event, they played little direct part in surface engagements, although the threat of their presence commanded respect, and imagined submarine sightings affected the course of many battles. Submarines were far deadlier outside of set-piece battles, accounting for more than forty warships sunk with torpedoes, and navies learned that big ships needed flotilla craft to screen routine movements. The implementation of convoying in 1917 resulted in a shortage of destroyers and inhibited the operations of Britain's fleet during the war's last year. Postwar developments (such as sonar) would give the escorts better tools to use against submarines, but the submarines would improve as well. The need to deal with hostile submarines influenced the mix of ships that a navy would deploy and the formations that they would use.

Night fighting received increased attention both during and after the war. At the outset, the Royal Navy viewed battle at night as an evil to be avoided wherever possible. But in the course of the war the British concluded that they needed to develop and then hone night fighting skills and to adopt technologies such as starshells. The Royal Navy entered World War II trained and ready to fight at night. The Germans had emphasized night fighting from the first and maintained their night fighting superiority throughout the war and on into World War II. Much to the contrary, Italy's war experience led it to conclude that night combat was generally inconclusive and was the purview of light forces only. It found itself at a disadvantage in both equipment and doctrine when World War II missions forced it to fight at night.

In sum, it is striking how little changed from the start of World War I to its conclusion. Despite profound advances in the technology of fire control and communications, despite the development of aircraft and submarines, despite the testing of tactical concepts and the accumulation of combat experience, the dreadnought battleship began as and remained the dominant measure of sea power. The importance of the screening and scouting functions filled by cruisers and flotilla craft had been recognized before the start of the war; those roles were even more important by the conflict's end. Submarines had been a wild card in the beginning. They proved to be effective commerce-killers—once allowed to discard legal restrictions—but did not fulfill expectations regarding surface combat. Submarines mostly affected surface operations by forcing navies to bolster their screens and devote resources to antisubmarine warfare. Mines and minesweeping played major roles, but somehow mines emerged from the war as a disregarded system (once they were all swept, that is) just as they had been undervalued going in. Aircraft were seen as enhancing the role of battleships and assisting surface units and submarines in scouting, but not as capable of exerting decisive force in themselves. Navies had not spent World War I in stasis, and they would not be in stasis during the interwar years, but it would take the experience of the Second World War to produce the next revolution in naval warfare.

Appendix I
Ship Specifications

Austro-Hungarian Navy (Kaiserliche und Königliche Kriegsmarine)

CB: *Budapest, Wien* 1895, 5,547t, 4x24cm/40 & 6x15cm/40 G, 2x45cm TT 10.6in B, C/VTE, 17.5k

CA: *Kaiser Karl IV:* 1898 6,166t, 2x24cm/40 & 8x15cm/40 G, 2x45cm TT 8.7in B, C/VTE, 21k

CA: *Sankt Georg:* 1903, 7,289t 2x24cm/40 & 5x19cm/42 G 2x45cm TT, 8.3in B, C/VTE, 22k

CP: *Aspern, Zenta* 1897, 2,503t, 8x12cm /40 G, 2x45cm TT 2in B, C/VTE, 20.5k

CLS: *Säida, Novara Helgoland:* 1912 3,500t, 9x10cm/50 G 2.4in B, O/Tb, 27k

DD: *Balaton, Csepel, Dukla, Lika* (i & ii), *Orjen, Tátra, Triglav* (i & ii), *Uzsok:* 1912 850t, 2x10cm/50 & 6x66mm/45 G, 4x45cm TT, M/Tb, 33k

DD:*Csikós, Dinara, Huszár, Ulan, Reka, Scharfschütze, Streiter, Turul, Velebit, Wildfang, Warasdiner, Pandur:* 1905, 400t 6x66mm G, 2x45cm TT, C/VTE, 28k

TB: *83F-96F*, 1914, 244t, 2x66mm/30 G 4x45cm TT, M/Tb, 28k
TB: *98M-99M* 1914, 250t, Tb, 29.5k

TB: *74T-81T* 1913, 262t 2x66mm/30 G 2x45cm TT 1913, Tb, 28k

TB: *54T, 68F, 70-71F, 73F* 1905, 210t 4x47mm/33 G 3x45cm TT C/VTE, 26k

---

Ottoman Navy (Osmanli Donanmasi)

BC: *Yavuz Sultan Selim* 1913, 23,100t, 10x28cm/50 & 10x15cm/45 G, 2x50cm TT, 10.7in B, C/Tb, 27k

OBB: *Torguid Reis* 1891, 10,500t, 6x28cm & 7x10.5cm/35 G, 5x45cm TT, 16in B, C/TE, 16.5k

CP: *Medjidieh, Hamidieh* 1903, 3,330-3,830t, 2x6 in/45 & 8x4.7/45in G, 2x 18in TT, 4in D, C/VTE, 22k

CL: *Midilli:* 1912, 4,725t 10x10.5cm/45 G, 2x50cm TT, 2.4in B, C/Tb, 27.5k

TGB: *Berk-i-Satvet* 1906, 760t, 2x10.5cm G 3x45cm TT, C/VTE, 21k

DD: *Muavenet, Jadhigar, Numene, Gairet:* 1909 665t, 2x88mm G, 3x45cm TT, M/Tb, 32k

TB: *Basra, Tasoz, Samsun:* 1907, 284t 1x67mm & 6x47mm G 2x45cm TT, C/VTE, 28k

TB: *Demirhisar, Hamidabad* 100t, 2x57mm G 3x45cm TT, C/TE, 26k

GB: *Yozgat* 185t, 2x57 mm G, 12k

GB: *Taşköprü* 192t, 2x47mm G 1x18in TT, 12k

German Navy (Kaiserliche Marine)

OBB: *Braunschweig, Elsass:* 1902-4, 14,167t 4x28cm/40 & 14x17cm/40 G 6x45cm TT, 10in, C/TE, 18k

BB: *Nassau, Posen* 1908, 15,570t, 12x28cm/45 & 12x15cm/45 G, 6x45cm TT, 12in B, C/VTE, 19.5k

BB: *Kaiser, Kaiserin:* 1911, 24,330t 10x30.5cm/50 & 14x15cm/45 G 5x50cm TT, 14in B, M/Tb, 21k (*König, Kronprinz* similar)

BC: *Seydlitz:* 1912, 24,590t 10x28cm/50, 10x15cm/45 G 2x50cm, TT, 12in B, C/VTE, 26.5k

BC: *Goeben, Moltke:* 1913, 23,100t, 10x28cm/50 G, 10x15cm/45 G, 2x50cm TT, 10.7in B, C/Tb, 27k

BC: *Von der Tann:* 1909, 19,064t, 8x28cm/45 G, 4x45cm TT, 10in B, 27k

CA: *Blücher:* 1908, 15,590t 12x21cm/45 & 8x15cm/45 G 4x45cm TT, 7in belt, Coal, VTE, 24k

BC: *Derfflinger, Lützow:* 1913, 26,180t 8x30.5cm/50 & 12x15cm/45 G, 4x50cm TT, 12in B, M/Tb, 26.5k

CA: *Gneisenau, Scharnhorst:* 1906, 12,781t 8x21cm/40 & 10x15cm/40 G 4x450 TT, 4in B, C/TE, 23.5k

CA: *Roon:* 1903, 10,104t 4x21cm/40 G, 21k

CA: *Prinz Heinrich* 1900, 9,650t, 2x24cm/40 &10x15cm/40 G,4x45cm TT, 4in B, C/TE, 20k

CL: *Ariadne, Frauenlob, Gazelle, Thetis:* 1898 3,033t, 10x10.5cm/40 G 2x45cm TT, 2in D, C/VTE, 21k

CL: *Königsberg, Nürnberg, Stettin, Stuttgart:* 1905, 3,390t 10x10.5cm/40, G,2x45cm TT, 1.2in D, C/VTE 23k

CL: *Dresden, Emden* 1906, 3,665t, 23.5k

CL: *Kolberg, Mainz, Köln, Augsburg:* 1908, 4,362t 12x10.5cm/45 G, 2x50cm TT 1.6in D, C/Tb, 26k

CL: *Bremen, Danzig, Hamburg, Leipzig, Lübeck, München* 1903, 3,750t, 10x 10.5cm/40 G, 2x45cm TT, 2in D, C/VTE, 23k

CL: *Breslau, Magdeburg Strassburg, Stralsund:* 1912 4,570t, 10x10.5cm/40 G 2x45cm TT, 3in D, M/Tb, 24k

CL: *Pillau, Elbing:* 1914, 4,390t 8x15cm/45 & 2x88mm/45 G 2x50mm TT, 3in D, O/Tb, 27.5k

CM: *Brummer, Bremse* 1916, 4,385t, 4x15cm/45 2x50cm TT, 400 mines 1.6in B, M/Tb, 28k

CL: *Karlsruhe, Rostock* 1914, 4,900t, 12x10.5cm/45 G, 28k. (*Graudenz, Regensburg* similar)

CL: *Wiesbaden, Frankfurt* 1915 5,180t, 8x15cm/45 & 2x88 mm/45 G, 4x50mm TT, 3in D, M/Tb, 27k

CL: *Königsberg, Nürnberg:* 5,440t

CM: *Albatross*, 1907
2,200t, 2x88mm/45
200 mines, C/VTE, 20k

MS: *M1-26*
1915, 425t
1x88mm
C/VTE, 16k

MS: *M27-56:* 1916, 480t
2x10.5cm/45, C/VTE, 16.5k
M57-95: 1917, 500t
2x10.5cm/45, C/VTE, 16k

DD: *S141-144*
1906, 533t,1x88mm/
35 & 3x52mm G, 3x
45cm TT, C/VTE, 30k
DD: *G135:* 1905
412t, 27k

DD: (all 2x88/30 G, M/Tb)
V150-160: 1907, 558t, 3x45cm TT, 30k
V161: 1908, 596t, 3x45cm TT, 32k
G175: 1908, 654t, 4x50cm TT, 31.5k
S176-V185: 1909, 636t, 4x50cm TT, 32k
V186-191: 1910: 666t, 4x50cm TT, 32k
V192-G197: 1910, 656t, 4x50cm TT, 32.5k
V1-G12: 1911, 565t, 4x50cm TT, 32.5k
S13-S24: 1911, 570t, 4x50cm TT, 32.5k

DD: (all 6x50cm TT, O/Tb)
V25-30: 1913, 812t, 3x88mm/45 G, 33.5k
S31-36: 1913, 802t, 3x88mm/45 G, 33.5k
G37-42: 1914, 822t, 3x88mm/45 G, 34k
V43-48: 1914, 852t, 3x88mm/45 G, 34.5k
S49-52: 1914, 802t, 3x88mm/45 G, 34k
S53-59: 1915, 919t, 3x88mm/45 G, 34k
S60-66: 1916: 919t, 3x10.5mm/45 G, 34k
V67-81: 1914, 924t, 3x88mm/45 G, 34k
V82-83: 1915, 924t, 3x10.5cm/45 G, 34k
G85-91: 1915, 960t, 3x88mm/45 G, 33.5k
G92-96: 1915, 960t, 3x10.5cm/45 G, 33.5k
(*G42, G85-89, G91, V47-48, V67-71, V73-74,
V77-81 & S53-56* to 10.5cm/45 G mid-late 1916)

DL: *B97-98, V99-100,
B109-112:* 1914
1,374t, 4x88mm/45 G
6x50cm TT, O/Tb, 36.5k
(both 4x10.5cm/45 from spring 1916.)

DL:*G101-104*
1914, 1,136t, 4x88
mm/45 G, 6x50cm
TT, O/Tb, 33.5k

TB: *S90:* 1898
310t, 3x50mm
G, 3x45cm TT
C/TE, 26k

TB: (all 3x50 mm G,
3x45cm TT, C/TE)
S115-119: 1902, 315t, 26k
S130: 1903 371t, 27k

TB: *A1-25*
1915, 109t, 1x
50mm/40 or 52
mm/55 G ,2x45cm
TT, C/VTE, 20k

TB: *A26-55:* 1916,
230t, 2x88mm/30 G
1x45cm TT, O/Tb, 25.8k
TB: *A56-95*
1917, 330t, 28k

French Navy (Marine Nationale)

OBB: *République* class: 1908
14,500t, 4x305mm/40, 10x194mm/50 G
2x457mm TT, 11in B, C/VTE, 19k

BB: *Coubet, Jean Bart:* 1913, 22,189t
12x305mm/45, & 22x138mm/55 G
4x17.7in TT, 10.6in B, M/Tb, 20kts

DD: *Bouclier, Boutefeu,Cap Mehl,
Cimeterre,Casque, Cdt Rivière,
Cdt Bory, Dehorter:* 1910, 750t, 2x
100mm/45 G, 4x450mm TT, C/TE, 30k

DD: *Bisson, Cdt Lucas, Magon,
Protet, Renaudin,* 1913, 775t

DD: *Ens Roux:* 1915, 850t

TB: *Branlebas,
Étendard,
Oriflamme*
1907, 339t
1x67 & 6x47mm
G, 2x450mm
TT, C/TE, 27.5k

TB: *Fronde,
Mousquet,
Pistolet,* 1902
298t, 1x65mm
& 6x47mm,G
2x380mm TT
C/TE, 28k

TGB:
D'Iberville
1896, 925t
1x100mm/45
3x65mm G
4x450mm TT
C/TE, 21k

Italian Navy (Regia Marina)

CP: *Puglia:* 1901
2,850t, 6x120mm/40 G
1in D, C/VTE, 19k

CLS: *Quarto* 1911, 3,271t
6x120mm/50 & 6x76/50 G
2x450mm TT, 1.5in D, M/Tb, 28k

CLS: *Nino Bixio, Marsala:* 1911
3,575t, 6x120mm/50 & 6x76/50 G
2x450mm TT, 1.5in D, M/Tb, 27k

DL: *Poerio,*
Pepe, Rossarol
1914, 1,028t, 6x102
mm/35 G, 4x450mm
TT, Tb, 31.5k

DL: *Mirabello,*
Racchia, Riboty: 1915
1,784t, 1x152mm/40
& 7x102mm/35 G
4x450mm TT, Tb, 35k

DL: *Aquila,Nibbio,*
Sparviero: 1917
1,594t, 3x152mm/40
& 4x76mm/40 G
4x450mm TT, Tb, 34k

DD: *Aquilone, Borea,*
Turbine: 1901, 325t
4x76mm/40 G, 2x450
mm TT, O/TE, 30k

DD: *Abba, Bronzetti,*
Missori, Mosto, Nievo,
Nullo, Pilo, Schiaffino
1915, 770t, 6x76mm/40 G
4x450mm TT, O/Tb, 30k

DD: (all 1x120mm/40 & 4x76mm/40
G, 4x450mm TT, O/Tb, 30k)
Indomito, Impavido, Impetuoso,
Insidioso, Irrequieto: 1910, 670t
Ardente, Ardito: 1912, 695t
Animoso, Audace: 1912, 750t

DD: *Acerbi, Orsini, Stocco*
1916, 790t, 6x102mm/35 G
4x450mm TT, O/Tb, 30k

DD: *La Masa:* 1917, 785t,
4x102mm/45 G

TB: *1, 3, 4, 8-12PN, 21-22, 24OS, 35-38PN*
1911, 120t, 1x57mm/43 G, 2x450mm TT, O/VTE, 28k

TB: PN series 2: *42PN, 67PN:* 1911, 129t
2x76mm/30 G, 2x450mmTT, O/VTE, 30k

Russian Navy (Rossiiskii imperatorskii flot)

BB: *Imperatritsa Mariia,*
Imperatristsa Ekaterina Velikaia
1913, 22,600t, 12x12in/52 &
20x5.1in/55 G, 4x18in TT
10.5in B, M/Tb, 21k

OBB: *Tri Sviatitelia*
1893, 13,318t,
4x12in/40 & 12x6in/45
G, 18in B Harvey
C/VTE, 17k

OBB: *Rostislav:* 1896
8,880t, 4x10in/45 &
12x6in/45 G, 6x18in
TT, 14in B Harvey
C/VTE, 15.6k

OBB: *Slava:* 1901, 12,915t
4x12in/40 &12x6in/45 G
7.5in B C/VTE, 17.5k
OBB: *Tsesarevich:* 1903
13,105t, 10in B,18.5k
OBB: *Panteleimon:* 1900
12,582t, 16x6in/45 G, 9in B, 16.6k

OBB: *Evstafii, Ioann*
Zlatoust: 1906, 12,840t
4x12in/40, 4x8in/50 &
12x6in/45 G,3x18in TT
9in B, C/VTE, 16.5k

CA: *Riurik:* 1906, 15,190t
4x10in/50 & 8x8in/50 G
6in B, C/VTE, 21k

CVS: *Almaz:* 3,285t, 7x4.7in
G, 4 a/c, C/VTE, 19k

CA: *Rossiia:* 1896
13,675t, 4x8in/45 &
22x6in/45 G, 8in B
Harvey-nickel, C/VTE, 22.2k

CA: *Gromoboi*
1899, 13,220t
4x8in/45 & 22x6in/45 G
6in B, C/VTE, 20k

CA: *Baian, Pallada,
Admiral Makarov:* 1906
7,775t, 2x8in/45 & 8x6in/45 G
2x18in TT, 7in B, C/VTE, 21k

CP: *Diana:* 1899
6,657t, 8x6in G
2in D, C/VTE, 19k

CP: *Bogatyr, Oleg, Kagul,
Pamiat Merkuriia:* 1901, 6,645t
16x6in/45 G, 3.3in D, C/VTE, 23k

CP: *Zhemchug:* 1903
3,103t, 8x4.7in/45 G, 3x
18in TT, 3in D, C/VTE, 24k

GB: *Khivinets*
1905, 1,340t
4x4.7in G
C/VTE, 13.5k

GB: *Koreets,
Sivuch:* 1905
875t, 2x4.7in
G, C/VTE, 12k

GB: *Khrabryi*
1895, 1,735t
5x5.1in/55 G
5in B,14k

GB: *Groziashchii*
1890, 1,672t
3x6in/45 G
5in B, C/VTE, 13k

GB: *Kubanbets,
Donets:* 1887, 1,300t
2x6in/45 & 1x4.7in/45
G, C/Cp, 12k

DD: *Amurets, Vsadnik, Emir Bukharskii,
Finn, Gaidamak, Moskvitianin, Ussuriets,
Dobrovolets:* 1904, 570t, 2x4in/60
3x18in TT, C/VTE, 25k

DD: *Gen Kondratenko, Okhotnik,
Pogranichnik, Sibirskii Strelok:* 1905
615t, 2x4in/60 G, 3x18in TT, C/VTE, 25.5k

DD: *Kapt Saken, K Lt Baranov, Lt
Shestakov, Lt Zatsarennyi:* 1905, 640t
1x4.7in/30 & 5x3in G, 3x18in TT, C/VTE, 25k

TB: (all 2x3in/38 G, C/VTE, 27K)
*Pylkii, Rianyi, Silnyi, Steregushchii,
Stremitelnyi, Strogii, Svirepyi, Smetlivyi*
1896, 220t, 2x15in TT
*Zavetnyi, Zavidnyi, Zharkii, Zhivoii,
Zhivuchii, Zhutkii, Zorkii, Zvonkii:*
1902, 350t, 2x15in TT, 26k
Lt. Burakov: 1904: 335t, 2x18in TT
Bditelnyi 1904, 380t, 3x18in TT
Storozhevoi 1904, 350t , 2x18in TT

DD: *Donskoi Kazak, Kazanets, Strashnyi,
Steregushchii,Turkmenets-Stavropolskii,
Ukraina, Voiskovoi, Zabaikalets:* 1904
580t, 2x4in/60 G 2x18in TT, C/VTE, 26k

DD: *Novik* 1911, 1,280t
3x4in/60 G, 10x18in TT, O/Tb, 34k

DD: *Bespokoinyi, Derzkii, Gnevnyi,
Gromkii, Pronzitelnyi, Bystryi, Schastlivyi,
Pospeshnyi:* 1913, 1,100t, 3x4in/60 G
10x18in TT, O/Tb, 30-32k

DD: *Desna, Gavriil, Grom, Lt. Ilin,
Konstantin, Orfei, Pobeditel, Samson,
Zabiiaka:* 1915, 1,260t, 4x4in/60 G
9x18in TT, O/Tb, 32k

DD: *Avtroil, Iziaslav:* 1915, 1,350t
5x4in/60 G, 9x18in TT, O/Tb, 33k

United Kingdom, Royal Navy

OBB: *Canopus, Goliath* 1897, 13,150t, 4x12in & 12x6in G, 4x18in TT, 6in B, C/TE, 18k

OBB: *Triumph:* 1903, 12,370t 4x10in &14x7.5in G, 2x17.7in TT, 7in B, C/VTE, 19k

OBB: *Lord Nelson:* 1908 15,360t, 4x12in/45 & 10x9.2in G, 5x18in TT, 12in B, C/TE, 18k

BB: *Queen Elizabeth* 1913, 27,500t, 8x15in/42 & 16x6in/45 G, 4x21in TT, 13in B, O/Tb, 23k

BC: *Invincible, Indomitable, Inflexible:* 1907, 17,373t 8x12in/45 & 16x4in/45 G, 5x18in TT, 6in B, M/Tb, 25.5k

BC: *Australia* (RAN), *Indefatigable, New Zealand* 1909, 18,500t, 3x18in TT, 25k

BC: *Lion, Princess Royal, Queen Mary* 1910, 26,270t, 8x13.5in & 16x4in/50 G, 2x21in TT, 9in B, M/Tb, 27k

BC: *Tiger:* 1913, 28,230t, 8x13.5in/45 & 12x6in/45 G, 4x21in TT, 9in B, M/Tb, 28k

BC: *Courageous, Glorious:* 1916 19,230t, 4x15in/42 &18x4in/44.3 G 2x21in TT, 3in B, O/Tb, 32k

BC: *Repulse:* 1916, 27,650t, 6x15in/42 & 17x4in/44.3 G, 2x21in TT, 6in B, O/Tb, 30k

CA: *Good Hope:* 1901 14,150t, 2x9.2in & 12x6in G 2x18in TT, 6in B, C/TE, 23k

CA: *Cornwall, Kent, Monmouth, Suffolk* 1903, 9,800t, 14x6in G 2x18in TT, 4in B, C/TE, 23k

CA: *Carnarvon* 1903, 10,850t, 4x7.5in & 6x6in G, 2x18in TT, 6in B, C/TE, 22k

CA: *Warrior* 1905, 13,550t, 6x9.2in & 4x7.5in G, 3x18in TT 6in B, C/TE, 23k

CA: *Defence:* 1907 14,600, 4x9.2in & 10x7.5in G, 5x18in TT

CP:*Pegasus* 1896, 2,135t, 8x4in G, 2x18in TT, 2in D C/TE, 20k

CLS: *Patrol, Forward* 1904, 2,900t 9x4in G, 2x18in TT 2in B, C/TE, 25k

CLS: *Amphion, Fearless:* 1911, 3,440t 10x4in/50 G, 2x18in TT 1in D, M/Tb, 25k

CL: *Arethusa, Aurora, Galatea, Inconstant, Penelope, Royalist, Undaunted:* 1913, 3,750t, 2x6in/45 & 6x4in/45 G, 2-4x21in TT, 3in B, O/Tb, 28.5k

CL: *Bristol, Glasgow, Gloucester, Liverpool:* 1909 4,800t, 2x6in/50 & 10x4in/50 G 2x18in TT, 2in D, M/Tb, 25k

CL: *Dartmouth, Falmouth, Weymouth, Yarmouth:* 1910 5,250t, 8x6in/50 G, 2x21in TT

CL: *Birmingham, Dublin, Chatham, Southampton, Sydney, Lowestoft, Nottingham:* 1911, 5,400t, 8 or 9x6in/45 G, 2x21inTT, 2in B, M/Tb, 25.5k

CL: *Canterbury, Carysfort, Cleopatra, Conquest:* 1914 4,300t, 2x6in/45 & 8x4in/45 G 2x21in TT, 4in B, O/Tb, 28.5k

CL: *Cardiff, Caledon, Ceres, Calypso, Caradoc, Centaur, Concord:* 1916, 4,120-90t, 5x6in /45 G, 2x21in TT, 3in B, O/Tb 29k

DL: *Swift:* 1907 2,170t, 4x4in/45 G 2x18in TT, O/Tb 35k (1x6in & 2x4in/45 in 1916)

DL: *Botha, Broke, Faulknor, Tipperary:* 1914, 1,610t 6x4in/45G, 4x21in TT, M/Tb, 31k

DL: *Lightfoot, Marksman, Nimrod:* 1915, 1,440t 4x4in/45 G, 4x21in TT, O/Tb, 34.5

DD: *Valentine*, Vanquisher, Vehement, Vendetta, Vimiera* 1917, 1,095t (*1,188t),4x4in/45 G, 4x21in TT, O/Tb, 34k

DD: *Flirt, Leopard, Leven, Lively* 1896, 310t-390t 1x3in/40 & 5x57mm G, 2x18in TT C/TE or Cp, 17-23k

DD: *Doon, Jed, Moy, Test, Kennet, Waveney, Wear* 1904, 550t, 4x3in/ 40 G, 2x18in TT, C/VTE, 25.5k

DD: *Wolverine, Beagle, Bulldog, Scorpion, Pincher* 1909, 945t,1x4in/45 & 3x3in/40 G, 2x 21in TT, C/Tb, 27k

DD: *Amazon, Cossack, Crusader, Mohawk, Nubian, Tartar, Viking** 1907, 850t-1,045t 3x3in/40 or 2x4in/45 2x18in TT, O/Tb, 33k *1x6in in 1916

DD: *Acheron, Acorn, Alarm, Ariel, Archer, Attack, Badger, Beaver, Cameleon, Comet, Defender, Druid, Ferret, Firedrake, Forester, Fortune,Goshawk, Hind, Hornet, Hydra, Jackal, Lapwing, Lizard, Lurcher, Nymphe, Nereide, Phoenix, Sandfly, Tigress, Torrens** 1910, 772t, 2x4in/45 & 3in/40 G 2x21in TT, O/Tb, 27-32k *RAN, 3x21" TT.

DD: *Laertes, Laforey, Lance, Landrail, Lark, Lassoo, Laurel, Laverock, Lawford, Legion, Lennox, Leonidas, Liberty, Linnet, Llewellyn, Lochinvar, Lookout, Louis, Loyal, Lucifer, Lydiard, Lysander* 1913, 965t, 3x4in/45 G, 4x21in TT, O/Tb, 29k

DD: *Acasta, Ambuscade, Hardy, Lynx, Unity, Shark, Spitfire, Sparrowhawk, Paragon* 1912, 1,072t, 3x4in/45, G, 2x21in TT, O/Tb, 29k

DD: *Medea, Medusa, Melampus, Melpomene:* 1914, 1,010t, 3x4in/45 G, 4x21in TT, O/Tb, 32k

DD: *Manly, Matchless, Mansfield, Mastiff, Mentor, Meteor, Milne, Minos, Miranda, Moorsom, Morris, Murray* 1914, 850t, 3x4in/45 G, 4x21in TT, O/Tb, 34k

DD: *Termagant, Turbulent* 1915, 1,098t, 5x4in/45 G, 4x21in TT, O/Tb, 32k

DD: *Mary Rose, Medway, Michael, Nerissa, Nestor, Nomad, North Star, Nugent, Partridge, Pellew, Phoebe* 1915-16, 895-1,025t, 3x4in/45 G, 4x21in TT, O/Tb, 35k

DD: *Redgauntlet, Recruit, Redoubt, Sceptre, Setter, Sharpshooter, Simoon, Surprise, Skilful, Springbok, Strongbow, Stark, Starfish, Sturgeon, Sybille, Sylph, Taurus, Teazer, Tempest, Tetrarch, Thisbe, Thruster, Torrent, Torrid, Truculent, Urchin, Umpire, Ursa* 1916, 975t, 3x4in/45 G, 4x21in TT, O/Tb, 36k

BM: *Erebus, Terror* 1916, 8,000t 2x15in/42 & 2x6in/40 4in B, O/VTE, 12k

BM: *General Wolfe, Lord Clive, Prince Eugene:* 1915, 6,150t 2x12in/35 & 4x6in G 6in B, C/VTE, 6.5k

BM: *Marshal Ney* 1915, 6,670t 1x9.2in/45 & 4-6in/40 G, 4in B, Diesel, 6k

BM: *M24, M26, M27, M28* 1915, 540t 1x9.2in & 1x7.5in or 6in G, 11k

BMR: *Severn, Mersey* 1914, 1,260t 2x6in/50, 3in B C/TE, 9.5k

DS:*Alyssum, Arabis, Buttercup, Poppy* 1915, 1,250t 2x4in or 4.7in G C/TE, 16k

TGB:*Halycon* 1895, 1,070 2x4.7in G 3x18in TT C/VTE, 19k

ATM: Mersey class:1916 440t, 1x12pdr G, 11k

Drifter 1916, 175t 1x6pdr G, 9k

Japanese Navy

CM: *Takaschio* 1898, 3700t, 8x6in/40 G 4x18in TT, 2in D, C/DE, 18k

AMC: *Otranto:* 1909, 12,124 grt 8x4.7in G, C/QE, 18k

Abbreviations:
a/c- aircraft; B- belt (armor); C- coal (fuel); Cp- compound (engine); D- deck (armor); DE-double expansion (engine); G- guns (weapons); k -knots (speed); M- mixed oil and coal (fuel); RAN -Royal Australian Navy; O- oil (fuel); QE quadruple expansion (engine); t- tons (normal displacement); Tb- turbine (engine); TE- triple expansion (engine); TT-torpedo tubes (weapons); VTE- vertical triple expansion (engine).

Ship types: ATM -armed trawler; BB -dreadnought battleship; BC -battlecruiser; BM -monitor; CA -armored cruiser; CL-light cruiser; CLS -scout cruiser; CM -cruiser-minelayer; CP -protected cruiser; DD -destroyer; DL -destroyer leader or large destroyer; DS -sloop; GB -gunboat; ML -minelayer; TB -torpedo boat; TGB -torpedo gunboat.
Armament shown as initially equipped unless otherwise noted. Armor values (deck or belt) are maximum thickness in inches and are for Krupp cemented armor or equivalent unless otherwise stated.

Appendix II
Conversions and Abbreviations

Conversions

Imperial to Metric

1 nautical mile = 2,205 yards, 1,852 meters, or 1.151 statute miles

1 knot = 1.852 km/hour or 1.151 statute miles/hour

1 meter = 1.094 yards

1 yard = .9144 meters

1 centimeter = .3937 inches

1 inch = 2.54 centimeters

1 kilogram = 2.205 pounds

1 pound = 0.4536 kilograms

Gun Equivalents (Most of these are rounded according to contemporary usage. For example, a 10-cm gun is actually 3.94 inches.)

1.85-inch = 47-mm

2-inch = 50-mm

2.6-inch = 66-mm (designated as 7-cm by Austrians)

3-inch = 75-mm

3.45-inch = 88-mm

3.9-inch = 10-cm

4-inch = 10.5-cm

4.7-inch = 12-cm

5.9-inch = 15-cm

8-inch = 20.3-cm

8.2-inch = 21-cm

9.2-inch = 23.4-cm

10-inch = 25.4-cm

11-inch = 28-cm

12-inch = 30.5-cm

13.5-inch = 34.3-cm

15-inch = 38-cm

Abbreviations

General

AA	antiaircraft
AH	Austro-Hungarian
AP	armor-piercing
ASW	antisubmarine warfare
AU	Australian
Aux	auxiliary
BEF	British Expeditionary Force
BL	breech loading
BR	British
BS	battle squadron
Cal	caliber
DA	Danish
D/F	direction finding
Div	Division

ER	effect ratio	CL	light cruiser
FR	French	CLS	scout cruiser
GRT	gross registered tons	CP	protected cruiser
HE	high-explosive (or high effect)	CV	aircraft carrier
		CVS	seaplane carrier
IT	Italian	DC	corvette
JA	Japanese	DD	destroyer
KM	Kaiserliche Marine	DL	destroyer leader
K.u.K.	Kaiserliche und Königliche	DS	sloop/escort
		GB	gunboat
MFR	modified force ratio	MAS	*motoscafi armati siluranti* (Italian motor torpedo boat)
MN	Marine Nationale		
NO	Norwegian		
ONI	Office of Naval Intelligence	ML	minelayer
		MM	merchant ship
OT	Ottoman	MS	minesweeper
RM	Regia Marina	MTB	motor torpedo boat
RN	Royal Navy	OBB	predreadnought battleship
RNR	Royal Navy Reserve	PB	patrol boat
RU	Russia	PC	patrol craft
SIGINT	signals intelligence	SC	submarine chaser
SNIS	*Sluzhba nabliudeniia isviazi* (Service of Observation and Communications)	SS	submarine
		TB	torpedo boat
		TGB	torpedo gunboat
		U-boat	*unterseeboot* (German or Austrian submarine)
SW	Swedish		
US	United States		
USN	U.S. Navy	*Ship Formations*	
W/T	wireless [telegraphy]	ASWF	antisubmarine flotilla
		BCS	battlecruiser squadron
Ship Types		BS	battle squadron
AMC	armed merchant cruiser	CS	cruiser squadron
AMT	armed trawler	DDHF	destroyer half flotilla
BB	dreadnought battleship	DF	destroyer flotilla
BC	battlecruiser	LCS	light cruiser squadron
BM	monitor	MSF	minesweeper flotilla
BMR	river monitor	MSHF	minesweeper half flotilla
CA	armored cruiser	SG	scouting group
CB	coastal battleship (obsolete)	TBF	torpedo boat flotilla
		TBHF	torpedo boat half flotilla
CD	coastal defense armored ship		

Appendix III
Les Petit Combats

Because of the fleeting nature of some encounters, not all are mentioned by official histories. Indeed, the French official history lists an example and remarks without elaboration that there were more "*petit combats*" like it. Even where one source mentions an encounter, others may not. The body of this work described those actions for which reasonably complete details could be found. Thus not all actions for which any information was found are described. The following table lists actions where complete information was lacking.[1]

Table A3.1 Petit Combats Not Further Described

Date	Location	Description
6-Feb-15	Black Sea	Turkish CL *Midilli* fires at four Russian TBs off Batum without results.
4-Jul-15	Black Sea	Turkish DDs *Gairet* and *Numene*, in Zonguldak harbor, surprise two Russian DDs on a bombardment mission. The Russians depart after firing thirty rounds.
12-Sep-16	Baltic Sea	German CL *Strassburg* and Russian GB *Khrabryi* briefly exchange salvos.
13-Sep-16	Adriatic	Italian TB *1PN* chases a small convoy escorted by two Austrian TBs to the cover of shore batteries off Porto Quieto.

Table A3.1 (cont.)

Date	Location	Description
11-May-17	Adriatic	Two Italian DDs chase one Austrian DD and three TBs toward Cattaro. There was a brief exchange of fire.
19-Jun-17	North Sea (Flanders)	German DDs *G91*, *V71*, *V73*, and *V81* chase one Entente DL and two DDs.
26-Aug-17	North Sea (Flanders)	German DDs *V70* and *V73* are fired on by a British BM while patrolling.
24-Sep-17	North Sea (Flanders)	One British DL and four DDs have a brush with German DDs *V71* and *V73* and TBs *A40* and *A50*.
1-Nov-17	North Sea (Flanders)	Two British BMs and seven Entente DDs skirmish with German DDs *V70* and *V71*.
13-Nov-17	North Sea (Flanders)	One British DL and four Entente DDs attack German DDs *V70* and *G91* protecting minesweepers.
15-Nov-17	North Sea (Flanders)	Two British BMs and six Entente DDs attack German DDs *S54* and *S55* and TBs *A39*, *A40*, *A42*, and *A45* covering minesweepers.
23-Dec-17	North Sea (Flanders)	Nine Entente DDs skirmish with German DDs *S55*, *G91*, and *V77*.

1 Thomazi, *Zone des Armées*, 127. For mentions of other patrol actions, see Gladisch, *Nordsee*, 7:154, 165–69; Naval Staff, *Monographs*, 19:181–82; Thompson, *War at Sea*, 381–84; Greger, *Russian Fleet*, 50; Lorey, *Mittelmeer*, 1:170–71; Cernuschi, *Battaglie sconosciute*, 79.

Notes

Chapter 1. The Fleets

1. Brooks, *Dreadnought Gunnery,* 66–70; Friedman, *Naval Firepower,* 87–89.
2. This section relies on Brooks, *Dreadnought Gunnery,* 19.
3. ADM 186/238, "Progress in Naval Gunnery," 28.
4. Ibid., 33–34.
5. Lott, *Dangerous Sea,* 8.
6. See Crossley, *Hidden Threat,* for an overview of the weapons and sweeping techniques.
7. The early history of the torpedo is covered in Gray, *Devil's Device.*
8. Marder, *Dreadnought,* 1:43–44.
9. Cradock, *Whispers from the Fleet,* http://www.gwpda.org/naval/wff01.htm.
10. See Brown, "Royal Navy's Fuel Supplies," for a discussion of the oil versus coal issue.
11. Keegan, *Intelligence in War,* 101–2.
12. Corbett, *Maritime Operations in the Russo-Japanese War,* 1:145, 193, 339, 346, 416.
13. Cost figures from *Jane's, 1914,* 41.
14. Hattendorf, ed., *Mahan,* 31.
15. Schleihauf, ed., *Jutland: The Naval Staff Appreciation,* 10.
16. Mahan, *Influence of Sea Power,* 2.
17. Quotes: C. Q. I., "Naval Tactics," 12.
18. Quotes: Anon., "Fleet in Action," 35–46. See also Gill "Gun Fire," 699–704; Knox, "Dispersion and Accuracy of Fire," 951–58.
19. See Bernotti, "Day Torpedo-boat Attack," 1157; C. Q. I., "Naval Tactics," 208; Frost, "Long-Range Torpedoes," 682–83. Quote: Anon., "Torpedo Fire in Future Fleet Actions," 47.
20. Friedman, *Naval Firepower,* 85–86; Jellicoe, *Grand Fleet,* 394–95.

21. Quotes: Knox, "Accuracy of Fire," 951. See C. Q. I., "Naval Tactics," 221; Anon., "Evolution of Naval Warfare," 31; Friedman, *Great War at Sea,* 109–11.

22. Quote: C. Q. I., "Naval Tactics," 216.

23. This section follows the Mission/Function, Organization, and Doctrine sections of each navy in O'Hara, et al, *To Crown the Waves.*

24. Jellicoe, *Grand Fleet,* 392.

25. Spencer, "Conduite du Tir Part 2," 62.

26. Quote: Pavlovich, *Fleet,* 275.

Chapter 2. 1914

1. Chickering and Förster, *Great War,* 183.

2. Scheer, *High Sea Fleet,* 19–20, says such interference could come only at the price of a decisive battle; Massie, *Castles,* 80, and Wolz, *Imperial Splendor,* 28, assert that the German General Staff did not believe the BEF would make a difference. In fact, the range of Germany's destroyers would barely permit them to reach the crossing points whereupon they would need to immediately return. See Halpern, *World War I,* 28–29; Scheer, *High Sea Fleet,* 63–64; Goldrick, *Before Jutland,* 83.

3. Halpern, *World War I,* 65.

4. Quote: Goldrick, *Before Jutland,* 96.

5. Quote: ONI, *Bulletin,* March 1921, 49.

6. Quote: Ibid., 47. Also, Corbett, *Operations,* 1:80–81; Groos, *Nordsee,* 1:101–11; Naval Staff, *Monographs,* 10:92–95; Patterson, *Tyrwhitt,* 41, 297n5; Scheer, *High Sea Fleet,* 42; Staff, *Seven Seas,* 4.

7. Quote: ONI, *Bulletin,* May 1921, 80.

8. Quotes: Ibid., 128, 130.

9. Ibid., 89.

10. Naval Staff, *Monographs,* 3:151.

11. Ibid., 3:129.

12. Thompson, *War at Sea,* 67.

13. Keyes, *Memoirs,* 87–88.

14. ONI, *Bulletin,* August 1921, 92.

15. Quote: Koblinski, "Light Cruiser," 33. Also, Corbett, *Operations,* 1:99–120; Groos, *Nordsee,* 1:131–224; Marder, *Dreadnought,* 2:50–54; Naval Staff, *Monographs,* 3:108–66; Osborne, *Heligoland Bight,* 47–99; Scheer, *High Sea Fleet,* 42–55; Staff, *Seven Seas,* 1–27.

16. ONI, *Bulletin,* February 1919, 36–37.

17. Corbett, *Operations,* 1:217–18; Goldrick, *Before Jutland,* 164–65; Groos, *Nordsee,* 2:191–200; Naval Staff, *Monographs,* 11:117–19; Patterson, *Tyrwhitt,* 78–79.

18. Beesly, *Room 40,* 7. The *Signalbuch der Kaiserlichen Marine,* recovered from the wreck of *Magdeburg,* arrived in London on 13 October while the *Handels-verkehrsbuch,* a code designed for use between warships and merchant vessels, was captured on 11 August off Melbourne, Australia, and arrived in London that same month. Some question if the *Verkehrbuch* was recovered as described. See Keegan, *Intelligence in War,* 146n6.

19. Koerver, ed. *Room 40,* 1:62.

20. Quote: Staff, *Battlecruisers,* 33.

21. Quote: Merrin, "German Raid on the East Coast," 303.

22. Corbett, *Operations,* 1:250–53; Groos, *Nordsee,* 2:260–76; Massie, *Castles,* 309–13; Naval Staff, *Monographs,* 12:1–17; Scheer, *High Sea Fleet,* 65–66. Staff, *Battlecruisers,* 33–34, 81, 157.

23. Times vary by source and by report. For example, vol. 12, p. 109 of the Naval Staff, *Monographs,* gives 0755 as the time the Germans opened fire, vol. 3, p. 186 says 0805, and the German history shortly after 0800.

24. See Staff, *Battlecruisers,* 81 and 159 for damage.

25. Quote: King-Hall, *Diary,* 76.

26. Quote: Ibid., 76–77.

27. Quote: Naval Staff, *Monographs,* 12:117.

28. Hase, *Kiel,* 66.

29. Corbett, *Operations,* 2:21–42; Goldrick, *Before Jutland,* 196–222; Groos, *Nordsee,* 3:50–121; Massie, *Castles,* 319–60; Naval Staff, *Monographs,* 3:167–208; Naval Staff, *Monographs,* 12:94–124.

30. Firle, *Ostsee,* 1:64–68; Greger, *Russian Fleet,* 13; Pavlovich, *Fleet,* 74–75.

31. Beesly, *Room 40,* 4–5; Firle, *Ostsee,* 1:79–85; Graf, *Russian Navy,* 4–7; Greger, *Russian Fleet,* 13; Kahn, "Magdeburg," 97–103; Pavlovich, *Fleet,* 76. Stephen McLaughlin, correspondence.

32. Graf, *Russian Navy,* 9.

33. Firle, *Ostsee,* 1:102–4; Graf, *Russian Navy,* 7–9; Greger, *Russian Fleet,* 13; Pavlovich, *Fleet,* 80.

34. Firle, *Ostsee,* 1:116–17; Pavlovich, *Fleet,* 80–81.

35. Firle, *Ostsee,* 1:232–33; Graf, *Russian Navy,* 4, 18; Greger, *Russian Fleet,* 14–16; Pavlovich, *Fleet,* 90–93.

36. Greger, *Russian Fleet,* 45; Lorey, *Mittelmeer,* 1:48–57; Pavlovich, *Fleet,* 284–89; Strachan, *To Arms,* 671–78; Staff, *Battlecruisers,* 118.

37. ADM 137/754, 13 describes a prewar test of the system against a target ship.

38. Ewin, "Cape Sarych," 214.

39. McLaughlin, "Predreadnoughts vs a Dreadnought," 129.

40. Greger, *Russian Fleet,* 46; Ewin, "Cape Sarych", 211–17; Halpern, *World War I,* 226–27; Lorey, *Mittelmeer,* 1:64–66; McLaughlin, "Predreadnoughts vs a Dreadnought," 117–40; Pavlovich, *Fleet,* 296–99; Staff, *Seven Seas,* 46–52.

41. Greger, *Russian Fleet,* 46–47; Halpern, *World War I,* 228; Lorey, *Mittelmeer,* 1:71–72; Pavlovich, *Fleet,* 302–5.

42. Churchill, *Crisis,* 1:242–43.

43. Corbett, *Operations,* 1:65.

44. Quote: Churchill, *Crisis,* 1:274. See also Corbett, *Operations,* 1:54–71; Lorey, *Mittelmeer,* 1:1–28; H. Sokol, *Seekrieg,* 80–84; Van der Vat, *Ship that Changed the World,* 51–120; Staff, *Battlecruisers,* 116–17.

45. Cunningham, *Odyssey,* 57.

46. Naval Staff, *Monographs,* 8:52; H. Sokol, *Seekrieg,* 80–84, 111–12, 122–31; Thomazi, *L'Adriatique,* 39–40.

47. Thomazi, *L'Adriatique,* 62–63.

48. Anon. *"China Station,"* 317–18; Naval Staff, *Monographs,* 5:49; Raeder, *Kreuzerkrieg,* 1:158.

49. Anon. "Seige of Tsingtau," 330–31.

50. Naval Staff, *Monographs,* 9:18–19; Raeder, *Kreuzerkrieg,* 2:239–43.

51. Pattee, *Distant Waters,* 172.

52. Edwards, *Salvo,* 66–75; Naval Staff, *Monographs,* 2:32–33; Raeder, *Kreuzerkrieg,* 2:152–57. Quote: Bennett, *Naval Battles,* 116.

53. Corbett, *Operations,* 1:288.

54. All quotes: von Mücke, "Emden," 811.

55. Naval Staff, *Monographs,* 5:90–93; Raeder, *Kreuzerkrieg,* 2:50–62. Quote: von Mücke, "Emden," 814.

56. The landing party escaped on a commandeered schooner and eventually made it back to Germany.

57. Quote: von Mücke, "Emden," 1197.

58. Quote: Naval Staff, *Monographs,* 5:210. See also Corbett, *Operations,* 1:382–83; Naval Staff, *Monographs,* 5:154–55, 210–12; Raeder, *Kreuzerkrieg,* 2:70–82.

59. Caresse, "von Spee," 74.

60. The *Times, Documentary History,* 4:7.

61. Millington-Drake, *Graf Spee,* 26.

62. Corbett, *Operations,* 1:341–57; Marder, *Dreadnought,* 2:112–18; Naval Staff, *Monographs,* 9:225–35; Raeder, *Kreuzerkrieg,* 1:197–224. Quote: Massie, *Castles,* 236.

63. Quote: Massie, *Castles,* 239. The best summary of why the battle was fought can be found in Jordan, *Naval Warfare,* 70–90. Also see Marder, *Dreadnought,* 2:115–19.

64. Millington-Drake, *Graf Spee,* 24. Nearly every British history also emphasizes that the crews of *Good Hope* and *Monmouth* were largely reservists and Spee's crew were long-service professionals. Nonetheless, the British crews had been together three months by that time and were hardly raw.

65. Naval Staff, *Monographs,* 9:241.

66. Quote: Millington-Drake, *Graf Spee,* 46.
67. Quotes: Beaumont, *Kent,* 22. See also Naval Staff, *Monographs,* 9:245.
68. Naval Staff, *Monographs,* 9:251.
69. Ibid., 258.
70. Ibid., 263.
71. Bennett, *Battles,* 97–123; Corbett, *Operations,* 1:414–36; Marder, *Dreadnought,* 2:118–29; Naval Staff, *Monographs,* 9:238–63; Raeder, *Kreuzerkrieg,* 1:269–336; Staff, *Seven Seas,* 58–81.

Chapter 3. 1915
1. O'Hara et al., *To Crown the Waves,* 121.
2. See Gibson and Prendergast, *Submarine War,* 107.
3. Greger, *Russian Fleet,* 52; *Jane's, 1914,* 409.
4. Italy produced 0.6 million tons of coal in 1910 compared to British, French, and German production of 270 million, 38 million, and 150 million tons respectively. The Entente's power to supply coal was crucial to Italy's decision to join them as an associated power. See Liesner, *Economic Statistics,* tables UK.3, F.2, G.2, and I.2.
5. USRM, *Marina italiana,* 1:331–35.
6. The fog of war can linger long after an event. The British chart of the action in Naval Staff, *Monographs,* shows the German line turning north while the German official history's chart shows it turning south. Naval Staff, *Monographs,* 3: Plan 2; Groos, *Nordsee,* 3: Karte 18.
7. *Inflexible* only reached 26 knots while the three leaders were hitting 29 knots by 0854. *Derfflinger's* captain claimed his ship could not exceed 24 knots due to a problem with the low-pressure turbine blades. See Goldrick, *Before Jutland,* 264; and Staff, *Battlecruisers,* 218.
8. http://wwi.lib.byu.edu/index.php/Battle_of_Dogger_Bank.
9. Staff, *Battlecruisers,* 161.
10. Quote: ADM 137/305, "Reports of Action," 34. For *Blücher* see Professional Notes, "Echo of the Dogger Bank," 1190.
11. Quote: Goldrick, *Before Jutland,* 276.
12. Quote: http://wwi.lib.byu.edu/index.php/Battle_of_Dogger_Bank.
13. Quotes: ADM 137/305, "Reports of Action," 18. See also Thompson, *War at Sea,* 101.
14. Quotes: ADM 186/2128, *Progress in Naval Gunnery,* 29.
15. Campbell, *Jutland,* 82–83, 373–74; Scheer, *High Sea Fleet,* 86.
16. ADM 137/305, "Dogger Bank, Reports of Action"; Corbett, *Operations,* 2:82–99; Goldrick, *Before Jutland,* 255–84; Groos, *Nordsee,* 189–249; Marder, *Dreadnought,* 2:156–75; Massie, *Castles,* 375–425; Naval Staff, *Monographs,* 3:209–26; Roskill, *Beatty,* 108–19; Scheer, *High Sea Fleet,* 76–83; Staff, *Seven Seas,* 82–103, and *Battlecruisers,* 83, 159–64, 217–18.

17. Corbett, *Operations,* 2:401–2; Naval Staff, *Monographs,* 13:224–25; Karau, "Marinekorps Flandern," 121–22. Groos, *Nordsee,* 4:124–25.

18. Corbett, *Operations,* 3:127; Naval Staff, *Monographs,* 14:145–54; Groos, *Nordsee,* 4:271–75; Patterson, *Tyrwhitt,* 130.

19. Campbell, *Jutland,* 277–78. Quotes: Steel and Hart, *Jutland 1916,* 294–95.

20. Brown, "British Mines"; Halpern, *World War I,* 345.

21. Chack, *Mer du Nord,* 121–34; Corbett, *Operations,* 3:149; Groos, *Nordsee,* 4:306–7; Thomazi, *Zone des Armées,* 95–96.

22. ONI, CA889, 3/39.

23. Quotes: Koblinski, "Light Cruiser," 35.

24. ONI, CA889, 3/42.

25. Greger, *Russian Fleet,* 16–17; Pavlovich, *Fleet,* 137; Rollmann, *Ostsee,* 2:74–83.

26. ONI, CA889, 6/40.

27. Quote: Ibid. Also Graf, *Russian Navy,* 41; Greger, *Russian Fleet,* 17; Pavlovich, *Fleet,* 141; Rollmann, *Ostsee,* 2:166–69.

28. Staff, *Seven Seas,* 113.

29. Gribovski, "Boi u Gotlanda," 46.

30. Staff, *Seven Seas,* 120.

31. Graf, *Russian Navy,* 42–48; Greger, *Russian Fleet,* 18; Pavlovich, *Fleet,* 142–46; Rollmann, *Ostsee,* 2:173–83; Staff, *Seven Seas,* 110–122.

32. Quote: ONI, CA889 8/22. Graf, *Russian Navy,* 49; Rollman, *Ostsee,* 2:215.

33. At this time the flotilla likely consisted of *G135* (leader), four *S130*-type torpedo boats, and five *S141*-type small destroyers. It is unclear how many participated in this action. Rollman, *Ostsee,* 2:44.

34. ONI, CA889, 9/10, 10.

35. Quote: Nekrasov, *Expendable Glory,* 45.

36. Fomin, "Zashchite Irbenskogo," 3–19; Graf, *Russian Navy,* 50–51; Greger, *Russian Fleet,* 18; Nekrasov, *Expendable Glory,* 43–46; Pavlovich, *Fleet,* 148–54; Rollmann, *Ostsee,* 2:243–47; McLaughlin, correspondence.

37. Graf was in *Novik,* and implies that the rest of the destroyer force in the gulf was there as well. At maximum strength, this would have included eight ships of the *Ukraina* and *Giadamak* types and four ships of the *Okhotnik* type. The ships listed in the order of battle were all specifically named as being present. Fomin, "Zashchite Irbenskogo," 19–20; Graf, *Russian Navy,* 51–52.

38. Pavlovich, *Fleet,* 149; Rollmann, *Ostsee,* 2:248–49.

39. Pavlovich, *Fleet,* 149; Rollmann, *Ostsee,* 2:250–51; Staff, *Battlecruisers,* 40–41; McLaughlin, correspondence.

40. ONI, CA889, 10/3.

41. Graf, *Russian Navy,* 53; Rollmann, *Ostsee,* 2:258.

42. Greger, *Russian Fleet*, 19; Pavlovich, *Fleet*, 151–54; Rollmann, *Ostsee*, 2:269–73; Tucker, *Encyclopedia*, 1:179. Quote: Nekrasov, *Expendable Glory*, 50.

43. Graf, *Russian Navy*, 55–56; Greger, *Russian Fleet*, 19; Pavlovich, *Fleet*, 151–53; Rollmann, *Ostsee*, 2:263–67; McLaughlin, correspondence.

44. CA889 9&10/38; Greger, *Russian Fleet*, 19; Pavlovich, *Fleet*, 153; Nekrasov, *Expendable Glory*, 52; Rollmann, *Ostsee*, 2:267; McLaughlin, correspondence.

45. Quotes: ONI, CA889, 9&10/43.

46. Ibid., 44.

47. Graf, *Russian Navy*, 57; Greger, *Russian Fleet*, 19; Pavlovich, *Fleet*, 154; Rollmann, *Ostsee*, 2:270–73; McLaughlin, correspondence.

48. ONI, CA889, 9&10/28.

49. Greger, *Russian Fleet*, 19–22; Pavlovich, *Fleet*, 172.

50. Greger, *Russian Fleet*, 47; Lorey, *Mittelmeer*, 1:75; Pavlovich, *Fleet*, 315.

51. Greger, *Russian Fleet*, 47–48; Lorey, *Mittelmeer*, 1:75–76; Pavlovich, *Fleet*, 315.

52. Greger, *Russian Fleet*, 48; Lorey, *Mittelmeer*, 1:78–80.

53. Greger, *Russian Fleet*, 48.

54. ADM 137/754, 48.

55. Ibid., 45–50; Greger, *Russian Fleet*, 48–49; Lorey, *Mittelmeer*, 1:94–100; Pavlovich, *Fleet*, 322–24; Staff, *Battlecruisers*, 122.

56. ADM 137/754, 27, 70–71. Greger, *Russian Fleet*, 49; Lorey, *Mittelmeer*, 1:131–33; Pavlovich, *Fleet*, 327–29. Staff, *Seven Seas*, 53–57, and *Battlecruisers*, 123–24.

57. Halpern, *World War I*, 232.

58. Ibid., 232–35; Lorey, *Mittelmeer*, 1:135–38.

59. Greger, *Russian Fleet*, 50; Lorey, *Mittelmeer*, 1:166–67; Nekrasov, *North of Gallipoli*, 58; Pavlovich, *Fleet*, 333–34.

60. Greger, *Russian Fleet*, 50; Lorey, *Mittelmeer*, 1:170–71. See Appendix II.

61. Greger, *Russian Fleet*, 50; Lorey, *Mittelmeer*, 1:171–72.

62. Greger, *Russian Fleet*, 51; Lorey, *Mittelmeer*, 1:176–77; Pavlovich, *Fleet*, 335–36; Staff, *Battlecruisers*, 125.

63. Lorey, *Mittelmeer*, 1:177.

64. ADM 137/754, 130–31; Greger, *Russian Fleet*, 51; Lorey, *Mittelmeer*, 1:193–95. Staff, *Battlecruisers*, 125.

65. Greger, *Russian Fleet*, 51–52; Lorey, *Mittelmeer*, 1:203–4.

66. ADM 137/754, 190; Greger, *Russian Fleet*, 52; Lorey, *Mittelmeer*, 1:206; Pavlovich, *Fleet*, 345.

67. Quotes: Stevens and Westcott, *Sea Power*, 374; Marder, *Dreadnought*, 2:211. See also Halpern, *World War I*, 109–11.

68. Marder, *Dreadnought*, 2:230. Quote: Ibid., 2:245.

69. Corbett, *Operations*, 2:213–30; Halpern, *World War I*, 114–15; Marder, *Dreadnought*, 2:246–47.

70. Naval Staff, *Monographs*, 8:123–24.

71. Corbett, *Operations*, 2:300–1; Lorey, *Mittelmeer*, 1:107–11.

72. Naval Staff, *Monographs*, 8:131.

73. Corbett, *Operations*, 2:323, 359, 370; Lorey, *Mittelmeer*, 1:118–19, 121.

74. Corbett, *Operations*, 2:406–8; Lorey, *Mittelmeer*, 1:138–45. Quote: Stern, *Destroyer Battles*, 48.

75. H. Sokol, *Seekrieg*, 101–4. Thomazi, *L'Adriatique*, 74–76.

76. See USRM, *Marina italiana*, 2:9–11; O'Hara et al., *To Crown the Waves*, 43; A. Sokol, *Austro-Hungarian Navy*, 195–214; H. Sokol, *Seekrieg*, 193–218.

77. H. Sokol, *Seekrieg*, 210–14. USRM, *Marina italiana*, 2:51–65. Quote: USRM, *Marina italiana*, 2:64.

78. A. Sokol, *Austro-Hungarian Navy*, 109, states the operation delayed the deployment of Italian troops by two weeks. USRM, *Marina Italiana*, 2:66fn, asserts that most movements from south to north had already been completed. See also Sondhaus, *Naval Policy*, 274–77.

79. See O'Hara et al., *To Crown the Waves*, 46.

80. See Naval Staff, *Monographs*, 8:206, for a description of the drifters at work.

81. Quote: Horthy, *Memoirs*, 85.

82. Quote, USRM, *Marina italiana*, 2:447.

83. Ibid., 452. Compare German comments regarding British shells at the 1914 Heligoland Bight battle.

84. Naval Staff, *Monographs*, 8:224.

85. Quote, USRM, *Marina italiana*, 2:461.

86. Thomazi, *L'Adriatique*, 111–13; USRM, *Marina italiana*, 2:433–465; Naval Staff, *Monographs*, 8:215–225; H. Sokol, *Seekrieg*, 250–63. Quote: Anon., "Four Months in the Adriatic," 353. Regarding Seitz and Haus see Sondhaus, *Naval Policy*, 285. Seitz returned to command after Haus's death.

87. Corbett, *Operations*, 2:250; Raeder, *Kreuzerkrieg*, 1:399–406.

88. ONI, *Bulletin*, January 1919, 3.

89. Corbett, *Operations*, 3:65–66; Naval Staff, *Monographs*, 2:97–99; Raeder, *Kreuzerkrieg*, 2:176–206.

90. For losses see Willmott, *Last Century of Seapower*, 1:259, and Ellis and Cox, *Databook*, 278.

Chapter 4. 1916

1. Halpern, *World War I*, 310; Scheer, *High Sea Fleet*, 96–112, 129–30; Sondhaus, *Great War*, 206–7.

2. Halpern, *Mediterranean*, 245, 250, 253.

3. Naval Staff, *Monographs*, 15:74.

4. Beesly, *Room 40*, 69–70, 145–46, 254n1; Corbett, *Operations*, 3:275–76; Groos, *Nordsee*, 5:35–47; Naval Staff, *Monographs*, 15:73–80; Patterson, *Tyrwhitt*, 148–49.

5. These ships had 10.5-cm guns by June 1916. It is likely that they had them in March. Gardiner, ed., *Conway's 1906–1921,* 168–69; Groos, *Nordsee,* 6:194.

6. Quotes: Naval Staff, *Monographs,* 15:160; Corbett, *Operations,* 3:290. See also Groos, *Nordsee,* 5:56–57; Karau, *Marinekorps Flandern,* 150–51.

7. Corbett, *Operations,* 3:290–96; Groos, *Nordsee,* 5:73–99; Naval Staff, *Monographs,* 15:160–74; Patterson, *Tyrwhitt,* 152–54; Scheer, *High Sea Fleet,* 118–19. The Germans also lost *S22* to a mine, while British destroyer *Michael* was badly damaged in a collision.

8. All quotes: Dorling, *Endless Story,* 116.

9. Quote: Ibid., 118.

10. Bacon, *Dover Patrol,* 1:197–98; Corbett, *Operations,* 3:299–300; Dorling, *Endless Story,* 115–123; Groos, *Nordsee,* 5:133; Naval Staff, *Monographs,* 15:142.

11. Naval Staff, *Monographs,* 16:68.

12. Quote: Ibid., 16:68–69.

13. Corbett, *Operations,* 3:300–9; Groos, *Nordsee,* 5:134–52; Naval Staff, *Monographs,* 16:21–31; Patterson, *Tyrwhitt,* 157–58; Scheer, *High Sea Fleet,* 126–28; Staff, *Battlecruisers,* 44, 91, 222, 270.

14. Quote: Jellicoe, *Grand Fleet,* 397–98.

15. This account is drawn largely from Campbell, *Jutland;* Gordon, *Rules of the Game;* Tarrant, *Jutland: The German Perspective;* and the March 1924 "Jutland" Supplement to the ONI Reports. Many more sources exist.

16. Corbett, *Operations,* 4:22; Gladisch, *Nordsee,* 6:204–6; Karau, *Marinekorps Flandern,* 174–75; Naval Staff, *Monographs,* 17:46.

17. Technically, the British were not escorting Dutch ships, as that would have deprived the Dutch of their neutral status. In practice, however, the patrol arrangements served the same function. Naval Staff, *Monographs,* 17:47, 61.

18. Corbett, *Operations,* 4:27–29; Gladisch, *Nordsee,* 6:209–11; Karau, *Marinekorps Flandern,* 177–80; Naval Staff, *Monographs,* 17:62–63; Patterson, *Tyrwhitt,* 166–67.

19. Naval Staff, *Monographs,* 6:130–31. For drifter dispositions see Naval Staff, *Monographs,* 6:70.

20. All the German ships likely had 10.5-cm guns except that *S55, S54, G42, V70, G91,* and possibly *S53* had 88-mm pieces. Corbett, *Operations,* 4:52n2; Gladisch, *Nordsee,* 7:146.

21. Quote: Keyes Papers, 123:10, "Enemy activity and Dover Patrol operations."

22. Quote: Thompson, *War at Sea,* 373–74.

23. Corbett, *Operations,* 4:55–64; Gladisch, *Nordsee,* 6:219–31; Karau, *Marinekorps Flandern,* 197–205; Naval Staff, *Monographs,* 6:66–87; and 17:185–89, 258–60.

24. See Campbell, *Jutland:* 277–78. ONI, *Bulletin,* March 1924 Supplement 1, 78–81.

25. Groos, *Nordsee*, 6:233–35; Karau, *Marinekorps Flandern*, 207–9; Naval Staff, *Monographs*, 17:194–95.

26. Naval Staff, *Monographs*, 17:216–220.

27. Gagern, *Ostsee*, 3:31–33; Graf, *Russian Navy*, 84–85; Greger, *Russian Fleet*, 23; Pavlovich, *Fleet*, 193–99. Sources vary as to the number of merchantmen in the convoy. *Jurgens* and each patrol boat mounted an 88-mm gun.

28. Gagern, *Ostsee*, 3:34–35; Graf, *Russian Navy*, 87; Greger, *Russian Fleet*, 23. Pavlovich, *Fleet*, 197–201.

29. Gagern, *Ostsee*, 3:70–72; Greger, *Russian Fleet*, 24.

30. Gagern, *Ostsee*, 3:94–97; Greger, *Russian Fleet*, 25. This single operation accounted for more than a quarter of all German destroyers sunk from mines during the war.

31. ADM 137/754, 217.

32. Ibid., 218; Greger, *Russian Fleet*, 52; Lorey, *Mittelmeer*, 1:212–14; Nekrasov, *North of Gallipoli*, 65, 68; Pavlovich, *Fleet*, 395.

33. Greger, *Russian Fleet*, 53; Lorey, *Mittelmeer*, 1:218–20; Pavlovich, *Fleet*, 400, 419–20. After repair for mine damage, *Midilli* returned to service with a 15-cm gun mounted fore and aft replacing the pair of 10.5-cm pieces that previously occupied each of those positions.

34. ADM 137/754, 300–301; Greger, *Russian Fleet*, 54; Lorey, *Mittelmeer*, 1:224, 228–30; Pavlovich, *Fleet*, 369–70; Van der Vat, *Ship that Changed the World*, 199.

35. Greger, *Russian Fleet*, 56; Lorey, *Mittelmeer*, 1:261–62; Pavlovich, *Fleet*, 425–28.

36. Greger, *Russian Fleet*, 56; Lorey, *Mittelmeer*, 1:263–66; Pavlovich, *Fleet*, 428–30. The destroyers probably included *Bystryi* and *Pospeshnyi* and all were likely *Bespokoinyi* class. See ADM 137/754, 377.

37. Greger, *Russian Fleet*, 60–61; Nekrasov, *North of Gallipoli*, 101, 106, 115–17, 128; Pavlovich, *Fleet*, 421.

38. O'Hara and Cernuschi, "Adriatic," Part 1, 166; H. Sokol, *Seekrieg*, 273–74.

39. Quote: Newbolt, *Operations*, 4:122. Halpern, *Mediterranean*, 217; Cernuschi, *Battaglie sconosciute*, 135–36; H. Sokol, *Seekrieg*, 274–76, 285.

40. Halpern, *Mediterranean*, 216.

41. A. Sokol, *Austro-Hungarian Navy*, 118.

42. Fatutta, *Oltre Adriatico*, 58; Cernuschi, *Battaglie sconosciute*, 137.

43. H. Sokol, *Seekrieg*, 453; USRM, *Marina italiana*, 3:96–98.

44. H. Sokol, *Seekrieg*, 454; USRM, *Marina italiana*, 3:100–102.

45. Cernuschi, *Battaglie sconosciute*, 139; H. Sokol, *Seekrieg*, 422.

46. H. Sokol, *Seekrieg*, 361–62.

47. H. Sokol, *Seekrieg*, 362–63; USRM, *Marina italiana*, 3:410.

48. Cernuschi, *Battaglie sconosciute*, 141–42; H. Sokol, *Seekrieg*, 402–6; Thomazi, *L'Adriatique*, 128.

49. Cernuschi, *Battaglie sconosciute*, 79.

50. Ibid., 143–44; H. Sokol, *Seekrieg*, 422.

51. Halpern, *Otranto Straits*, 27–28; Cernuschi, *Battaglie sconosciute*, 144; H. Sokol, *Seekrieg*, 367–76; Thomazi, *L'Adriatique*, 138–39. Sokol proudly notes that the K.u.K. destroyers were commanded by a Pole, a Slovene, a Czech, and a Romanian.

Chapter 5. 1917

1. Halpern, *World War I*, 337–39; Scheer, *High Sea Fleet*, 234–54; Sondhaus, *Great War*, 242–47.

2. Scheer, *High Sea Fleet*, 251–52.

3. Marder, *Dreadnought*, 4:102–3, 115–66, 181–82, 277–78.

4. Pavlovich, *Fleet*, 219.

5. Halpern, *Mediterranean*, 312.

6. These ships likely received 10.5-cm guns in December 1916 if not before. Groos, *Nordsee*, 6:154. Quote: Thompson, *War at Sea*, 376.

7. Quote: Thompson, *War at Sea*, 377.

8. Groos, *Nordsee*, 6:157–68; Karau, *Marinekorps Flandern*, 293–97; Naval Staff, *Monographs*, 18:92–99; Newbolt, *Operations*, 4:73–79.

9. Halpern, *World War I*, 350; Marder, *Dreadnought*, 4:316; Naval Staff, *Monographs*, 6:130–31.

10. Groos, *Nordsee*, 6:299–302; Karau, *Marinekorps Flandern*, 310–12; Keyes Papers, "Dover Patrol operations," 34–37; Naval Staff, *Monographs*, 6:88–91 and 18:189–92; Newbolt, *Operations*, 4:352–55.

11. ADM 137/3239, 11.

12. Ibid., 14.

13. Groos, *Nordsee*, 6:303–7; Karau, *Marinekorps Flandern*, 313–16; Keyes Papers, "Dover Patrol operations," 38–43; Naval Staff, *Monographs*, 6:91–96 and 18:271–78; Newbolt, *Operations*, 4:361–65.

14. Groos, *Nordsee*, 6:309; Naval Staff, *Monographs*, 18:278–79.

15. Groos, *Nordsee*, 6:312–13; Naval Staff, *Monographs*, 18:393–94.

16. Keyes Papers, "Destroyer Raid on the Dover Straits," 47.

17. ADM 137/3237, 12.

18. Ibid. Groos, *Nordsee*, 6:314–22; Karau, *Marinekorps Flandern*, 322–25; Keyes Papers, "Dover Patrol operations," 44–48; Naval Staff, *Monographs*, 6:96–99; Naval Staff, *Monographs*, 18:394–401; Newbolt, *Operations*, 4:373–78; Dorling, *Endless Story*, 214–18.

19. Chack, *Mer du Nord*, 238–40; Groos, *Nordsee*, 6:308–9, 322–23; Karau, *Marinekorps Flandern*, 320; Naval Staff, *Monographs*, 18:402; Newbolt, *Operations*, 4:378; Thomazi, *Zone des Armées*, 176–77.

20. Groos, *Nordsee*, 6:323–24; Karau, *Marinekorps Flandern*, 325–26; Naval Staff, *Monographs*, 18:402–3.

21. ADM 137/2802, 13.

22. ADM 137/2802; Groos, *Nordsee*, 6:328–31; Karau, *Marinekorps Flandern*, 326–27; Naval Staff, *Monographs*, 19:4–6.

23. Quote: Naval Staff, *Monographs*, 19:10fn.

24. Groos, *Nordsee*, 6:333–34; Karau, *Marinekorps Flandern*, 327; Naval Staff, *Monographs*, 19:10–11.

25. Chack, *Mer du Nord*, 240–54; Groos, *Nordsee*, 6:334–35; Karau, *Marinekorps Flandern*, 321–22. Quote: Thomazi, *Zone des Armées*, 178.

26. Groos, *Nordsee*, 6:292; Naval Staff, *Monographs*, 19:13. 2 Flanders DDHF order of battle as of January 1917.

27. Gladisch, *Nordsee*, 7:148–52; Naval Staff, *Monographs*, 19:121–23, 290; Newbolt, *Operations*, 5:45–47. Gladisch does not mention the intervention by four additional destroyers, although the Naval Staff Monograph does, and says that *V47* was severely damaged. That is plausible as *V47* (the flagship of the Flanders flotilla) does not appear in subsequent operations.

28. ADM 137/2085; Bacon, *Dover Patrol*, 1:210–11; Gladisch, *Nordsee*, 7:154–55; Naval Staff, *Monographs*, 19:181–82.

29. The Germans lost four armed trawlers in a third raid. See Gladisch, *Nordsee*, 7:50–51.

30. ADM 137/2084; Gladisch, *Nordsee*, 7:62–65; Staff, *Seven Seas*, 193–94; Thompson, *War at Sea*, 382. The M-boats collectively had eight 10.5-cm/45 and eight 88-mm pieces.

31. ADM 137/3723, 50. The German cruiser's reports in http://www.hmsstrongbow.org.uk state that *Strongbow* was leading two columns of merchantmen.

32. Quotes: http://www.hmsstrongbow.org.uk; ADM 137/3723, 5, 53, 56.

33. Quotes: http://www.hmsstrongbow.org.uk; ADM 137/3723, 94.

34. ADM 137/3723, 18, 60.

35. Ibid., 50, 86.

36. Ibid., 64.

37. Gladisch, *Nordsee*, 7:83–88; Marder, *Dreadnought*, 4:293–99; Newbolt, *Operations*, 5:149–57.

38. Brown, *Grand Fleet*, 148; Buxton, *Monitors*, 152–53; Gladisch, *Nordsee*, 7:173–74; Karau, *Marinekorps Flandern*, 415–16; Thomazi, *Zone des Armées*, 185–86.

39. Gladisch, *Nordsee*, 7:166; Thomazi, *Zone des Armées*, 183.

40. Brown, *Grand Fleet*, 148; Gladisch, *Nordsee*, 7:167–69; Karau, *Marinekorps Flandern*, 414–15.

41. Anon, "Narrative of HMS *Caradoc*," 642.

42. ADM 137/548, *Umpire*, Report, 1.

43. The various British ships reported submarines, sweepers, destroyers, and light cruisers. See their respective reports in ADM 137/584. Quotes: ADM 137/584, *Courageous*, Report, 1, and Napier, Report, 3.

44. Quote: ADM 137/584, *Courageous*, Report, 2.

45. Ibid., *Glorious*, Report, 4.

46. Ibid., *Repulse*, Report, 1.

47. Ibid., "Heligoland Bight;" Gladisch, *Nordsee*, 7:96–127; Koerver, *Room 40*, 1:345–47; Marder, *Dreadnought*, 4:299–311; Newbolt, *Operations*, 5:164–76; Staff, *Seven Seas*, 190–207.

48. Quotes: Koerver, ed., *Room 40*, 345, 347.

49. The damaged ship was Swedish steamer *Nike*. She had been previously captured by a British submarine in the Baltic and released by the Russians when the Swedes protested. Halpern, *World War I*, 202.

50. Beesly, *Room 40*, 280–81; Gladisch, *Nordsee*, 7:132–39; Halpern, *World War I*, 378–79; Marder, *Dreadnought*, 4:311–3, 335–7; Newbolt, *Operations*, 5:185–98; Scheer, *High Sea Fleet*, 312–13.

51. Barrett, *Albion*, 56–87, 122–24; Beesly, *Room 40*, 181; Greger, *Russian Fleet*, 28. See Gagern, *Ostsee*, 3:413–23 for order of battle information.

52. The T-boats were older destroyers, redesignated with a "T" letter prefix but keeping the same numbers. The A-boats did not receive torpedoes until (at the earliest) the afternoon of 15 October. Gagern, *Ostsee*, 3:251; Barrett, *Albion*, 124; Gagern, *Ostsee*, 3:222–23; Staff, *Baltic Islands*, 28–29.

53. Gagern, *Ostsee*, 3:222–23; Greger, *Russian Fleet*, 28; Pavlovich, *Fleet*, 245–46; Staff, *Baltic Islands*, 29–31.

54. Gagern, *Ostsee*, 3:225–28; Graf, *Russian Navy*, 148–49; Greger, *Russian Fleet*, 28; Pavlovich, *Fleet*, 246; Staff, *Baltic Islands*, 35–38.

55. Barrett, *Albion*, 159–60; Gagern, *Ostsee*, 3:233–36; Graf, *Russian Navy*, 148–49; Greger, *Russian Fleet*, 28–29; Pavlovich, *Fleet*, 247–49; Staff, *Baltic Islands*, 52–59.

56. Gagern, *Ostsee*, 3:247–49; Greger, *Russian Fleet*, 29; Staff, *Baltic Islands*, 84–85.

57. Gagern, *Ostsee*, 3:253–55; Staff, *Baltic Islands*, 96–99.

58. Gagern, *Ostsee*, 3:259–67, 269–71; Greger, *Russian Fleet*, 29–30; Nekrasov, *Expendable Glory*, 101–8; Pavlovich, *Fleet*, 252–56; Staff, *Baltic Islands*, 107–16.

59. Gagern, *Ostsee*, 3:277–78; Pavlovich, *Fleet*, 255; Staff, *Baltic Islands*, 132–33.

60. Greger, *Russian Fleet*, 63; Lorey, *Mittelmeer*, 1:308–11; Pavlovich, *Fleet*, 460–3.

61. Greger, *Russian Fleet*, 64; Lorey, *Mittelmeer*, 1:321–22; Pavlovich, *Fleet*, 468.

62. See Van der Vat, *Ship that Changed the World*, for example.

63. Cernuschi, *Battaglie sconosciute*, 175–77; Halpern, *Otranto Straits*, 54–58.

64. Quote: UCSMM, "Azione Navale," 19.

65. Horthy, *Memoirs*, 96. The chemical apparatus was invented by the Germans the year before and premiered in the Mediterranean by Horthy.

66. UCSMM, "Azione Navale," 23; USRM, *Marina italiana*, 6:537.

67. Halpern, *Otranto Straits*, 87.

68. USRM, *Marina italiana*, 6:547.

69. Halpern, *Otranto Straits*, 94.

70. Cernuschi, *Battaglie sconosciute*, 172–202; Halpern, *Otranto Straits*, 49–122; Horthy, *Memoirs*, 93–98; Newbolt, *Operations*, 4:297–306; H. Sokol, *Seekrieg*, 376–93; Thomazi, *L'Adriatique*, 148–152; UCSMM, "Azione Navale del 15 Maggio"; USRM, *Marina italiana*, 6:532–53.

71. Halpern, *Otranto Straits*, 133–34; H. Sokol, *Seekrieg*, 549–50.

72. Cernuschi, *Battaglie sconosciute*, 83–84.

73. H. Sokol, *Seekrieg*, 606–7; USRM, *Marina italiana*, 4:77–80.

74. H. Sokol, *Seekrieg*, 484; USRM, *Marina italiana*, 4:271–74.

75. Cernuschi, *Battaglie sconosciute*, 88–89; Halpern, *Mediterranean*, 411; H. Sokol, *Seekrieg*, 484–86; USRM, *Marina italiana*, 4:271–75.

Chapter 6. 1918

1. Chickering and Förster, *Great War*, 187.

2. Gardiner, ed., *Conway's 1906–1921*, 186–87; Koerver, ed., *Room 40*, 1:347; Köppen, *Überwasserstreitkräfte*, 120–21; ONI, *Bulletin*, April 1924, 74; Crossley, *Hidden Threat*, loc. 1838; Tucker, *Encyclopedia*, 3:1103–4.

3. These numbers are based on Halpern, *World War I*, 423; O'Hara et al., *To Crown the Waves*, 124–25; Willmott, *Seapower*, 261.

4. Sondhaus, *Great War*, 311–18, 339–48.

5. ADM 137/3464; Buxton, *Monitors*, 134; Gladisch, *Nordsee*, 7:167; Newbolt, *Operations*, 5:208–9.

6. Gladisch, *Nordsee*, 7:237–43; Halpern, *World War I*, 408–9; Keyes Papers, "Dover Patrol operations," 50–69; Marder, *Dreadnought*, 5:42–45; Newbolt, *Operations*, 5:210–19.

7. Admiralty, *Navy List February 1918 Supplement*, 13,15; Jellicoe, *Grand Fleet*, 443; Halpern, *World War I*, 359; Naval Staff, *Monographs*, 18:378–80. The number of 68 destroyers cited comes from the *Monographs*; Newbolt, *Operations*, 5:387–88 gives 65.

8. Chack, *Mer du Nord*, 272–80; Gladisch, *Nordsee*, 7:287–90; Newbolt, *Operations*, 5:224–26; Thomazi, *Zone des Armées*, 191–2. Thomazi and Chack say that *Morris* also launched a torpedo at *Botha* "*parallèlement, fraternellement*" with *Mehl's*. Newbolt only mentions *Mehl's* torpedo and suggests that *Morris* was not then in company.

9. ADM 137/343; Gladisch, *Nordsee*, 7:257–60.

10. Gladisch, *Nordsee*, 7:269–76; Koerver, ed., *Room 40*, 1:354–56; Newbolt, *Operations*, 5:230–40.

11. Cunningham, *Odyssey*, 91–92 (he mistakenly dates the action as late May); Gladisch, *Nordsee*, 7:389–90. Keyes Papers, "Dover Patrol operations," 201.

12. ADM 137/2090, 118; Gladisch, *Nordsee*, 7:389–90, 403–4; Halpern, *World War I*, 444.

13. Halpern, *World War I*, 444–47; Sondhaus, *Great War*, 342–48.

14. Halpern, *Otranto Straits*, 138–40; Newbolt, *Operations*, 5:287–88; H. Sokol, *Seekrieg*, 550–51; Stevens, *In All Respects Ready*, 320–21; Thomazi, *L'Adriatique*, 184–85.

15. Quote: ONI, *Bulletin*, October 1922, 69–70.

16. Halpern, *Mediterranean*, 501–2; Bagnasco et al, "Italian Fast Coastal Forces," 91; H. Sokol, *Seekrieg*, 553–63. Otto Hersing in *U21* sank *Triumph* and *Majestic* off the Dardanelles.

17. H. Sokol, *Seekrieg*, 611–13; USRM, *Marina italiana*, 4:641–42.

18. Cernuschi, *Battaglie sconosciute*, 267; H. Sokol, *Seekrieg*, 503.

19. Cernuschi, *Battaglie sconosciute*, 217–18; Halpern, *Mediterranean*, 556–58; A. Sokol, *Austro-Hungarian Navy*, 136; H. Sokol, *Seekrieg*, 636–46. Quotes: ONI, *Bulletin*, January 1919, 55–57.

20. Kemp, *Admiralty Regrets*, 64.

21. Newbolt, *Operations*, 5:85–91. Staff, *Battlecruisers*, 130–32. Quote: ONI, *Bulletin*, March 1919, 83.

22. Halpern, *World War I*, 221–22; Sondhaus, *Great War*, 318–24.

23. Halpern, *World War I*, 258.

24. Ibid., 256–58.

Chapter 7. Summing Up

1. Schleihauf, *Jutland*, 13.

2. Most are described in O'Hara, *Struggle for the Middle Sea, German Fleet at War*, and *U.S. Navy against the Axis*.

3. For information on these actions, see Historical Section, *Official History of the Russo-Japanese War*, vols. 1–3; Corbett, *Maritime Operations in the Russo-Japanese War*, vols. 1–2; Willmott, *Seapower*, 74–133.

Bibliography

Official and Primary Sources

Admiralty. *Navy Lists.* London: His Majesty's Stationery Office, various dates. Online at http://www.navy.gov.au/media-room/publications/navy-list.

Admiralty, Naval Staff, Training and Staff Duties Division. *Naval Staff Monographs (Historical).* Volumes 1–19, 1920–1939. Online at http://www.navy.gov.au/media-room/publications/world-war-i-naval-staff-monographs.

———. *Review of German Cruiser Warfare, 1914–1918.* 1940.

Ayres, Leonard. *The War with Germany: A Statistical Summary.* Washington, D.C.: GPO, 1919.

British Library. Keyes Papers. Volume 123, "Enemy Activity and Dover Patrol Operations; October 1916–13 April 1919."

———. Jellicoe Papers.

Corbett, Julian S., and Henry Newbolt. *Naval Operations: History of the Great War Based on Official Documents.* 5 vols. London: Longmans, Green, 1920–1931.

Fayle, Charles E. *Seaborne Trade.* London: John Murray, 1920.

Firle, Rudolf, Heinrich Rollman, and Ernst Gagern. *Der Krieg in der Ostsee.* 3 vols. Berlin and Frankfurt: E. S. Mittler, 1921–1964.

Groos, Otto, and Walter Gladisch, *Der Krieg in der Nordsee.* 7 vols. Berlin, Frankfurt, and Hamburg: E. S. Mittler, 1920–2006.

Historical Section of the Committee of Imperial Defence. *Official History (Naval and Military) of the Russo-Japanese War.* 3 vols. London: His Majesty's Stationery Office, 1910–1920.

Lorey, Hermann. *Der Krieg in den Türkischen Gewässern.* Vol. 1, *Die Mittelmeer-Division.* Berlin: E. S. Mittler, 1918.

The National Archives. ADM 137/305. "Reports of Action 24th Jan. 1915." 1st Battle Cruiser Squadron, 11 February 1915.

——. ADM 137/343. "Harwich Force, Diary of Events, 30 December 1917 to 19 April 1919."

——. ADM 137/584. "Heligoland Bight Operation, 17 November 1917, Reports."

——. ADM 137/754. *Black Sea Russian Fleet: Reports of Eng: Lieut Commdr: G.W. Le Page. February 1915–September 1916.*

——. ADM 137/940. *Black Sea Russian Fleet: Reports of Engineer Lieut Commdr: G.W. Le Page. 11 September 1916–26 December 1916.*

——. ADM 137/2090. "Interception of Enemy Vessels, etc."

——. ADM 137/2802. "Action between Harwich Force and German TBDs. 10th May, 1917."

——. ADM 137/2804. "Minelaying Operation 'W.9' and subsequent engagement between the Harwich Force and enemy minesweepers."

——. ADM 137/2085. "3rd Division After Action Reports, 25 July 1917."

——. ADM 137/3237. "Report on Raid by German Destroyers on Straits of Dover on 20th/21st April 1917."

——. ADM 137/3239. "Report of Raid by Enemy Destroyers on the Dover Straits Patrol Line. 17th/18th March 1917."

——. ADM 137/3464. "Action with Enemy Destroyers off Belgian Coast 23-1-1918."

——. ADM 137/3654. "Report of Court of Enquiry to Investigate the Circumstances Attending the Attack on Dover Destroyers by the Enemy on the Night of 17th/18th March, 1917."

——. ADM 137/3659. "Report of Court of Enquiry to Investigate the Circumstances Attending the Action between HMS *Swift*, HMS *Broke* with Enemy Destroyers on the night of 20th/21st April, 1917."

——. ADM 137/3723. "Convoy Action between HMS *Mary Rose* and HMS *Strongbow* and Enemy Cruisers."

——. ADM 186/238. *Progress in Naval Gunnery 1914–1918.* July 1919.

——. ADM 186/339. *Progress in Naval Gunnery 1914–1936.* December 1936.

Pavlovich, N. B., ed. *The Fleet in World War One.* Vol. 1, *Operations of the Russian Fleet.* New Delhi, India: Amerind Publishing, 1979.

Raeder, Erich, and Eberhard Mantey. *Der Kreuzerkrieg in den Ausländischen Gewässern.* 3 vols. Berlin: E. S. Mittler, 1922–1937.

Thomazi, A. *La guerre navale aux Dardanelles.* Paris: Payot, 1927.

——. *La guerre navale aux Méditerranée.* Paris: Payot, 1929.

——. *La guerre navale dans l'Adriatique.* Paris: Payot, 1927.

——. *La guerre navale dans la Zone des Armées du Nord.* Paris: Payot, 1925.

Ufficio del Capo di Stato Maggiore della Marina (UCSMM). *Cronistoria documentata della guerra marittima Italo-Austriaca 1915–1918,* Azione Navale del 15 maggio 1917 nel'basso Adriatico. Rome: Ufficio Storico, 1927.

Ufficio Storico della Regia Marina (USRM). *La marina italiana nella Grande Guerra*. 8 vols. Florence: Vallecchi, 1935–1942.

United States Navy, Office of Naval Intelligence (ONI). *Monthly Intelligence Bulletins*. 1919–1923.

——. CA 889. Translation of *The German History of the Naval War Baltic*. Vol. 2. 27 March 1930.

Secondary Sources

Bacon, Reginald. *The Dover Patrol, 1915–1917*. 2 vols. New York: Doran, 1919.

Balincourt, Raoul de. *Les flottes de combat en 1914*. Paris: Augustin Challamel, 1914.

Barrett, Michael B. *Operation Albion: The German Conquest of the Baltic Islands*. Bloomington, Ind.: Indiana University Press, 2008.

Beesly, Patrick. *Room 40: British Naval Intelligence 1914–18*. New York: Harcourt Brace Jovanovich, 1982.

Bennett, Geoffrey. *Naval Battles of the First World War*. London: Penguin, 1968.

Brooks, John. *Dreadnought Gunnery and the Battle of Jutland: The Question of Fire Control*. Milton Park, England: Routledge, 2006.

——. *Warrior to Dreadnought: Warship Development 1860–1905*. London: Chatham Publishing, 1997.

Brown, David. *The Grand Fleet: Warship Design and Development 1906–1922*. Annapolis, Md.: Naval Institute Press, 1999.

Brown, Warwick M. "The Royal Navy's Fuel Supplies, 1898–1939: The Transition from Coal to Oil." PhD thesis, King's College, London, 2003.

Buxton, Ian. *Big Gun Monitors: Design, Construction and Operation 1914–1945*. Annapolis, Md.: Naval Institute Press, 2008.

Campbell, John. *Jutland: An Analysis of the Fighting*. New York: Lyons Press, 2000.

Cernuschi, Enrico. *Battaglie sconosciute: Storia riveduta e corretta della Regia Marina durante la Grande Guerra*. Vicenza, Italy: In Edibus, 2014.

Cernuschi, Enrico, and Andrea Tirondola. *Noi e Loro: La Grande Guerra in Adriatico Strategie, tecnologie e battaglie*. Rome: Ufficio Storico della Marina Militare, 2015.

Chack, Paul. *Marins á la bataille*. Vol. 4, *Mer du Nord 1914–1918*. Paris: Éditions du Gerfaut, 2002.

Chesneau, Roger, and Eugene Koleskik, eds. *Conway's All the World's Fighting Ships 1860–1906*. London: Conway Maritime Press, 1979.

Chickering, Roger, and Stig Förster, eds. *Great War, Total War: Combat and Mobilization on the Western Front 1914–1918*. Washington, D.C.: Cambridge University Press, 2000.

Churchill, Winston S. *The World Crisis*. Vol. 1, *1911–1914*. Toronto: Macmillan, 1923.

——. *The World Crisis*. Vol. 2, *1915*. Toronto: Macmillan, 1923.

Coletta, Paolo E. *Sea Power in the Atlantic and Mediterranean in World War I*. New York: Lanham, 1989.

Corbett, Julian S. *Maritime Operations in the Russo-Japanese War, 1904–1905*. 2 vols. Annapolis, Md.: Naval Institute Press, 1994.

Crossley, Jim. *The Hidden Threat: Mines and Minesweeping in WWI*. Barnsley, England: Pen & Sword, 2011.

Cunningham, Andrew. *A Sailor's Odyssey*. London: Hutchinson, 1951.

Darr, Karl. "The Ottoman Navy 1900–1918." PhD thesis, University of Louisville, Kentucky, 1998.

Dorling, Taprell (writing as Taffrail). *Endless Story*. London: Hodder and Stoughton, 1931.

Edwards, Bernard. *Salvo: Classic Naval Gun Actions*. Annapolis, Md.: Naval Institute Press, 1995.

Ellis, John, and Michael Cox. *The World War I Databook: The Essential Facts and Figures for all the Combatants*. London: Aurum, 1993.

Fatutta, Francisco. *Oltre Adriatico: Cronologia delle operazioni navali in Istria, nel Carnaro e in Dalmatia durante il primo conflitto mondiale Tomo I (1915–1916)*. Rome: Rivista Marittima Supplement, 2006.

Faulkner, Marcus. *The Great War at Sea: A Naval Atlas 1914–1919*. Annapolis, Md.: Naval Institute Press, 2015.

Ferguson, Niall. *The Pity of War*. New York: Basic Books, 1999.

Fitzsimons, Bernard. *Warships & Sea Battles of World War I*. New York: Beekman House, 1973.

Fraccaroli, Aldo. *Italian Warships of World War I*. London: Ian Allen, 1970.

Friedman, Norman. *British Destroyers from Earliest Days to the Second World War*. Annapolis, Md.: Naval Institute Press, 2009.

———. *Fighting the Great War at Sea: Strategy, Tactics, and Technology*. Annapolis, Md.: Naval Institute Press, 2014.

———. *Naval Firepower: Battleship Guns and Gunnery in the Dreadnought Era*. Annapolis, Md.: Naval Institute Press, 2011.

———. *Naval Weapons of World War One: Guns, Torpedoes, Mines, and ASW Weapons of all Nations. An Illustrated Directory*. Barnsley, England: Seaforth, 2011.

Gardiner, Robert, ed. *Conway's All the World's Fighting Ships 1906–1921*. London: Conway, 1985.

Gibson, R. H., and Maurice Prendergast. *The German Submarine War*. Annapolis, Md.: Naval Institute Press, 2003.

Gilbert, Martin. *The First World War: A Complete History*. New York: Henry Holt, 1994.

Goldrick, James. *Before Jutland: The Naval War in Northern European Waters, August 1914–February 1915*. Annapolis, Md.: Naval Institute Press, 2015.

Gordon, Andrew. *The Rules of the Game: Jutland and British Naval Command.* Annapolis, Md.: Naval Institute Press, 1996.

Graf, H. *The Russian Navy in War and Revolution: From 1914 up to 1918.* Honolulu, Hawaii: University Press of the Pacific, 2002.

Gray, Edwyn. *The Devil's Device: Robert Whitehead and the History of the Torpedo.* Annapolis, Md.: Naval Institute Press, 1991.

Greger, René. *The Russian Fleet, 1914–1917.* Shepperton, England: Ian Allen, 1972.

Gröner, Erich. *German Warships, 1815–1945.* 2 vols. London: Conway, 1990–1991.

Halpern, Paul G. *The Battle of the Otranto Straits: Controlling the Gateway to the Adriatic in WWI.* Bloomington, Ind.: Indiana University Press, 2004.

———. *A Naval History of World War I.* Annapolis, Md.: Naval Institute Press, 1994.

———. *The Naval War in the Mediterranean 1914–1918.* Annapolis, Md.: Naval Institute Press, 1987.

Hase, Georg. *Kiel and Jutland.* London: Skeffington, 1921.

Hattendorf, John B., ed. *The Influence of History on Mahan.* Newport, R.I.: Naval War College Press, 1991.

Herwig, Holger H. *'Luxury' Fleet: The Imperial German Navy 1888–1918.* London: George Allen & Unwin, 1980.

Horthy, Nicholas. *Memoirs.* London: Hutchinson, 1956.

Hough, Richard. *Great Naval Battles of the 20th Century.* Woodstock, N.Y.: Overlook Press, 2001.

———. *The Great War at Sea 1914–1918.* Oxford: Oxford University Press, 1983.

Hughes, Wayne P., Jr. *Fleet Tactics and Coastal Combat.* 2nd ed. Annapolis, Md.: Naval Institute Press, 2000.

Jane, Fred T. *Jane's Fighting Ships 1914: A Reprint of the 1914 Edition of Fighting Ships.* New York: Arco, 1969.

Jellicoe, John R. *The Grand Fleet, 1914–1916: Its Creation, Development, and Work.* New York: George H. Doran, 1919.

Jordan, Gerald, ed. *Naval Warfare in the Twentieth Century.* London: Croom Helm, 1977.

Karau, Mark. "'Lost Opportunities': The Marinekorps Flandern and the German War Effort 1914–1918." PhD thesis, Florida State University, Tallahassee, Florida, 2000.

Keegan, John. *Intelligence in War: Knowledge of the Enemy from Napoleon to Al-Qaeda.* New York: Alfred A. Knopf, 2003.

Kemp, Paul. *The Admiralty Regrets: British Warship Losses in the 20th Century.* Phoenix Mill, England: Sutton, 1999.

Keyes, Roger. *The Naval Memoirs of Admiral of the Fleet Sir Roger Keyes: The Narrow Seas to the Dardanelles 1910–1915.* New York: E. P. Dutton, 1934.

King-Hall, Stephen. *A North Sea Diary 1914–1918.* London: Newnes, n.d.

Koerver, Hans J., ed. *Room 40: German Naval Warfare 1914–1918.* Vol 1, *The Fleet in Action.* Berlin: Schaltungsdienst Lange o.H.G., 2009.

Köppen, Paul. *Die Überwasserstreitkräfte und ihre Technik.* Berlin: E. S. Mittler & Sohn, 1930.

Laurens, Adolphe. *Précis d'historie de la guerre navale 1914–1918.* Paris: Payot, 1929.

Liesner, Thelma. *Economic Statistics 1900–1983.* New York: Facts on File, 1985.

Lott, Arnold S. *Most Dangerous Sea: A History of Mine Warfare.* Annapolis, Md.: Naval Institute Press, 1959.

Mahan, A. T. *The Influence of Sea Power upon History 1660–1783.* Boston: Little Brown, 1918.

Marder, Arthur, J. *From the Dreadnought to Scapa Flow.* 5 vols. Annapolis, Md.: Naval Institute Press, 2013.

Massie, Robert K. *Castles of Steel: Britain, Germany, and the Winning of the Great War at Sea.* New York: Random House, 2003.

——. *Dreadnought: Britain, Germany, and the Coming of the Great War.* New York: Random House, 1991.

Millington-Drake, Eugene. *The Drama of Graf Spee and the Battle of the Plate: A Documentary Anthology: 1914–1964.* London: Peter Davies, 1964.

Nassigh, Riccardo. *La Marina Italiana e l'Adriatico: Il potere marittimo in un teatro ristretto.* Rome: Ufficio Storico della Marina Militare, 1998.

Nekrasov, George M. *Expendable Glory: A Russian Battleship in the Baltic, 1915–1917.* New York: Columbia University Press, 2004.

——. *North of Gallipoli: The Black Sea Fleet at War, 1914–1917.* New York: Columbia University Press, 1992.

O'Hara, Vincent P. *The German Fleet at War, 1939–1945.* Annapolis, Md.: Naval Institute Press, 2004.

——. *Struggle for the Middle Sea: The Great Navies at War in the Mediterranean Theater, 1940–1945.* Annapolis, Md.: Naval Institute Press, 2009.

——. *The U.S. Navy against the Axis: Surface Combat 1941–1945.* Annapolis, Md.: Naval Institute Press, 2007.

O'Hara, Vincent P., W. David Dickson, and Richard Worth, eds. *To Crown the Waves: The Great Navies of the First World War.* Annapolis, Md.: Naval Institute Press, 2013.

Osborne, Eric W. *The Battle of Heligoland Bight.* Bloomington, Ind.: Indiana University Press, 2006.

Padfield, Peter. *The Battleship Era.* New York: David McKay, 1972.

Pattee, Phillip G. *At War in Distant Waters: British Colonial Defense in the Great War.* Annapolis, Md.: Naval Institute Press, 2013.

Patterson, A. Temple. *Tyrwhitt of the Harwich Force: The Life of Admiral of the Fleet Sir Reginald Tyrwhitt.* London: MacDonald, 1973.

Ruge, Friedrich. *SM Torpedo Boat B110.* Windsor, Canada: Profile Publications, 1973.

Scheer, Reinhard. *Germany's High Sea Fleet in the World War.* London: Cassel, 1920.

Schleihauf, William, and Stephen McLaughlin, eds. *Jutland: The Naval Staff Appreciation.* Barnsley, England: Seaforth, 2016.

Sokol, Anthony. *The Imperial and Royal Austro-Hungarian Navy.* Annapolis, Md.: Naval Institute Press, 1968.

Sokol, Hans H. *Österreich-Ungarns Seekrieg 1914–18.* Graz, Austria: Akademische Druck-u. Verlagsanstalt, 1967.

Sondhaus, Lawrence. *The Great War at Sea.* Cambridge, England: Cambridge University Press, 2014.

———. *The Naval Policy of Austria-Hungary, 1867–1918: Navalism, Industrial Development, and the Politics of Dualism.* West Lafayette, Ind.: Purdue University Press, 1994.

———. *Naval Warfare 1815–1914.* London and New York: Routledge, 2001.

Staff, Gary. *Battle for the Baltic Islands 1917.* Barnsley, England: Pen & Sword Maritime, 2008.

———. *Battle on the Seven Seas: German Cruiser Battles 1914–1918.* Barnsley, England: Pen & Sword Maritime, 2011.

———. *German Battlecruisers of World War One: Their Design, Construction, and Operations.* Annapolis, Md.: Naval Institute Press, 2014.

Steel, Nigel, and Peter Hart. *Jutland 1916: Death in the Grey Wastes.* London: Cassell, 2004.

Stern, Robert C. *Destroyer Battles: Epics of Naval Close Combat.* Annapolis, Md.: Naval Institute Press, 2008.

Stevens, David. *In All Respects Ready: Australia's Navy in World War One.* South Melbourne, Australia: Oxford University Press, 2014.

Stevens, William Oliver, and Allan Westcott. *A History of Sea Power.* New York: George H. Doran, 1920.

Stevenson, David. *With Our Backs to the Wall: Victory and Defeat in 1918.* Cambridge, Mass.: Belknap, 2011.

Still, William N., Jr. *Crisis at Sea: The United States Navy in European Waters in World War I.* Gainesville, Fla.: Florida University Press, 2006.

Strachan, Hew. *The First World War.* Vol. 1, *To Arms.* Oxford: Oxford University Press, 2001.

Sumida, Jon Tetsuro. *In Defense of Naval Supremacy: Finance, Technology, and British Naval Policy 1889–1914.* London and New York: Routledge, 1993.

———. "The Quest for Reach: the Development of Long-Range Gunnery in the Royal Navy, 1901–1912." In *Tooling for War: Military Transformation in the Industrial Age*, edited by Stephen D. Chiabotti, 49–96. Chicago: Imprint Publications, 1996.

Tarrant, V. E. *Jutland: The German Perspective*. Annapolis, Md.: Naval Institute Press, 1995.

Thompson, Julian. *The Imperial War Museum Book of the War at Sea 1914–1918*. London: Pan Books, 2005.

The *Times. Documentary History of the War.* Vol. 3, *Naval Part I*, and Vol. 4, *Naval Part 2*. London: Printing House Square, 1917.

Tuchman, Barbara W. *The Guns of August*. New York: Macmillan, 1962.

Tucker, Spencer C. *World War I: The Definitive Encyclopedia and Document Collection*. Santa Barbara, California: ABC-CLIO, 2014.

Van der Vat, Dan. *The Ship that Changed the World: The Escape of the Goeben to the Dardanelles in 1914*. Edinburgh, Scotland: Birlinn, 2000.

Weyer, B. *Taschenbuch der Kriegsflotten XV. Jahrgang 1914*. Munich: J. F. Lehmann's, 1914.

Willmott, H. P. *The Last Century of Seapower.* Vol. 1, *From Port Arthur to Chanak, 1894–1922*. Bloomington, Ind.: Indiana University Press, 2009.

Wolz, Nicholas. *From Imperial Splendor to Internment: The German Navy in the First World War*. Annapolis, Md.: Naval Institute Press, 2015.

Magazines and Journals

Anon. "Action of May 15th, 1917, in the Adriatic; and the Torpedoing of the Dartmouth." *Naval Review* 7, no. 3 (1919): 379–384.

——. "Four Months in the Adriatic." *Naval Review* 4, no. 2 (1916): 352–360.

——. "Narrative of Events during Attacks on the German Cruiser Konigsberg." *Naval Review* 4, no. 2 (1916): 335–344.

——. "Narrative of HMS *Caradoc* 1917–1920." *Naval Review* 9, no. 4 (1921): 641–663.

——. "Narrative of the Events in Connection with the Siege, Blockade and Reduction of the Fortress of Tsingtau." *Naval Review* 3, no. 3 (1915): 322–335.

——. "Offence not Defence." *Naval Review* 1, no. 4 (1913): 224–229.

——. "Some Remarks on the Evolution of Naval Warfare." *Naval Review* 1, no. 1 (1913): 53–56.

——. "The Fleet in Action." *Naval Review* 2, no. 1 (1914): 35–46.

——. "The Allied China Station." *Naval Review* 3, no. 3 (1915): 312–321

——. "Torpedo Fire in Future Fleet Actions." *Naval Review* 2, no. 1 (1914): 47–57.

Bagnasco, Erminio, Enrico Cernuschi, and Vincent P. O'Hara. "Italian Fast Coastal Forces: Development, Doctrine and Campaigns 1914–1986, Part One: From the Beginning to 1934." *Warship 2008*. London: Conway, 2008: 85–98.

Beehler, W. P. "A Lesson from the War: A Study of German Naval Communications on August 28, 1914." U.S. Naval Institute *Proceedings* 53, no. 4 (April 1927): 440–454.

——. "The Torpedo on Capital Ships." U.S. Naval Institute *Proceedings* 40, no. 6 (November–December 1914): 1775–1786.

——. "The Day Torpedo-boat Attack." U.S. Naval Institute *Proceedings* 40, no. 4 (July-August 1914): 1156–1162.

Bernotti, Romeo. "Concentration of Fire and the Numerical Strength of a Division." U.S. Naval Institute *Proceedings* 40, no. 2 (March-April 1914): 404–412.

Brooks, John. "The Admiralty Fire Control Tables." *Warship 2002–2003*. London: Conway, 2003: 69–93.

Brown, David K. "HMS *Invincible:* The Explosion at Jutland and Its Relevance to HMS *Hood.*" *Warship International* 40, no. 4 (2003): 339–349.

——. "The Russo-Japanese War: Technical Lessons as Perceived by the Royal Navy." *Warship 1996*. London: Conway, 1996: 66–77.

——. "Some Thoughts on the British Mines of the First World War." *Warship 2001–2002*. London: Conway, 2001: 99–102.

Caresse, Philippe. "The Odyssey of Von Spee and the East Asiatic Squadron, 1914." *Warship 2008*. London: Conway, 2008: 67–84.

Cernuschi, Enrico, and Alessandro Gazzi. "Canale d'Otranto, 15 maggio 1917." *Storia Militare*, no. 250 (July 2014): 56–66.

Cernuschi, Enrico, and Vincent O'Hara. "The Naval War in the Adriatic, Part 1: 1914–1916." *Warship 2015*, 161–173. "Part 2: 1917–1918." *Warship 2016*, 62–75. London: Conway, 2015–2016.

C. Q. I. "Studies in the Theory of Naval Tactics." *Naval Review* 1, no. 1 (1913): 12–25; no. 2 (1913): 82–95; no. 4 (1913): 208–221; 2, no. 2 (1914): 79–89.

Cuniberti, Vittorio. "All Torpedoes!" U.S. Naval Institute *Proceedings* 40, no. 1 (January-February 1914): 29–31.

Ejstrud, Bo. "A Near Miss: Heavy Gun Efficiency at Jutland." *Warship International* 41, no. 2 (2004): 159–171.

Ewin, Toby. "A British Account of the Action off Cape Sarych, 1914." *The Mariner's Mirror* 102, no. 2 (May 2016): 211–217.

Fomin, N. "Eshche o zashchite Irbenskogo proliva v kampaniiu 1915 goda" [More about the Defense of the Irben Strait during the Campaign of 1915], trans. Stephen McLaughlin. *Morskie zapiski* 20, no. 1/2 (1962): 3–20.

Frost, H. H. "The Problem of Firing at a Fleet under way with Long-Range Torpedoes." U.S. Naval Institute *Proceedings* 39, no. 2 (March-April 1913): 681–98.

Gill, C. C. "Rapidity of Gun Fire." U.S. Naval Institute *Proceedings* 39, no. 2 (March-April 1913): 699–704.

Goldrick, James. "Coal and the Advent of the First World War at Sea." *War in History* 21, no. 3 (2014): 322–337.

——. "The Impact of War: Matching Expectation with Reality in the Royal Navy in the First Months of the Great War at Sea." *War in History* 14, no. 1 (2007): 22–35.

Gribovski, V. Yu. "Boi u Gotlanda 19 Iiunia 1915" [Battle of Gotland, 19 July 1915]. *Gangut* 11 (1996): 35–55.

Kahn, David. "The Wreck of the Magdeburg." *MHQ* 2, no. 2 (1990): 97–103.

Knox Dudley W. "'Column' as a Battle Formation." U.S. Naval Institute *Proceedings* 39, no. 3 (May-June 1913): 951–958.

———. "Discussion: Dispersion and Accuracy of Fire." U.S. Naval Institute *Proceedings* 39, no. 4 (July-August 1913): 951–958.

Koblinski, G. "On a Light Cruiser during the War." U.S. Naval Institute *Proceedings* 57, no. 1 (January 1931): 33–39.

Langenberg, William H. "Rise and Fall of the Dreadnought." *MHQ* 11, no. 2 (1999): 37–42.

Layman, R. D. "Air vs. Sea in World War I." *Warship International* 19, no. 3 (1982): 215–223.

———. "Naval Warfare in a New Dimension 1914–1918." *Warship 1989.* Annapolis, Md.: Naval Institute Press, 1989: 56–73.

McCallum, Iain. "The Riddle of the Shells: The Test of Battle, Heligoland to the Dardanelles." *Warship 2004.* London: Conway, 2004: 9–20.

———. "The Riddle of the Shells: The Approach to War, 1882–1914." *Warship 2002–2003.* London: Conway, 2003: 3–25.

———. "The Riddle of the Shells: Disappointment in the North Sea." *Warship 2005.* London: Conway, 2005: 9–24.

McLaughlin, Stephen. "'Equal Speed Charlie London': Jellicoe's Deployment at Jutland." *Warship 2010.* London: Conway, 2010: 122–139.

———. "Predreadnoughts vs a Dreadnought: The Action off Cape Sarych, 18 November 1914." *Warship 2001–2002.* London: Conway, 2002: 117–140.

Merrin, H. "The German Raid on the East Coast, November 3, 1914." U.S. Naval Institute *Proceedings,* 42, no. 1 (January-February 1916): 301–303.

Mücke, Hellmuth von. "Emden." U.S. Naval Institute *Proceedings* 42, no. 3 (May-June 1916): 774–823; no. 4 (July-August 1916): 1194–1207.

Nottelman, Dirk. "From Ironclads to Dreadnoughts: The Development of the German Navy 1864–1918. Part V: The Kaiser's Navy." *Warship International* 51, no. 1 (March 2014): 43–90.

Professional Notes. "An Echo of the Dogger Bank." U.S. Naval Institute *Proceedings* 48, no. 7 (July 1922): 1188–1190.

Seligmann, Matthew. "The Battle Cruisers *Lion* and *Tiger* at Dogger Bank: The View of the Ship's Medical Officers." *Warship 2013.* London: Conway, 2013: 67–77.

Sieche, Erwin F. "L.S.M.S. *Helgoland.*" *Storia Militare,* no. 49 (October 1997): 37–44.

———. S.M.S. *Szent István:* Hungary's Only and Ill-Fated Dreadnought." *Warship International* 23, no. 2 (1991): 113–146.

Sokol, Anthony. "Austria-Hungary's Naval Building Projects 1914–1918. Part I Cruisers." *Warship International* 15, no. 3 (1978): 185–211.

———. "Austria-Hungary's Naval Building Projects 1914–1918. Part II Destroyers." *Warship International* 19, no. 4 (1982): 324–341.

Spector, Ronald H. "The First Battle of the Falklands." *MHQ* 3, no. 2 (1991): 76–85.

Spencer, John. "Conduite du Tir Part 2: 1900–1913." *Warship 2012*. London: Conway, 2012: 52–64.

Stankovic, Nicholas. "The War in the Adriatic, 1914–1918." *Naval Review* 11, no. 3 (1923): 459–475.

Sumida, Jon Tetsuro. "British Naval Operational Logistics." *The Journal of Military History* 10, no. 10 (July 1993): 447–480.

Williams, M. W. "The Loss of HMS *Queen Mary* at Jutland." *Warship 1996*. London: Conway, 1996: 111–132.

Zorini, Decio. "S.M.S. *Viribus Unitis.*" *Storia Militare*, no. 239 (August 2013): 18–33.

Online Sources

Beaumont, Adrian. "HMS *Kent:* Her part in the Battle of the Falkland Islands 8th December 1914." www.canterbury-cathedral.org/2014/10/27/hms-kent/

Cradock, Christopher. "Coaling Ship from a Collier." In *Whispers from the Fleet.* 2nd ed. J. Griffin, 1908. http://www.gwpda.org/naval/wff01.htm.

Grant, Heathcoat. *My War at Sea 1914–1916: A Captain's Life with the Royal Navy during the First World War.* Warletters.net.

Naval History, World War I at Sea. "Ships of the Royal Navy, Location/Action Data, 1914–1918, Admiralty 'Pink Lists,' 1 October 1916." http://www.naval-history.net/

The World War I Document Archive, 1915 Documents. "Battle of Dogger Bank." 24 January 1915. http://wwi.lib.byu.edu/index.php/Battle_of_Dogger_Bank.

WW1NavyBritishShips-Locations2PL1610.htm. HMS *Strongbow.* http://www.hmsstrongbow.org.uk.

WWI: The War at Sea. "Fleet Deployments//Fleet Lists." http://www.gwpda.org/naval/n0000000.htm#swt.

Index

Page numbers followed by a t *indicate tables.*

About the Authors

Vincent O'Hara is an independent scholar and the author of eleven works, most recently *Torch: North Africa and the Allied Path to Victory* (Naval Institute Press, 2015). His articles have appeared in *Naval War College Review, Warship, MHQ,* and other publications. He holds a history degree from the University of California, Berkeley, and lives in Chula Vista, California.

Leonard Heinz is a retired financial services lawyer with a strong interest in naval affairs. He has designed and published many wargames with an emphasis on tactical naval simulations. He holds a degree in history from the University of Pennsylvania and lives in Corrales, New Mexico, with his wife Meg.